T0192149

Communications
in Computer and Information Science

2025

Rationale

The CCIS series is devoted to the publication of proceedings of computer science conferences. Its aim is to efficiently disseminate original research results in informatics in printed and electronic form. While the focus is on publication of peer-reviewed full papers presenting mature work, inclusion of reviewed short papers reporting on work in progress is welcome, too. Besides globally relevant meetings with internationally representative program committees guaranteeing a strict peer-reviewing and paper selection process, conferences run by societies or of high regional or national relevance are also considered for publication.

Topics

The topical scope of CCIS spans the entire spectrum of informatics ranging from foundational topics in the theory of computing to information and communications science and technology and a broad variety of interdisciplinary application fields.

Information for Volume Editors and Authors

Publication in CCIS is free of charge. No royalties are paid, however, we offer registered conference participants temporary free access to the online version of the conference proceedings on SpringerLink (http://link.springer.com) by means of an http referrer from the conference website and/or a number of complimentary printed copies, as specified in the official acceptance email of the event.

CCIS proceedings can be published in time for distribution at conferences or as post-proceedings, and delivered in the form of printed books and/or electronically as USBs and/or e-content licenses for accessing proceedings at SpringerLink. Furthermore, CCIS proceedings are included in the CCIS electronic book series hosted in the SpringerLink digital library at http://link.springer.com/bookseries/7899. Conferences publishing in CCIS are allowed to use Online Conference Service (OCS) for managing the whole proceedings lifecycle (from submission and reviewing to preparing for publication) free of charge.

Publication process

The language of publication is exclusively English. Authors publishing in CCIS have to sign the Springer CCIS copyright transfer form, however, they are free to use their material published in CCIS for substantially changed, more elaborate subsequent publications elsewhere. For the preparation of the camera-ready papers/files, authors have to strictly adhere to the Springer CCIS Authors' Instructions and are strongly encouraged to use the CCIS LaTeX style files or templates.

Abstracting/Indexing

CCIS is abstracted/indexed in DBLP, Google Scholar, EI-Compendex, Mathematical Reviews, SCImago, Scopus. CCIS volumes are also submitted for the inclusion in ISI Proceedings.

How to start

To start the evaluation of your proposal for inclusion in the CCIS series, please send an e-mail to ccis@springer.com.

Wenxing Hong · Geetha Kanaparan

Editors

Computer Science and Education

Educational Digitalization

18th International Conference, ICCSE 2023
Sepang, Malaysia, December 1–7, 2023
Proceedings, Part III

Springer

Editors
Wenxing Hong (iD)
Xiamen University
Xiamen, China

Geetha Kanaparan (iD)
Xiamen University Malaysia
Sepang, Malaysia

ISSN 1865-0929   ISSN 1865-0937 (electronic)
Communications in Computer and Information Science
ISBN 978-981-97-0736-2   ISBN 978-981-97-0737-9 (eBook)
https://doi.org/10.1007/978-981-97-0737-9

Preface

Welcome to the proceedings of the 18th International Conference on Computer Science & Education (ICCSE 2023), held December 1–7, 2023, at Xiamen University Malaysia in Selangor, Malaysia. We proudly present these volumes encompassing both online and in-person presentations.

Since its inception in 2006, ICCSE has served as a premier international forum for sharing and exploring cutting-edge advances in computer science, education, and allied fields like engineering and advanced technologies. It bridges the gap between industry, research, and academia, fostering dynamic information exchange and collaboration.

Under the theme "Empowering development of high-quality education with digitalization", ICCSE 2023 invited and received 305 submissions in total, culminating in 106 high-quality manuscripts accepted for these proceedings. Each underwent a rigorous double-blind peer-review process (three reviews per submission) by an esteemed international panel consisting of organizing and advisory committee members and renowned experts.

The proceedings are organized into three volumes reflecting the diversity of submissions: Computer Science and Technology, Teaching and Curriculum, and Educational Digitalization. These reflect the latest developments in computing technologies and their educational applications. Volume 1 covers topics like data science, machine learning, and large language models, while Volume 2 delves into curriculum reform, online learning, and MOOCs. Finally, Volume 3 explores digital transformation and new digital technology applications.

ICCSE 2023 had a dynamic technical program, brimming with cutting-edge insights from renowned figures and diverse opportunities for engagement. Three captivating keynote speeches kicked off the conference:

- Xu Rongsheng, from the Chinese Academy of Sciences, delved into the intricate interplay between the internet, China, and cybersecurity, sparking thought-provoking discussions.
- Andrew Ware, of the University of South Wales, shed light on the transformative potential of generative AI in education, inspiring new perspectives on learning and teaching.
- Zhou Aoying, from East China Normal University, navigated the complexities of digital transformation and its impact on smart education, offering practical guidance for navigating the evolving landscape.

Beyond the keynotes, a dedicated workshop titled "Digitalization Capability Level Certification" provided participants with valuable tools and frameworks for assessing and enhancing their digital skills. Additionally, two Best Paper sessions and 11 parallel sessions offered platforms for researchers to showcase their groundbreaking work and engage in stimulating dialogue with peers.

This comprehensive program ensured that every author had the opportunity to present their research to a receptive audience, fostering a vibrant exchange of ideas and fostering meaningful collaborations.

In closing, we express heartfelt gratitude to everyone who made ICCSE 2023 possible. Our thanks go to the program chairs for their program expertise, the publication committee for their meticulous review process, and the local organizing committee led by the School of Computing and Data Science at Xiamen University Malaysia. We hope these proceedings inspire further discourse and collaboration in the ever-evolving world of computer science and education.

December 2023

Geetha Kanaparan
Wenxing Hong

Organization

Honorary Chairs

Jonathan Li   University of Waterloo, Canada
Wang Huiqiong   Xiamen University Malaysia, Malaysia
Li Maoqing   Xiamen University, China

General Chairs

Geetha Kanaparan   Xiamen University Malaysia, Malaysia
Hong Wenxing   Xiamen University, China

Organizing Chairs

Miraz Mahdi Hassan   Xiamen University Malaysia, Malaysia
Hu Jie   Zhejiang University, China
Yang Chenhui   Xiamen University, China

Program Chairs

Li Xin   Louisiana State University, USA
Li Chao   Tsinghua University, China
Wang Qing   Tianjin University, China

Publications Chairs

Weng Yang   Sichuan University, China
Yang Fan   Xiamen University, China

Industry Chairs

Ding Yu   Netease Fuxi AI Lab, China
Cui Binyue   Xiamen Digital Twin Information Technology Co,
                           China

Regional Chairs

Lang Haoxiang   Ontario Tech University, Canada
Xia Min   Lancaster University, UK.

Program Committees

Adam Saeid Pirasteh   Xiamen University Malaysia, Malaysia
Ben M. Chen   Chinese University of Hong Kong, Hong Kong
                           SAR, China
Cen Gang   Zhejiang University of Science and Technology,
                           China
Chen Zhibo   Beijing Forestry University, China
Chen Zhiguo   Henan University, China
Ching-Shoei Chiang   Soochow University, Taiwan
Clarence de Silva   University of British Columbia, Canada
Deng Zhigang   University of Houston, USA
Ding Yu   Netease Fuxi AI Lab, China
Dong Zhicheng   Xizang University, China
Farbod Khoshnoud   California State University, Pomona, USA
Geetha Kanaparan   Xiamen University Malaysia, Malaysia
He Li   Software Guide Magazine, China
He Liang   East China Normal University, China
Hiroki Takada   University of Fukui, Japan
Hiromu Ishio   Fukuyama City University, Japan
Hong Wenxing   Xiamen University, China
Wang Huiqiong   Xiamen University Malaysia, Malaysia
Hu Jie   Zhejiang University, China
Huang Jie   Chinese University of Hong Kong, Hong Kong
                           SAR, China
Jiang Qingshan   Shenzhen Institutes of Advanced Technology,
                           CAS, China
Jin Dawei   Zhongnan University of Economics and Law,
                           China

Jonathan Li	University of Waterloo, Canada
Koliya Pulasinghe	Sri Lanka Institute of Information Technology, Sri Lanka
Lang Haoxiang	Ontario Tech University, Canada
Li Chao	Tsinghua University, China
Li Taoshen	Nanning University, China
Li Teng	University of British Columbia, Canada
Li Xiaohong	Tianjin University, China
Li Xin	Texas A & M University, USA
Li Ying	Beihang University, China
Lin Xianke	Ontario Tech University, Canada
Lin Zongli	University of Virginia, USA
Liu Renren	Xiangtan University, China
Liu Tao	Anhui University of Engineering, China
Liu Tenghong	Zhongnan University of Economics and Law, China
Luo Juan	Hunan University, China
Peng Yonghong	Manchester Metropolitan University, UK
Peter Liu	Carleton University, Canada
Qiang Yan	Taiyuan University of Technology, China
Qiao Baojun	Henan University, China
Sena Seneviratne	University of Sydney, Australia
Shao Haidong	Hunan University, China
Shen Xiajiong	Henan University, China
Tom Worthington	Australian National University, Australia
Wang Chunzhi	Hubei University of Technology, China
Wang Jiangqing	South-Central University for Nationalities, China
Wang Ming	Lishui University, China
Wang Ning	Xiamen Huaxia University, China
Wang Qing	Tianjin University, China
Wang Yang	Southwest Petroleum University, China
Wang Ying	Xiamen University, China
Wang Zidong	Brunel University London, UK
Wei Shikui	Beijing Jiaotong University, China
Wen Lifang	China Machine Press, China
Weng Yang	Sichuan University, China
Wu Xinda	Neusoft Institute Guangdong, China
Xi Bin	Xiamen University, China
Xi Chunyan	Computer Education Press, China
Xia Min	Lancaster University, UK
Xiangjian (Sean) He	University of Technology Sydney, Australia

Xiao Huimin	Henan University of Finance and Economics, China
Xie Lihua	Nanyang Technological University, Singapore
Xu Li	Fujian Normal University, China
Xu Zhoubo	Guilin University of Electronic Technology, China
Xue Jingfeng	Beijing Institute of Technology, China
Yang Li	Hubei Second Normal College, China
Yang Mei	Southwest Petroleum University, China
Yu Yuanlong	Fuzhou University, China
Zeng Nianyin	Xiamen University, China
Zhang Dongdong	Tongji University, China
Zhang Yunfei	ViWiStar Technologies Ltd, Canada
Zhao Huan	Hunan University, China
Zheng Li	Tsinghua University, China
Zhou Qifeng	Xiamen University, China
Zhou Wei	Beijing Jiaotong University, China
Zhu Shunzhi	Xiamen University of Technology, China

Additional Reviewers

Aditya Abeysinghe	University of Sydney, Australia
Ahmad Affandi Supli	Xiamen University Malaysia, Malaysia
Akihiro Sugiura	Gifu University of Medical Science, Japan
Al-Fawareh Hejab Ma'azer Khaled	Xiamen University Malaysia, Malaysia
Cen Yuefeng	Zhejiang University of Science & Technology, China
Chen Lina	Zhejiang Normal University, China
Chen Linshu	Hunan University of Science and Technology, China
Chen Zhen	Tsinghua University, China
Ding Qin	Anhui University of Science & Technology, China
Fumiya Kinoshita	Toyama Prefectural University, Japan
Gou Pingzhang	Northwest Normal University, China
Hironari Sugai	University of Fukui, Japan
Huang Tianyu	Beijing Institute of Technology, China
Jiang Huixian	Fujian Normal University, China
Jin Ying	Nanjing University, China
Kenichiro Kutsuna	Thaksin University, Thailand
Lee Sui Ping	Xiamen University Malaysia, Malaysia
Li Ji	Guangdong University of Foreign Studies, China

Li Sibei	Sichuan University, China
Li Xiaoying	Hunan University, China
Li Yifan	University of Sanya, China
Liu Yiwen	Huaihua University, China
Ma Ji	Xiamen University, China
Mahdi Miraz	Xiamen University Malaysia, Malaysia
Mao Jiali	East China Normal University, China
Mallikarachchi Dilshani Hansika	Xiamen University Malaysia, Malaysia
Mailasan Jayakrishnan	Xiamen University Malaysia, Malaysia
Moubachir Madani Fadoul	Xiamen University Malaysia, Malaysia
Qiu Tianhao	Zhejiang University of Science and Technology, China
Subashini Raghavan	Xiamen University Malaysia, Malaysia
Tian Song	Beijing Institute of Technology, China
Wang Ji	Xiamen University, China
Wang Junlu	Liaoning University, China
Wang Ying	Xiamen University, China
Xiong Yu	Chongqing University of Posts and Telecommunications, China
Yasuyuki Matsuura	Gifu City Women's College, Japan
Yu Niefang	Huaihua University, China
Yuan Haomiao	Nanjing Normal University, China
Yue Kun	Yunnan University, China
Zamratul Asyikin	Xiamen University Malaysia, Malaysia
Zhang Ping	Anhui Polytechnic University, China
Zhang Yupei	Northwestern Polytechnical University, China
Zhong Ping	Central South University, China
Zhou Yujie	Henan University, China

Contents – Part III

Frontiers in Educational Digitalization

Policies and Theories of Educational Digitalization

Discussion on Construction of the Progressive Practice Teaching for Computer Majors Under the New Engineering Background

Xiangyu Dai[1] , Juan Luo[2]([⊠]) , and Ke Li[3]

[1] Hunan Vocational College of Commerce, Changsha, China
[2] Hunan University, Changsha, China
juanluo@hnu.edu.cn
[3] Changsha Preschool Teachers College, Changsha, China

Abstract. In order to make the talents trained by vocational education more suitable for the needs of new engineering construction. This paper proposes a teaching model based on the concept of achievement oriented education. We have constructed a progressive practical teaching model based on School-enterprise cooperation. Through the continuous improvement and optimization of teachers' team, curriculum system, resource platform and practical teaching process, the engineering ability of vocational education talents can be cultivated.

Keywords: New engineering · Vocational education · School-enterprise cooperation · Practical teaching

1 Introduction

With the background of new economy and new industry, new engineering is developed from engineering education. On the one hand, it is necessary to set up and develop a number of new engineering majors, on the other hand, it is necessary to promote the reform and innovation of existing engineering majors [1, 2]. Under the background of new engineering construction, how computer majors should adapt to the requirements of new engineering construction, deepen the reform of engineering education, and cultivate professionals who can meet the needs of current industrial development is the key problem to be solved in the connotation construction of computer majors. Vocational education is the main body of training skilled and applied talents, and computer major is a discipline major with strong practicality. Under the background of new engineering construction, how to play the role of practical teaching in training computer professionals in vocational education is becoming more and more important.

At present, more than 1,000 colleges and universities in China offer engineering majors, and the number of students accounts for about 30% of the total number of college students. At present, domestic vocational colleges are actively exploring and practicing the training mode of engineering talents, but there are still some problems, such as the lack of close integration of students' theoretical study and practice, and the mismatch with the actual employment needs of enterprises [3]. There are various reasons for this phenomenon, but one of the main reasons is that the practical teaching effect can't meet the requirements of enterprises. OBE (Outcomes-Based Education) theory is an educational idea that guides the training of engineering talents in order to adapt to the current economy and industry [4, 5]. Through defining the goal of talent training, reasonably formulating the graduation requirements, scientifically constructing the curriculum system, and persisting in continuous improvement and other teaching links, we can promote the reform of engineering education and improve the quality of engineering talent training [6]. Based on this, this paper takes the construction method of progressive practice teaching mode as an example, expounds that under the guidance of OBE concept of achievement-oriented education, aiming at output-oriented, ability-oriented, and employment innovation-oriented, it explores a school-enterprise cooperation mode that adapts to the cultivation of vocational education talents in new engineering construction.

2 Training of Computer Majors Under School-Enterprise Cooperation

2.1 Short-Board of Practical Teaching in the Training of Computer Majors

As a typical application-oriented talent training major, vocational computer major emphasizes the organic combination of "teaching, learning and doing" in educational practice, and the training mode should be closely combined with theory and practice. Under the background of new engineering construction, the training goal of computing major in vocational education is to enable students to master the appropriate depth and breadth of professional knowledge, and be able to work as engineers in enterprises. Students are required to have strong engineering practice ability (to solve engineering problems in their current positions), strong learning ability (to deal with new problems derived from new technologies), good communication skills and technical communication skills (to understand and correctly describe problems and needs). At present, there are some problems in the cultivation of students' engineering practice ability, such as the lack of close integration between students' theoretical study and practice, the mismatch with the actual employment needs of enterprises, and their weak sense of innovation. The main reasons are: lack of pertinence of teaching methods, inaccurate positioning of teaching objectives, lack of relevant engineering practice training experience of teaching staff, and imperfect joint training mode between schools and enterprises [7].

2.2 School-Enterprise Cooperation is the Necessity of Training Computer Profession Talents

There is no fixed mode of education. Based on the current development trend of higher education, the orientation of national education policy and the educational achievements of various colleges and universities, it is not necessarily the inevitable mode of talent cultivation in China's higher education. However, in terms of the new characteristics of new engineering and the choice of talent cultivation path in vocational education, it is the inevitable trend of talent cultivation reform in new engineering through school-enterprise cooperation guided by the government, driven by market demand and actively responded by schools.

From the new characteristics of new engineering, the "new" means the emerging, the late-model and the newly born. New engineering has the characteristics of cross-border integration, advancement, derivation, innovation-driven and practical application. The new features need to introduce the new concept of engineering education, the new structure of disciplines and specialties, the new mode of personnel training, the new quality of education and teaching, and the new system of classified development. However, the traditional combination of production and education is lagging behind, and the new technologies, new processes and new norms of enterprises are often not reflected in schools in time. The relationship between enterprises and schools, which is similar to' friends help', requires the direction of national policies and the guidance of the government to promote the deep participation of enterprises and their integration with schools. Enterprises and schools jointly invest, work out talent plans and cultivate talents to achieve a win-win situation.

From the perspective of training high-quality talents in schools, China's higher education has entered a new stage of popularization. An important feature of the new stage of popularization is the individualization of talent cultivation, respecting the uniqueness of individual students, helping each student to grow into an adult, and truly teaching students in accordance with their aptitude. However, at present, higher education still adopts a single curriculum for different educational objects, which can't take into account students of different foundations and meet the demand of industry for talents of different levels. One of the effective ways to solve these problems is to create a new mechanism of "co-construction, co-management and sharing" of high-quality educational resources: government-led, overall planning, multi-input, linkage between schools and enterprises, breaking the institutional barriers of schools and enterprises, industries and departments, integrating high-quality educational resources, co-constructing training bases and public technical service platforms, and ensuring the efficient and sustainable operation of resource sharing platforms.

2.3 Requirements for Practical Teaching Mode of School-Enterprise Cooperation

The training of computer talents under the new engineering construction needs the deep participation of enterprises. As shown in Fig. 1, on the one hand, the key teachers of school teaching need to participate in the discussion of regional industrial development, and understand the industrial ecology, development trend, characteristics of emerging industries and the demand for talents. On the other hand, under the leadership of the competent government departments, social organizations and enterprises are deeply involved in the training activities of professional talents in colleges and universities, empowering advanced technologies, concepts and experiences into the talent training base in real time, building a talent training program jointly by schools and enterprises, developing a platform for practical teaching resources according to teaching needs, keeping close empowering contact between school teachers and industry enterprises, building a team of practical teaching teachers together, participating in the whole process of talent training, and achieving the training goal that the trained talents meet the needs of the industry, that is, having a certain depth and breadth of professional knowledge. In terms of engineering ability, he has the professional skills to be competent for a position in the computer field, and comprehensive abilities such as practice of incident handling, organization and management, etc. It has patriotic quality and innovative ability in comprehensive literacy.

Industry	Enterprise	School and Enterprise	Training Objective
Joint research on regional industrial development	Advanced productivity tools and experience empowerment	School-enterprise co-construction of practical teaching teachers	Professional knowledge Depth + Breadth
		School-enterprise co-construction of practical resource platform	Engineering ability Skill + Synthesis
		School-enterprise co-construction talent training program	Talent accomplishment Patriotism + Innovation
School-enterprise Cooperation in Training Computer Talents			

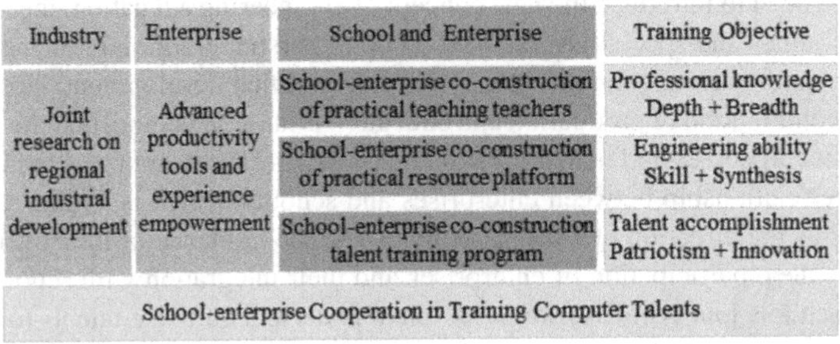

Fig. 1. New requirements for computer talents training in school-enterprise cooperation

3   Construction of Progressive Practical Teaching for Computer Majors

At present, the problems existing in the cultivation of students' engineering practice ability mainly focus on the lack of pertinence of teaching methods, inaccurate positioning of teaching objectives, lack of relevant engineering practice training experience of teachers, and imperfect school-enterprise joint training mode. Therefore, under the guidance of OBE concept, we reverse design and construct the talent training system with output orientation, as shown in Fig. 2. The post talent demand (social demand) of the joint industrial enterprise of the school determines the talent training goal of the school, takes this goal as the criterion, designs the professional knowledge requirements, skill requirements and comprehensive literacy requirements required for graduation, and on this basis, reconstructs the curriculum system and carries out teaching links. In the process of teaching, we need reasonable teachers and perfect supporting conditions to help students with teaching output meet the needs of the society.

The construction model of practical teaching for computer majors is shown in Fig. 3. First of all, it is necessary to build a talent training mode of school-enterprise cooperation, relying on school-enterprise cooperation to build a team of double-qualified school-enterprise tutors with practical teaching ability and teaching experience, so as to ensure the smooth development of talent training activities. Secondly, the school-enterprise tutor team is used to reconstruct the curriculum system and form the support of students' ability cultivation. Once again, build a school-enterprise resource platform to help students achieve their ability efficiently and with high quality; Finally, the platform is used as a carrier for classroom teaching and assessment, so as to cultivate students' ability.

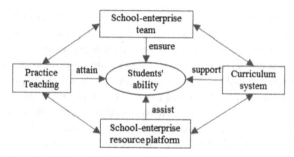

Fig. 2. OBE output-oriented teaching model

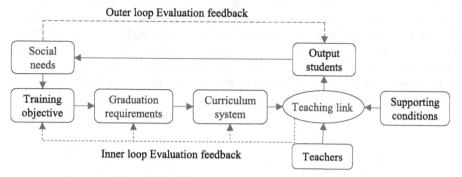

Fig. 3. Construction model of practical for computer majors

3.1 Build a Team of School and Enterprise Mentors with the Mutual Growth of Teaching and Learning

Under the OBE concept, the cultivation of students' computer professional ability requires not only teachers' practical skills, but also teachers' experience in cultivating computer engineering ability. Double-qualified teachers are an important guarantee for the quality and level of computer professionals. Relying on the cooperation between universities and enterprises, on the one hand, we should strengthen the training of double-qualified teachers in schools, encourage professional teachers to take temporary training in enterprises, guarantee six months' training time every three years, work or study in enterprises full-time for one year, learn about the management and operation mode of modern enterprises, study and study new technologies and new processes, and at the same time make use of their own professional knowledge and skills to serve the production and operation of enterprises and strengthen teachers' engineering practice ability. On the other hand, increase the exchange of human resources between schools and enterprises, and hire senior engineers with rich practical experience to cooperate with teachers in schools to jointly complete the teaching of some specialized courses, restricted courses and other courses; Regularly hire enterprise experts and engineering technicians to hold special lectures for students; Or hire enterprise managers to explain knowledge about innovation and entrepreneurship to students and participate in guiding the whole process of innovation and entrepreneurship. Enterprises employ teachers and enterprise engineers to jointly carry out project research and so on. Teachers are enriched in the production line of enterprises, and the talents of enterprises are transferred to schools, so as to realize the sharing of teachers between schools and enterprises.

Mutual improvement of teaching and learning creates an ecological chain of teachers with specialty in schools and enterprises that supports the common growth of teachers and students, as shown in Fig. 4. Taking the School-enterprise cooperation of Huawei ICT Institute as an example, relying on Huawei's school-enterprise cloud platform and Huawei's vocational certification system, we set up a team of school-enterprise joint training teachers, train practical teachers for colleges and universities, build an adequate and comprehensive enterprise real project resource bank, and integrate Huawei certification curriculum system into the cloud platform. Realize the sharing of teaching resources and digitalization of talents through artificial intelligence and big data technology; Through the double methods of school-enterprise joint training teachers, enterprise teaching resources and enterprise real environment, students' engineering practice ability can be efficiently cultivated, and new engineering construction can be helped; Through the implementation of curriculum design, professional certification of teachers and students, enterprise project team service and other means, to create an ecological chain for teachers and students to grow together.

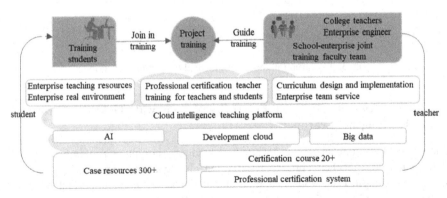

Fig. 4. Ecological chains of mutual improvement of teaching and learning

3.2 Re-Constitute a Result-Oriented Practical Teaching Curriculum System

Based on the idea of result-oriented reverse design, starting from the development needs of students and the needs of enterprises for talents, and according to the characteristics of the knowledge system of computer courses, the content of course practice teaching can be divided into three categories: cognition and foundation, experience and total sum, and research and innovation. They focus on the cultivation of basic knowledge, practical ability and innovative ability respectively. Teaching practice is a necessary supporting condition for cultivating advanced applied innovative talents. This paper takes Routing and Switching Technology as an example to illustrate. This course is the core course of computer network technology specialty. In the professional curriculum system, the practice teaching links related to this course include cognitive practice, basic practice teaching based on project-driven integration of theory and practice, comprehensive practice, national vocational college students' skill competition and graduation design. In order to achieve the training goal of applied innovative talents, it is necessary to build a practice teaching system that is organically integrated with theoretical teaching, hierarchical, multi-module and connected with each other on the basis of the original practice teaching links (see Table 1). Finally, a new practical teaching curriculum system with "cognition and foundation-experience and synthesis-research and innovation" will be formed step by step, with the cultivation of students' engineering practice ability and innovation ability as the core.

Table 1. Practical teaching curriculum system for computer majors.

	Cognitive practice teaching	Cognitive practice
Practical Teaching Curriculum System of Computer-related Specialty	Basic practice teaching	Integration of theory and practice teaching
		Project-driven teaching
	Comprehensive practical teaching	Comprehensive practice
		Internship
	Innovative practice teaching	Skill competition
		Internet + Innovation and Entrepreneurship Competition
		Research projects of teachers in this field
	Applied practice teaching	Curriculum design
		Graduation project

3.3 School-Enterprise Cooperation Resource Platform with Co-Built Output-Orientation

With the promotion of students' comprehensive ability, professional ability, innovation and entrepreneurship as the main line, the school-enterprise joint practice teaching resource platform will be jointly built. The front-line technology, enterprise model and employment resources of enterprises are organically integrated into the process of professional construction, teaching implementation and employment security of schools. The teaching resource construction model is shown in Fig. 5.

The platform construction includes two main parts of teaching content resources and teaching environment resources. Teaching content resources are dominated by schools, including reconstructed and integrated curriculum resources, processing and optimizing enterprise case resources. Teaching environment resources are dominated by enterprises, including enterprise operation and experience environment, and enterprise development and opening laboratory. On the basis of resources and environment, we will build courses that are closely coupled with posts, loose-leaf textbooks that update technology in real time, classroom activities that combine theory with practice, and teaching services that integrate post, class, certificate and creation.

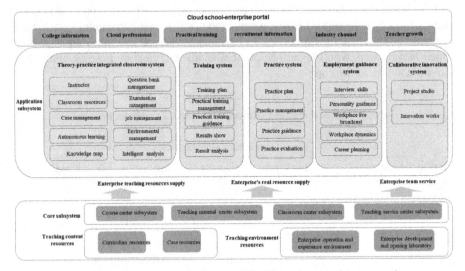

Fig. 5. Teaching resource platform model of School-enterprise cooperation

3.4   Implement Ability Oriented Progressive Practical Teaching

We analyzed the ability requirements of new economy and new industry application, including professional quality, professional foundation, skill application, collaborative ability, innovation ability, expansion ability, etc. With the participation of industry tutors, a modular curriculum system is constructed for the post, and a progressive practical teaching mode of "combination of work and study and project-oriented" is formed on this basis, as shown in Fig. 6. The model is divided into four stages, three modules and four objectives. First, pay attention to and train students' basic skills and professional skills. In the first academic year, the virtual simulation technology is combined to train the course experiment. Through the training of basic skills, we can achieve the goal of skillfully using theoretical knowledge. In the second year, we will train the application ability of professional knowledge. Through school-enterprise cooperation, classic projects or daily small projects of enterprises are designed into professional comprehensive experiments to try to understand the actual engineering positions. In the third academic year, students will train their engineering ability with the platform of school-enterprise cooperation. In the fourth year, the training of scientific research and innovation ability will be carried out. Four-year practice training is uninterrupted, and a progressive training mode is constructed. In this way, students can basically achieve the goal of cultivating high-quality compound new engineering talents by graduation.

Fig. 6. Progressive practical teaching model

4 Conclusion

One of the key points of new engineering construction is the reform and practice of multi-party collaborative education mode. This paper attempts to construct a progressive practice teaching mode based on school-enterprise cooperation from the perspective of OBE achievement-oriented education. To make it mature and applied to vocational higher education, more people need to participate in it, and further improve the theory and strategy of new engineering construction, so that new engineering personnel can better meet the needs of new economy and new industry construction.

Acknowledgment. The author is grateful for the support of Hunan Education Science Foundation under Grant. The content of this paper is one of the research results of Hunan educational science project of Research on the network practice teaching mode of higher vocational education under the background of new engineering. No. of project approval is XJK22CZY038.

References

1. Denghua, Z.: Connotation and action of new engineering construction. Res. High. Eng. Educ. **1**, 1-6 (2017)
2. Bogoslowski, S., Geng, F., Gao, Z., Rajabzadeh, A.R., Srinivasan, S.: Integrated thinking - a cross-disciplinary project-based engineering education. In: Auer, M.E., Centea, D. (eds.) Visions and Concepts for Education 4.0, ICBL 2020, Advances in Intelligent Systems and Computing, vol. 1314, pp. 260–267. Springer, Cham (2021). https://doi.org/10.1007/978-3-030-67209-6_2
3. Jiali, Z.: Hybrid teaching design based on OBE teaching concept. Sci. Technol. Wind **2021**(35), 178–180 (2021)
4. Wang, J., Dong, M., Lou, X., Yan, B.:Reform of diversified talents training mode against the background of engineering education accreditation. In: proceedings of the 2019 International Conference on Advanced Education and Social Science Research (2019)
5. Kaliannan, M., Chandran, S.D.: Empowering students through outcome-based education (OBE). Res. Educ. **87**(10), 50–63 (2012)

6. Wang, Y.: Research on the Design of Learning Activities to Promote the Development of College Students' Design Thinking under the Concept of OBE. Jiangnan University, Wuxi (2021)
7. Li, Y., Wang, Z.: Strategies for improving students engineering practice ability based on OBE concept. China Arab Sci. Technol. Forum (Chinese and English) **2022**(02), 144–148 (2022)

Research on the Cognitive Dimension of Overseas Students in China and from Countries Along "the Belt and Road" on the Image of Ningbo

Li Jun[✉]

School of International Studies, NingboTech University, Ningbo, China
kevindoodoo@163.com

Abstract. This paper carries out a free association test of words on overseas students from countries along "the Belt and Road" in Ningbo, and studies their cognitive dimensions on the image of Ningbo and the influencing factors, so as to further consolidate Ningbo's status as a node city of "the Belt and Road Initiative" and as the bridgehead of Chinese and Western culture, and provide valuable reference for local governments to formulate publicity policies for China and Central and Eastern European Countries Economic and Trade Cooperation Demonstration Zone in Ningbo and to effectively spread the image of Ningbo to the world.

Keywords: the Belt and Road Initiative · city image · cognitive dimension

1 Introduction

Being one of China's earliest coastal cities to open its port to the world, Ningbo serves not only as a focal point for the convergence and interaction of Chinese and Western cultures but also as a showcase for presenting China's national image globally. As a Demonstration Zone for China-Central and Eastern European Countries Economic and Trade Cooperation, Ningbo is steadily establishing an international "circle of friends" for educational and cultural cooperation related to the "Belt and Road Initiative." By the end of 2021, universities in Ningbo had enrolled over 3,000 international students from 113 countries worldwide, with approximately 60 percent of them from countries along the "Belt and Road." [1] These overseas students are not only international audiences in the communication path of Ningbo image, but also the spokespersons for the communication by Ningbo city. In contrast to individual audiences in China who passively receive media information, these overseas students have the conditions and opportunities to closely perceive Ningbo. They serve as active carriers, participating in the promotion of the city's image and influencing public opinion. These individuals genuinely understand

Fund: This paper is the result of the research project supported by a social science planning project of Ningbo in 2023 (project No.: G2023-2-17).

Ningbo and have the potential to become friends of the city. Therefore, studying Ningbo's image through the eyes of overseas students from countries along "the Belt and Road" in Ningbo, along with understanding its dissemination routes, can contribute to enhancing Ningbo's cultural soft power and international image communication capabilities. This is particularly significant as Ningbo holds a crucial position as an important city along "the Belt and Road," offering a unique and effective external perspective for the city's aspirations to become a "functional international city."

2   Research Methods and Data Statistics

2.1   Research Methods

1) *Research design:* In this research, a free association test involving words was administered to overseas students from countries along "the Belt and Road" in Ningbo, aiming to investigate their perceptions of Ningbo's image and their emotional orientation. The word association test, grounded in the associative network memory model in psychology, delves into the cognitive structure of the target concept held by the interviewees. It prompts them to generate several associated words immediately upon encountering the target word. A total of 120 overseas students from six universities in Ningbo, originating from countries along "the Belt and Road," were chosen for the study. The participants, with an average age of 24–30 years, had studied Chinese for an average duration of 24–72 months and resided in China for an average period of 12–48 months. The study took place in a university classroom where the survey was conducted. Using "Ningbo" as the target word, participants were instructed to write eight associated words without any specific format restrictions, language and content of words.

   To ensure accuracy in translating non-Chinese words, professional translators were engaged for the task. Additionally, high-level Chinese learners from the relevant native countries were invited to verify and confirm the translations. This comprehensive approach aimed to enhance the precision and cultural appropriateness of the translations, taking into account both linguistic nuances and cultural context.

2) Data Processing:

   a) *Synonym merger:* The objective of the word association test is to understand the conceptual significance held by the individual being tested. The words used in the test merely serve as external expressions of these concepts. Examining how words with similar meanings converge can provide a more insightful view of the testee's cognitive framework regarding the image of Ningbo.

   b) *Word frequency and weight statistics:* Two indicators are employed to gauge the proportion of words in the cognition of overseas students. The first is word frequency, reflecting the number of times a word is associated. A higher word frequency suggests a greater association by individuals. To ensure representativeness, only words with a frequency greater than or equal to 2 are considered. The second indicator is the weighted score, taking into account the order of association, which impacts its significance. The initial word in the association holds a score of 1, indicating a stronger cognitive connection. Subsequent words are scored as 0.9, 0.8, 0.7, and 0.6, respectively. The score after weighted statistics provides another measure of significance. Both indicators are consistent and can be cross-referenced for a comprehensive understanding.

3) Questionnaire

    a) *Questionnaire design:* This research, utilizing a word association test conducted on overseas students from countries along "the Belt and Road" in Ningbo, employed questionnaires to investigate the subjects' inclination to promote the image of Ningbo and their methods of acquiring and comprehending this image. Primarily, through interviews focusing on the ways for overseas students to familiarize themselves with Ningbo, a questionnaire comprising seven options was administered. Participants assigned scores ranging from 1 to 5 based on their individual circumstances, representing various levels of agreement: very disagreement, disagreement, uncertainty, consent, and complete consent. Subsequently, the average value for each option was computed through statistical analysis, facilitating an examination of the approaches to understanding Ningbo and the willingness to disseminate its image.

    b) *Questionnaire contents:* 1. Daily life in Ningbo; 2. Chinese language class; 3. Chinese friends; 4. Mobile phones, micro media, Internet; 5. Chinese publications and news reports; 6. Publications and news reports of home country

B. *Data Statistics*

    The statistics of high frequency words about Ningbo based on free association test of words are as shown in "Table 1":

Table 1. Statistics of High Frequency Words About Ningbo Based on Free Association Test of Words (More Than 10% Frequency)

More people 76 63%	The Bund 68 57%	Fine food and seafood 56 47%	Friendly 51 43%	High-speed railway 49 41%
Mobile payment 47 39%	Weather 46 38%	Tianyi Pavilion 41 34%	Chinese 40 33%	Ningbo dialect 35 29%
Museum 27 23%	Nottingham 2 1 18%	Batterycart 18 15%	Park 14 12%	Takeout (convenience)12 10%

3   Data Analysis and Survey Findings

3.1   The Constitutional Dimension and Positive Recognition of Ningbo Image by Overseas Students from Countries Along "The Belt and Road " in Ningbo

The notion of "city image" was initially introduced by the American communication scholar Kevin Lynch. He posited that the city image comprises five essential elements: path, edge, district, node, and landmark. (K.Lynch, 1960) [2]. Later, P.Kotler and others defined the image of a place as "a combination of people's beliefs, ideals and impressions on a place". [3] In contemporary times, the prevailing belief is that a city's image encompasses a comprehensive impression and perception conveyed to the public in political, economic, environmental, and cultural dimensions. People's perception of a city's image is derived not only from tangible elements such as urban form, architecture, and infrastructure but also from the intangible aspects of urban culture, customs, and spiritual civilization. [4]

In this study, the author collected a total of 1065 valid responses through a word association test conducted on 120 overseas students from 6 universities in Ningbo, representing countries along "the Belt and Road." Following the consolidation of synonyms and statistical analysis of word frequencies, 15 groups of high-frequency words, each with an occurrence of more than 10%, were identified (refer to "Table 1"). By considering the relevance of these high-frequency words, it becomes feasible to encapsulate the image of Ningbo as perceived by overseas students, delineating it across five dimensions. (See "Table 2").

Table 2. The Image of Ningbo in the Eyes of Overseas Students from Five Dimensions

Culture dimension	The Bund	Fine food	Tianyi Pavilion	Chinese	Ningbo dialect	Museum	Nottingham	47%
Economic dimension	High-speed railway	Mobile payment	Battery cart	Takeout				27%
Ecological dimension	More people	Weather	Park					20%
Citizen dimension	Friendly							6%
Political dimension								0%

According to the statistics, the historical culture of Ningbo emerges as the most crucial dimension in shaping the city's image among overseas students from countries along "the Belt and Road" in Ningbo. The enduring historical culture consistently stands out as a primary symbol in the external portrayal of China's image. [5] For a city, historical culture stands out as the most pivotal factor in shaping its image. The well-known slogan encapsulating Ningbo's city image, "a city of culture and a gateway to the world," succinctly captures the historical and cultural essence of Ningbo as perceived by overseas students. Tianyi Pavilion library, the earliest private library in China and the oldest existing library in Asia, holds significance as one of the world's earliest three family libraries. It also marks the earliest port opening to the outside world and lease area in China's "Five-port Trading." Among overseas students from countries along "the Belt and Road" in Ningbo, Tianyi Pavilion and Ningbo Bund are widely recognized. The Bund has evolved into a landmark gathering spot for leisure among many overseas students in Ningbo. Furthermore, elements such as Ningbo cuisine (including seafood and sweet dumplings), the Ningbo dialect, and the Ningbo Museum are frequently mentioned, contributing to the dissemination of Ningbo's urban characteristics and image. An interesting highlight is the mention of "Nottingham" as the sole content related to Ningbo's education in the high-frequency words of the cultural dimension. This signifies that the University of Nottingham has become a paradigm of Sino-foreign cooperation in higher education and stands as an international brand in China's higher education landscape. Its success has significantly propelled the international development of Ningbo.

The economic dimension emerges as the second-ranking factor in shaping the image of Ningbo city, with economic high-frequency words constituting over a quarter of the statistical data across the five dimensions. Terms such as high-speed railway, mobile payment, battery cars, and takeouts serve as reflections of China's achievements in economic development, infrastructure construction, and scientific and technological innovation. Overseas students' perceptions of Ningbo in the economic dimension align with the city's dominant functions. With a well-developed manufacturing industry, high trade status, and a prominent position in harbor, traditional manufacturing, and certain high-tech industries in China, Ningbo boasts the third-highest total foreign trade volume among the 15 sub-provincial cities. Its strengths in industrial and commercial enterprises, industrial technology, brand recognition, market share, and internationalization levels are generally leading. As a developed coastal open city and a hub city for "the Belt and Road Initiative" in China, Ningbo's level of economic development leaves a lasting impression on many overseas students. These students, hailing from countries along "the Belt and Road," can play a vital role in disseminating their firsthand experiences in Ningbo and China, thereby significantly contributing to the international image of Ningbo. This not only aids in the continual global promotion of China's "the Belt and Road Initiative" but also contributes to the ongoing enhancement of the initiative in practical terms.

Ningbo, positioned as a quintessential water town and harbor city in the Yangtze River Delta, boasts distinctive advantages in ecological livability and lifestyle. The survey reveals that over 80% of interviewed overseas students consider Ningbo to be an ecological and livable city. The city's moderate pace of work and life, efficient water, road, and air transportation options, riverside promenades, abundant urban parks, favorable warm and humid climate, and overall high-quality ecological and living environment contribute to the satisfaction of most overseas students with their study and life experiences in Ningbo. Notably, the term "Ningbo man" is frequently mentioned by overseas students, reflecting a characteristic feature of the city's population. Interestingly, the comment "although there are many people, the public security and order are kept" underscores the ecological livability traits of Ningbo. Undoubtedly, the ecological dimension of Ningbo's city image has emerged as a prominent and positive aspect for the city's external communication, setting it apart as a distinctive feature among the many Chinese cities visited by overseas students.

It is unfortunate that many foreigners, particularly those who have not personally visited China, may harbor significant prejudices against Chinese people. This bias often stems from the highly skewed and biased narrative surrounding China's image perpetuated by modern and contemporary Western countries. [6] Even with our neighboring country, South Korea, achieving a positive perception is challenging. A survey conducted in South Korea indicates that 92% of respondents believe Chinese people are unclean, while 80% perceive them as inconsiderate, highly self-respecting, and difficult to trust. Additionally, 78.9% express the opinion that Chinese individuals are generally not trustworthy. [7] At times, physical presence can be the most effective means of mutual understanding. In this context, overseas students in Ningbo express positive sentiments towards the local residents. A notable 43% of them explicitly describe Ningbo citizens as "friendly." Moreover, a significant proportion of overseas students view Ningbo citizens as "polite," "orderly," "kind," "hardworking," and possess other positive qualities. Fewer than 3% of overseas students in Ningbo hold the belief that Ningbo people are "noisy" and "do not queue." An example from a Polish student underscores the positive impression gained during their time in Ningbo. The student notes that Chinese people in Ningbo appeared more civilized and friendly, in stark contrast to the portrayal in Polish media, films, and literary works. Historically, as one of China's earliest ports open to the world, Ningbo was influenced by Westerners who brought material, systemic, and spiritual aspects of European and American civilization. Over time, Ningbo evolved into a Western cultural enclave and a showcase for Western culture. [8] This has significantly expanded the international perspective of the residents of Ningbo and fostered their tolerance towards foreign cultures.

The only thing that does not appear in the high-frequency words of Ningbo city image is the content of political dimension. The political dimension of city image mainly refers to the external image and administrative efficiency of government agencies. There are two main reasons why the government dimension is seldom involved in the association test and questionnaire survey for overseas students in Ningbo. One is that overseas students have less direct contact with government agencies and lack relevant knowledge of Ningbo municipal government agencies; the other is that the core of this survey is the image of Ningbo city rather than that of China. Therefore, the political dimension is rarely mentioned by overseas students.

3.2 Negative Cognition of Overseas Students from Countries Along "the Belt and Road" in Ningbo on Ningbo Image

While the majority of high-frequency words in the free association test about "Ningbo" convey positive sentiments, it's crucial to address a few negative words that warrant attention. Data analysis reveals that the term "noisy" constitutes 6.1% of all counted words, "not queuing" makes up 5.3%, "toilet sanitation" is at 4.65%, and "spitting everywhere" stands at 3.1%. Numerous overseas students in Ningbo acknowledge the city's adherence to rules and regulations, surpassing many other cities in China. However, occasional instances of people not forming lines for buses or shopping and disregarding traffic rules at intersections lead to dissatisfaction among overseas students, diminishing their favorable impression of Ningbo. Some students also bring up concerns such as "taxi refusal," "relationship," "pollution," and "smoking." The negative image perceived by certain overseas students may stem from cultural differences, but it also reflects longstanding habits and urgent issues that need attention in the process of social development or transformation.

All Ningbo citizens should attach importance to these problems. Ningbo people should accept the criticism from the outside frankly, put aside the so-called matter of ego, and work together to start from their own. Meanwhile, they should begin with every little thing around them, love Ningbo, and make Ningbo beautiful. Only in this way can Ningbo become a more beautiful, harmonious and charming Chinese port city in the eyes of more and more overseas students and friends.

4 Implications and Suggestions

4.1 Integrating into Ningbo History and Culture and Daily Life to Cultivate Overseas Students' Cross-cultural Adaptability

In the process of internationalization of higher education in Ningbo, excellent overseas students have been continuously added. Upon entering a novel and unfamiliar culture, individuals often experience varying degrees of discomfort in a cross-cultural environment due to their unfamiliarity with the code of conduct and social norms of the new cultural setting. Overseas students in Ningbo consistently face "culture shock," causing them headaches or trouble. Failure to effectively address these challenges can significantly impact their academic and personal lives. In severe cases, some students may even develop serious mental health issues, ultimately resulting in a negative impression not only of Ningbo but of China as a whole. Therefore, the integration of Ningbo stories into daily campus life and international Chinese classes will help them fully understand Ningbo's history and culture and their own behavior and emotional tendencies, be conducive to their smooth learning and life in a different cultural environment, and improve their understanding of the culture and local customs of Yongcheng, thus providing beneficial enlightenment for the healthy development of internationalization of higher education in Ningbo.

4.2 Constructing Multi-lingual Convergence Media Information Dissemination Channels to Provide Efficient and Accurate Information Window for Overseas Students

The "convergence media" is a new type of media that makes full use of media carriers, and integrates radio, television, newspapers and other media that have both common ground and complementarity in terms of manpower, content and publicity, so as to realize "resource accommodation, content compatibility, publicity integration and co-fusion of interest". [9] In the survey, numerous overseas students in Ningbo highlighted the lack of effective channels to access information about local customs and current affairs in Ningbo. Presently, there are only a few foreign-language radio stations, TV programs, newspapers, and other media outlets offering information on Ningbo's history and culture for overseas students and foreigners. There is a notable absence of mobile apps or multi-language platforms on micro-media for this purpose. The limited communication channels provided by convergent media significantly impede the internationalization process of Ningbo city. Moreover, the lack of accessible information and the potential spread of hearsay contribute to cross-cultural misunderstandings among foreigners regarding the image of Ningbo city. Therefore, it is urgent for us to build a convergence media platform with the characteristics of Ningbo's local "cultural business card", establish the "international concept" of communication of Ningbo culture, pay close attention to the "user experience" of overseas students in the convergence media, and constantly improve and promote the "Ningbo model" spreading to the outside to improve Ningbo's international image.

4.3   Further Enhancing the Civilized Quality of Ningbo Citizens and Improving the Public Civilized Image of Ningbo as an "International Functional City"

Citizens' quality decides the level of a city, and relates to the image and operation efficiency of a city. [10] The quality of citizens is central to urban civilization and plays a fundamental role in its construction. The good manners exhibited by citizens serve as a tangible representation of urban civilization. The public consciousness and moral standards of citizens directly impact the collective behavior of urban residents, influencing the public environment within a city. These factors also reflect the spiritual temperament and external image of a city. Improving the overall civilization quality of citizens is not only a pressing need for achieving a well-off society comprehensively but also essential for enhancing a city's level of civilization and meeting the necessary requirements for the harmonious development of both its soft and hard environments. The key to elevating the civilization of a city lies in the continuous improvement of citizens' quality. Building Ningbo into an "international functional city" is the goal of Ningbo's urban development. Improving citizens' civilization quality and changing the inherent prejudice against us by overseas students and international friends played a vital role in this process.

5   Conclusion

Predictably, as China's "the Belt and Road Initiative" continues to develop, an increasing number of overseas students from countries along "the Belt and Road" in Ningbo will be regarded as ambassadors to represent Ningbo. This will have a significant and positive impact on the international dissemination of Ningbo's image, contributing to the ongoing promotion and enhancement of China's "the Belt and Road Initiative" globally. Such efforts will not only strengthen Ningbo's position as a cultural bridgehead between China and the West but will also serve as valuable guidance for relevant governments in formulating publicity policies for the China-Central and Eastern European Countries Economic and Trade Cooperation Demonstration Zone in Ningbo. This, in turn, will effectively promote and broadcast the image of Ningbo to a global audience.

Acknowledgment. The author gratefully acknowledges the research project supported by a social science planning project of Ningbo in 2023 (project No.: G2023-2-17).

References

1. http://www.ningbo.gov.cn/art/2021/7/2/art_1229096013_3747635.html
2. Lynch, K.: The Image of the City. The MIT Press, Cambridge (1960)
3. Kotler, P., Haider, D.H.: Marketing Places: Attracting Investment, Industry, and Tourism to Cities, States, and Nations. The Free Press, New York (1993)

4. Smith, A.: Conceptualizing city image change: the 're- imaging' of Barcelona. Tour. Geogr. **74**, 98–423 (2005)
5. Chan, B.: Virtual communities and Chinese national identity. J. Chin. Overseas **21**, 1–32 (2006)
6. William, C.: Prejudice against prejudices": China and the limits of Whig Liberalism. Eur. Romant. Rev. **24**, 509–529 (2013)
7. Dong, X.R., Wang, X.L.: The Image of China through the Eyes of Koreans. Social Sciences Academic Press, Beijing (2012). (in Chinese)
8. Yong, H.: Ningbo: a city with stories. Modern Chin. Popul. **28**, 2 (2011)
9. Huang, E.: Facing the challenges of convergence media professionals' concerns of working across media platforms. Convergence **12**, 83–98 (2006)
10. Xuan, L.I.: Improve citizens' quality and reinforce national soft-strength. J. Dali Univ. **7**, 38–40 (2008)

Research on Teaching Model Innovation in the Context of Smart Learning

Hao Wang[1] and Huiyan Li[2(✉)]

[1] Hospitality Institute of Sanya, Sanya, China
[2] Sanya Universtiy, Sanya, China
109375642@qq.com

Abstract. Information technology is an important source and force for the current education reform and development. It has improved the innovation of teaching methods and teaching strategies as a tool; It has expanded the scope of teaching resources as the content; It has leaded the development of education as a tendency. It has spawned a new educational form——smart education. The concept of smart education has contributed to the occurrence of smart learning, and smart learning can be realized in a smart learning context. In the smart learning environment, not only the educational philosophy, models, and forms has changes greatly, but also the methods in teaching and learning will appear revolutionary changes. Therefore, research on the teaching strategy in the smart learning context is one of the issues that must be studied and solved by the current teaching model innovation and reform environment, and it is also the prerequisite for ensuring the implementation of smart learning.

Keywords: Smart Learning · Teaching Mode · Human Anatomy · Innovation

1 Introduction

The smart learning context is guided by the concept of smart education, relying on modern educational technologies such as the Internet of Things, artificial intelligence, big data and cloud computing, to promote the personalized development of learners. Different learning environments have certain effects on learning behavior. Under the background of "Internet + ", in order to meet the demands of the development of smart education, the method of teaching and learning change with the learning environment, so their teaching strategies are also changing. In the era of "Internet + education", the smart learning environment, with its advantages of intelligence, relies on the support of new information technology, takes learners as the center, and pushes learning resources intelligently according to their needs to meet their personalized development. Under such an environmental background, teachers should adopt appropriate teaching strategies and carry out corresponding teaching activities according to the teaching content and the different performance and needs of learners, so as to provide learners with more personalized and intelligent services.

W. Hong and G. Kanaparan (Eds.): ICCSE 2023, CCIS 2025, pp. 22–29, 2024.
https://doi.org/10.1007/978-981-97-0737-9_3

The emergence of smart learning has solved some of the problems that cannot be solved in the traditional teaching environment, and better satisfies the personalized learning and development of learners. However, smart learning is a new learning form. How to use personalized teaching strategies and innovative teaching models in a smart learning environment, to promote students' smart learning and improve learners' problem-solving ability, and cultivate higher-order thinking ability, these are important problems that needs to be solved urgently in the current development of smart education.

2 The Definition of Smart Learning

At present, the definition of "smart learning" in the international academic circle has not been unified. Relevant literature statistics show that South Korea is the country that pays more attention to smart learning abroad. Hwang believes that "smart learning" is a more flexible learning in which learners use open learning resources to enhance their ability to change behavior through smart technology.

According to Kaur, "smart learning" is the process of using multiple information technologies (multimedia, Internet, agent technology) to promote learning. Kwon believe that "smart learning" is that learners can use portable wireless handheld devices to install and operate various applications on a specific platform.

There are many relative studies on smart education in China, but few studies on smart learning practice. Chen Lin believes that smart learning enables learners to make full use of the smart learning environment, seamlessly access smart devices, and cultivate learners' good value orientation and agile thinking ability. Professor Zhu Zhiting believes that smart learning is a learning activity in which learners can use relevant technologies to promote knowledge construction and innovative practice. He Bin believes that smart learning is a new learning paradigm with learner-centered and self-directed learning experience.

To sum up, the definition of smart learning can be understood from the multi-perspective of human and technological environment itself. From the perspective of learners, "smart learning" is a learning process that takes learners as the center, participates in various learning activities, and realizes personalized learning development and self-reflection. From a technical point of view, "smart learning" is an autonomous exploration activity in which learners using intelligent devices (Smart phone, iPad and various mobile terminals, etc.), by means of social networks and sensors. From the perspective of the relationship between people, technology and the environment, "smart learning" is the process of making full use of intelligent equipment, enabling seamless access to technology, prompting learners to implement personalized learning activities and supply personalized services for them so as to improve the learners' higher-order thinking ability.

3 The Characters of Smart Learning

Constructivism theory believes that learning is the interaction between people and the environment. For individual students, the learning environment includes the hard environment of teaching resources and teaching media, the soft environment of different teaching modes. The smart learning supported by information technology has more prominent features of technology-promoting changes in the learning environment. Mainly reflected in the following aspects.

3.1 Easy Access to Learning Resources

In the cloud computing technology in the smart learning, a large number of highly virtualized computing and storage resources are stored and managed to form a huge information resource pool, which can be stored and extracted by users at any time. After AI technology identifies students' learning style or cognitive ability level, it can intelligently push relevant learning resources on demand to promote the effective occurrence of smart learning.

3.2 Intelligence of Learning Media

One of the manifestations of technology-driven changes is the change in learning media, from blackboards and chalks to projectors in the past to smart terminal media in the current, such as e-book bags, smart phones and iPad. These intelligent devices are light and dexterous, but their functions are powerful, and the convenience they provide for learning and teaching cannot be achieved by traditional teaching aids.

3.3 Personalized of Learning Methods

Learning methods in smart learning environment rely on the support of technology, students can use intelligent learning media equipment, through augmented reality technology, to obtain real learning experience and interaction, and promote the meaning construction of knowledge. The smart learning can satisfy learners to connect with the learning community anytime, anywhere and find a learning community. Based on the same learning knowledge points, mutual exchanges and discussions, under the individual guidance of teachers, the needs of individualized development are well met, thereby promoting the development of lifelong learning.

3.4 Dynamics of Learning Evaluation

The smart learning constructed by new generation of information technology, can comprehensively and accurately carry out pre-school diagnostics for students. Use big data to record learners' learning process data, use artificial intelligence technology to identify learners' cognitive style and learning status, use learning analysis technology to analyze students' learning process data, and then realize students' process evaluation. At the same time, teachers can make summative evaluations based on students' learning results over a period of time. Teachers can understand the progress of different students' learning through the information of different students' learning process stored in the system. Based on this, teachers can propose staged personalized and applicable evaluations for each student, so as to improve students' learning initiative and enthusiasm.

4   Reform and Innovation of Teaching Mode in the Context of Smart Learning

The smart learning can support learners to create a variety of scenarios to carry out personalized learning, so as to meet the self-adaptive learning needs of learners in different scenarios and play the main role of learners. Through the analysis of the evolution and comparison of the learning environment and the development trend of teaching strategies, based on the characteristics of the smart learning, the following suggestions are put forward for the reform and innovation of teaching strategies in smart learning.

4.1   Highlight the Role of the Learner's in the Smart Learning

Under the support of the new generation of information technology, learners carry out adaptive learning in the smart learning environment. The main role of learners in the smart learning environment is mainly reflected in the following aspects:

First, learners can choose learning resources and tools independently, create learning situations according to the learning content, with the assistance of technical means and teachers, and conduct free group collaborative learning. In this process, self-determined learning goals can be achieved.

Second, according to learning needs, the situational awareness in smart learning can automatically and intelligently push corresponding learning resources, so that autonomous learning can proceed smoothly.

Third, big data real-time monitoring of learner learning process, dynamic evaluation, real-time feedback of learning information, these can all promote learners complete learning tasks independently and achieve personalized development.

4.2   Expand the Utilization of Digital Learning Resources in Smart Learning

Under the background of "Internet + education", with the continuous updating of information technology and the arrival of the era of smart education, the demand for personalized learning is constantly expanding due to the development of information technology. How to make digital learning resources meet the personalized learning needs of learners better and realize the intelligent development of resources requires further thinking.

In the new round of educational informatization construction, the continuous updating of teachers' educational concepts, the continuous improvement of teaching resources, and the continuous improvement of teaching strategies have provided a good theoretical basis for educational reform. The environment, teaching methods and learning methods have changed greatly in smart learning which supported by technology. Digital learning resources have developed from convenience, diversity, and interactivity to sharing and intelligence, and learning resource construction has developed from computer-based terminals to all kinds of mobile smart terminals, from teaching assistants to student assistants to widespread use, from assisting formal learning to supporting informal learning and even the smart learning. Technology promotes educational innovation and brings about the intelligence of the learning environment. At the same time, learning resources also tend to develop intelligently, realizing the intelligent recommendation of personalized learning resources, which is conducive to the personalized development of learners.

4.3 Strengthen the Design of Deep Teaching Interaction in Smart Learning

The teaching interaction in smart learning can form different interactive relationships according to the teaching elements involved in the teaching process. The teaching elements in smart learning mainly include teachers, learners, environment, resources, educational technology, etc. The interaction relationship between the elements can be divided into learners and teachers, learners and learning environment, learners and resources, learners Interactions with themselves, and interactions between teachers and environment, teachers and resources, and teachers themselves. In the interactive relationship between the above elements, teachers and learners are collectively referred as subjects, which can be divided into teaching interaction relationships such as subject and environment, subject and resources, subject and subject, and subject itself. Because of its intelligent characteristics, the smart learning can support different interactive relationships. For example, it can provide learning situation diagnosis, intelligently push learning resources according to their needs, and conduct scientific and comprehensive teaching evaluation.

4.4 Emphasis on Data Mining in the Process of Learning Activities in Smart Learning

The smart learning is an intelligent and efficient learning space built on the basis of constructivist learning theory and using new-generation information technologies such as big data, cloud computing, and the Internet of Things. It uses dynamic learning data in the learning process to digitize teaching decision-making, conduct real-time evaluation and feedback, realize three-dimensional interaction, and push intelligent resource, comprehensively change the traditional teaching form, and propose a new information-based teaching model in the era of smart education.

Smart learning can use the Internet of Things to perceive the learning environment, use artificial intelligence technology to analyze the characteristics of learners, provide learning resources through cloud computing, and use big data learning analysis technology to comprehensively and deeply mine the information of the learners' learning process, so as to realize the personalized and effective study. Based on the support of technology, the smart learning can provide learning resource management services, intelligent management of educational information, and multiple evaluation of learning effects. Through the seamless connection of various technical terminals, it can continue to pay attention to the individual differences of each learner, understand the learning materials, assessment and feedback through the media technology, and then further analyze the situation and optimize the teaching design, which is convenient for teachers to teach accurately. In the process of learning activities, the big data learning analysis technology is used to collect real-time dynamic learning data and real-time analysis and feedback to improve teaching strategies, adjust the teaching process, and achieve three-dimensional communication and exchange between teaching and learning. Through feedback data analysis, smart learning can push real-time relevant learning materials for learners on demand to achieve personalized learning support. The close combination of teaching evaluation and practice promotes the formation of generative teaching strategies and improves the teaching effect.

4.5 Highlighting the Research Process of Teaching Strategies in Smart Learning

The research on teaching strategies in smart learning is based on the concept of smart education, combined with the characteristics and advantages of the smart learning environment, and puts forward suggestions on the design of teaching strategies in smart learning environment from the following three aspects.

Teaching Activity Design Strategies: The teaching design the decision-making process of proposing the best solution to the problem (such as the determination of teaching objectives, the design of teaching content, and the selection of teaching methods and strategies) based on the analysis of learning needs, so as to improve the system of education and teaching performance. That is, while improving the quality of teaching, it should also further improve the teaching effect. Teaching design in smart learning mainly refers to the organization and management of teaching activities with the guidance of smart education concepts and the purpose of promoting learners' training. Based on this, the setting of teaching objectives in the design should take the learner as center and reflect the learner's dominant position, should create a learning situation with the cultivation of learners' higher innovative thinking as the core, should pay attention to the individual needs and realize the individual development of learners guided by questions or tasks.

The Implementing Strategies for Teaching Activities: To Teaching strategy is one of the main links in teaching design. According to the characteristics of different media and their impact on teaching, the design and the implementation of teaching activities have a direct correlation and impact on the quality of teaching. The implementation of teaching activities in the smart learning requires scientific and rational use of the network environment to truly realize that the environment serves for teaching and learning, fully considers the selection of teaching resources and tools, connects relevant learning communities, and pays attention to the individual differences of learners, to recommend related learning resources.

The Evaluation Strategies for Teaching Activities: The evaluation of teaching activities is the feedback of learning results, and it is also the measurement and evaluation of the teaching quality. The smart learning supports technical evaluation of teaching activities, collects and analyzes students' learning effects in time through big data, and realizes personalized process evaluation of students' learning. The intelligent robots can analyze teachers' voices, expressions, movements and interactive information during teaching, so as to provide teachers' real-time diagnosis and advice to achieve accurate teaching evaluation. Because of the intelligent characteristics of smart learning, when proposing corresponding teaching strategies, it is necessary to focus on the research process of strategy formation, and then reflect the scientific nature of strategy formation. Different teaching strategies have their own key functions, and there is no one-size-fits-all strategy. Therefore, to propose a scientific and effective teaching strategy requires a research-based verification process.

5   Reform and Innovation of Teaching Mode in the Context of Smart Learning

"Human Anatomy" course in Sanya University uses inquiry-based teaching. Its key advantage lies in the relationship between teaching and learning, correctly handling the dialectical relationship between "teacher-led" and "student-subject". The teaching of course pays attention to the initiative of both teachers and students, and emphasize the dominant position of students. In this link, every student is the master of learning. Therefore, they take the initiative to acquire knowledge, and the learning goals of each of them are different and open-ended.

The teaching of the "Human anatomy" course is based on individualized learning model reconstruction with students as the main body. The learning task is to choose the 3D reconstruction of the body part of interest. As far as the knowledge system is concerned, although the existing knowledge system is complete, if you want to innovate, you must try to break the rules. Smarter classrooms provide students with sufficient space for in-depth thinking and appropriate space for independent thinking, allowing students to have the opportunity to put forward various questions so as to break the original shackles and achieve the purpose of innovation. Students can choose the content they are interested in, and use 3D reconstruction technology to think and explore independently, and design the structure, composition, and disassembly of objects.

Under the technology of smart classroom, each student selectively learns the knowledge of anatomical muscles and bones according to their own learning interests. These human body knowledge will become omni-directional, horizontal and vertical, 360-degree cognition without dead ends. The deep learning function of human anatomy is conducive to the knowledge internalization and optimization of human bones, muscles, organs and other knowledge learning in students' minds. In the process of teaching, human-computer interaction is enhanced, and the core of this interaction is "user-centered". In this part, students think deeply and need more immersion, presence and experience, so that they can learn and practice for a longer time. The use of enhanced interaction makes our teaching objects more three-dimensional, vivid and interesting. The main purpose is also to improve students' self-efficacy, so that they can form self-learning and independent learning.

The following pictures are the homework of the students.

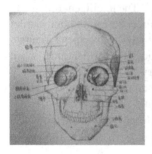 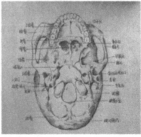 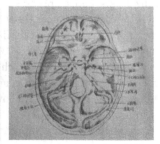

6 Conclusion

Compared with the traditional learning environment, the smart learning has the character-istics of intelligence, personalization and innovation. The essence of the smart learning is the mutual integration of physical learning space and virtual learning space, forming an immersive experience learning method, which urges learners to achieve deep learning. The smart learning not only retains the advantages of classroom teaching in the traditional environment, but also provides convenient conditions for learners to achieve higher-order cognitive goals and promote the development of innovative thinking, making it possible for learners to develop in the true sense.

Acknowledgments. A This research was financially supported by 2021 Research Project of Higher Education and Teaching Reform in Hainan Province (Grant NO. Hnjg2021-98); by 2020 Research Project of Higher Education and Teaching Reform in Hainan Province (Grant NO. Hnjg2020-104).

References

1. Xie, X., Xiao, M., Shen, J.: Optimization of wisdom classroom teaching resources based on visualization software. In: Journal of Physics: Conference Series, p. 1881, no. 3 (2021)
2. Dai, D.: Wisdom class learning task design. Sci. Insights Educ. Front. **8**(S1), 9 (2021)
3. Feng, H.H., Gong, Y.D., Dai, J.: Exploring students' preferences toward the smart class-room learning environment and academic performance. In: 2020 International Symposium on Educational Technology (ISET), Bangkok, Thailand (2020)

Training Methods of Innovative Talents in Medical Imaging Informatics Under the Background of New Engineering

Jin Liu, Qian Bi[✉], Ping Zhong, Hong-Dong Li, Fei Guo, and Junwen Duan

School of Computer Science and Engineering Central, South University Changsha, Changsha, China
970347301@qq.com

Abstract. It is crucial to cultivate the innovative ability of graduate students under the background of new engineering. In this article, we recommend training students' innovative ability from three aspects. Firstly, Follow the particularity Training Methods of medical imaging informatics. Secondly, Compare and study the talent training methods and joint training models in different countries. Thirdly, Establish an effective innovation ability evaluation method. The purpose of improving medical imaging informatics training methods is designed to improve the ability of interdisciplinary science of graduate students, Innovation capabilities and international vision, build a reasonable evaluation indicator to guide and promote the development of interdisciplinary medical imaging informatics.

Keywords: New Engineering · Cultivation Mode · Innovative Talents · Medical Imaging Informatics

1 Introduction

Medical imaging informatics is an emerging interdisciplinary subject formed with the rapid development of computer science and medical imaging [1]. It mainly studies the acquisition of medical images, storing, transmitting, processing and analyzing, and then revealing the mysteries of life endowed by large and complex medical imaging data, it is a major frontier of natural science today and one of the core fields of natural science in the 21st century. As a new interdisciplinary subject, medical imaging informatics still lacks systematic design for its development. At present, they are still distributed under different disciplines, lacking the high degree of interdisciplinary emphasis on their disciplines, and lack of corresponding support policies, so that the development of medical imaging information field has always lagged behind developed countries [2, 3]. At the same time, the field of medical imaging informatics research talents is relatively scarce, the knowledge structure of postgraduates is incomplete, and the international perspective is generally lacking [4]. Therefore, how to accurately locate medical imaging informatics and provide corresponding courses for students at different training stages for directional training will greatly promote the growth of students and the development of interdisciplinary subjects.

© The Author(s), under exclusive license to Springer Nature Singapore Pte Ltd. 2024
W. Hong and G. Kanaparan (Eds.): ICCSE 2023, CCIS 2025, pp. 30–36, 2024.
https://doi.org/10.1007/978-981-97-0737-9_4

At present, all "double first-class" colleges and universities are actively exploring the cultivation of first-class talents. The cultivation of first-class talents in medical imaging informatics is crucial to seize the commanding heights of natural science. In recent years, medical imaging informatics has become a hot research issue that is widely concerned by academia, industry and application industries, setting off an unprecedented upsurge in research and application over the world.

2 Review of Related Literature

At present, the education of medical imaging informatics in most colleges and universities is mainly concentrated in postgraduate education. In order to explore a more reasonable talent training model, improve the curriculum and teaching plans, we analyze and compare the differences in curriculum setting and personnel training among different colleges and universities.

2.1 Teaching System of Medical Imaging Informatics

Through the comparison of disciplinary structure, there are similarities and differences in the parent discipline, related disciplines and potential branch disciplines of medical imaging informatics, indicating that medical imaging informatics has common disciplinary foundation, disciplinary support and disciplinary differentiation and have their own characteristics [5]. Therefore, medical imaging informatics should improve the teaching system on the basis of seeking common ground while reserving differences, drawing on the advantages of foreign medical structure [6]. Specifically, it is reflected in three aspects: allocation of teacher resources, improvement of enrollment plans, and optimization of curriculum structure. First of all, the differences between the parent disciplines will help to optimize the curriculum structure. In terms of curriculum layout, strengthening the setting of biology, engineering technology and mathematics related courses will also help to improve the enrollment plan. The training of graduate students majoring in medical imaging informatics can be oriented towards medicine, Biology, engineering technology, information management and other majors are recruited; secondly, the comparison of related disciplines will help to allocate teacher resources, that is, on the basis of medical imaging, to increase the introduction of teachers in the field of computer applications; thirdly, for potential branches It is suggested should further increase the research on the subject of medical imaging informatics and highlight Chinese characteristics.

2.2 Medical Imaging Informatics

Through the comparison of domestic and foreign literature analysis, although domestic research has shown a good development trend, the quantity and quality of scientific research papers are higher than domestic research [7]. It provides many enlightenments for the research on the development of medical imaging informatics from perspective of discipline development. Specifically, according to the situation of publications, to increase the quantity and quality of domestic academic research results, researchers should enhance their own scientific research capabilities and the ability to absorb the scientific research results of others; for the half-life period, speed up the update of scientific and technological documents to keep pace with the international, each college should strengthen the construction of literature resources, especially should introduce more high-quality foreign research results, and update the aging resources in time; For the core group, strengthen cooperation with foreign core groups, combine the strong with the strong, cooperate with the strong and the weak, and replace the weak with the strong), the national scientific research management department should increase investment, encourage cooperation with high-influence scientific research groups, and establish a good academic atmosphere.

2.3 Development Direction of Medical Imaging Informatics

At present, the position of medical imaging informatics is to realize the full utilization and sharing of medical imaging information through the effective management of medical imaging information, and improve the efficiency and quality of medical decision-making and management [8]. Through the comparison of the development context and research topics of medical imaging informatics, the development direction of medical imaging informatics should be based on continuing to improve the efficiency and quality of medical decision- making and management, strengthen intelligent electronic medical care, data mining, machine learning and the application of knowledge graphs in the field of medical imaging information, so as to build a medical imaging information discipline with Chinese characteristics and an international perspective. This requires the joint efforts of countries, colleges and individuals. Specifically, at the national level, invested resources in human, financial and material should be increased to create a favorable environment for the development of medical imaging informatics; at the college level, efforts should be made to cultivate high-end talents in these fields; at the individual level, continuous learning and strengthen scientific research cooperation with foreign countries to improve their own research level.

To sum up, in view of the shortcomings in the development of medical imaging informatics, we will conduct research on the teaching courses, training models, and evaluation systems and aiming to propose a reasonable training system for first-class graduate students.to provide high-quality innovative talents in the field of medical imaging informatics, and also provide a reference for the training of first-class graduate students in other interdisciplinary disciplines.

3   Methodology of Research

3.1   The Goal of Research

Under the background of "Double First-Class" and "Integration of Medicine and Engineering", this project studies the construction of a first-class talent training system in the direction of medical imaging informatics as shown in Fig. 1. The goal of this project is to establish a complete training system for postgraduates in the direction of medical imaging informatics, include: facing the new trend of "combination of medicine and engineering", through comparative research on the training modes of postgraduates in the field of medical imaging informatics between China and foreign countries, obtain relevant strategies for improving the training model of medical imaging informatics graduate students. Combined with the advantages of computer science and medical imaging to build a new training model for interdisciplinary medical imaging informatics; relying on International Science and Technology Innovation Cooperation Base and clinical Medical Research Center, to carry out Sino-foreign joint training of postgraduates, improve the quality of postgraduate, enhance their scientific research capabilities and international perspective; from the perspective of "medicine-industrial integration", establish a new interdisciplinary medical imaging informatics Orientation graduate student innovation ability evaluation system.

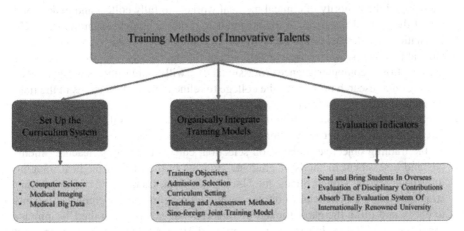

Fig. 1. Training Methods Construction Diagram

3.2 The Key Point

As an important frontier and hot research direction under the background of new engineering, there are many challenges in the talent training system in the direction of medical imaging informatics, among which the key issues are:

- How to reasonably set up the curriculum system so as to optimize the knowledge structure of postgraduates and enable to have the ability to engage in interdisciplinary research.
- How to organically integrate the domestic and foreign postgraduate training models, so as to improve the innovation ability and international vision of postgraduates.
- How to construct Reasonable evaluation index of innovation ability, so as to guide and promote the development of interdisciplinary medical imaging informatics.

3.3 Main Contents

In this study, the main contents are as follows:

- Facing the new trend of "combination of medicine and engineering", research the first-class postgraduate training mode suitable for the interdisciplinary development of medical imaging informatics. As an interdisciplinary subject, medical imaging informatics has certain particularities in its training methods. Combining the advantages of medicine and computer science and technology, we try to study the new training model of interdisciplinary medical imaging informatics. Utilize the advantages of computer science, medical images and medical big data to promote the interdisciplinary construction of medical imaging informatics under the background of combining medicine and engineering, especially big data research which based on medical data. We should combine the medical big data research and application to carry out the discipline construction of medical imaging informatics under the background of big data. The major changes in medicine at the age of information science encouraged the majority of clinical medical workers to fully collect and make good use of the clinical resources of the hospitals to promote clinical scientific research, translational medicine research, and drive the development of basic medicine through clinical practice. However, the construction of the big data system also requires the participation of computer science professionals. we will combine the relevant biomedical big data research projects of the college to refine the scientific issues in the field of medical imaging informatics.
- A comparative study on the training mode of postgraduates in the field of medical imaging informatics between different countries. To carry out a comparative analysis on the training objectives, admission selection, curriculum setting, teaching methods and assessment methods of graduate students in the field of medical imaging informatics in the United States, the United Kingdom, Canada and obtain relevant strategies that are beneficial to improving the training model for graduate students to check and fill in the gaps. Linked by international experts from the Disciplinary Innovation and Talent Introduction Program of Higher Education Institutions and the International Joint Laboratory of Biological Data Processing, through research with these experts, investigations in internationally renowned universities such as the United States, the United Kingdom, and Canada, and the personal experience of joint training of postgraduates, the festival Carry out a comparative study on the postgraduate training mode of medical imaging informatics and these internationally renowned universities and obtain relevant strategies that are beneficial to improving the training model of medical imaging informatics graduate students.
- Relying on International Science and Technology Innovation Cooperation Base and the Clinical Medical Research Center, a Sino-foreign joint training model for medical imaging informatics postgraduates is carried out. Joint postgraduate training with well- known universities in the United States, the United Kingdom, Canada and other countries, adopt the strategy of "send students out and bring in overseas scholars", and teach by an international team of professors, improve the quality of postgraduate training, and enhance their research capabilities and international vision. There is a big gap between domestic medical imaging informatics education and research and developed countries and regions in Europe and the United States. Joint training is an important way to improve the quality of postgraduates. This project will rely on the existing disciplinary innovation and intelligence introduction plan of "Medical Big Data Analysis Theory and Application" in colleges and universities, conduct

lectures by an international professor team and personally guide research projects. By complementing their advantages, they can enhance the professional foundation of postgraduates and enhance their scientific research capabilities. Every year, according to the training direction and specific cooperation topics, students can be sent out to conduct short-term or medium-term visits and academic exchanges in foreign universities, so that students can go overseas to learn about and experience different training models and expand their international horizons.

- An effective method for evaluating the innovation ability of graduate students in the interdisciplinary direction of medical imaging informatics. As an interdisciplinary subject, the disciplinary contribution of medical imaging informatics is not limited to computer science, and it is difficult to evaluate its innovation ability. The traditional evaluation that only looks at the contribution to the discipline is unfair to the interdisciplinary students. The establishment of a new interdisciplinary comprehensive evaluation system can effectively promote the innovation ability of graduate students.

4 Conclusion

Deepening the reform of innovation and entrepreneurship education in colleges and universities, promoting the deepening reform of innovation and entrepreneurship in the field of intelligent medical imaging, and providing reference for the reform of other cross-category talent training models.

Acknowledgments. The authors gratefully acknowledge the research funding from the following programs: Central South University Graduate Education and Teaching Reform Research Project (No. 2022JGB113); Central South University Innovation and Entrepreneurship Education Teaching Reform Research Project (No. 2022–15).

References

1. Xiaoqiu, S., Yingying, X.: Construction of talent training system driven by engineering education certification and industry education integration. Res. High. Educ. Eng. **2**, 33–39 (2019)
2. Li, W., Hei, X., Wang, L., Wang, X.: Exploration and practice on the construction of computer first-class major. In: 2021 16th International Conference on Computer Science & Education, ICCSE, pp. 281–285. IEEE (2021)
3. Zhang, Z., Liu, Y., Mao, G.: Research on the cultivation of innovative and entrepreneurial talents based on cooperative education in application-oriented universities. In: 2020 International Conference on Big Data and Informatization Education, ICBDIE, pp. 187–190. IEEE (2020)
4. Zhang, M., Xiande, H. U., Xie, B., Li, H.: Research on the core capabilities cultivation mode of software engineering talents for new engineering. In: 2020 International Conference on Big Data and Informatization Education, ICBDIE, pp. 225–228. IEEE (2020)
5. Panayides, A., et al.: AI in medical imaging informatics: current challenges and future directions. IEEE J. Biomed. Health Inf. **24**(7), 1837–1857 (2020)
6. Pezoulas, V., Exarchos, T., Fotiadis, D. I.: Medical data sharing, harmonization and analytics. 1nd edn. Academic Press (2020)

7. Xiaoming, Z., Lin, H., Donghui, Z., Yungang, W.: Research on talent cultivation mode of computer between China and America. In: 2019 14th International Conference on Computer Science & Education, ICCSE, pp. 11–16. IEEE (2019)
8. Zhang, X., Luo, H., Wu, J.: Thoughts on cultivating applied and innovative talents in computer majors of universities. In: 2019 14th International Conference on Computer Science & Education, ICCSE, pp. 216–221 IEEE (2019)

Exploration and Practice of Promoting High-Quality Development of Higher Education with Digitization

Chong Teng[✉][ID], Fei Li[ID], and Donghong Ji[ID]

School of Cyber Science and Engineering, Wuhan University, Wuhan, China
{tengchong,lifei_csnlp,dhji}@whu.edu.cn

Abstract. Digitalization of higher education is an important pathway for advancing the high-quality development of higher education. This article explores the exploration and practice of promoting high-quality development in higher education with digitalization from three aspects: building digital teaching platforms, deepening educational and teaching reforms, and enhancing teaching management and services. It also shares the talent cultivation philosophy and the design and practice of the teaching platform at Wuhan University, along with some thoughts and recommendations on information literacy for teachers and undergraduates, particularly in the context of higher education digital reform.

Keywords: Digitalization of Education · Digital Literacy · Information Literacy · Higher Education · High-Quality Development

1 The International Context of Education Digital Transformation

In recent years, with the deepening of the new round of technological revolution and industrial transformation, human activities in various fields have rapidly evolved towards networking, informatization, intelligence, and digitization. Digital technology has become a driving force for fundamental changes and comprehensive reshaping of human social thinking, organizational structures, and operational models. Countries and international organizations around the world have successively introduced digital strategies, such as Germany's "Innovative Germany" Future Research Program launched in 2020, the National Digital Strategy formulated by the UK, and the "2030 Digital Compass Plan" launched by the European Commission in 2021.

The COVID-19 pandemic and the trend of internationalization have greatly accelerated the pace of embracing digitization in the field of education in many countries. Numerous countries have introduced education digital transformation strategies. UNESCO released "Education Digital Transformation: School Connectivity, Student Empowerment" in 2020 and "Reimagining our Futures Together: A New Social Contract for Education" in 2021, explicitly stating that

W. Hong and G. Kanaparan (Eds.): ICCSE 2023, CCIS 2025, pp. 37–50, 2024.
https://doi.org/10.1007/978-981-97-0737-9_5

"digital technology holds enormous transformative potential, and we need to find realistic paths to turn this potential into a driving force for educational transformation" [1]. The European Union published the "Digital Education Action Plan (2021–2027)" emphasizing the integration of educational resources and the promotion of the construction of EU online teaching platforms in higher education [2]. The Organisation for Economic Co-operation and Development (OECD) released "Back to the Future of Education: Four Scenarios for the OECD Schooling Scenarios" which strategically integrates digitization into the entire process of lifelong education system construction, considering digital innovation as an important means of reforming lifelong education supply and digital development as an important way to achieve sustainable development in lifelong education [3]. The Russian Ministry of Science and Higher Education issued the "Digital Transformation Strategy for Higher Education and the Technology Industry" [4], Australia released the "Australia's International Education Strategy (2021–2030)", and Singapore issued the "Education Technology Decade Plan (2020–2030)" and so on.

In February 2023, the World Digital Education Conference will discuss how to promote educational recovery in the post-pandemic era, ensure equitable access to quality educational resources, and advance the achievement of the United Nations Sustainable Development Goals through educational digital transformation.[1] The conference, with the theme of "Digital Transformation and the Future of Education," will focus on exploring educational digital transformation, enhancing digital literacy of teachers and students, digital governance in education, as well as assessing the digital development in basic education, vocational education, higher education, and other fields.

China has also fully recognized the profound impact of information technology and digital technology on higher education concepts, teaching models, and educational systems. It has successively issued landmark documents such as the "New Generation Artificial Intelligence Development Plan," "China's Education Modernization 2035," and the "Education Informatization 2.0 Action Plan." The "2022 Work Points of the Ministry of Education" also proposed the implementation of an education digitalization strategy, emphasizing the leveraging of advantages in networking, digitization, and artificial intelligence, enriching the supply of digital educational resources and services, innovating education and learning methods, and accelerating the realization of balanced, personalized, and lifelong education [5]. General Secretary Xi Jinping mentioned in the report of the 20th National Congress, "Promote education digitalization and build a learning society and a learning country for all."

Therefore, the digital transformation of education is a common need for countries worldwide. It is the top-level design of educational institutions and organizations worldwide and represents the new trend in the development of the education sector in the digital age.

---

[1] https://wdec.smartedu.cn/.

2   Mission and Goals of High-Quality Development in Higher Education

At the 2022 Global MOOC and Online Education Alliance, it was mentioned that the digital transformation of higher education will advance in both physical and human terms to create a more inclusive and equitable higher education system that provides quality education and accomplishes new missions and objectives [6]. There are six specific points as follows:

First, we need to adopt a more people-centered education philosophy. Second, we need to build a more intelligent education process. Third, we need to adopt more diversifified approaches in education evaluation. Fourth, we need to foster an educational culture that values openness and connectivity. Fifth, we need to provide individualized education services. Sixth, we need to build a higher education system that values sustainability.

Back in 1998, the World Conference on Higher Education adopted the Declaration on Higher Education in the Twenty-First Century: Vision and Action. The declaration stated that in today's rapidly changing world, higher education clearly needs a new perspective and new models that prioritize a student-centered approach. It emphasized the importance of focusing on students and their needs, considering them as the main and responsible participants in educational reform. This was the first time that the concept of "student-centeredness" appeared in an official document of United Nations agencies. This is also the educational philosophy of "people-oriented" proposed by the digital development of higher education worldwide.

In the context of the new era, global economic development remains imbalanced. The digital divide amplifies the issue of unequal access to education. To bridge this digital gap and ensure that education is accessible to everyone, everywhere, and at all times, the education system must become more open, equitable, and of higher quality. Digitization is driving education, including higher education, into a stage of high-quality development.

Digitalization promotes the updating and iteration of the knowledge system in higher education, the upgrading and optimization of instructional design, and the transformation and innovation of teaching methods. It enables the educational process to fully align with new advancements in disciplines, new demands in industry development, and new goals in talent cultivation. With the help of digital technology and digital thinking, the higher education system autonomously constructs and aggregates the most cutting-edge and high-quality teaching resources of various disciplines. It actively creates immersive and scenario-based teaching environments and strengthens autonomous, inquiry-based, and collaborative teaching activities. Adhering to the student-centered educational philosophy, students are regarded as the important subjects of all educational activities, emphasizing their growth and development. Resource allocation revolves around the central position of students, providing them with diverse choices and personalized educational services. This allows digital resources to autonomously match students, enabling them to learn and develop independently, thus unleashing their maximum vitality and potential. The goal is to establish a sustainable and high-quality higher education system.

3   Exploration and Practice of Digital Transformation in Higher Education

Higher education research is a transformation and upgrade in response to the high demands of the digital age for talent development. The transformation of the human society's mindset, organizational structure, and operational mode based on digital technology, led by digitization, paves the way for innovation, reshapes the landscape, and promotes the high-quality development of education.

Digital education is not a replacement for the traditional teaching model; each has its own characteristics and different areas of applicability. The reform of digital education should adopt an open and inclusive attitude, adhering to a development logic that combines the strengths of traditional teaching with diverse innovative models.

The higher education system encompasses many aspects and components. Here, we will only explore and practice the digital transformation of higher education from three core elements of the higher education system: the learning environment, educational reforms (curriculum, teaching resources, teaching methods, and teaching models), and educational support (management and services).

3.1   Strengthening the Foundation of Education Digital Transformation

"Teaching and learning" is the core issue in higher education, and the related teaching environment, teaching space, and teaching platforms are the foundation of education digital transformation, which is particularly important as they directly impact teaching models and the development of teaching resources.

In 2022, the strategic action for education digitalization was launched, and the world's largest national higher education smart education platform, Smart Education of China of Higher Education,[2] was constructed and launched, as shown in Fig. 1. The award ceremony for the 2022 UNESCO Education ICT Prize was held at the UNESCO headquarters in Paris, France, on September 7, 2023, local time. The project "Smart Education of China," the national smart education platform,[3] and the "National Resource Centre" project of Ireland were jointly awarded. In his speech, Jiani Ni, Assistant Director-General for Education at UNESCO, stated that the "Smart Education of China" project is an outstanding initiative to ensure universal access and effective use of public digital learning platforms. It showcases how digital technology can be utilized to make teaching and learning more accessible and provides valuable experience for global digital education transformation. Our representative who received the award stated

---

[2] https://higher.smartedu.cn/.
[3] https://www.smartedu.cn/.

Fig. 1. Platform of Smart Education of China of Higher Education

that the Chinese government attaches great importance to the development of digital education and considers it an important component of Digital China. In 2022, the Chinese Ministry of Education launched the implementation of the National Education Digitalization Strategy, focusing on student learning, teacher instruction, school governance, and educational innovation. The national smart education platform was launched and put into operation, creating one of the most important education public service products in China. The launch and large-scale application of the platform reflect the sustained spillover effects of digital technology on education development, effectively serving the construction of a lifelong education system for all citizens, promoting educational equity, and facilitating high-quality education development. This award also reflects the international community's high recognition of China's digitalization of education.

In addition, many universities have digital teaching platforms for their faculty and students, such as Zhejiang University's "Learn at Zhejiang" course management platform and Wuhan University's "Luo Jia Online" course management platform[4]. These platforms facilitate access to official high-quality education platforms like the national higher education smart education platform and also provide access to top-notch course resources. The primary function of these platforms is to serve the faculty and students of the respective universities. They serve as spaces for managing courses taught by teachers and include features like materials, statistics, activities, assignments, exams, discussions, and management sections, as shown in Fig. 2. They make it convenient for faculty and students to share course materials, for teachers to assign and students to submit homework, for organizing discussions and Q&A sessions, and for managing class students, monitoring their learning progress, and facilitating personalized management. These platforms also serve as spaces for students to manage the courses they are taking, allowing them to view course content, check and submit assignments, and access the platform easily on both desktop and mobile devices. Such teaching platforms greatly enhance the quality of teaching and learning.

This type of teaching environment has transformed the traditional, single physical space into an intelligent, hybrid online and offline teaching space with enhanced functionality. Teaching platforms and teaching spaces directly deter-

---

[4] http://www.mooc.whu.edu.cn/.

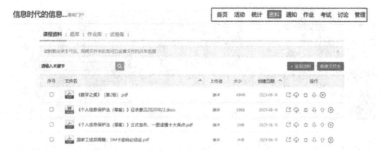

Fig. 2. "Luojia Online" Course Management Platform Interface at Wuhan University

mine the richness of teaching resources and have a significant impact on the conduct of teaching activities, teaching methods, and other aspects of teaching. They are closely related to the quality of talent development at universities. Therefore, high-quality teaching platforms are the foundation and solid guarantee for the high-quality development of education in the digital age.

3.2 Deepening Systemic Education and Teaching Reform

Teaching reform is of paramount importance in higher education. Schools are keeping pace with the times by promoting the optimization of curriculum design, teaching method reform, high-quality resource development, and organization, with a focus on building a high-quality education system characterized by digitalization and centered on student growth.

Optimizing Training Programs to Enhance the Quality of Future Talent for Society. Higher education, especially undergraduate education, is an important period for students to transition from adolescence to adulthood and cultivate their complete intellectual and moral development. The group of individuals who have received higher education is the main driving force in exploring the laws of nature and society and promoting the progress of human civilization. Higher education needs to lay the foundation for students' comprehensive development and help them transition from learning basic knowledge to exploring "profound knowledge" and be prepared to inherit and lead human civilization and values.

What kind of people should higher education cultivate? Professor Zhang Pingwen, President of Wuhan University and Academician of the Chinese Academy of Sciences, emphasized three points in his article "The Responsibilities and Obligations of Universities in the Digital Age" [7]: universities should focus on enhancing students' digital thinking abilities in the talent cultivation process, universities should further promote the digital empowerment of scientific and technological innovation and cultural dissemination, and universities should actively participate in global digital governance.

Talent development programs are the top-level design for talent cultivation in higher education. They should be oriented towards the digital transformation of the era and industries, conduct research, and clearly define talent development goals and competency dimensions. Guided by the concept of student growth, under the guidance of discipline categories and professional training goals, and based on overall requirements for academic years and credits, a curriculum system and knowledge structure should be constructed reasonably and scientifically. Emphasis should be placed on general education courses, foundational courses, and practical teaching, ensuring that the teaching content fully reflects the new features of the digital age, disciplinary knowledge foundations, and new developments. It is important to adhere to a solid foundation, physical and mental health, and the basic requirements of comprehensive development with both moral character and talent.

At Wuhan University, all undergraduate students must complete at least 12 credits of general education courses (according to the 2023 version of the training program). Efforts are made to strengthen students' "information literacy" and enhance their ability to adapt to the information age and the era of numerical intelligence in terms of daily life, learning, innovation, and overall capabilities. Wuhan University's general education courses and teaching reform projects on information literacy have been continuously offered, developed, and optimized in terms of knowledge structure since the beginning of the 21st century. The forward-looking design of Wuhan University's training program lays a solid foundation and fosters innovative abilities for students to face the digital age and future society.

Integrating and Optimizing Digital Resources to Eliminate the Digital Divide. In 2022, at the World MOOC and Online Education Conference, the ten-year journey of Chinese MOOCs was reviewed. From the initial 5 MOOCs and a hundred registered users in 2013, to November 2022, the number of online courses has exceeded 61,900, with 402 million registered users and 9.79 billion learning instances. The recognition of MOOC credits for students has reached 352 million instances. Both the number of MOOCs and the number of learners in China rank first in the world. Over the past decade, MOOCs have broken down the walls of universities and brought knowledge out of the ivory tower.

"In the past, a teacher's knowledge could only reach a few thousand students throughout their lifetime. Now, a single MOOC can benefit millions of learners, and MOOC teachers can be regarded as educators with influence worldwide." At the 2022 World MOOC and Online Education Conference held recently, a representative from a MOOC platform summarized the changes of the past decade in a single statement.

During the last ten years, the digital transformation of higher education in China has shown initial results: the foundation for digital transformation in education has been strengthened. In 2022, the strategic action for digital education was launched, and the construction of the largest national higher education smart education platform was initiated. Online teaching has formed a Chinese model, and reforms in teaching methods such as online learning and flipped classrooms have continued to promote the deep integration of information technology and education. Efforts have been made to promote fairer and higher-quality education. The "Westward Expansion of MOOCs" has facilitated the collaborative construction and sharing of high-quality courses between universities in the eastern and western regions, effectively improving the educational level of teachers in western universities.

In addition to creating MOOC courses, in the face of the digital age, Wuhan University is actively constructing and organizing high-quality digital resources. By applying for national-level first-class courses and promoting high-quality development through digitalization, the university is continuously taking action.

Reforming Teaching Methods and Pedagogical Models, Putting Students at the Center. In the digital age, the roles of university teachers and students are being repositioned. Under the concept of "student-centered", the focus of teaching design, practice, and reform in universities is gradually shifting from being "teacher-centered" to being "student-centered." In the new teaching format, teachers are organizers, supporters, and guides, while students are collaborators, explorers, and discoverers. Both parties interact and learn from each other. These new roles in the new era will drive changes in teaching and educational models both inside and outside the classroom.

The existence of established digital resources and open sharing formats have provided a new form of learning for people around the world, achieving the goal of "learning for all, everywhere, and at all times." At the same time, it offers all learners the option of a blended learning mode combining online and offline learning.

Furthermore, the high-quality development of higher education primarily refers to the "quality" of talent cultivation in higher education institutions rather than a mass-produced and standardized training model. In the face of the digital age, both international and domestic higher education institutions, including Wuhan University, have adopted a more small-class approach, which is more conducive to personalized education.

Wuhan University has enriched its teaching resources, learning materials, and the previously mentioned on-campus course management platform in the process of educational informatization. This has inevitably led to improvements in teaching methods and teaching models. Currently, technologies like ChatGPT and other artificial intelligence generation methods can generate endless digital materials and "KNOWLEDGE". Research on how to effectively utilize AI assistants and human-computer collaborative teaching methods is an emerging area of study. Especially in terms of optimizing the integration and systematization of teaching resources, this presents a challenging task for educators in the era of digital education.

3.3   Continuously Improving Teaching Management and Services

Higher education management services urgently need to make coordinated use of digital technology and digital thinking. This includes strengthening the perception, collection, analysis, and utilization of teaching information, promoting the improvement of management service mechanisms based on digital technology and thinking, and constructing a more scientific, precise, and efficient higher education development and governance system.

In terms of teaching evaluation, it is important to adhere to the "student-centered" educational philosophy and consider student learning outcomes as a key indicator of educational quality. With the support of digital technology, big data analysis, digital assessment, integrated system management, and service systems can provide more accurate assistance to teachers, students, and administrators, ensuring the quality of education and promoting high-quality development through digitization.

The digital transformation of higher education is a massive systemic project. Currently, under the joint development and exploration practices of international organizations and national digital development strategies in the field of higher education, significant achievements and experiences have been gained, and a common understanding of the implementation path has been reached. Digitalization has created new infinite possibilities for the high-quality development of higher education. Technologies such as virtual space break the limitations of physical space and create multidimensional interactive teaching scenarios. Learning process analysis based on big data provides a technological foundation for formative assessment. AI teaching assistants liberate teachers from heavy repetitive and mechanical labor. The flourishing development of digitalization is driving the high-quality development of higher education.

4   Challenges and Suggestions

However, we must also recognize that some problems still exist, such as the construction and sharing of high-quality digital resources, the digital divide in education, the quality of university talent cultivation, the level of digitalized university governance, the new challenges posed by artificial intelligence in teaching and talent cultivation, teacher digital literacy, digital literacy and innovation ability of university students, the quality culture and quality assurance capacity of higher education, and the issues of digital technology, network security, and ethics.

4.1   Quality Talent Development and Digital Literacy

In the digital age, in the process of high-quality development of higher education, the quality of talent cultivation is the most reflective of a school's educational standards and soft power. It is the most essential element for promoting science and education, and realizing the strength of education in our country. All faculty and staff in higher education institutions should focus on this central point to improve teaching and management services. Enhancing digital literacy is a requirement for everyone, and the digital literacy of every faculty and staff member in higher education is closely related to the quality of talent cultivation, and its significance cannot be ignored.

We give a suggestion that categorizes the evaluation criteria for digital literacy of teachers, administrators, and laboratory personnel based on workplace scenarios.

4.2 Teachers Actively Respond to Educational Digital Transformation, Enhancing Digital Literacy

The main battlefield of educational reform is the classroom, and classroom teaching is the core of digital transformation [8]. Empowering teaching with information technology has become a focus both domestically and internationally, specifically manifested in the accelerated integration of information technology with the teaching process and teaching content, starting from both the "teaching" aspect of teachers and the "learning" aspect of students to achieve comprehensive digitization. On the one hand, it is necessary to promote flexible and open teaching organizational models supported by information technology, such as course selection, cross-school collaboration, home-school cooperation, and school-enterprise linkage, to promote personalized development and collaborative education. On the other hand, efforts should be made to strengthen and deepen the application of online learning spaces, build effective models for blended online and offline teaching, and promote the normalization of their use [2].

In the new teaching format, teachers are organizers and guides of teaching. By conducting heuristic, inquiry-based, discussion-based, participatory, and performance-based classroom activities, they create a networked, immersive, and intelligent smart teaching model to promote deep learning and cultivate students' core competencies.

Additionally, it is important to actively utilize AI-based intelligent teaching assistants, intelligent learning companions, and other teaching products, and explore the application of new technologies such as virtual reality and augmented reality in teaching. At the same time, teachers should be prepared to respond to the impact of Artificial Intelligence Generated Content (AIGC) technologies like ChatGPT on student autonomy and provide proper guidance.

In February 2023, the World Digital Education Conference was held, during which the Ministry of Education officially released the Teacher Digital Literacy standards to solidly promote the national education digitalization strategy and improve the standard system for educational informatization. As shown in Fig. 3, the framework for teacher digital literacy includes five primary dimensions, thirteen secondary dimensions, and thirty-three tertiary dimensions. In the digital era, teacher digital literacy has evolved from early education technology skills, information technology application abilities and information literacy to today's "digital literacy." From the framework for teacher digital literacy, it is evident that being a university teacher who adapts to digital transformation

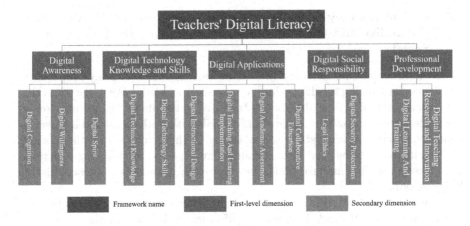

Fig. 3. Framework for Teacher Digital Literacy

requires learning new requirements, actively adapting to the development trend of digital transformation, effectively implementing differentiated teaching, and personalized student development, as well as actively promoting the deep integration of technology and teaching.

Looking at the international higher education field, as early as 2011, the United Nations Educational Scientific and Cultural Organization (UNESCO) issued the "Framework for Teacher ICT Competency", which detailed the abilities teachers should possess to effectively use digital technology in teaching. In 2017, the Joint Research Centre of the European Commission issued the "European Framework for Digital Competence of Educators", enabling educators at all levels to comprehensively assess and develop their digital competence. In addition, in 2020, the European Commission published the "Self-Reflection Tool for the European Digital Competence Framework," which measures citizens' digital competence levels through knowledge, skills, and attitudes. Furthermore, the European Union's "Digital Education Action Plan (2021–2027)" issued in 2020 specifically emphasizes the establishment of the "European Digital Skills Certification" system to strengthen the assessment of teachers' digital skills. The International Society for Technology in Education (ISTE) released the "ISTE Standards for Educators" in 2017, which analyzes the various roles teachers play in education in the information age and defines the responsibilities and competency standards for teachers to promote innovative teaching using digital technology.

Given these factors, enhancing teacher digital literacy is an urgent and challenging task in promoting the high-quality development of higher education in the digital age.

We give a suggestion that universities should establish a training and exchange working group within an alliance of teachers with experience in information literacy teaching. Through demonstrations and sharing, they can collectively enhance teachers' information literacy.

4.3 Digital Literacy of College Students: The Source of Innovation Capability and the Foundation for Adapting to the Future Society

In the discussion of digitalizing education, I have not yet heard any proposals or research on enhancing the digital literacy of college students. We understand that the core mission of higher education is to cultivate talents for the future, preparing students to become well-rounded individuals with both moral and intellectual qualities, capable of innovation and adapting to the demands of future society. "Advancing educational digitalization and creating a lifelong learning society for all" places a greater emphasis on the need for college students to possess lifelong learning skills.

How can we effectively improve the digital literacy of college students? Digital literacy is an upgraded version of information literacy in the digital age. Wuhan University's general education course on information literacy has been continuously offered and updated since the beginning of the 21st century [9]. The philosophy of this course at Wuhan University is to enhance students' innovative and critical thinking skills, computational thinking, cybersecurity literacy, data literacy, and research literacy, laying a solid interdisciplinary foundation for adapting to today's and future society.

We give a suggestion that in the process of educational digitalization, experienced teachers with expertise in information literacy should share digital resources and bridge the gap in digital literacy among college students from different regions and different types of schools. Additionally, it is advisable for every university to offer general education courses on information literacy and digital literacy. University faculty should also pay attention to the content and teaching methods of these general education courses, as this is a firsthand experience gained after practicing information literacy general education courses.

4.4 Assessing and Certifying Digital Competence: An Important Means to Accelerate High-Quality Development in Higher Education

Due to the high-quality development of higher education and digital transformation being a complex undertaking, there are numerous challenges involving human, financial, and material resources, all of which require significant investment. Globally, each country and university faces unique and unpredictable difficulties. Compared to physical infrastructure development, the challenges of software development are even greater. During a certain period, the digital literacy of students, faculty, and administrators will encounter numerous obstacles.

We suggest quantifying soft power and establishing various personnel digital literacy assessment criteria. Use capability certification[5] to accelerate the enhancement of digital literacy, promote innovation in talent development, and contribute to the high-quality development of higher education.

---

[5] www.dclc.org.cn.

5   Conclusion

Regarding the topic of promoting high-quality development in higher education through digitalization, the following statements are provided at the end of the article:

First, digitization is a means, and talent development is the goal. Second, teaching and learning are at the core of what knowledge to teach, what skills to teach, and how to teach knowledge and skills. What to learn and how to learn are always the key points for the high-quality development of universities. Third, digital education reform can take various, diverse, and multidimensional approaches for reform and enhancement. It should avoid creating a path dependency and explore multiple effective paths. Fourth, digital literacy is an upgraded version of information literacy in the digital age. To enhance the digital literacy of the entire population, we need to break down disciplinary boundaries, strengthen interdisciplinary collaboration between relevant fields, and collaborate with industries to collectively promote the improvement of digital literacy for all [10].

The digital reform in higher education is a long-term, progressive, and evolving process. In the long run, by developing forward-looking top-level planning, focusing on the core elements of reform, identifying key paths and breakthroughs, every university in the country can embark on a distinctive path of educational digital reform. This will provide strong impetus for accelerating the construction of a high-quality higher education system and enhancing the ability to independently cultivate outstanding innovative talents.

Finally, I'd like to share a quote from Minister Huai Jinpeng of the Ministry of Education at the World Digital Education Conference as the concluding remark of this article: "Promoting digital education and driving educational digital transformation is not only a global trend and developmental necessity but also a reform imperative. It is a shared aspiration, a duty, and a remarkable achievement that every educator should pursue."

References

1. UNESCO: reimagining our futures together: a new social contract for education. UN (2022)
2. Wu, D., Li, H., Wei, X.: Digital transformation in education: international context, development needs and paths to advancement. China Dist. Educ. **7**, 21–27 (2022). in chinese
3. Li, W., Fan, X., et al.: OECD digital strategy for lifelong learning: Highlights and features (2022). (in Chinese)
4. Du, Y., Tang, X.: A realistic picture and strategic planning of digital transformation of Russian higher education for 2030. Comparative Education Studies (2022). (in Chinese)
5. Editorial Board of the Journal: Ministry of education 2022 work points deploying strategic actions to implement digitalization of education. China Educ. Inf. **28**(2) (2022). (in Chinese)

6. Secretariat of the global MOOC and online education alliance: report on the digital development of global higher education (2022). https://www.chinadaily.com.cn/a/202212/11/WS6395d5c4a31057c47eba3d18.html

7. Zhang, W.: Responsibilities and obligations of universities in the digital age. Chinese Society of Higher Education, 12 Sep 2023. (in Chinese)

8. Huang, R., Yang, J., et al.: Connotations and implementation path of educational digital transformation. Chinese Education Newspaper (2022). (in Chinese)

9. Teng, C., He, N.: Integration of information literacy and higher education computer fundamentals education. Forum on Modern Education and Teaching (2006). (in Chinese)

10. Pan, Y., et al.: A major leap from information literacy for all to digital literacy. Libr. J. **41**(10), 4 (2022). in Chinese

Construction and Evaluation of the Five-in-One Practice Teaching Model

Zhicheng Dong[1], Donghong Cai[2(✉)], Yonghao Shi[1,3(✉)], Qing Wang[4], and Lan Ding[5]

[1] Tibet University, Lhasa, Tibet Autonomous Region, China
2818536836@qq.com
[2] Jinan University, Guangzhou, Guangdong, China
dhcai@jnu.edu.cn
[3] Zhengzhou University of Economics and Trade, Zhengzhou, Henan, China
[4] Tianjin University, Tianjin, China
[5] Tibet Agricultural and Animal Husbandry University, Linzhi, Tibet Autonomous Region, China

Abstract. In response to the economic and social development of Tibet Autonomous Region and the demand for information technology construction in the new engineering era, this paper analyzes the communication engineering major at Tibet University, a Five-in-One practical teaching talent training system model is proposed, and a first-class undergraduate professional talent training system with Tibetan characteristics is formed. The aim is to enhance practical innovation capabilities and improve the process of building innovative and entrepreneurial talent training systems. It explains that deepening the reform of the curriculum system not only requires updating concepts but also innovating practical teaching models. Finally, cluster analysis and identification models were used to evaluate the effectiveness of the Five-in-One practical teaching model adopted by the Advanced Technology Research Center of Tibet University. The results showed that the practical teaching model had significant advantages.

Keywords: Talent Training System · Practical Teaching Model · Communication Engineering · Five-in-One

1 Introduction

Tibet University, which has been rooted in the plateau for seventy years, adheres to the guidance of president Xi Jinping Thought on Socialism with Chinese Characteristics for a New Era, conscientiously implements instructions of president Xi Jinping's on Tibetan education in the new era, keeping in mind president Xi Jinping's reply to the medical students of Tibet University, comprehensively implement the CPC's education policy, strengthen the party's overall leadership, strengthen the correct direction of running schools, implement the fundamental task of cultivating people with moral integrity, intensify efforts to cultivate

W. Hong and G. Kanaparan (Eds.): ICCSE 2023, CCIS 2025, pp. 51–61, 2024.
https://doi.org/10.1007/978-981-97-0737-9_6

"unity, diligence, pragmatism and innovation" talents who are "reliable, useful and retainable", and explore Multi-dimensional practical teaching model. Tibet University Advanced Technology Research Center (TUATRC), under the purpose of "building a university that satisfies the people", is guided by the new engineering concept and focuses on improving students' skills, and actively explores the Five-in-One talent training system model, achieved remarkable results, and cultivated a large number of outstanding information talents who "take root in Tibet and serve Tibet".

2   Practicing the Thoughts of Educational Reform

The importance of informatization in economic and social development is increasingly evident. As the forefront "gateway" for cultivating informatization talents, the classroom holds a crucial role. Only by firmly grasping the pulse of the times and innovating with the traditional can we cultivate well-qualified information talents [1]. In the talent training system, we are guided by the spirit of the 20th National Congress of the Communist Party of China and steered by the "China Education Modernization 2035" and the "Implementation Plan for Accelerating Education Modernization (2018–2022)" issued by the Central Committee of the Communist Party of China and the State Council in early 2019. This allows us to comprehensively implement the Party's education policy, stay on course in running a socialist school, closely focus on the fundamental questions of "who to train, how to train, and for whom", execute the essential task of fostering individuals with moral integrity, and delve into professional courses. In each teaching segment, we prioritize human functionality, realize the organic unity of shaping values, transferring knowledge, and cultivating abilities. We strive to nurture builders and successors of the socialist cause who demonstrate comprehensive development in moral, intellectual, physical, artistic, and labor aspects [2].

3   The Relationship Between Practical Teaching and Course Teaching

Practical teaching is inseparable from curriculum teaching, which is mainly reflected in three aspects. Firstly, curriculum teaching serves as the foundation for practical teaching, providing the content and framework for classroom teaching and learning activities, as well as the subject foundation and theoretical support for practical teaching. By participating in practical teaching activities, students combine the knowledge learned in the classroom with practice to deepen their understanding and application of knowledge. Secondly, practical teaching serves as an extension of course teaching. Practical teaching encourages students to apply what they have learned through practical operations and activities. This helps them solve practical problems and enhances their practical and innovative abilities. Practical teaching also provides examples and cases for course teaching, allowing students to better understand and apply the knowledge learned in the classroom. Finally, practical teaching serves as the basis for course teaching, with evaluation standards developed through practical teaching activities able to evaluate students' learning effects and abilities. The results and performance of practical teaching can be fed back into course teaching, helping teachers understand students' learning situations, adjust course teaching content and methods in a timely manner, and improve teaching effects. Practical teaching and course teaching are complementary and mutually reinforcing. Practical teaching provides a practical foundation and application scenarios for course teaching, while course teaching provides theoretical support and subject knowledge for practical teaching.

In the era of new engineering, the TUATRC has redesigned and comprehensively harmonized the practical elements of the student ability training system. Through continuous exploration and optimization in practice, we have gradually formed a system called "Five-in-One," which places students as the center, teachers as guides, projects as motivators, institutions as guarantors, and fair and equitable evaluation as the foundation.

4   Five-in-One Practical Education System

The TUATRC has effectively transformed the traditional educational paradigm that emphasizes theory over practice and knowledge teaching over ability cultivation. We have embraced a new concept that prioritizes the integration of learning and thinking, the unity of knowledge and action, and individualized education based on students' aptitude. Guided by the implementation of relevant requirements for practical teaching, we have actively mobilized and integrated resources from all sectors to form a Five-in-One practical education team. This team works collaboratively to establish a long-term mechanism for practical education and create a new era for practical education.

Firstly, students are the main body, signifying that the focus of education is to cultivate students' comprehensive qualities and abilities, encompassing knowledge, skills, attitudes, and values. The TUATRC designs targeted education programs based on students' characteristics and needs, providing personalized learning support and guidance. Additionally, we encourage students to actively participate in the management and decision-making of practical teaching in the TUATRC, exercising their autonomy and participation, and cultivating self-management abilities and a cooperative spirit.

The TUATRC establishes a personalized practice archive for each student, creating a file data system that documents their practical process and core literacy growth. This supports students in improving their unique skills through independent learning and practice, tailored to their individual abilities, providing quick and convenient access. This promotes the rapid improvement of students' practical abilities.

Secondly, under the guidance of teachers. College students are influenced by multiculturalism, and the formation of values is at a critical period. Implementing "cultivating people with moral integrity" urgently requires teachers' professional skills and ideological guidance. As guides, teachers raise open questions during the teaching process, leading students to consider different viewpoints and solutions. They harness students' initiative and creativity, guiding them to analyze problems, reason, and demonstrate, assessing the reliability of information. This cultivates students' lifelong learning ability and overall development.

The guidance of teachers not only establishes a positive teacher-student relationship but also enables students to exert their initiative and creativity, engage in speculative and critical thinking, and achieve personalized learning and comprehensive development.

Thirdly, driven by projects. Utilizing projects as a motivating force, we aim to inspire and drive students to actively participate in practical activities and endeavors. Each project is accompanied by clear objectives and measurable outcomes, enabling students to fully grasp the significance of their contributions to the organization and concentrate on achieving project goals. This sense of achievement not only enhances team morale but also serves as a powerful motivator. Project-driven not only stimulates division of labor and specialization, with each project assigned a specific team member to handle specific tasks, but also enhances efficiency and quality. It also motivates team members to face challenges and seek solutions.

Project-driven learning leads to higher efficiency, better teamwork, and better results. It links students' efforts to clear goals and motivates them to strive for the best outcome of a project, thereby achieving the goal of comprehensive skill development.

Fourthly, system as a guarantee. Taking the system as a guarantee refers to ensuring that the rights of every individual within the TUATRC are upheld through the formulation, implementation, and execution of a series of systems, enabling the TUATRC to develop soundly and rapidly. The TUATRC has formulated a series of guiding and binding rules and systems, such as the attendance system, training and selection system, final elimination system, asset management system, equipment sharing system, equipment and software resource allocation system, reward and punishment system, and so on.

The implementation of the aforementioned systems ensures fair and equal opportunities, provides a good balance of power and supervision mechanism, and establishes an institutionalized long-term mechanism for the TUATRC within the entire practical education system.

Fifthly, supported by a fair and unbiased evaluation system. A fair and unbiased evaluation system focuses on objective, verifiable, and unbiased evaluation criteria to avoid the influence of individual subjective opinions and unfair factors. The evaluation criteria and methods of the TUATRC are transparent, which fairly evaluates students' academic abilities and potential, ensuring that every teacher and student has equal opportunities and resources. This not only stimulates students' practical interests but also promotes the elevation of instructors' guidance.

To support a fair and unbiased evaluation system, the TUATRC has established transparent evaluation criteria and processes. It has also recruited evaluators with professional knowledge and a sense of fairness to participate in the evaluation. Additionally, it has established a supervision mechanism and appeal channels to ensure the fairness and transparency of the evaluation.

The implementation of the Five-in-One practical education system enables students to achieve comprehensive development in practice, allowing them to better understand and apply the knowledge they have learned. This system cultivates students' innovative abilities, practical abilities, organizational abilities, and social responsibility. Additionally, practical activities help to enhance students' self-confidence, team awareness, and social skills, providing them with more competitiveness and choices for their future development.

5   Model and Data Processing

Mathematical models and data analysis can offer intuitive and quantitative representations of the inherent laws of the research object. In the modern era, many colleges and universities have made numerous explorations and attempts to enhance the quality of talent training. Evaluating the correlation between a particular training method and changes in students' academic performance quantitatively holds significant importance in optimizing training methods and enhancing the quality of education.

5.1   Data Preprocessing

LI M investigated the impact of non-intellectual factors on college students' English scores using decision tree algorithms to predict changes in future performance trends [3]. Ren Ge employed the Apriori algorithm to analyze the correlation between students' failing scores and establish a set of academic warning rules [4]. Huang Jianming and Sun Jie studied the future development trend of students' performance through Bayesian network and deep neural network [5,6]. Jin Xiankai established a model to predict student performance through fully connected neural network [7]. Unlike the aforementioned studies, this paper focuses on exploring the correlation between student performance change factors and teaching models. We selected average, median, passing rate, excellence rate, distinction, and other student performance indicators to form a comprehensive Index-gain coefficient. Based on this, cluster analysis and the identification information model were chosen to evaluate the effectiveness of the Five-in-One teaching system.

5.2   Model Selection

The data set representing students' test scores serves as the evaluation object, where N,C,Y, and A represent the number of students, the set of courses, grades, and the transcript for a particular course. For example, N_{cy} denotes the number of test takers in grade y for course c. $A_{cy}(i)$ denotes the score of the student indexed i who is in grade y ($y \in Y$) in course c ($c \in C$) [8]. The variables AVE,MID,EXC and QUA represent the scores for average, median, excellence rate, and passing rate, respectively, before implementing the Five-in-One practical teaching model. On the other hand, AVE', MID', EXC', and QUA' indicate the corresponding values after choosing this model [6]. defines the grade y ($y \in Y$) in course c ($c \in C$) gain coefficient ρ_{cy} as

$$
\rho_{cy} = \frac{\gamma_1 \left(\frac{AVE'_{cy}}{100}\right)^2 + \gamma_2 \left(\frac{MID'_{cy}}{100}\right)^2 + \gamma_3 \left(EXC'_{cy}\right)^2 + \gamma_4 \left(QUA'_{cy}\right)^2}{\gamma_1 \left(\frac{AVE_{cy}}{100}\right)^2 + \gamma_2 \left(\frac{MID_{cy}}{100}\right)^2 + \gamma_3 \left(EXC_{cy}\right)^2 + \gamma_4 \left(QUA_{cy}\right)^2}, \tag{1}
$$

where $\gamma_1, \gamma_2, \gamma_3$ and γ_4 represent the importance of each statistical indicator in the effectiveness coefficient of the measure. These weights allow the evaluation system to be adjusted according to the preference for different indicators. Since the value range of the average score AVE_{cy} and the median MID_{cy} is $[0, 100]$, and the value range of the excellence rate EXC_{cy} and passing rate QUA_{cy} is $[0,1]$, the values are normalized accordingly. The AVE_{cy} is calculated as $AVE_{cy} = (\sum_{i=1}^{N_{cy}} A_{cy}(i))/N_{cy}$, which represents the average score for students in grade y ($y \in Y$) in course c ($c \in C$). When the scores are not evenly distributed, the median is used to reflect the average level, and the course scores are sorted in descending order, with the middle rank defined as MID_{cy}. The $EXC_{cy} = N(A_{cy} \geq 90)/N_{cy}$ represents the proportion of students with a score of 90 or above in grade y ($y \in Y$) in course c ($c \in C$). The QUA_{cy} is defined as $QUA_{cy} = N(A_{cy} \geq 60)/N_{cy}$, which represents the proportion of students who have passed the course.

The gain coefficient ρ_{cy} has the following property:

Property 1. $\rho_{cy} > 1$, *it indicates that the teaching reform measures adopted have shown effective statistical trends; conversely, if $\rho_{cy} \leq 1$, the measures are considered ineffective.*

5.3   Cluster Analysis

Cluster analysis is an unsupervised learning method that partitions a data set into distinct groups or clusters by gathering similar data samples together. Its objective is to reveal hidden patterns or structures within the data, enabling a more profound understanding. This paper employs the $K-$means clustering algorithm to cluster the observations (n) into k sets ($k \leq c$), minimizing the sum of squares of deviations between the data in each cluster and its mean. In other words, clustering must satisfy.

$$
\min \sum_{i=1}^{k} \|x_i - \mu_i\|^2, \tag{2}
$$

where x_i represents a point that belongs to the ith class, and μ_i denotes the mean of all points in the i-th class.

By taking students' grades A_{cy} as feature values, we cluster students' grades into n clusters to obtain this type of central feature value. In this context, the feature corresponds to the course, and the feature value corresponds to the grade.

It is approximately believed that the feature value of the cluster center feature can reflect the performance of this type of student. The larger the clustering center value, the higher the overall achievement level of the students. The change in the proportion of the number of different types to the total reflects the change in the performance distribution.

5.4 Information Discrimination

Information discrimination (ID) is a metric that gauges the correlation between information sources [9]. Assuming the range of random variable X is given by $F = (f_1, f_2, \ldots, f_m)$ and the probability distribution of X is associated with hypotheses H_1 and H_2, the conditional probability distribution (CPD) $P_1(X)$ under hypothesis H_1 is characterized as follows

$$\begin{bmatrix} X \\ P_1(X) \end{bmatrix} = \begin{bmatrix} f_1 & f_2 & \cdots & f_m \\ P_1(f_1) & P_1(f_2) & \cdots & P_1(f_m) \end{bmatrix}. \tag{3}$$

The CPD $P_2(X)$ under the assumption H_2 is formulated as

$$\begin{bmatrix} X \\ P_2(X) \end{bmatrix} = \begin{bmatrix} f_1 & f_2 & \cdots & f_m \\ P_2(f_1) & P_2(f_2) & \cdots & P_2(f_m) \end{bmatrix}. \tag{4}$$

Obviously , there is $P_1(f_i) = P(f_i|H_1)$, $P_2(f_i) = P(f_i|H_2)$. Furthermore, we define the ID as

$$I(P_1|P_2) = ln \frac{P_1(f_i)}{P_2(f_i)}, \tag{5}$$

which is the amount of information provided when the random variable X taking f_i, that tends to H_1 when identifying hypotheses H_1 and H_2 . It is easy to get the following property.

Property 2. *When the ID is positive, the information provided by the event f_i is positively correlated with hypothesis H_1; conversely, when the identification information is negative, the information provided by the event f_i is negatively correlated with hypothesis H_1.*

6 Evaluation

6.1 Basic Statistical Analysis

We select the average score, median score, excellent rate, pass rate, and increase rate of the scores for 7 courses-Digital Circuit, Program Analysis and Design, Signal and System, High-Frequency Electronic Circuit, Digital Signal Processing and Principles of Communications-for 11 grades of students from 2011–2021, as shown in Tables 1, 2, 3 and 4.

The Five-in-One practical teaching reforms were introduced in 2017. To facilitate comparative analysis of the Five-in-One practical teaching effect, students in grades 2011–2016 are grouped together, and grades 2017–2021 are grouped separately.

As Tables 1 and Tables 2 reveal, the average scores and median scores of each course have increased post the implementation of the Five-in-One. Tables 3 and 4 reflect an increase in the passing rate after the implementation of the Five-in-One education system, along with an increase in the excellent rate, indicating an overall improvement in student performance. The effective coefficients of measures are obtained based on the statistical data in Tables 1, 2, 3 and 4 as shown in Table 5, $\rho > 1(\gamma_1 = \gamma_2 = \gamma_3 = \gamma_4 = 1)$. According to Property 1, the Five-in-One is an effective Teaching reform measures.

Table 1. Analysis of the average numbers for grade 2011–2021.

Grade	Analog Circuit	Digital Circuits	Program Analysis and Design	Signals and Systems	High Frequency Electronic Circuit	Digital Signal Processing	Principles of Communications
2011–2016	79.25	74.63	78.95	82.28	74.65	76.73	74.86
2017–2021	85.36	80.32	86.73	90.58	80.12	82.18	82.36
Increases%	7.71	7.62	9.85	10.09	7.33	7.10	10.02

Table 2. Center of clustering and proportion of Digital Circuit for grade 2011–2021.

Grade	Failed	Proportion%	Pass	Proportion%	Medium	Proportion%	Good	Proportion%	Excellent	Proportion%
2011–2016	38.50	3.57	64.57	18.24	76.95	27.38	84.36	31.26	93.14	19.55
2017–2021	40.12	2.16	67.52	19.12	79.68	28.64	86.73	32.16	94.68	17.92
Increa-ses%	4.21	−39.50	4.57	4.82	3.55	4.60	2.81	2.88	1.65	−8.34

Table 3. Analysis of the pass rates for grade 2011–2021.

Grade	Analog Circuit	Digital Circuits	Program Analysis and Design	Signals and Systems	High Frequency Electronic Circuit	Digital Signal Processing	Principles of Communications
2011–2016	84.23	80.6	83.23	87.63	83.25	84.38	83.12
2017–2021	91.35	86.13	88.25	95.26	89.68	91.12	90.16
Increases%	8.45	6.86	6.03	8.71	7.72	7.99	8.47

Table 4. Analysis of the excellent rates for grade 2011–2021.

Grade	Analog Circuit	Digital Circuits	Program Analysis and Design	Signals and Systems	High Frequency Electronic Circuit	Digital Signal Processing	Principles of Communications
2011–2016	19.23	18.68	19.56	17.35	16.73	15.58	15.23
2017–2021	22.32	23.28	24.36	21.98	19.28	18.86	20.26
Increases%	16.07	24.63	24.54	26.69	15.24	21.05	33.03

Table 5. Analysis of the excellent rates for grade 2011–2021.

Course	Analog Circuit	Digital Circuits	Program Analysis and Design	Signals and Systems	High Frequency Electronic Circuit	Digital Signal Processing	Principles of Communications
ρ	1.16	1.18	1.19	1.21	1.16	1.16	1.19

6.2 Cluster Analysis

The 7 courses selected from grades 2011–2021 are clustered into failing, passing, medium, good, and excellent categories using K−means clustering. The cluster centers and proportions are shown in Tables 6, 7, 8, 9, 10, 11 and 12. Although the proportion of outstanding students in individual courses has decreased, the cluster centers and proportions of different grades have increased, and the cluster center is higher. This indicates that the learning ability of outstanding students has improved. Meanwhile, the number of students in the low-segmented category has significantly decreased, demonstrating that the Five-in-One approach plays a prominent role in cultivating students' abilities.

Table 6. Center of clustering and proportion of Analog Circuit for grade 2011–2021.

Grade	Failed	Proportion%	Pass	Proportion%	Medium	Proportion%	Good	Proportion%	Excellent	Proportion%
2011–2016	46.78	5.12	64.23	18.32	76.02	27.36	84.28	31.02	93.12	18.18
2017–2021	48.63	1.20	68.74	18.02	78.24	28.76	86.73	32.58	95.12	19.44
Increa-ses%	3.95	−76.56	7.02	−1.64	2.92	5.12	2.91	5.03	2.15	6.93

Table 7. Center of clustering and proportion of Digital Circuit for grade 2011–2021.

Grade	Failed	Proportion%	Pass	Proportion%	Medium	Proportion%	Good	Proportion%	Excellent	Proportion%
2011–2016	38.50	3.57	64.57	18.24	76.95	27.38	84.36	31.26	93.14	19.55
2017–2021	40.12	2.16	67.52	19.12	79.68	28.64	86.73	32.16	94.68	17.92
Increa-ses%	4.21	−39.50	4.57	4.82	3.55	4.60	2.81	2.88	1.65	−8.34

Table 8. Center of clustering and proportion of Program Analysis and Design for grade 2011–2021.

Grade	Failed	Proportion%	Pass	Proportion%	Medium	Proportion%	Good	Proportion%	Excellent	Proportion%
2011–2016	51.21	5.42	66.13	16.78	73.45	28.16	84.31	28.96	93.12	20.68
2017–2021	53.21	1.26	67.56	18.24	78.32	31.02	86.29	29.68	95.16	19.80
Increa-ses%	3.91	−76.75	2.16	8.70	6.63	10.16	2.35	2.49	2.19	−4.26

Table 9. Center of clustering and proportion of Signal and System for grade 2011–2021.

Grade	Failed	Proportion%	Pass	Proportion%	Medium	Proportion%	Good	Proportion%	Excellent	Proportion%
2011–2016	52.64	3.12	66.32	19.28	76.59	29.12	85.26	30.12	93.26	18.36
2017–2021	54.21	2.13	68.12	18.24	78.68	30.21	86.39	31.26	95.61	18.16
Increa-ses%	2.98	−31.73	2.71	−5.36	2.73	3.74	1.33	3.78	2.52	−1.09

Table 10. Center of clustering and proportion of High-Frequency Electronic Circuit for grade 2011–2021.

Grade	Failed	Proportion%	Pass	Proportion%	Medium	Proportion%	Good	Proportion%	Excellent	Proportion%
2011–2016	38.26	5.36	64.25	18.63	73.96	28.24	84.02	30.12	93.24	17.65
2017–2021	48.62	3.18	67.61	18.76	77.62	29.35	87.32	31.02	96.02	17.69
Increa-ses%	27.08	−40.67	5.23	0.70	4.95	3.93	3.93	2.99	2.98	0.23

Table 11. Center of clustering and proportion of Digital Signal Processing for grade 2011–2021.

Grade	Failed	Proportion%	Pass	Proportion%	Medium	Proportion%	Good	Proportion%	Excellent	Proportion%
2011–2016	38.26	5.23	64.26	18.78	75.62	26.35	84.25	30.28	93.21	19.36
2017–2021	46.38	2.36	68.72	19.28	78.64	27.43	86.59	31.26	95.34	19.67
Increa-ses%	21.22	−54.88	6.94	2.66	3.99	4.10	2.78	3.24	2.29	1.60

Table 12. Center of clustering and proportion of Principles of Communications for grade 2011–2021.

Grade	Failed	Proportion%	Pass	Proportion%	Medium	Proportion%	Good	Proportion%	Excellent	Proportion%
2011–2016	48.76	4.86	64.35	19.32	76.02	25.36	82.56	30.24	93.21	20.22
2017–2021	51.23	3.40	66.53	20.13	78.63	26.76	86.35	31.28	94.37	18.43
Increa-ses%	5.07	−30.04	3.39	4.19	3.43	5.52	4.59	3.44	1.24	−8.85

6.3 Using ID

We analyze the scores of the selected 7 courses from 2011–2021 grades using ID, and categorize the scores into five categories: less than 60 points, 60–69 points, 70–79 points, 80–89 points, and 90–100 points. We then calculate ID, which is the proportion of students in each fraction of the 2011–2016 grade compared to the total number of students, and compare it to the proportion of students in the 2017–2021 grade compared to the total number of students (Table 13). $I\left(P_1|P_2\right)$ indicates that the proportion of students in this grade group has decreased after implementing the Five-in-One approach; conversely, it indicates that the proportion has increased. Overall, the proportion of low-scoring students in the selected courses has decreased, while the high-scoring students have increased except for High-Frequency Electronic Circuits and Digital Signal Processing. The survey found that the difficulty of the two courses' test papers in 2019

Table 13. Information discrimination of courses for grade 2011–2021.

FractionCourse	Analog Circuit	Digital Circuits	Program Analysis and Design	Signals and Systems	High Frequency Electronic Circuit	Digital Signal Processing	Principles of Commu- nications
<60 points	0.60	0.34	0.36	0.96	0.48	0.56	0.54
60–69 points	0.24	0.27	0.04	0.09	−0.10	0.07	0.05
70–79 points	−0.18	0.01	0.03	−0.17	−0.12	−0.21	0.05
80–89 points	−0.15	−0.28	−0.06	−0.03	0.05	0.07	−0.18
90–100 points	−0.15	−0.22	−0.22	−0.24	−0.14	−0.19	−0.29

and 2020 increased compared to other years. The ID in Table 13 clearly shows that the Five-in-One system has a relatively significant impact on overall ability improvement.

7 Conclusion

The practical education system of Five-in-One can provide students with a good practical environment, improve their ability to effectively analyze and solve problems, and support teaching and research. It contributes to the cultivation of "reliable, useful, and available" talents with "unity, diligence, realism, and innovation" qualities.

Acknowledgment. This work was supported by the key research project of higher education teaching reform in Tibet Autonomous Region Education Department in 2021 (Grant Number: JG2021-02), the third batch of the National University Huang Danian Teacher Team by the Ministry of Education of the People's Republic of China for the Border Security Information Transmission and Processing Faculty Team, and the Science and Technology Major Project of Tibetan Autonomous Region of China (Grant Number: XZ202201ZD0006G).

References

1. Wenxing, C.: Construction and practice of the "Three Innovations" talent training system in colleges and universities. Chin. Univ. Teach. **390**(3), 52–55 (2022)
2. Renzhong, D., Kaicheng, G., Zhixiang, X.: Construction of the "six-in-one" training model for top talents in basic economics disciplines. Chin. Univ. Teach. **368**(2), 89–93 (2021)
3. Li, M.: A study on the influence of non-intelligence factors on college students' English learning achievement based on C4.5 algorithm of decision tree. Wirel. Person. Commun. **102**(2), 1213–1222 (2018)
4. Ren Ge, Wu Meng, Khan Guli Litifu, et al: Construction of college course early warning rule base based on improved Apriori algorithm. Comput. Syst. Appl. **30**(7), 290–295 (2021)
5. Jianming, H.: Application of Bayesian network in student performance prediction. Comput. Sci. **39**(3), 280–282 (2012)
6. Jie, S.: Research on the application of Gaussian Naive Bayes algorithm in college student performance prediction. Comput. Knowl. Technol. **17**(20), 23–26 (2021)
7. Xiankai, J., Wei, S.: Research on the prediction method of college students' academic performance based on DNN: taking the electronic information major of a university in Beijing as an example. J. North China Univ. Technol. **33**(5), 134–140 (2021)
8. Jin Xin, Yu., Feifan, D.Y., et al.: Analysis of teaching effect evaluation model based on cluster analysis and discriminant information. J. Shandong Univ. (Sci. Edn.) **58**(7), 115–120 (2023)
9. Ye, L., Huijuan, C., Kun, T.: Speech endpoint detection algorithm based on energy and identification information. J. Tsinghua Univ. (Nat. Sci. Edn.) **46**(7), 1271–1273 (2006)

The Role of Science and Technology Innovation Competition in Talent Cultivation and Development

Zhirui Zuo(iD), Jie Zhang(iD), and Ying Jin(✉)(iD)

Nanjing University, Nanjing, China
191300087@smail.nju.edu.cn, {zhangj,jinying}@nju.edu.cn

Abstract. Nowadays, the science and technology innovation competitions (hereinafter referred to as STICs) geared towards undergraduate students is booming, exemplified by events like the College Student "Internet+" Innovation and Entrepreneurship Competition in China, and Mathematical Contest in Modeling overseas, both of which are high-level and high-quality events. These STICs offer students an opportunity to practically apply their academic knowledge and build a solid foundation for future employment prospects. At the same time, the continuous enhancement of students' aptitude requires that STICs evolve in tandem with the development of various industries and specializations. Hence, to ensure the continuous supply of innovative talents to society, it is crucial to investigate the evolution of the STICs. In this paper, our study processes the competition data of the Chinese Collegiate Computing Competition(hereinafter called 4C) in Jiangsu division from 2017 to 2022 with modules such as Pandas and Pyecharts in Python. Based on visualization and modeling results, combined with employment distribution data and national educational policies, the development of the competition is analyzed, and suggestions are made for the future development of the STICs, in order to better utilize the talent cultivation function of the competition and promote the future development of talents.

Keywords: Science and Technology Innovation Competition · Higher education · Employment and entrepreneurship of undergraduates · Discounted Utility Model

1 Introduction

Since the 1980s, the STICs in Chinese colleges and universities have been increasingly popular. Every year, millions of college students demonstrate their enthusiasm and ability to apply their knowledge creatively and make a positive impact

Supported by 1. University Computer Course Teaching Steering Committee of the Ministry of Education, Research on the reform of university computer empowerment education in the new era project- Research on the reform of university computer empowerment education in New Liberal Arts. 2. Computer Education Research Association of Chinese Universities, Projects in the direction of education in 2021 - Research on the connection between universities and K12 information technology teaching.

on the world through the STICs. Not only does the recognition of the STICs among students continue to increase, but the Guiding Opinions on Further Supporting Innovation and Entrepreneurship among College Students issued by the General Office of the State Council in 2021 also specifically pointed out the need to create innovation and entrepreneurship competition brands and play their role as educational practice platforms. As an important component of talent training in China, the STICs have provided a practical platform for college students to develop and exercise their "four creativities" abilities. Consequently, examining the development of the STICs for college students in China carries significant implications for talent cultivation and future development.

Among numerous competitions, the 4C, as one of the earliest competitions for undergraduate students in China, is held to cultivate innovative, compound and applied talents with all-round development. As a practical form of learning computer knowledge and skills related to undergraduate majors, the 4C aims to improve the comprehensive quality of college students, specifically implement and further promote the reform of the knowledge system, curriculum system, teaching content, and teaching methods in undergraduate computer teaching. In addition, unlike competitions that prioritize students' abilities in specific fields, such as the "Pilot Cup" that emphasizes creative ability in digital media, the 4C offers nine categories and thirty sub-categories of entries, allowing students to choose the entry position that best suits their interests and strengths.

Among the divisions of the 4C, the Jiangsu division not only actively participated (with a total of 1287 submitted works in 2022), but also had a high quality of participation (with an overall award rate of 33.10% in 2022). Considering the difficulty of obtaining data nationwide, the subsequent analysis of this article uses the participation data of the 4C in Jiangsu province from 2017 to 2022 as a representative of the national data.

As for the tools used for analyzing data, due to the obtained data is in Excel format, it is very suitable to use the DataFrame data type in pandas for data processing. In addition, analyzing sub-categories belonging to the same category is a process of data aggregation, and the groupby method provided in the pandas module can conveniently achieve the purpose of analyzing different categories. In terms of visualization, pyecharts provides a variety of chart types, so we use pyecharts for visualization.

Based on the above reasons, by utilizing the pandas and pyecharts modules in Python, this article takes the 4C in Jiangsu division as an example to analyze the development trend of the competition by processing and visualizing the data of the competition from 2017 to 2022, combined with the employment distribution data of some universities and national educational policies. Finally, the current situation of the STICs is discussed, and suggestions for future development are provided.

2   The Role of the STICs in Talent Development

2.1   Analysis of the Trend of the 4C

We drew a stacked graph of the registration data for various categories of the 4C in Jiangsu from 2017 to 2022, and then analyzed the development trend of the competition based on the visualization results. Due to space limitations, the article only displays visualization results for some categories, with columns from left to right representing the number of registrations for each category from 2017 to 2022. (Note: Due to the fact that artificial intelligence applications and information visualization design were only opened after 2018 and 2019, the visualization results for both categories are only 5 and 4 columns, respectively), as shown in Fig. 1:

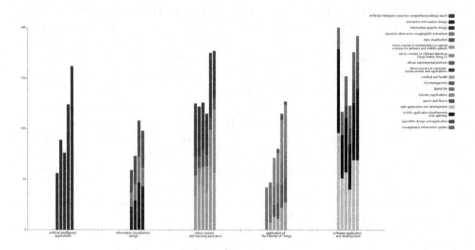

Fig. 1. Registration status for some categories from 2017 to 2022

By analyzing the visualization results, the following conclusions can be drawn:

1. Software application and development, micro courses and teaching assistance have always maintained a high level of participation enthusiasm, and in the early stage of the 4C in Jiangsu, they far surpassed other major categories. Over time, the two categories still have the highest number of participants, but no longer have an absolute leading position. On the other hand, although artificial intelligence was only launched after 2018, its popularity has been increasing year by year, the application of the Internet of Things and information visualization design are also showing a growth trend, which is closely related to the continuous development of majors such as artificial intelligence, big data technology, and Internet of Things engineering. It also indicates that the hot topics of competition projects are constantly becoming more technological and information-based [1].

2. At the sub-category level, the participating students have a high enthusiasm for the artificial intelligence practice competition (ordinary track) and web application and development. Based on this trend, the STICs (not only the 4C) can encourage students to introduce science literacy and application works to the public, so as to play the role of discipline competition in repaying the society [2], and also can exercise the knowledge transformation and application ability of the participants, thus preparing for their future employment in advance.

2.2 The Connection Between Competition Development and Employment

First we collected and organized data on the employment distribution of some universities from 2017 to 2022, and calculated the Pearson correlation coefficient between the proportion of industries with higher employment and corresponding categories of the 4C. The results showed a strong correlation between the employment distribution of universities and the proportion of popular competition categories in the overall competition, For example, the employment proportion in the information transmission, software, and information technology service industries of Nanjing University has maintained a consistent growth trend in the past six years, and reached a significant proportion of 28.31% in the overall industry distribution in 2022. The correlation coefficients between this employment data and the application of the Internet of Things and big data practice are 0.794 and 0.852, respectively, indicating a strong correlation between competition development trends and employment flows.

In addition to employment flow, the establishment of majors in universities and social demand are also important indicators reflecting the changing trends in the industry. In terms of professional settings, since the first batch of 35 universities opened the artificial intelligence specialty in 2019, a total of 4 batches of 440 universities have opened the AI specialty to date. In terms of social demand, according to the "2022 Future Talent Employment Report" released by Liepin [3] and the "2023 Talent Migration Report" released by Maimai [4], the growth of new job opportunities in some industries in the past four years is shown in Table 1. It is not difficult to find that the artificial intelligence industry that has emerged in recent years has always maintained a very high growth rate, and traditional industries such as education and training have gradually stabilized. Although the growth rate of new job opportunities in the production and manufacturing industry has slowed down in 2020, with the support and influence of the "smart reform and digital transfer" policy, a large number of job opportunities have been provided to society again. For example, XCMG Group has launched a quality and efficiency improvement project based on big data, utilizing industrial data to analyze defects in production, resulting in a 68% improvement in the overall efficiency of XCMG equipment. Enterprises have increased their production capacity through intelligence and digitization, and in order to further improve their level of intelligence, more job opportunities have emerged, forming a virtuous cycle. The changes in these industries are consistent with the emergence and rapid development trends of artificial intelligence, big data applications, information visualization design, and other categories in competitions.

Table 1. Year-on-year growth of new positions in some industries in the past four years

Industry	2019	2020	2021	2022
Artificial Intelligence	13.96%	28.12%	51.39%	57.60%
Manufacturing	32.88%	12.20%	32.73%	28.24%
Education and training	22.14%	4.44%	−8.45%	−0.86%

In summary, The STICs have honed students' practical and innovative abilities, serving as a testing ground for students to understand and apply their professional knowledge. They have provided project experience for future job interviews and laid a solid foundation [5]. At the same time, with the changes in employment trends and social needs, the competition itself is constantly adapting, providing better exercise platforms for contestants by opening new categories and other adjustments.

2.3   Discussion on the STICs and Entrepreneurship

In terms of direct impact, considering the impact of STICs on college students' entrepreneurial intention, in the questionnaire survey of senior students by Huang et al. [6], eight questions were set in the form of Likert five-point scale under the dimension of entrepreneurial intention, and the results showed that the average of 3.18 points (out of 5 points) of students with experience in STICs was significantly higher than the average of 2.74 of students who had not participated in STICs. It can be seen that the STICs have greatly improved the innovative ability of the participating students, enhanced their entrepreneurial confidence and willingness by providing students with complete project practice experience, further played a good role in creating a social atmosphere of mass entrepreneurship and mass innovation in China.

In terms of indirect impact, consider the role of STICs in cultivating the ability of college students to start their own businesses. First of all, the STICs have strengthened the cooperation ability of college students. For example, in the 4C in Jiangsu, there were 5666 works from 2017 to 2022, of which only 637 were completed by individuals independently, and the award rate of these works was only 25.27%. Among the remaining 5029 team entries, 1837 were awarded, with the award rate as high as 36.53%. It's obvious that team participation has more opportunities to gain in the competition, which encourages players to produce high-quality works through team cooperation, thus exercising students' cooperation ability. In addition, by creating works for practical problems, students can also be promoted to apply the theoretical knowledge learned in class to extracurricular practice and improve their application ability.

In a word, whether directly or indirectly, the STICs have played a positive role in college students' entrepreneurship.

3   Analysis of Competition Results and Suggestions for the Development Direction of Colleges

Since the Ministry of Education, the Ministry of Finance and the National Development and Reform Commission of the People's Republic of China issued the Implementation Measures for the Overall Promotion of the Construction of World-class Universities and First-class Disciplines (Provisional) in 2017, the division of "double first-class" and "application-oriented" colleges has further reflected the talent training ideas in different directions, and the two types of colleges have also exhibited distinct characteristics in the STICs.

In this section, the discount utility model is introduced to calculate the award rates of two types of universities in each category of the 4C during the past several years. Based on the results, the characteristics of "double first-class" and "application-oriented" universities are analyzed, and suggestions are provided for the future talent cultivation of these two types of universities.

3.1   Introduction of Discounted Utility Model

When examining the award rates of provincial competitions over the years, due to the incomplete setting of categories of the 4C in its early stages and the fact that the 4C itself is also adjusted with changes in employment trends, the reference value of early data of the competition is weaker than that of recent data. Therefore, it is necessary to balance the reference significance of different annual award rates by setting weights.

The earliest approach to characterizing this long-term process was the Discounted Utility Model (DU), which provides more of an analytical framework and provides a relatively simple description of intertemporal selection behavior. Subsequent researchers have also proposed a hyperbolic discount function that is more in line with human time preferences. After 2015, an incremental discounted utility model considering the interrelationship between the utility obtained in different time periods appeared [7], However, due to the limited amount of data in this article and the main purpose being to balance the impact of long-term and short-term data, the most basic DU model is adopted, which includes a constant discount factor β. The mathematical form is as follows:

$$U = u(x_0) + \sum_{t=1}^{\infty} \beta^t \cdot u(x_t) \tag{1}$$

In the presented formula, the term $u(x_0)$ denotes the award rate of entries for a certain category in 2022, while $u(x_t)$ refers to the award rate of the same category in 2022-t. The final weighted award rate is represented by U.

According to this idea, we model the calculation of the weighted award rate as arranging the weights of exponential decay for award rates of different years from the perspective of 2022 and summing them, finally obtains the overall award rate of a category on the entire historical series.

3.2   Analysis of Competition Results and Characteristics of Colleges and Development Suggestions

Result of the Weighted Award Rate. With the DU model introduced in Sect. 3.1, the overall weighted award rate of each category for "double first-class" and "application-oriented" colleges in the years 2017–2022 can be calculated. Based on this weighted award rate, the performance of the "double first-class" and "application-oriented" colleges in each category can be evaluated.

In order to examine the educational characteristics of the two types of universities, it is only necessary to focus on the participating categories that perform well. Table 2 and 3 shows the top ten categories with weighted award rates from the two types of colleges(to prevent result overflow, the calculation results of each category have been proportionally scaled down, and this operation does not affect the size order relationship between the weighted award rates of different categories).

Table 2. "application-oriented" colleges

Category	Sub-category	Weighted-award rate
micro course and teaching assistance	virtual experimental platform	65.608%
digital media static design	environmental design	63.747%
digital media anime and short films	documentary	59.508%
digital media anime and short films	new media comics	55.075%
application of the Internet of Things	digital life	53.335%
digital media anime and short films	microfilm	53.324%
digital media games and interactive design	interactive media design	51.632%
application of the Internet of Things	medical and health	50.832%
digital media games and interactive design	game design	50.697%
digital media anime and short films	animation	47.247%

Table 3. "double first-class" colleges

Category	Sub-category	Weighted-award rate
micro course and teaching assistance	virtual experimental platform	71.008%
application of the Internet of Things	medical and health	56.696%
digital media games and interactive design	game design	54.524%
software application and development	web application and development	51.570%
application of the Internet of Things	digital life	50.147%
digital media anime and short films	documentary	50.078%
micro course and teaching assistance	micro courses in mathematics or natural sciences for primary and middle schools	49.381%
software application and development	mobile application development(non gaming)	48.967%
digital media static design	product design	47.644%
software application and development	algorithm design and application	46.526%

Analysis of the Characteristics and Development Suggestions for "Application-Oriented" Colleges. The characteristics of "application-oriented" colleges are extremely prominent. Seven out of ten of their outstanding performance categories are related to digital media, which is consistent with their policy of focusing on the cultivation of application-oriented talents.

According to the List of National Colleges and Universities issued by the Ministry of Education, as of May 31, 2022, there were 3013 colleges and universities nationwide, an increase of 571 compared with 2442 in 2012. Under the real environment of the growing number of colleges, local colleges can only make the most efficient use of educational resources by giving full play to their characteristic advantages in serving the local area, meeting the needs of local industrial transformation and upgrading, adapting to the needs of local economic construction [8] and cultivating high-level application-oriented innovative talents different from the training goals of research universities and polytechnic college.

In order to further build "application-oriented" colleges and cultivate high-quality specialized talents, we must first grasp the general direction of "industry-education city integration, economic science and education linkage, school-govern- ment-enterprise cooperation, and industry-university-research integration" [9], chan-ge the traditional academic-oriented thinking to market-oriented. In terms of specific details, it is necessary to strengthen the construction of practical teaching, such as encouraging students to participate in competitions directly related to employment, such as service outsourcing for Chinese college students competition.

This comprehensive pattern helps to cultivate students who possess both professional skills and innovative thinking and practical abilities, promote deep integration between schools and society, which providing society with high-quality talents that better meet practical needs, thus promoting industrial innovation and social progress.

Analysis of the Characteristics and Development Suggestions for "Double First-Class" Colleges. Different from "application-oriented" colleges, "double first-class" universities have demonstrated strong comprehensive capabilities and shown high quality of participation in various categories such as digital media, programming applications, and micro-courses which is also in line with the "double first-class" colleges' concept of paying more attention to the cultivation of innovative, general-purpose rather than specialized talents. In order to continuously deliver corresponding talents to the society, "double first-class" colleges should achieve three "linkages".

1. The first is the linkage between scientific research and teaching, meaning that "double first-class" colleges shoule grasp their own scientific research advantages and teach through scientific research activities so as to further improve students' innovation and engineering capabilities.
2. The second is the linkage between in-class and out-of-class, which inplies the ability of college students to cooperate, innovate, solve problems and other abilities can be improved through science and technology competitions, and the comprehensive development of college students can be promoted.
3. The final is the linkage between teaching and learning, conveying that the development of talents is not only a unilateral task of the school, students also need to exert subjective initiative, only combining teaching and learning can we achieve twice the training effect with half the effort [10].

By achieving the three "linkages", we can implement a comprehensive talent cultivation pattern to improve students' practical abilities, stimulate innovative thinking, cultivate teamwork spirit. This not only has a positive impact on individual students, but also has a positive effect on society, such as promoting social innovation and development. By providing students with a comprehensive educational experience and cultivating more competitive and innovative talents, we can build a society that combines innovation and practical abilities.

4   Analysis on the Current Situation of Competition and Suggestions for Future Development

Based on the Catalog of Undergraduate Programs in General Colleges and Universities (2022), there are a total of 413 majors in the fields of science, engineering, agronomy, and medicine. Hence, the STICs have a broad target audience among students, but the distribution of disciplines in competitions is more concentrated in electronic information competitions. Upon analyzing the ranking list of the STICs, statistical results indicate that the overall development of the competitions is stable and progressing, and the number of awards distributed is proportional to the number of events, ensuring the quality of the contests. Notably, electronic information competitions hold a significant position, accounting for 65.79% of all events and 72.78% of all awards.

The reason for this is firstly that the education department focuses on cultivating new engineering talents. By integrating computer, artificial intelligence, big data and other technologies with traditional majors, it promotes the cross integration of disciplines and upgrades and transforms traditional disciplines. Among the 31 new majors added in 2021, 14 new majors were added in the engineering category, with "intelligence" and "wisdom" appearing 7 times. Secondly, the country advocates for the process of "intelligent transformation and digital transformation" of enterprises, which aims to improve production efficiency through highly intelligent transformation and digital transformation of the manufacturing industry. This requires digital and networked improvements in production. The emergence of categories such as artificial intelligence applications and information visualization designs in the 4C is also closely related to this policy. Finally, in the current environment, artificial intelligence applications have penetrated into various industries. The distribution of demand for artificial intelligence talents in the "Talent Blue Book" shows that the demand for artificial intelligence talents in four industries: information transmission, computer services and software industry, finance industry, manufacturing industry, leasing and business services industry all accounts for over 10% [11]. It can be seen that using computer and AI technology to improve efficiency and increase production capacity is significant for all industries.

In summary, on the basis of maintaining the overall supply of the STICs, there is a need to optimize their internal structure. The large number of electronic information competitions can be integrated, guided and standardized to a certain extent. On the one hand, it can increase the scale of the competition, improve its visibility, and cover more universities, thus guiding and assisting universities to better export computer application talents to society and filling the talent gap in relevant positions. On the other hand, it can also improve the quality of the competition and provide students with a higher quality competition environment.

5   Conclusion

As a crucial component of talent cultivation, the evolution of STICs mirrors the trend of talent mobility and societal demand. The performance of different colleges in the competition also indicate their respective training direction. Therefore, it is necessary to promote the diversified development of competitions in the future, expand the coverage of competitions, and provide diverse competitions for university students to better play the role of the STICs in talent cultivation and promoting the future development of talents.

Acknowledgements. We thank Nanjing university and University Computer Course Teaching Steering Committee of the Ministry of Education for supporting the project.

References

1. Wu, W., Zhang, X., Ye, Y., Shi, J., Lu, G., Zhang, K.: Evaluation of innovation and entrepreneurship education based on contest data portrait-data analysis of china international college students "internet+" innovation and entrepreneurship competition. Res. High. Educ. Eng. (2), 5 (2022)
2. Li, G., Hu, X., Hu, Q.: Data analysis and prospects of the national college students' life science competition. Chin. J. Biotechnol. **36**(11), 7 (2020)
3. 2022 future talent employment trends report. Liepin Big Data Research Institute (2022)
4. 2023 talent migration report. Maimai Research Institute (2023)
5. Huang, J.: Study on the double-integration and double-improvement mechanism of college students' discipline competition and employment and entrepreneurship. J. Huainan Vocat. Tech. Coll. **21**(70–72) (2021)
6. Huang, Y., Zhu, J., Zhang, Z., Yu, T.: The impact of engaging in technological innovation and entrepreneurship competitions on engineering undergraduates' entrepreneurial intention. Res. High. Educ. Eng. (6), 7 (2021)
7. Zhang, N., Li, K.: Can government subsidies increase farmers' willingness towards pension contribution? A simulation analysis based on discount incremental utility model. Econ. Sci. (3), 14 (2020)
8. Wang, F., Ye, M., Hong, L.: Idea remodeling and position shaping: application-oriented development of local colleges and universities. Appl.-Oriented High. Educ. Res. **2**(2), 6 (2017)
9. Song, Q., Zhou, Y., Wang, F., Lu, Y., Hong, L.: High-quality development of application-oriented universities: connotation, principles and practical paths. J. Yangzhou Univ. (High. Educ. Study) **26**(4), 28–34 (2022)
10. Chen, L.: Talent cultivation: the "institutionalized arrangement" of "double world-class" universities in china. Mod. Educ. Manag. (1), 1 (2020)
11. Mo, R., Zhan, M., Wu, J.: Talent blue book: report on the development of artificial intelligence talents in china (2022)

Reform of the Teaching Mode of "Four-in-One" Integrated Graduate Programs Research and Practice

Yan Wang, Shi Bai, DaPeng Qu, AiPing Tan, and Junlu Wang[✉]

Liaoning University, Shenyang 110036, Liaoning, China
{wang_yan,shibai,dapengqu,tanaiping,wangjunlu}@lnu.edu.cn

Abstract. Postgraduate courses usually lack real problem-oriented experimental and practical components, and most do not integrate the elements of Civics and Politics. To deepen the integration of industry and education, and to cultivate cross-discipline-oriented applied professionals, this paper proposes a four-in-one integrated postgraduate course teaching mode reform plan to research the teaching reform of postgraduate courses. The research is carried out from four aspects: the design of postgraduate course teaching program integrating Civic-Political elements, the reform of postgraduate course content based on the integration of industry-academia-research and utilization, the cultivation of applied professional degree postgraduate students oriented to real problems, and the cultivation of talents based on the deep integration of innovation and entrepreneurship. The research results are tested in the master course "Principles of Distributed Database" of the School of Information of Liaoning University. The academic-related experimental design and classroom teaching are completed through a cloud platform to cultivate the students' hands-on ability and innovation ability.

Keywords: problem-oriented · curriculum Civics · school-enterprise collaboration · innovation and entrepreneurship

1 Introduction

At present, the general problem of education and teaching of computer courses in China is that the courses favor theoretical teaching, without the real problems of the industry as a leader; lack of cultivation of ideological education and awareness of independent intellectual property rights, mostly relying on foreign software for operation and experimental sessions; single knowledge structure, not focusing on the cultivation of students' innovation and entrepreneurship [1], which in turn leads to the following contradictions:

1.1 The Contradiction Between Non-autonomous Knowledge and Ideological Education

Currently, in the process of computer education and teaching, database courses, for example, in the student experimental sessions are more willing to learn, use Oracle, DB2 and other non-domestic database software as the basic software for classroom teaching, students subconsciously favor foreign products, the domestic independent intellectual property rights of the system and the database products on the "poor performance," "technologically backward" label. Students will subconsciously prefer foreign products and label domestic proprietary intellectual property systems and database products as "poor performance" and "technologically backward". According to statistics, domestic and foreign software from the market share alone, non-independently developed operating systems and various types of professional software has occupied more than 70% of China's market share, the majority of users have been accustomed to using foreign mature software, which leads to the promotion of China's independent software, the use of technology, human resources and other [2]. However, the fact is that, along with the rapid development of China's database technology and the improvement of software security needs, more and more enterprises pay more attention to the issue of independent intellectual property rights [3], the market demand for talent in the information and innovation industry is also increasing, a number of China's science and technology has been ranked among the world's leading level. Therefore, while cultivating students' professional knowledge, the integration of Civic and political education, patriotism education should not be delayed.

1.2 The Contradiction Between Traditional Theoretical Teaching and the Cultivation of Practical Ability

In the traditional theoretical teaching process, students mainly passively accept and digest knowledge, focusing only on the transmission and understanding of knowledge, the teacher is often the main source of knowledge, students only need to accept and memorize, and seldom provide opportunities for students to practice and apply what they have learned, which leads to the weak practical application of knowledge, and students may encounter difficulties and lack of problem-solving ability when facing the real problems of enterprises.

1.3 The Contradiction Between the Single Knowledge Structure and the Cultivation of Compound Application-Oriented Talents

At this stage, China's computer class education concept is still generally stay in the theoretical teaching level [4]. Teachers in the teaching process, mostly only focus on a single theoretical knowledge on the textbook, the lack of students' composite ability to cultivate, but also did not docking the real problems faced by enterprises as a guide, resulting in the professional knowledge learned by students cannot be applied, cannot cope with the various industries on the demand for composite knowledge structure.

1.4 Contradiction Between Test-Taking Training and Innovation and Entrepreneurship Training

The contradiction between test-taking cultivation and the cultivation of innovative and entrepreneurial ability is an important issue facing the field of education today. Test-taking training emphasizes the memorization and application of knowledge and focuses on students achieving good results in exams, while innovation and entrepreneurship training focuses more on students' creativity, cooperation and practical ability. Test-taking cultivation tends to measure students' learning performance by standardized test evaluation, which makes students' learning focus mainly on test-taking skills and knowledge memorization. This education model will limit the development of students' innovation ability, because innovation requires students to have the ability to think, question and practice independently, which are not well cultivated in the test; although a small number of universities independently opened off-campus innovation and entrepreneurship practice courses, but only the cooperative enterprises are simply used as an extracurricular internship and practice bases, which does not really give full play to the value of school-enterprise cooperation in innovation and entrepreneurship ability cultivation [5]. At the same time, the design and development of such innovation and entrepreneurship courses are also rarely supported by specific industry backgrounds, resulting in the process of enterprise cooperation, the combination with the professional education system is not close enough [6], so that the sustainable development of school-enterprise cooperation lacks the support of professional knowledge.

In summary, at the present stage of computer education and teaching process, the teaching concept is more biased towards theoretical teaching, resulting in the separation of production and education; lack of integration of the elements of ideology and politics, there is no training on the awareness of autonomy property rights and innovation [7]; all these problems have seriously affected the cultivation of high-end talents of composite computer in China.

2 Status

In view of the above problems, in terms of course teaching reform, Xia Ying [8] addresses the social demand for high-level innovative talents with large-scale data management and processing capabilities of enterprises, combines with the construction of advanced database system technology course, elaborates on the reform and practice in the aspects of teaching content, resource platform, teaching methodology, teaching team, etc., and provides reference for the construction of the same kind of courses. Jia Bin [9] and others analyzed the enterprise demand and domestic and international database course teaching problems, elaborated on the enterprise demand based on the application of database course teaching reform practice, and gave the relevant database course teaching reform proposals. In terms of the use of domestic independent software in teaching practice, Wang Wenxin [10] elaborated on the value, challenges and strategies of domestic software innovation and emphasized the necessity of domestic software innovation. Pei Ligong [11] provided a detailed analysis of the process of domestic database substitution evolution and migration process, which promoted the speed of domestic database migration at the realistic level. Ye [12] and others analyzed the influential compute and storage separation technologies of domestic and foreign cloud service providers, including the compute and storage separation architectures of Amazon AWS Aurora, Microsoft AzureHyperscale, AliCloud PolarDB, and Huawei Cloud TaurusDB, and summarized the progress of compute and storage separation technologies, which can help developers of cloud database in their architectural design and summarize the progress of compute-storage separation technology, which can help cloud database developers in architecture design and practical research. However, the existing education and teaching reforms are mostly carried out for undergraduate courses, strengthening related experiments and practical courses, and achieving good reform results. In postgraduate courses, the lack of separate experimental courses and supporting hardware and software environments has led to the fact that the above contradiction has never been well resolved. Therefore, this course reform proposes a "four-in-one" integrated postgraduate course teaching mode reform in the teaching of postgraduates in computer science, relying on the collaborative education program, and oriented to the real problems of enterprises, through the introduction of the cloud native distributed database platform with independent intellectual property rights.

Joint school-enterprise co-construction of interactive teaching oriented to real problems is a hot spot of higher education reform research in recent years [13]. Policies such as the Ministry of Education's Education Informatization 2.0 Action Plan clearly state that we should actively carry out research and demonstration of wisdom education innovation, innovate new models of school-enterprise cooperation in research and development and cooperative education [14], and build gold classes of high order, innovation and challenge [15]. The concept of student-centered design of teaching links [16], emphasizing the students, weakening the teacher's teaching, the real problems of the enterprise as the guide, the student's "analysis, synthesis, evaluation" in the main position, around the students to carry out classroom internships and practical links [17], to help and promote student learning. The so-called "higher-order" is the organic integration of knowledge, ability and quality, which is to cultivate students' comprehensive ability to solve complex problems and advanced thinking. The so-called "innovativeness" means that the content of the courses reflects the cutting-edge and modernity, the form of teaching is advanced and interactive, and the results of learning are exploratory and personalized. The so-called "challenge degree" means that the course is difficult and requires a certain degree of jumping to reach, and the teacher's preparation and the students have higher requirements in class. Therefore, this teaching reform takes the distributed database course as the entry point, comprehensively applies a variety of practical teaching methods such as online and offline hybrid "gold class", cultivates students' hands-on ability by means of modern information technology, gives full play to students' creativity, strengthens students' ability to cope with the real problems of the enterprise, emphasizes the innovative evaluation, weakens the test-taking evaluation, and opens up a new way of teaching and learning. At the same time, the curriculum reform positively responds to the national development strategy of "information and innovation industry" [18], grasps two social practice classes [19, 20], and vigorously promotes the in-depth integration process of Civic and Political Education. In the current process of vigorously promoting the deep integration of ideological and political education, the distributed database course is deeply integrated with the cloud native platform of independent intellectual property rights, exploring the reform of the teaching mode of postgraduate courses with the integration of problem orientation, course ideological and political education, school-enterprise collaboration, and innovation and entrepreneurship in a "four-in-one" way.

3 *Four-in-One* Pedagogical Reforms

Aiming at the above problems and contradictions, we take the distributed database course as the pilot course for reform, integrate the elements of Civic and Political Science in the course, deeply cooperate with the domestic autonomous cloud native database, and carry out the co-construction reform relying on the collaborative education program of Ali-Cloud, and put forward the reform of the teaching mode of "four-in-one" integrated postgraduate courses to cultivate cross-disciplinary applied professionals and improve the innovative and entrepreneurial ability of the students. It proposes the reform of "four-in-one" integrated postgraduate course teaching mode to cultivate interdisciplinary applied professionals and improve students' innovation and entrepreneurship ability, and makes deep efforts in the design of postgraduate course teaching program integrating elements of Civic and Political Studies, postgraduate course co-construction reform relying on collaborative nurturing project, real problem-oriented interdisciplinary-oriented applied postgraduate degree cultivation, and the cultivation of talents through the in-depth integration of innovation and entrepreneurship with postgraduate courses, which make the teaching and learning of computer education more professionalized, nationalized and practiced to further enhance the efficiency of student learning, the specific process is shown in Fig. 1.

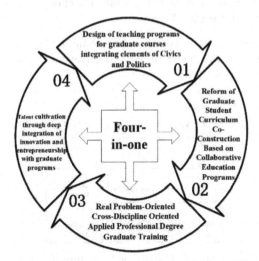

Fig. 1. General map of the "four-in-one" teaching reforms

3.1 Design of Teaching Programs for Graduate Courses Integrating Elements of Civics and Politics

Compared with undergraduate courses, postgraduate courses are more research-oriented and deeply specialized, focusing on academic research and professional development, and helping students to acquire more in-depth knowledge and skills in specific fields.

The knowledge taught in the traditional classroom focuses more on the sharing of static or teaching resources such as graphics, videos, etc., and lacks the enterprise real problem orientation and the element of ideology; at the same time, for the teachers and students in the process of knowledge exchange, the classroom interaction resources generated at anytime and anywhere lack of the necessary storage, to a large extent, ignoring the students' own subjective initiative. In view of these problems, the theoretical teaching content of this teaching reform centers around distributed database courses, cultivates students' patriotism, adds patriotism education and domestic software development into the curriculum, actively learns the relevant construction and development of domestic software, and brings domestic software into classroom teaching, and at the same time, it will cooperate with the industry-leading Aliyun, and bring China's independent technology cloud-native database At the same time, we will cooperate with the industry-leading Aliyun to integrate the technology of "PolarDB-X" into the classroom teaching content in an efficient and standardized way, so as to build a complete system of distributed database teaching and training. Through the construction of the cloud native teaching platform, the platform for students to acquire knowledge is no longer limited to the school classroom, realizing more efficient sharing of teaching resources, and creating an excellent course integrating elements of Civics and Politics and a computer gold course.

3.2 Reform of Graduate Student Curriculum Co-construction Based on Collaborative Education Programs

The reform of postgraduate course co-construction relies on the collaborative education program and aims to promote the quality and effectiveness of postgraduate education. The content of the reform is shown in Fig. 2.

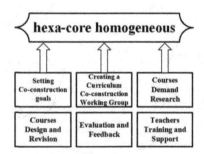

Fig. 2. Reform of Graduate Student Curriculum Co-construction Relying on Collaborative Education Programs Content structure diagram

As shown in Fig. 2, first of all, in the process of postgraduate training, the goal of co-creative reform is formulated. Based on the requirements of the collaborative education program with Aliyun, the goals and directions of the co-creative reform are clarified, and the content of the co-creative reform is formulated, and the training of experimental and practical contents is increased in the process of theoretical course lectures, so as to improve the graduate students' ability to understand and solve the actual enterprise problems. Innovation ability, cultivating interdisciplinary ability, etc.

The establishment of a curriculum co-construction working group will be the cornerstone of the reform in the collaborative parenting program. There will be a working group composed of faculty members and graduate students who will be responsible for the specific implementation of the collaborative parenting program, such as course chapters, knowledge structure and so on. Then members of the project team will conduct demand research through questionnaires and symposiums to understand the needs and expectations of graduate students and enterprises for curriculum reform. According to the results of the research, the existing courses will be revised or new courses will be designed, focusing on the cultivation of students' practical ability and the ability to solve practical problems. Members of the Collaborative Educational Program Team will evaluate and give feedback on the courses on a regular basis, collect the opinions and suggestions from students and enterprises, and adjust and improve the course contents and teaching methods in a timely manner.

Training and support for lecturers is also an important part of the parenting reform. The project team will provide training and support throughout the process for teachers involved in the co-construction of the curriculum to improve their teaching ability and awareness, and to update their knowledge of the relevant fields in a timely manner.

3.3 Real Problem-Oriented Cross-Discipline Oriented Applied Professional Degree Graduate Training

Authentic problem-oriented cross-discipline-oriented applied professional degree graduate training is to promote the level of graduate study and further deepen the integration of graduate teaching and enterprise work, and the reform content is shown in Fig. 3.

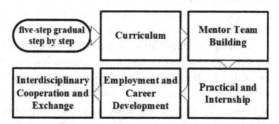

Fig. 3. Real Problem Oriented Applied Professional Degree for Cross-disciplines Cultivation Content Structure of Graduate Students

As shown in Fig. 3, in the collaborative education program based on the collaborative education program with Aliyun, we take the real problem-oriented interdisciplinary-oriented applied professional degree graduate training as an important part of this reform. In this, the first issue is to establish what kind of graduate curriculum, so it is important to design an interdisciplinary distributed database course that covers the basic knowledge and methodology of multiple disciplines. At the same time, the content of the application technology specialization direction will also allow students to further deepen their knowledge of cloud-native databases according to their own interests and needs.

Upon completion of the curriculum, mentor team building for the entire program will take place, creating a team of individuals with interdisciplinary backgrounds and research experience to provide comprehensive guidance and support to students. The mentor team will include professors with experience in related disciplines. In the training, Aliyun Platform will provide practical and internship sessions to provide students with the opportunity to work on real projects, so that they can apply what they have learned in practice and improve their ability to solve real-world problems. By participating in relevant studies, students will be able to understand the industry needs and the actual working environment. Students will be fully provided with the opportunity to communicate and present their research results with Aliyun and other well-known platforms in China.

Real Problem Oriented Cross-Discipline Oriented Applied Professional Degree Graduate Cultivation will understand the actual needs through close cooperation with AliCloud platform, students will get better employment and career development opportunities, and help students to further understand the information of the domestic cloud-native platform. Meanwhile, career planning and development guidance will be provided to help students plan their career path.

3.4 Talent Cultivation Through Deep Integration of Innovation and Entrepreneurship with Graduate Programs

Talent cultivation mode of deep integration of innovation and entrepreneurship with graduate courses is a cultivation mode that organically combines innovation and entrepreneurship education with graduate courses, aiming at cultivating senior talents with innovation and entrepreneurship ability and professional research ability.

First of all, at the level of curriculum, we will add some practice-related contents in the postgraduate curriculum system, such as cultivating students to build cloud independently through AliCloud platform in a teamwork way and other contents. These contents contain both theoretical knowledge and focus on practical operation and case analysis, with the purpose of cultivating students' thinking and hands-on ability. Through the way of practical teaching, students can participate in real innovation and entrepreneurship projects to grow their insights, so that students can learn the practical skills of innovation and entrepreneurship through the distributed database course, and at the same time apply the theoretical knowledge they have learned to solve real problems. Teachers of the course will provide personalized guidance and support, and through communication and guidance, students can better understand the practices and challenges of innovation and entrepreneurship promoted by the state nowadays, as well as obtain professional guidance and advice.

In the Distributed Database course, students will gain knowledge as well as experience in teamwork. Students will engage in teamwork and interdisciplinary cross-collaboration to further develop their teamwork spirit and interdisciplinary synthesis ability. Innovative entrepreneurship often requires multidisciplinary knowledge and skills, and through teamwork and interdisciplinary cross-collaboration, students can better meet the challenges of innovative entrepreneurship.

4 Effectiveness of Implementation

According to the social demand and actual situation, computer education in colleges and universities are required to choose different positioning of the training program and teaching plan for personnel training. In this "four-in-one" curriculum reform, we synthesize our own professional positioning and characteristics, and choose Alibaba Cloud as the collaborative education partner to evaluate the effect of the reform. The targets of the reform are master's degree students of software engineering in 2019, 2020, 2021 and 2022. The practical results have proved that the "four-in-one" integrated graduate course teaching mode reform program has played an important role in promoting students' learning, and we found that students' learning participation, theoretical mastery, and hands-on practical ability have been improved to different degrees through the comparison between this teaching reform and the previous training results, especially the effect of practical ability cultivation is remarkable. In particular, the effect of practical ability cultivation is remarkable.

4.1 Analysis of the Level of Student Participation

Students learn experimental tutorials online, complete experiments independently based on the Alibaba cloud native experimental platform, demonstrate and accept them in offline seminars, analyze and summarize them, and form experimental reports for project improvement and innovation. For students with extra capacity, they are encouraged to conduct in-depth research on cloud computing technology in the form of learning groups to enhance student participation.

Student participation is determined by, let the total number of students in the classroom be x_i, where $i = 1, 2, 3, 4$, representing the four grades. The number of students in the class of 2019 is $x_1 = 85$, the number of students in the class of 2020 is $x_2 = 110$, the number of students in the class of 2021 is $x_3 = 89$, and the number of students in the class of 2022 is $x_4 = 84$. The student engagement for each grade is Δi. The student participation is determined by the number of student check-ins d_1, the number of homework submissions d_2, and the number of classroom responses d_3. The distributed database course has 64 class hours, so the value range of d_1 is [0, 64]. The average number of homework assignments is once per class hour, so the value range of d_2 is [0, 64]. Each class uses a circular roll call, and each person generally answers 1 to 2 times, so the value range of d_3 is [50, 100]. These three indices are determined and multiplied by the weights ε_i, where $\sum_{i=1}^{3} \varepsilon_i = 1$. The weights are set by expert experience: $\varepsilon_1 = 0.4$, $\varepsilon_2 = 0.2$, $\varepsilon_3 = 0.4$. The calculation formula for student participation is as shown in formula (1):

$$\Delta_i = \sum_{i=1}^{4} \frac{\sum_{j=1}^{3} \varepsilon_j d_j}{x_i} \tag{1}$$

The implementation effect is shown in Fig. 4.

As can be seen in Fig. 4, the master's degree students of software engineering in the classes of 2019–2021 who participated in the teaching reform improved their participation by 4.4%, 5.6%, and 5.4%. Respectively, compared with those in the traditional

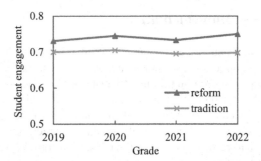

Fig.4. Comparative data on student engagement

teaching mode, the master's degree students of software engineering in the class of 2022 had the greatest degree of improvement in their participation, which amounted to 7.4%. Therefore, this teaching reform has a great advantage over the traditional teaching mode in terms of student engagement, with an average increase of 5.7%.

4.2 Theoretical Mastery

In order to broaden students' knowledge, the online classroom releases the latest technical literature in the field of computer science, cutting-edge technology lectures, innovative entrepreneurship development classes, and online resources, encouraging students to carry out extended learning. While expanding their professional knowledge, it integrates the elements of Civics and Politics while expanding professional knowledge, and introduces the excellent cases of domestic cloud computing enterprises into the course resource system. It guides students to deeply understand the innovation ability of China's cloud computing technology, stimulates students' sense of responsibility for learning, and reaches the higher-order goals of the course in terms of knowledge transfer, ability cultivation, quality and value leadership.

The student's theoretical mastery is determined by setting the total number of students in the classroom to be x_i, where $i = 1, 2, 3, 4$. Representing the four grades, the number of students in the class of 2019 is $x_1 = 85$, the number of students in the class of 2020 is $x_2 = 110$, the number of students in the class of 2021 is $x_3 = 89$, and the number of students in class 2022 is $x_4 = 84$. The theoretical mastery of students in each grade is θ_i. Theoretical mastery was determined by students' classroom problem grades e_1, homework grades e_2, teaching experiment grades e_3, and final examination results e_4, of which e_1, e_2, e_3, and e_4 take values in the range $[0, 100]$. These four indices determine and multiply the weights of the items τ_i, and $\sum_{i=1}^{4} \tau_i = 1$. Based on experience, the weights are set as follows: $\tau_1 = 0.2$, $\tau_2 = 0.2$, $\tau_3 = 0.2$, and $\tau_4 = 0.4$. The theoretical mastery is calculated as shown in Eq. (2):

$$\theta_i = \sum_{i=1}^{4} \frac{\sum_{j=1}^{4} \tau_j e_j}{x_i} \tag{2}$$

The implementation effect is shown in Fig. 5.

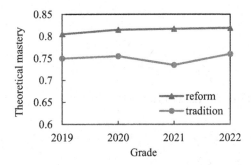

Fig. 5. Comparative data on students' theoretical mastery

As can be seen in Fig. 5, the master's degree students of software engineering in the classes of 2019–2022 who participated in the teaching reform improved their theoretical mastery by 7.3%, 7.9%, 11.1%, and 7.7%. Respectively, compared with those in the traditional teaching mode, the reformed group of master's degree students of software engineering in the class of 2021 increased instead of decreasing in the epidemic, and had the greatest improvement within the recent classes, which shows that the cloud-native database is useful for the online teaching with stability and reliability. Therefore, this teaching reform has a great advantage over the traditional teaching mode in terms of theory mastery, with an average improvement of 8.5%.

4.3 Comparison of Practical Skills

Based on the technical background and cloud resources of Alibaba Cloud, the extracurricular innovation and practice platform is constructed, and students are guided to carry out extracurricular practice projects using the industry training cases and data sets provided by the platform, so as to enhance their engineering practice ability. Through the cooperation between industries and universities in constructing innovation and practice resources, it effectively solves the problem of the shortage of practice platforms and case resources in colleges and universities, so as to support the cultivation of students' innovation and practice ability.

Student practice ability is determined by setting the total number of students in the classroom to be x_i, where $i = 1, 2, 3, 4$. Representing the four grades, the number of students in the class of 2019 is $x_1 = 85$, the number of students in the class of 2020 is $x_2 = 110$, the number of students in the class of 2021 is $x_3 = 89$, and the number of students in the class of 2022 is $x_4 = 84$. The practical mastery of students in each grade is σ_i. Practice mastery was determined by students' classroom problem grades f_1, homework grades f_2 and instructional lab grades f_3, of which f_1, f_2, and f_3 take values in the range of $[0, 100]$, these three indices are determined and multiplied by the weights of the items μ_i, where $\sum_{i=1}^{3}\mu_i = 1$, the weights of each item are set empirically: $\mu_1 = 0.3$, $\mu_2 = 0.3$, and $\mu_3 = 0.4$. The formula for calculating practical ability is shown in

Eq. (3):

$$\sigma_i = \sum_{i=1}^{4} \frac{\sum_{j=1}^{3} \mu_j f_j}{x_i} \tag{3}$$

The implementation effect is shown in Fig. 6.

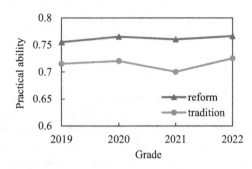

Fig. 6. Comparative data on students' practical skills

As can be seen in Fig. 6, the master's degree students in software engineering of grades 2019–2022 who participated in the teaching reform improved their practical ability by 5.6%, 6.3%, 8.6%, and 5.7%. Respectively, compared with those in the traditional teaching mode, the practical ability of grade 2021 decreased because of the epidemic online class, but the extent of the decrease in the reform group was smaller. Therefore, this teaching reform has a greater advantage over the traditional teaching mode in terms of practical ability, with an average improvement of 6.6%.

5   Conclusion

At present, China has a large number of colleges and universities with computer majors, and each college has its own development and positioning. How to cultivate students' practical ability according to their own situation, how to carry out problem-oriented education in accordance with local conditions, how to carry out ideological and political education in courses, how to achieve school-enterprise collaboration, and how to achieve the four-in-one training of innovation and entrepreneurship, so as to achieve the optimal combination of economic efficiency for students, schools, enterprises, and society, are topics worthy of in-depth research in future education and teaching reform. This attempt at teaching model reform can clearly show that by collaborating with corporate platforms to build courses, enhancing students' practical ability, improving their ideological and political awareness and national pride, and mobilizing their subjective initiative, students' theoretical and practical abilities have been significantly improved. In conclusion, the reform of the teaching mode of "four-in-one" integrated postgraduate courses provides an effective way of construction for the future development of computer education and teaching.

Funding. This work was supported by the Liaoning Province Graduate Education and Teaching Reform Research Funding Project (No. LNYJG2023010), "Cloud Native Distributed Open Source Database "PolarDB-X" Demonstration Course Construction Project" of the Ministry of Education's Industry University Collaborative Education Project (No. 220600643082102), Liaoning Province Graduate Education and Teaching Reform Research Funding Project (No. LNYJG2022012) and the Key Points of Liaoning University Graduate Teaching Reform Project (No. YJG202301055).

References

1. Zhang, X.L., Pang, J.F.: Teaching reform of database system course based on flipped classes. Comput. Educ. **340**(04), 181–185 (2023)
2. Chen, X.B.: An analysis of the reform of modularized construction of entrepreneurship basic course content for college students in local colleges and universities. Soc. Sci. **02**, 154–160 (2023)
3. Ye, C.L., Li, D.C., Tan, M., et al.: Teaching reform and practice of blended teaching model for "database principle and application" course based on MOOC. Exp. Technol. Manag. **37**(07), 217–221 (2020)
4. Pang, J.F., Zhang, X.L., Wang, Y.L., et al.: Research on the teaching reform of database system course oriented to "double first-class" and "new engineering." Comput. Educ. **329**(05), 150–154 (2022)
5. Sun, X.J.: Teaching reform of oracle database technology course based on OBE. Comput. Educ. **331**(07), 146–150 (2022)
6. Peng, Y.C., Jin, B.H., Yu, X.C.: Teaching reform of database principles course in the context of engineering education certification. Comput. Educ. **323**(11), 128–133 (2021)
7. Wang, D., Cao, S.S.: Exploration of teaching reform of computer courses under meta-universe empowerment. Comput. Educ. **335**(11), 11–14 (2022)
8. Xia, Y.: Construction and practice of advanced database system technology course for graduate students. Comput. Educ. **23**, 4–6 (2015)
9. Jia, B., Li, M., Ren, Z.H.: Teaching reform practice of applied undergraduate database courses based on enterprise needs. Western China Q. Educ. **6**(08), 110–112 (2020)
10. Wang, W.X.: Interpreting domestic software innovation: values, challenges and strategies. China's Informatiz. **07**, 38–40 (2022)
11. Pei, L.G.: Analysis of the evolution process of domestic databases replacing foreign databases. Financ. Technol. Time **31**(04), 94–97 (2023)
12. Ye, Z.W., Cai, D.B., Qian, L.: Progress of cloud-native relational databases with decoupled compute-storage architecture. Softw. Guide **20**(08), 236–240 (2021)
13. Zhang, X., Hu, D.H., Zhu, F.B.: Reform and practice of computer course system based on system ability training. Softw. Guide **21**(07), 142–146 (2022)
14. Wang, H.: Reform of blended teaching mode for object-oriented programming course. Softw. Guide **22**(06), 124–128 (2023)
15. Pan, L., Ye, H.W.: Research on the construction of hybrid "Gold Class" for basic computer courses under "two dimensions, one degree, three standards." Mod. Bus. Trade Ind. **43**(23), 219–220 (2022)
16. Xu, Y., Qin, M.P., Tang, Y.N., et al.: Reform and practice of multi-blended teaching of intelligent robot course under the background of new engineering. Softw. Guide **22**(05), 225–229 (2023)
17. Liu, B., Peng, Y.W., Yu, L., et al.: Teaching and practice reform of database principles in the era of localization. Softw. Guide **21**(11), 172–176 (2022)

18. Dong, J., Fan, Q.R., Zhang, S.J., et al.: Experimental teaching reform of database principle course oriented by engineering practice ability training. Res. Explor. Lab. **41**(09), 200–203 (2022)
19. Guan, X.D., He, S.X.: Curriculum reform on ideological and political education for postgraduates. J. North China Inst. Aerosp. Eng. **33**(04), 33–35 (2023)
20. Wen, P.W., Yang, L., Chang, Y.P., et al.: Research on reform of ideological and political education in curriculum of communication principle under background of gold lessons construction. China Educ. Technol. Equip. **40**(06), 1–4 (2023)

New Digital Technology's Application

Quantitative Research and Evaluation Innovation of College Tennis Teaching Based on Data-Driven

Huan Li[1], Tingting Wu[1], Dongmei Wei[2(✉)], and Tingting Zhang[1]

[1] School of Physical Education, Xihua University, Chengdu 610039, China
[2] School of Computer and Software Engineering, Xihua University, Chengdu 610039, China
7729904@qq.com

Abstract. With the promotion and development of tennis in the world, tennis is paid more and more attention at home and attracts more and more lovers. In recent years, the rapid development of tennis has prompted major colleges and universities in China to set up tennis courses and establish tennis associations. However, due to the late start, there are still some problems, such as lack of teachers, poor teaching effect, lack of perfect evaluation mechanism and so on. Taking data-driven as the core concept, this paper collects and records students' learning trajectory data in training, carries out data analysis and quantitative methods, constructs a scientific student evaluation index system, effectively sets weights and evaluation indexes, and uses data mining methods to cluster and predict students' learning. From the first attempt to apply the evaluation system, after three semesters of practice, good results have been achieved. The results show that the scientific and information-based evaluation system in data-driven tennis teaching can not only accurately quantify students' learning indicators, but also effectively improve the efficiency of physical education management, change the traditional form of physical education, improve students' learning satisfaction, and better achieve the skill objectives and comprehensive objectives in the teaching objectives, At the same time, it provides reference for the development of college sports precision and information education.

Keywords: Data Driven · tennis teaching · evaluation system · skill index · Quantitative research · data mining · cluster analysis

1 Introduction

Tennis, badminton and table tennis, as the national competitive sports advantage projects, are paid more and more attention in college physical education. Tennis, as a representative of competitive ball games, has developed rapidly in China in recent years. Through Baidu Index, take "tennis" as the keyword to count the attention (search volume) of domestic Internet users to tennis in recent 10 years. As shown in Fig. 1, the annual peak value of tennis is maintained at more than 10000 times, indicating that domestic Internet users pay very high attention to tennis, and even form a "small peak" in the short term. For example, from 2011 to 2014, the national attention to tennis was very high. It is speculated that the reason is that Li Na, a famous Chinese tennis player, won the runner up of the Australian Open and the French Open in 2011; Won the second place in the 2013 WTA year-end finals; In 2014, he won the Australian Open women's singles championship. It can be seen that domestic attention to tennis will increase due to the influence of athletes and events (Australian Open, Wimbledon, us open, Olympic Games, etc.).

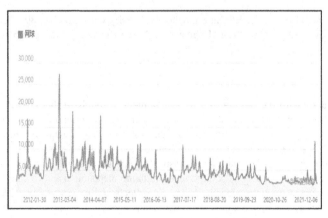

Fig. 1. Baidu search index of tennis

1.1 Domestic Research Status

As an important part of social sports, college physical education plays an important role in promoting the full implementation of the national strategy of national fitness. The strategic task of the outline for the construction of a sports power points out that we should improve the comprehensive strength of competitive sports and help build a healthy China.

Through China HowNet, VIP and other databases, and taking college tennis teaching as the key word to search the relevant literature, we can see that the reform and exploration of college tennis curriculum are increasing year by year. Among them, Liang Chengjun and others established the analysis model between the hitting point and the gain and loss point of tennis skills and tactics by using the association analysis data mining theory and relying on the Weka data mining platform in 2012, so as to provide objective and scientific decision support for the technical and tactical decision-making of tennis matches; In 2014, from the perspective of multiple intelligences theory, Liu Wenfang explored the teaching methods and paths of tennis courses of physical education major in Colleges and universities in China from multiple links; In 2017, Tao Yuanyuan and others discussed the impact of MOOC on College Sports in the era of big data; In 2020, taking Heilongjiang as an example, Li Mingyang put forward innovative opinions on the cultivation of tennis talents in Colleges and Universities under the background of network big data and artificial intelligence. In 2021, Liu Xiaolong and others proposed the use of "flipped classroom" in tennis teaching, and studied and innovated the tennis classroom teaching mode.

With the advent of the era of big data, big data technology has injected fresh blood into the innovation of college physical education concept, and the combination with the construction of college physical education teaching evaluation system has become a trend. The formation of this trend provides excellent development opportunities for the construction and innovation of college physical education curriculum and teaching evaluation system.

1.2   Research Status Abroad

Tennis was conceived in France, born in Britain and popularized in the United States. Now it is popular all over the world. Its popularity in western countries is much higher than that in China. There are many researches devoted to tennis. Representative: IBM has been supporting various public events with big data analysis technology. Among them, it has cooperated with the French Open for 28 years and brought a series of solutions to the French Open, all centered on real-time and historical Grand Slam event data. Foreign colleges and universities mostly refer to some indicators of NTRP or ITN tennis evaluation system for the evaluation of students' tennis learning effect and technology. However, most of these indicators use written description to judge tennis technology, which has great subjective differences and uncertainties.

Thus, China's tennis curriculum system and talent training are relatively backward, and there are still many weak links in the allocation of teachers, the construction of curriculum system and professional characteristics. There are few cases of applying quantitative methods to public sports tennis teaching, and most of them are teacher-centered or system centered subjective evaluation models. Summarize the main problems:

1) Tennis started late in China and the teaching system is not mature;
2) There are great differences in teaching methods and evaluation methods between colleges and universities in different regions;
3) The examination methods of tennis courses in Colleges and universities mostly take the final examination results or a final evaluation as the main reference standard. The examination and evaluation method is too single and unreasonable;
4) There is great subjectivity in the evaluation methods of students' tennis courses, and the evaluation methods are not objective enough, lack of quantitative analysis and management.

To sum up, under the background of the rapid development of big data and intelligent technology, it is imperative to build a scientific and reasonable curriculum system, take data-driven as the core, and form an accurate and quantitative evaluation mechanism.

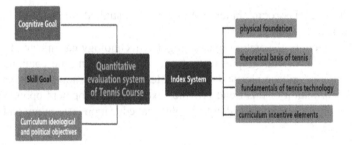

Fig. 2. Quantitative evaluation system

2 Constructing the Student Evaluation System of Tennis Teaching Based on Data-Driven and Intelligent Algorithm

According to the provisions of the outline for the construction of a sports power and the outline for the teaching guidance of physical education courses in national colleges and universities, there is an urgent need to establish a complete, scientific, operable, student-oriented and skill oriented evaluation standard and system for the basic objectives, comprehensive evaluation models and evaluation standards to be achieved by tennis courses.

Based on the data-driven perspective, it is of great practical significance to integrate the methods of data analysis and quantification into the research of college tennis public physical education curriculum. Constructing a scientific and reasonable evaluation system can enable students to clarify the learning objectives and basic action points of tennis, which is conducive to students' learning various skills and tactics in tennis at the fastest speed. Paying attention to the importance of data in the learning process can not only establish a scientific and quantitative evaluation method, but also accurately guide students' follow-up learning and training direction. It plays an important role in promoting students to develop good learning habits, sports spirit and learning interest.

It provides a practical and innovative perspective for the construction of tennis courses in Colleges and universities.

From the perspective of big data technology and intelligent analysis, guided by quantification and based on data-driven, this project carries out the construction and teaching research of high-quality tennis course evaluation system, so as to further establish the direction of professional characteristics and improve the implementation path of the course system. The basic view of the project is to adhere to the fact that students' process learning data contains a lot of value that can be mined. By building an evaluation framework and establishing a hierarchical index system, we can analyze students' learning data and accurately quantify the learning effect.

2.1 Construction of Evaluation Index System

The framework of tennis course student evaluation system is shown in Fig. 2. The goal is composed of cognitive goal, skill goal and course Ideological and political goal. In order to achieve various goals and accurately quantify student data, a hierarchical index system is set up, which is divided into primary indicators and secondary indicators.

Among them, the secondary index system, defined as index system, contains four main components, as shown in the Fig. 3.

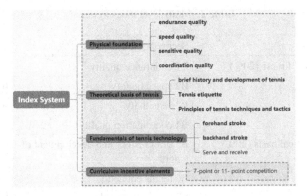

Fig. 3. Index System of Evaluation

Under the guidance of big data analysis and intelligent processing methods, around the optimized evaluation system, formulate curriculum teaching objectives, as shown in Table 1.

Table 1. Curriculum Objectives

Achieve Goals	Target Description
Cogonitive Goal	A. Students can master the essentials of technology B. enhance their ability to analyze technology, and apply it to practice
Skill Goal	Students can master the basic technical requirements of tennis and complete the basic movements of tennis: forehand stroke, double counterattack, receiving service in zone 1 and zone 2
Curriculum ideological and political objectives	A. Cultivate students' sports spirit and hard work spirit B. shape good spiritual character and practice the concept of lifelong sports

Based on the goal to be achieved, a two-level index system is set. The first level index is composed of four parts: the basic part of physical fitness, accounting for 20%; Theoretical basis of tennis, accounting for 20%; Basic tennis skills, accounting for 55%; The incentive element part accounts for 5%, which is the teaching incentive index of "practice with competition", that is, whether students participate in the competition with 7 points or 11 points. Scientific and reasonable weights are set through expert interviews and statistical quantification. As shown in Table 2 multi-level index system, the weights of 11 secondary indicators are set.

Table 2. Multi-level index system

Primary indicator	Secondary indicator	Weight setting
A1 basic physical fitness (20%)	B1 endurance quality	0.25
	B2 speed quality	0.40
	B3 sensitivity	0.20
	B4 coordination quality	0.15
A2 tennis theoretical basis (20%)	B5 brief history and development of tennis	0.25
	B6 tennis etiquette	0.15
	B7 tennis technical	0.60
A3 tennis technical foundation (55%)	B8 forehand stroke	0.50
	B9 backhand stroke	0.30
	B10 serving and receiving	0.20
A4 incentive elements (5%)	B11 competition participation	1.00

2.2 Quantitative Evaluation Process

Through analysis and planning, the research route to be developed for this subject is shown in Fig. 4:

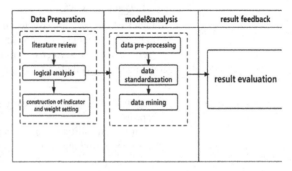

Fig. 4. Research procedure

1) Select important indicators that may affect students' final scores from the data, and conduct correlation analysis after normalization and standardization.

2) Extract the students' learning trajectory data of two semesters (2019–2021);
3) Data exploration, analysis and preprocessing. In this step, it is important to deal with missing data and abnormal data, data cleaning, data standardization and other key steps to prepare for further data mining;
4) According to the evaluation results, clustering algorithm is used for clustering analysis, and the students are divided into three categories. Different teaching instructions are customized for these three types of students.

The data-driven college tennis teaching evaluation system needs to be based on diversified channel data. The intelligent teaching data comes from the information-based teaching platform (super one learning pass), students' daily classroom performance records, student card records of learning behavior information and other channels, which provides rich data sources for intelligent teaching decision-making.

3   A Case Study of Tennis Intelligent Teaching Evaluation System in Colleges in Colleges and Universities Based on Data-Driven

According to the students' tennis teaching evaluation system, taking the collected data as the research object, using intelligent methods for data analysis and data mining, combined with quantitative and knowledge methods, this paper tests the comprehensive evaluation scheme of tennis.

Combined with the characteristics, the characteristics of each student are analyzed and clustered. K-Means clustering algorithm is used to cluster the standardized data as shown in Table 3:

Table 3. Weight of tennis technical foundation

A3 tennis technical foundation (55%)	B8 forehand stroke	0.50
	B9 backhand stroke	0.30
	B10 serving and receiving	0.20

According to the index system, through the two parts of data of students' learning trajectory, that is, the combination of online learning data and offline practical course data, the evaluation of students can be obtained through the relevant calculation of the index system.

3.1   Quantitative Methods Used in the Evaluation Model

In this case study, the main data used is mainly composed of online and offline parts. Course superstar platform. The data are selected from students from September 2019 to December 2022, with a total of 940 valid data. It mainly includes: Online (theoretical basis and video course learning), offline (skill basis and usual training results), etc. In order to better mine the learning effect of students hidden behind the data, combined with K-Means method, samples are classified according to data similarity. Select the three most relevant and important indicators of learning effect, and finally aggregate the comprehensive evaluation results into three categories.

In the part of measuring students' technical foundation (accounting for 55% of the primary indicators), the weighted sum and average are used as the final processed data through the five secondary scores recorded at ordinary times. For example, when evaluating forehand skill scores, use the Table 4, take the technical points of each secondary index as the main basis for scoring. For example, evaluate students' forehand skills. If the landing point is in the opponent's bottom line area, the attacker will get 8–10 points, as shown in Fig. 5.

If the landing point is in the middle of the field (good), get 6–7 points, as shown in Fig. 6. If the landing point is outside the boundary, as shown in Fig. 7, they will get 1–5 points, and 0 point will be used to record the absence of the test; Other technical and tactical scoring bases and standards are similar.

3.2 Data Preparation and Data Pre-processing

1) collect multiple data (Sports assessment performance data, sports training data and other information).
2) Implement unified normalization preprocessing for data, process and supplement missing data and reduce data redundancy.
3) Discretization of continuous data.
4) In the decision-making level of the system, analyze the physical education teaching plan and intelligently generate the decision-making plan.

Fig. 5. Excellent point of forehand stroke

3.3 Data Mining and Clustering Analysis

In the fourth step of the process, clustering algorithm is used to cluster the data. There are many available clustering algorithms, including Hierarchical clustering, K-means,

Fig. 6. Good point of forehand stroke

Fig. 7. Under-performing of forehead stroke

FCM, Neural network clustering and DBSCN, etc. The combination of data-driven and K-Means clustering algorithm is used to realize teaching evaluation and intelligent decision-making of scheme. The specific process is as follows:

- Step 1: After data acquisition and data cleaning, the collected data, randomly select k objects from n sample data as the initial clustering center;
- Step 2: Calculate the distance from each sample to each cluster center, and assign the object to the nearest class;
- Step 3: Recalculate the centers of K clusters;
- Step 4: Compared with the K cluster centers calculated last time, if the cluster center changes, go to step 2, otherwise go to step 5;
- Step 5: When the clustering center does not change, stop and output the clustering results.

3.4 Clustering Algorithm and Experiment

- *Through the Euclidean distance method, the distance between samples and the distance between samples and clusters are calculated*

- *There are p attributes to represent the matrix of n samples* $\begin{pmatrix} x_{11} & \dots & x_{1p} \\ \dots & & \dots \\ x_{n1} & \dots & x_{np} \end{pmatrix}$, *In this case, through*

  Euclidean distance From the calculation formula.

  SSE is used as the objective function to measure the clustering quality, and the smallest SSE calculation result is selected as the classification result.

$$SSE = \sum_{i=1}^{k} \sum_{x \in E_i} dist(e_i, x)^2 \tag{1}$$

The description of formula parameters is shown in the Table 4:

Table 4. Descriptive statistics

Clustering Class	Class-I	Class-II	Class-III
	Excellent	Good	Under-performing
Samples	455	458	27
Ratio	48.4%	48.7%	2.9%
Max Value	50	30	20
Min Value	5.5	3.3	2.4
Average Value	44.05	26.52	15.79

The data are selected from students from September 2019 to January 2021, with a total of 940 valid data. In order to ensure the convergence of the algorithm, the Euclidean distance is used to calculate and SSE is used as the objective function to obtain the clustering results.

According to the analysis, the characteristic data of students' scores are shown in the Table 5. As shown in. After normalizing the three main feature values, the k-means method is used to evaluate them from three levels, and the clustering center is shown in the Table 5.

Table 5. Clustering center

Cluster category	Clustering results	Clustering Center		
		B8	B9	B10
Cluster-I	excellent	0.1225	0.1308	−0.6418
Cluster-II	good	0.1527	0.1323	0.8234
Cluster-III	Under-performing	−4.6549	−4.4477	−3.1508

In the process of experimental operation, use SciPy for clustering, and then use the visualization tool tsne to visualize the results, as shown in the Fig. 8, in which red, blue and green represent excellent, good and under performing respectively.

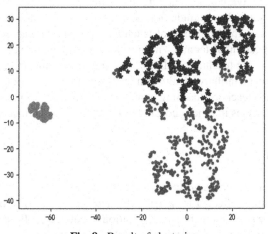

Fig. 8. Result of clustering

With the deep integration of data-driven learning and physical education, data-driven learning, as a new teaching model in the information age, has gradually become the core label of the new physical education teaching ecology. Through the data, we can realize the all-round fine management and guidance of all links of college courses and high-quality physical education. Quantification refers to comprehensively reshaping the structural relationship between college tennis education and classroom teaching.

4 Discussion

This thesis studies the tennis course teaching and student evaluation system based on data and the combination of quantification and knowledge. The preliminary idea of applying the new method to tennis teaching evaluation is to improve the quality of results through data-driven quantification prediction decision-making.

In order to evaluate the final learning effect of students more reasonably, this paper divides the goal into two levels, namely, the first level goal and the second level goal. The first level goal includes: cognitive goal, skill goal and curriculum ideological and political goal. And set different weights according to the importance. The purpose of this is to better improve the rationality and scientificity of the evaluation and increase the importance of the evaluation process elements.

We extract the learning track data of students from 2019 to 2021 semesters, select important indicators that may affect students' final scores from the data, and conduct correlation analysis and data mining after normalization and standardization. In the clustering analysis of the evaluation results, considering the large amount of data, the small number of clustering types and the priority of efficiency, K-means was selected as the clustering method of the experiment. Finally, the students were grouped into three categories, and different teaching guidance plans were customized for these three categories of students. Through the practice of this method, it is more conducive to the implementation of individualized teaching in teaching.

Based on this, solve the contradiction between the single evaluation method of traditional tennis course, the limitation of teaching concept and teaching means and the increasing diversification of tennis; Through accurate quantitative and digital teaching evaluation, optimize teaching feedback, teaching evaluation and goal achievement; Adhere to long-term quantitative evaluation and form a virtuous circle, be able to judge and predict students, teachers, teaching contents and teaching forms based on data, and adjust teaching strategies in time according to the data feedback mechanism.

5 Conclusions

The problems and research perspective of this topic are innovative. The innovation of the research is mainly reflected in: a scientific and reasonable quantitative evaluation system is conducive to promote the transformation of college public sports tennis teaching evaluation from "experience decision" to "data-driven decision", improve student evaluation, improve teaching effect and optimize teaching management.

The curriculum evaluation system takes data as the guidance and quantification as the means, examines the activities of various elements in the environment from the perspective of data, and establishes the relationship between various elements and between elements and objectives through data, which has good advantages. First, quantification can more accurately reflect the teaching effect and the achievement of objectives; Secondly, the evaluation results can be clustered according to the data, which can not only judge the teaching effect, but also predict the learning results to a certain extent. It helps to improve the feedback mechanism and adjust teaching strategies in time. Third, we should pay more attention to personalized learning needs, respect individual differences in learning, and be able to describe differences in a quantitative form.

But there are still some shortcomings. In the practice of the evaluation system, the model of intelligent decision evaluation is still relatively single. In the later research, we can try to realize the collaborative innovation of multimodal decision model; Further optimize the prediction model, combined with the problem reflected by the representation of students' behavior data. The implicit causes of learning and their integration with learning concepts and elements; Learn from Learning behavior and psychological cognition, Construct the reform path of learning and teaching evaluation of multimodal behavior data relationship.

Acknowledgement. This work has been funded by teaching reform projects of Xihua University (No: Xjjg2021060 and Xjjg2021115); Project of Sichuan Provincial Education Development Research Center (CJF23072); Sichuan Leisure Sports Industry Development Research Center (XXTYCY2023B04); the teaching research project of computer basic education of National Institute of computer basic education (no. 2022-AFCEC-559).

References

1. Wu, M.: Current situation and countermeasures of public elective tennis course teaching in colleges and universities. Front. Educ. Res. **3**(15) (2020)
2. Lai, Y.: The status quo and development research of tennis teaching in sports college. Int. J. High. Educ. Teach. Theory **1**(2) (2020)
3. Zhang, Y.F., Qian, Y.T., Liu, T.Y., Wu, S.Y.: Data mining clustering algorithm research and application. Adv. Mater. Res. **3181**(926) (2014)
4. Cheng, P., Ming, D., Man, X., Dai, D.: Optimized allocation of tennis teaching resources based on big data. J. Phys. Conf. Ser. **1744**(4) (2021)
5. Wang, H.: Research on design and implementation of computer 3D table tennis simulation animation. J. Phys. Conf. Ser. **1744**(3) (2021)
6. Sporting Activities - Tennis; Findings from C.X. Fu and Co-Researchers Advance Knowledge in Sporting Activities - Tennis (Research and Analysis of Tennis Teaching Strategy based on 3D Simulation). Journal of Engineering (2018)
7. Li, H., Wu, T., Wei, D.: Research and practice of student evaluation mechanism of College Tennis Course based on Quantification. In: 2021 International Conference on Big Data Engineering and Education (BDEE) (2021)
8. Cui, Y., Liu, H., Liu, H., et al.: Data-driven analysis of point-by-point performance for male tennis player in Grand Slams. Motricidade **15**(1), 49–61 (2019)

Design of Immersive Curriculum Learning Environment for Network Planning and Design Course

Xiuyu Chen[✉]

Higher Vocational Technical College, Dalian Neusoft University of Information, Dalian, China
chenxiuyu@neusoft.edu.cn

Abstract. In response to the need to explore the construction of a new environment for flexible and intelligent education and teaching, this paper proposes an immersive learning environment design method and a learning evaluation program. This paper first combines experiential learning theory and situational learning theory to discuss how to build an experiential learning environment based on interaction. Secondly, the evaluation index system of the learning environment is constructed, and the corresponding learning evaluation scale is formed. Finally, using the experiential design method, a case prototype and learning effect table for students' experience are designed taking "Network Planning and Design Course" as an example, which provides a reference for further improving the learning environment of related courses.

Keywords: Immersive · Experience feeling · Learning environment

1 Introduction

<<The action plan for educational informatization 2.0>> points out that "vigorously promote intelligent education and carry out the construction of learner-centered intelligent teaching support environment", "accelerate the reform of talent training mode and teaching method by using intelligent technology, and explore the construction and application mode of ubiquitous, flexible and intelligent new education and teaching environment" [1]. Among them, the new intelligent education and teaching environment mainly refers to the virtual learning environment (VLE), which combines remote interaction and face-to-face interaction in many ways. Including evaluation, student tracking, collaboration, communication and other functions, it is suitable for learning in and out of school at any time. It breaks through the limitations of time and space and can be regarded as the combination of curriculum management system and learning management system [2]. How to effectively integrate VLE technology into schools and education, so as to promote the development of a new teaching model focusing on experience, has become an important research topic in current teaching research.

At present, the application and research of VLE technology in education are still in the exploratory stage. How to use it to improve the learning environment and how to evaluate its application effect are still the focus of intelligent teaching environment research.

W. Hong and G. Kanaparan (Eds.): ICCSE 2023, CCIS 2025, pp. 102–109, 2024.
https://doi.org/10.1007/978-981-97-0737-9_10

Scholars from all over the world have completed many virtual learning models according to their core ideas and design schemes, and continued to improve in combination with the actual situation. For example, the Key Laboratory of intelligent information resource management, Institute of computing technology, Chinese Academy of Sciences, cooperated with the electronic computer management center of Yunnan Normal School and other units to develop a formal entity model of teaching system based on Web [3]. The personalized recommendation system of 3D virtual learning environment based on big data in Yongzhou vocational and technical college uses computer to simulate reality for learning. It is deeply loved by higher vocational students because of its situational, experiential and immersive characteristics [4].

In the course of network planning and design, the real working environment provides good support for the course teaching, but the school teaching environment has become the restriction and bottleneck of the real teaching environment of the course. The rapid development of VLE technology provides a feasible technical solution for the course, and an immersive virtual learning space based on VLE technology provides favorable support for the teaching of the course.

Based on the application of VLE technology in immersive virtual learning space, this paper discusses the teaching framework of network planning and design course, immersive course learning environment, and designs the corresponding evaluation scale to evaluate its teaching effect.

2   Construction of Immersive Learning Environments

The construction of immersive learning environment of network design and planning course aims to design and create a virtual space. Students enter the virtual space and participate in the whole process of network planning and design in the first person by choosing different network planning themes, so as to improve the sense of participation and interactivity, and then obtain the on-site experience.

This learning environment is conducted from the perspective of students, breaking the sense of boundary of the traditional learning mode, and learners change from passive viewing to active selection of content. These are the fundamental differences from the traditional learning environment. As a beneficial supplement to the traditional offline teaching mode, it is more suitable for online teaching environment, so that the whole teaching and experience form a complete closed-loop virtual learning environment (VLE) (see Fig. 1).

2.1   Feature Quantity Design of Immersive Curriculum Learning Environment

The construction of immersive learning environment needs reasonable interactive design, and realizes effective human-computer interaction through vision, voice and other interactive methods, so as to bring effective experience to learners and improve learning experience. In this process, as both students and VLE interact, students are the main body of interaction, how to stimulate students' interest in learning is the main content of immersive teaching environment design.

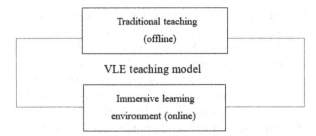

Fig. 1. VLE teaching model

From the perspective of students, an effective knowledge acquisition process is composed of these parts: simple cognitive process, complex cognitive process, knowledge structure formation process, knowledge system expansion process. These processes will form a cognitive closed loop, so that students can acquire new knowledge. In short, the acquisition of knowledge is the process of constantly obtaining new information and new knowledge. Brooks put forward the basic equation of information science, the formula is K[S] + ΔI = K[S + Δ S], Where k[S] represents the knowledge structure, ΔI represents information increment, ΔS stands for structural variable [5].

It can be seen that the learning process is an iterative process of adding new knowledge to the old knowledge. Therefore, determining the benchmark value of old knowledge and increasing the amount of new knowledge is the key to the whole teaching process. In other words, the key to the construction of immersive curriculum learning environment is to take students as observers of the learning process and use students' average learning level to formulate the baseline of old knowledge (learning basis) and the increment value of stimuli in the learning process, The design process of characteristic quantity of immersive course learning environment (see Fig. 2).

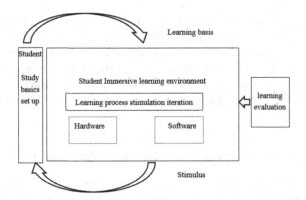

Fig. 2. Block diagram of immersive course learning environment

2.2 Learning Evaluation Process Design

As an important part of immersive classroom behavior, teachers' evaluation behavior plays an indispensable role in the development of students. Any evaluation in the classroom cannot be conducted at will. Evaluation should not only consider many factors such as the content, form and direction of evaluation from the subjective perspective of teachers, but also take into account students' own learning basis, learning attitude and other relevant factors from the perspective of students. General teaching evaluation divides teaching evaluation into formative evaluation and summative evaluation according to the role of evaluation, in these two evaluation methods, students' learning foundation, learning enthusiasm and other students' factors are not considered. According to Bloom's (1971) theory, on the basis of formative evaluation and summative evaluation, the third evaluation type, diagnostic evaluation, is proposed. The introduction of diagnostic evaluation makes teaching evaluation no longer a unilateral act of teachers, but uses the evaluation process to closely connect teachers and students, making the whole evaluation process more objective. In the design process of immersive classroom evaluation system, three kinds of evaluation will be introduced, among which: the purpose of diagnostic evaluation is to ensure that teaching is suitable for students' background, characteristics and emotions before learning; formative evaluation is used to evaluate the needs and progress of each student in the teaching process; summative evaluation is used to determine the different levels of students or their relative grades. Therefore, the evaluation system in the design of immersive curriculum learning environment is shown in Table 1.

Table 1. Immersion course learning evaluation form

Evaluation process	Purpose
Diagnostic evaluation	Evaluate students' background, characteristics and emotions before learning
Formative evaluation	In the teaching process, constantly evaluate students' learning and give timely feedback to help them correct
Summative evaluation	Determine the different levels of students or their relative grades

3 Application Case

Network planning and design course is a basic course of computer network specialty. The main teaching goal is to learn general network design methods, network architecture design methods, and LAN and WAN design related technologies, and finally plan and design a small and medium-sized enterprise network through case analysis.

Because the knowledge system of the course is more abstract, it has higher requirements for students' early knowledge reserve and students' learning state in the classroom. At present, the organization of classroom teaching content does not consider or cannot consider the learning basis of students. This situation makes a large amount of knowledge flow to students at the same time in the teaching process, which not only cannot form a strong supplement to classroom teaching, but also makes students more confused because it is too much, too detailed and difficult to understand. After the introduction of virtual technology based on VLE in the network planning and design class, we can make use of the advantages of VLE technology in modeling and simulation, learning accurate push, teaching intelligent control and so on to effectively case the whole teaching system, so as to enhance the students' sense of learning experience.

The whole construction process of immersive curriculum learning environment is divided into three parts: the basic analysis part of students' learning is used to measure the basic line of students' learning; teaching content analysis part designs the teaching content from three aspects: teaching scene design, teaching stimulus design and student learning activity design; the learning evaluation part of students throughout the whole teaching process dynamically and repeatedly adjusts the teaching content according to the evaluation results, so as to complete the whole teaching process. The design process (see Fig. 3).

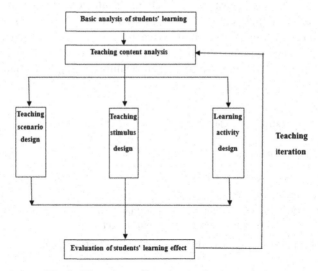

Fig. 3. Flow chart of learning environment design

3.1   Basic Analysis of Students' Learning

In the learning situation analysis stage, the digital twin technology is used to generate the digital twin objects corresponding to the students by using the relevant course information [6], and the knowledge points of this course are screened and layered (divided into basic layer and improvement layer) for use in the next stage. The acquisition of the basic line of student learning mainly comes from the collection of students' effective characteristics and the conversion of effective data of other related courses into virtual student information models, that is, based on the basic information of various student entities (such as age, interests and hobbies), students' historical achievements (such as the relevant achievements of various types of courses since admission), and students' relevant course achievements (the relevant achievements of previous courses), generate corresponding basic items of student learning data.

3.2 Teaching Scenario Setting

The design of learning situation is the key to the construction of immersion learning environment. In the virtual learning environment, real career scenes are used to improve learners' learning experience. The learning environment uses modeling technology to deal with different physical scenes required by the network planning course, and adds real scenes such as user communication. In the whole learning environment, according to the needs of students, it also provides other different functions, such as different business environment simulation function, demand analysis function, network and equipment selection function, scheme, network topology design function, etc. Various functions are cued in the learning environment, which can guide students to complete the corresponding functions step by step. The corresponding links are equipped with different background knowledge, FAQs and solutions; Each link is also equipped with a corresponding self-test for students' reference; After each link is completed, students can conduct corresponding diagnostic evaluation (see Fig. 4).

Fig. 4. Learning scenario design sample

3.3 Teaching Strategy Setting

Under the teaching strategy of case guidance and progressive training, this paper puts forward the idea of progressive teaching content design, updates the point and line knowledge dissemination model to the iterative learning model. The whole teaching strategy draws lessons from the concept of agile development in software engineering, advocates that the key content should be emphasized at the beginning of teaching, so that students can quickly start the design of the whole network, and then adjust the learning content of the next learning stage through different company types, constantly deepen and expand the depth and breadth of knowledge, and finally master the overall skills of network planning course.

3.4   Learning Activities and Interaction Design

Immersive network design and planning course learning environment uses operational learning activities to design the whole learning behavior. As a learning stimulus, in addition to ensuring the comprehensive coverage of teaching knowledge, it is also necessary to design the two-way interaction between students and VLE, stimulate students' interest in autonomous learning, and carry out the overall clue learning process and interaction design. The specific teaching resource incentive design sample is shown in Table 2.

Table 2. Sample table of incentive design of teaching resources.

Knowledge module	Incentives - knowledge points
Requirement analysis	Questionnaire survey method, demand verification and demand documentation
Network and equipment selection scheme	Layer 2 switch, layer 3 switch, router
Network topology design	Use of Huawei simulator
IP address planning and design	Intranet IP, extranet IP
Main equipment configuration scheme	ACL list, VLAN, virtual switching interface, OSPF
Network test analysis	Data flow blocking

3.5   Teaching Evaluation Design

As an important part of the whole learning environment, based on the traditional evaluation data, the immersive network design and planning course learning environment conducts student questionnaire survey before, during and after the semester to complete the diagnostic evaluation. As is shown in Table 3 is the specific contents.

Table 3. Sample student questionnaire.

Type	Problem
Teaching methods	Do you think the teaching mode of this course is reasonable
Active learning	1. Is this way of practicing network planning conducive to independent completion 2. Can you always follow the teacher to complete the teaching process of each module
Mastery of knowledge points	What knowledge points need to be strengthened in the next stage of teaching in the learning process

All students in 2020 participated in the questionnaire survey, and the results showed that the majority of students were satisfied with the teaching process (see Fig. 5).

Fig. 5. Survey Results Chart

4 Conclusion

Immersive learning environment is more flexible than face-to-face teaching. It is helpful for students to purposefully complete abstract learning plans and goals, make learning more personalized, and solve the limitations of classroom teaching mode. When applying VLE, teachers can not only use it as a storage tool for learning resources such as teaching materials and videos, but also for interactive functions such as online testing and discussion. The learning environment design of the immersive network planning course designed in this paper uses the hybrid teaching method to combine the traditional teaching and VLE virtual technology, create an active classroom atmosphere through the immersive learning scene, and mobilize the students' learning initiative and enthusiasm. In the next step, we need to further refine the implementation details in order to give full play to the role of VLE in the learning process.

References

1. Notice of the Ministry of education on printing and distributing the action plan for educational informatization2.0. http://www.moe.gov.cn/srcsite/A16/S3342/202804/t20180425_334 188.html. Accessed 20 June 2023
2. Learn about Virtual Learning Environment/Course Management System Content. http://glo bal.oup.com/uk/orc/learnvle/. Accessed 01 Dec 2015
3. Wang, H., Song, J.: Research on virtual learning environment model for personalized teaching process. Sci. Technol. Horizon (19), 35–36 (2021)
4. Tang, X.: Research on personalized recommendation system of 3D virtual learning environment based on big data. Digit. Commun. World (05), 94 (2020)
5. Zhang, Z.: Research on teacher-student interaction in effective classroom teaching. Shanghai Normal University, Shanghai (2015)
6. Chen, X.: Research on the reform of mixed teaching mode based on digital twin. Softw. Eng. (06), 49–51 (2020)

Design and Exploration of Digital Media Comprehensive Experiment Based on 3E

Huawei Pan[1](✉) and Li Li[2]

[1] College of Computer Science and Electronic Engineering, Hunan University, Changsha, Hunan, China
hw_pan@hnu.edu.cn
[2] College of Mechanical and Vehicle Engineering, Hunan University, Changsha, Hunan, China

Abstract. In order to enable college students to integrate the knowledge of various professional courses and break the experimental barriers between professional courses, and under the background of promoting the construction of Emerging Engineering Education (3E) by the Ministry of Education of China, this paper studies and explores the teaching contents and methods of comprehensive experiment of digital media courses, aiming at cultivating students' ability of innovative thinking, analyzing and solving complex problems, and improving students' ability of mutual cooperation and engineering practice. Based on Outcomes Based Education (OBE), a comprehensive experimental case of interaction between virtual objects and hand posture is designed. The case puts forward an assessment method focusing on the evaluation of students' comprehensive experimental practice ability. The experiment case can broaden students' horizons, cultivate students' innovative spirit, improve students' engineering practice ability. We achieved good teaching results in practice.

Keywords: Emerging Engineering Education · Multimedia · Comprehensive Experiment

1 Introduction

Emerging Engineering Education (3E) majors, mainly for emerging industries, focus on the Internet and industrial intelligence, including big data, cloud computing, artificial intelligence, blockchain, digital media technology and other related engineering majors. Compared with the traditional engineering talents, emerging industries and new economy in the future need high-quality compound 3E talents with strong practical ability, strong innovation ability and international competitiveness. The concept of 3E has been generalized and expanded by the MOE of China into "five new", namely, the new concept of engineering education, the new structure of disciplines and majors, the new mode of talent training, the new quality of education and teaching, and the new system of Classified Development [1]. After Fudan Consensus, Tianda Action and Beijing Guide have more systematically carried out the research and practice of 3E [2], focusing on disciplines and majors facing a new round of scientific and technological revolution and industrial reform. By building and improving the 3E specialty, we will cultivate professionals who can better meet the needs of the industry and society.

Digital media technology is a cross compound specialty. In the digital media curriculum system of Hunan University, its courses include Programming, Data Structure, Computer Animation and Graphics Engine, Introduction to Intelligent Graphics and Images, Computer Vision, Virtual Reality, Machine Learning, Computer Network, as well as Fundamentals of Art design, Human-Computer Interaction Technology, Software Architecture and Design Mode. The purpose of the curriculum system is to train compound talents with the ability of information communication theory, digital media technology and design management in the digital network era [3]. Under the background of 3E, digital media technology specialty is a highly applicable specialty. It should be committed to cultivating applied talents who can effectively solve the problems of actual production and demand [4]. It should have three quality characteristics: first, the talents should not only be proficient in research in a certain discipline, but also have the ability of interdisciplinary integration, and have a certain grasp of relevant discipline knowledge to promote its own development in the main learning direction; Second, the talents are able to use the knowledge to solve real problems, and have the ability to learn new knowledge and technology to deal with new problems that may arise in the future; Third, the talents are not only familiar with technology, but also need to know the knowledge of economy and management [5].

Therefore, it is necessary to cultivate students' professional skills and humanistic quality in the digital media courses. The best way to cultivate comprehensive ability is to let students really learn how to solve real demand problems through experimental practice courses [6]. How to practice and how to construct the comprehensive experimental course is particularly important.

2 Analysis of the Problems in the Design of Comprehensive Experiment Course

Digital media technology major should pay more attention to cultivating students' cross professional ability and practical ability. There are some existing problems in the curriculum arrangement and experimental curriculum design related to digital media:

1. Each specialized course in the digital media curriculum system offers experiments according to its syllabus to practice and realize. The experiment's content is relatively single and there is a lack of connection between different courses. As a result, it is difficult for students to use the knowledge they have learned, and the improvement of students' comprehensive ability is limited. When practical engineering problems need to be solved in the enterprise, the graduate student unable to start or start slowly, may leading to bad impression.
2. There are no courses on software architecture and design patterns, which leads to lack of knowledge on software requirements and software development cooperation, and to really establish and participate in promoting the development process.
3. The contents of study and experiment are boring, and students lack learning motivation this leads to students' lack of interest in using knowledge comprehensively and in learning and expanding knowledge independently.

The above problems make it difficult to effectively train students to truly master and skillfully use the knowledge learned in the classroom, and it is also difficult to train students' ability of cooperation and innovation. At the same time, students lack the motivation of active learning in the existing experimental courses.

3   Reform Ideas of Comprehensive Experiment Curriculum Design

In order to meet the social requirements and expectations of digital media technology specialty under the background of 3E, teachers need to enrich the skill of classroom teaching, and cultivate the students' cross knowledge system, problem-solving ability, innovation ability and cooperation ability. The OBE teaching mode is a good way for teachers to reference to cultivate the application-oriented talents of the specialty.

1. Involving different course contents in experiments content, such as image processing, 3D rendering engine, artificial intelligence, game / virtual reality development, etc.
2. Add relevant contents of software requirements management, design pattern, software engineering development to the experimental course.
3. The experiment content combined with the relevant competition to encourage students to participate in discipline competition, such as College Students Innovation and Entrepreneurship Competition, Chinese College Students Computer Design Competition, National Challenge Cup and other competitions. Encourage students to take participation in the competitions as the goal and to study independently
4. Information specialty may pay more attention to science and technology, and the weight for artistic is insufficient. But it is also important that the excellent visual effects are also one of the driving forces to software and games development. Fortunately, there are many art and artistic design related courses to learn on Bili website and MOORC website. In addition, we can also consider cooperate experiments with the Art and Design Institute, and the students of the two institutes work together to complete the experiments.
5. Adopting the OBE teaching mode to carry out the content reform of comprehensive experimental courses has important practical significance for cultivating engineering talents with the ability to solve complex engineering problems [11].

The main purpose of the comprehensive experimental curriculum is to optimize the experimental content, better improve students' practical ability. Combine with relevant college student competitions, the reform would further impel students to study independently and inspire students' teamwork ability.

4   Experimental Content Organization

4.1   Experimental Content Reform

According to the characteristics of centralized practice and engineering training, the experimental course is considered and designed to have a variety of positive effects on students' future learning and practice.

The contents of the comprehensive experiment are as follows: Course requires to use the camera embed in laptop, or USB-based webcam to capture and recognize the hand posture, and transfer the information into laptop or smartphone, and to control the behavior of an object in the virtual scene created by a rendering engine. So, student should construct story scene with their imagination and creativity in the rendering engine. Finally, the student should complete an interactive software applied between the virtual scene and real world. Unity rendering engine is adopted in the experimental courses. Teachers provide experimental teaching materials, allowing students to choose project topics and programming platform themselves. The teaching form is mainly based on students' practice, supplemented by special lectures, counseling, Q & A, lecture reports and etc. Students need to complete the usage of software and hardware tools, and complete program design training, creative and innovative design, etc.

The practical course is divided into several stage nodes, as shown in Fig. 1. It is include Topic Selection and Planning Document Writing stage, Application Scenario Construction stage, Gesture Recognition Implementation stage. In addition, students can choose data transmission trajectory and whether to establish C/S service mode.

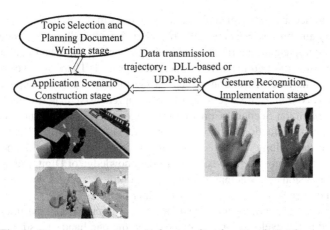

Fig. 1. Stage node arrangement of comprehensive experimental course.

There are multiple choices at each stage of the practical course. We take game project development as an example. The types of game topics for students to choose include competition, music rhythm, gunfight, intelligence type, Virtual Reality, as shown in Table 1; Gesture recognition has always been a technical hotspot for long time, and so there are many implementation method for student to choose. Therefore, as shown in Table 1, including traditional schemes based on color and morphology, methods based on deep learning, online or offline APIs provided by the company, machine learning tool library, etc. Considering that students are exposed to cross platform data exchange for the first time, Some learning materials and reference code for data communication are provided for students' reference and selection.

In this way, the students have an whole awareness to the methods adopted by each node. The student group can make choices according to individual abilities and wishes of the students in the group. Of course, it is available for students having other options and ideas not within this scope.

Table 1. Node options of comprehensive experimental courses.

Stage	selections
Topic type	Competition, music rhythm, gunfight, intelligence, Virtual Reality, etc.
Ability	based on color and morphology, online or offline companies' API, based on deep learning, based on machine learning tool library, etc.
Programming platform and data communication scheme	C/C++ and DLL-based, Python and UDP-based, etc.
Optional Selection	build C/S mode

The comprehensive experimental course integrates majority basic courses of computer specialty and professional curriculum of digital media, allowing students to organize teams to complete an interactive game design. And the practical operation of different courses runs through the whole experiment project. There are two main stages, Application Scenario Construction stage and Gesture Recognition Implement stage. The course involved in each stage node of the comprehensive experimental course are as follow: Application Scenario Construction stage maybe concern the knowledge of Human-Computer Interaction technology, Computer Graphics, Virtual Reality, 3D Rendering Engine technology, Computer Animation and Artificial Intelligence; Gesture Recognition Implement stage maybe concern the knowledge of Digital Image Processing, Computer Vision and Machine Learning; If multiple computers are networked, the experimental course should also involve Computer Networks.

In the process of learning and research, the comprehensive experimental course project is gradually developed and completed. On the one hand, the students are very interested to design their own personalized games. And at the same time, the students also understand the usefulness of the knowledge learned in relevant courses and learn how to use it. On the other hand, progressive 'visualizing' the theoretical knowledge they have learned, the students increase interest and get motivation for learning and research [8].

The course has the characteristics of inclusiveness and openness, It provides not only traditional scheme, but also opportunities for students to broaden their thinking and make breakthroughs and innovations at a certain point.

The whole experimental has many selections from easy to difficult, so that students can complete the experimental content with their individual selection step by step [9, 10].

According to teaching objectives, shown in Table 2, we have rescheduled the curriculum. The experiment course has a total of 64 class hours. We allocate it to 4 class hours of theoretical teaching, 6 class hours of discussion which is split to three times, 4 class hours of reporting experiment project, and 50 class hours of practice. All class hours are completed within 4 weeks.

The student's project report is scheduled before the end of the course. Through the report, each group study and discuss the technologies and methods used, and compare the algorithms used by other groups. Therefore the students can horizontally analyze the advantages and disadvantages of the technologies, methods and algorithms used by other groups.

Table 2. Course Teaching Objectives.

Target category	Objective description
knowledge	Based on the knowledge of basic and professional computer courses, the student should master a rendering engine software, program development language, master key algorithms, and realize an interactive application software
Ability	Be able to use appropriate knowledge and methods to study digital media problems, including designing experiments, analyzing and interpreting data, and obtaining reasonable conclusions through information synthesis; Complete the whole process of a digital media application system from demand to architectural design and final implementation in the way of team cooperation

4.2 Practice Scoring Mechanism

The experimental course adopts a multiple and echelon scoring mechanism. During the period, we have three regular face-to-face meetings and communicate with students, involving discussion, inspection and evaluation, stage scoring. So that teachers are aware of the progress of students' project and arrangements for the next step. At the same time, Teachers can also put forward some suggestions to each group. Discuss and answer questions can guide the group to promote thinking. If the group who is adopting new technology, teacher can consider to give extra score points to the group. Before the end of the experimental course, each group will make a final report, give students an chance to learn the project designed by the other groups. Final submission material are project's source code, demo video, operation manual, technical report and attached materials. The final score consists of four parts: General Grade, Group Report grade, Personal Report grade in Group and Final Submission Material grade. The student's final score is constituted by the four parts according to a certain percentage.

4.3 Student Feedback

Students are generally interested in the experimental courses and feel a sense of achievement in realizing a game software created by themselves. During the experiment, students' research attitude is obviously divided into three stages: Teachers' guidance and students' compliance; Actively independent inquiry planning scheme; Be more proactive, ask for technical solutions and actively modify design solutions.

Students usually have their own options. In addition to learning the arranged teaching contents, most students try to query and replace with new technologies and methods found on the Internet, gradually learn and apply algorithms, and try to explore and master the current advanced technology. In the process of learning and researching, many student groups plan to adopt the deep learning method at the initial stage. However, given the limited time and computational power conditions, most of them give up the plan of training new model. But still a few student groups insist on collecting and training samples in a relatively simple way for basic hand training.

Through practical operation, students complete the whole process of the input and output of the interactive application software system, which make students realize the importance of optimization of software architecture and the necessity of algorithm efficiency.

The comprehensive experimental course can further increase the diversity of projects. For example, gesture recognition can be replaced by face recognition and human posture recognition. Of course, this will further increase the complexity, and also require teachers to have a wide range of knowledge in this regard. However, it does guide students to think further.

5   Conclusion and Improvement Measures

The purpose of comprehensive experimental course is to organically unify multiple professional core courses and elective courses in the design of comprehensive courses, promote students' mutual cooperation and engineering practice ability, and lay a good foundation for students' future work.

This experimental course has been carried out for five years and has achieved remarkable results. Students use the knowledge learned in the classroom to realize a preliminary application system. The basic knowledge learned in the course do not meet Some students' curiosity. So they search ethernet, use SDK and enterprise API, and learn to call shared computing nodes to achieve the purpose of functional computing. The effect is that the project design among groups has personalized differences. The discussion and demonstration among students and groups enable students to promote each other, make them absorb extensive and far-reaching knowledge. The students are not only expand the scope of knowledge, and contact the frontier of knowledge, but also further improve the integration of different curriculum knowledge.

In addition, the practical experiment courses can be adjusted according to the requirements of relevant competitions in that year, and students are encouraged to combine the design of practical courses with competitions to complete experiments with higher quality.

Under the background of 3E, according to the requirements and expectations of society and industry for digital media technology specialty, we aim to cultivate compound application-oriented talents, and increase the interaction between teachers and students, improve students' learning interest, promote the Industry-University-Research Collaboration, integrate the needs of enterprises into the curriculum and experimental system, and provide digital media technology professions with strong practical ability for society and industry.

References

1. Quan, S., Cai, L.: Construction and practice of engineering training system for new engineering. Value Eng. 298–299 (2018)
2. Zhu, B., Wu, F.: Research on the training scheme of digital media technology talents from the perspective of new engineering. J. Zhejiang Shuren Univ. **2**, 42–46 (2018)
3. He, Y., Shi, B.: Practical research on project driven in program teaching of digital media technology specialty. J. Lanzhou Univ. Arts Sci. **5**, 117–119 (2017)
4. Liu, G., Li, W.: Thinking and exploration on the training of applied talents of digital media technology under the background of "new engineering." Educ. World **43**, 103–104 (2018)
5. Li, L., Zhang, Y., Du, J.: Research and Reform on the training mode of practical talent under the background of new engineering – take digital media technology specialty of Lanzhou University of Arts and science as an example. J. Lanzhou Univ. Arts Sci. (Nat. Sci.) **36**(2), 122–128 (2022)
6. Kang, H., Wang, G., Zhang, L.: Taking practical teaching as a platform to improve college students' scientific and technological innovation ability. China Adult Educ. **16**, 133–134 (2008)
7. Zhao, X., Ning, G.: Innovation of digital media education concept in the era of media convergence – thinking based on the practice of "project + competition" double drive teaching mode. Art Educ. **336**(20), 67–68 (2018)
8. Cheng, C., Wu, Y., Xiao, M.: Application of project case inspired teaching method in human-computer interaction course teaching. University Education, vol. 5 (2017)
9. Chen, A., Lu, M., Zheng, S.: Research on experimental teaching mode of digital media technology and application based on CDIO mode. Comput. Knowl. Technol. **15**(12) (2019)
10. Du, X.: Probe into the practical teaching reform of digital media design specialty based on project driving. China Packag. **11**, 65–68 (2015)
11. Li, L., Wang, N., Tang, S.: OBE based reform for software project management curriculum. In: The 14th International Conference on Computer Science & Education (ICCSE), pp. 1075–1079 (2019)

On Diversified Innovative Strategies of English Teaching Evaluation in Junior High School Based on "Internet Plus"

Liping Ju[✉] and Ying Shao

Suqian University, Suqian 223800, China
771712622@qq.com

Abstract. Based on the theory of multiple intelligences combined with the practical experience from teaching practice in the era of "Internet Plus", this paper mainly starts with the present background, application fields and functions of "Internet Plus" through adopting several research methods such as literature method, survey method, interview method, etc. to analyze the major problems of the existing junior high school English teaching evaluation model, arguing that in the era of "Internet Plus", the advantages of the Internet application can be drawn on effectively in the evaluation of English teaching in junior high schools. Some feasible multiple innovation strategies will be proposed for the existing junior high school English teaching evaluation.

Keywords: Internet Plus · junior high school · English teaching evaluation · diversified innovative strategies

1 Introduction

Teaching evaluation is a process of measuring the teaching process and results, giving valuable judgments according to scientific standards via all effective technical means based on teaching objectives. Effective teaching requires creativity, imagination, and innovation. The researches on teaching evaluation can be traced back to the western education measurement movement in the 1930s, which also had a great influence on China's education. Since the restoration of the college entrance examination system in China in 1977, in order to improve the quality of teaching faster and better, the government of China has attached great importance to teaching evaluation, and in recent years many researches and experiments have been conducted on teaching evaluation at various schools, which have exerted a very good effect on improving English teaching (Wang Qiyu, 2021, Yang Kaicheng et al., 2021, Chen Xia, 2021). In junior high school English teaching, it is an inevitable trend to break the tradition of looking on teachers as the main body of evaluation. With the advancement of science and technology and the continuous development of the Internet, the evaluation model that combines educational evaluation with the Internet has received more and more attention in the English educational field. In the study of teaching evaluation, various aspects of evaluation need to be taken into consideration, such as evaluation subject, evaluation method, evaluation content, evaluation means and so on. The application of Internet technology is already widely spread in English classroom teaching, but research concerning Internet plus in teaching evaluation may not be that extensive, which, in effect, can make teaching evaluation progressively up to date. Zhu, Q.F. (2017) argues that "Internet Plus" refers to the Internet-supported approach towards social and economic development, which advocates the seamless integration of digital tools, artificial intelligence, big data systems into daily work through the Internet to enhance performance and quality of service in all walks of life.

Therefore, taking the "Internet Plus" as the research background, combined with the previous practical experience and relevant knowledge, based on the existing problems in the evaluation of English teaching, this thesis aims to employ the superiority of the "Internet Plus Education" settings concerning the evaluation of English teaching at junior high school, trying to propose several innovation strategies, which are practicable to be implemented by using various advantages of the Internet technology.

2 Literature Review

2.1 Background of the Research

Starting from Microblog and WeChat, the Web system has begun to upgrade from 2.0 to 3.0. With the continuous development of the Internet, people have gradually entered the era of perception of all things that is called intelligent control or intellectualization. The all-round information interaction brings the material world much closer to human society. The communication between people is only a part of information exchange, and the communication between people and the material world will become a very rich part among information exchanges. Under this context, it has become a general trend to expand the Internet to the field of education. As an indispensable link in the teaching process, education evaluation must also be integrated with the Internet plus.

2.2 Previous Studies of English Evaluation

Domestic scholars have made preliminary research results on the Internet plus education model, which has involved many subjects such as ideology, politics, history, and English education, but the Internet plus education model still needs to be further developed. Innovative reform methods have been proposed by some scholars for multiple evaluations in teaching and learning from three following aspects: evaluation content, evaluation methods, and evaluation subjects. Zhang Fang (2014), Jia Zijing (2019) and Zhao Yanhong (2018) pointed out that the construction of the teaching evaluation system not only needs to clarify the evaluation subject, but also needs to clarify the content, the standard and the mode. They maintained that by making people clearer about this idea of evaluation system, teachers can realize the scientific evaluation of teaching evaluation in a very diversified way. Zhang Fang (2014) found out a host of shortcomings in the present "Internet Plus Education" evaluation system, such as lacking a suitable evaluation system matching with the positioning of the school, having no support from the school leaders, thus harboring poor operability. He pointed out that the present evaluation system needs to be optimized and perfected in the new era. Based on "Internet Plus Education", he launched a research on the construction of the teaching quality evaluation system in colleges and universities, putting forward some specific practical strategies.

Corresponding research has also been done on the evaluation of English teaching abroad. Foreign researches on educational evaluation can be traced back to the Western Educational Measurement Movement in the 1930s, which has gradually formed a system after nearly half a century of continuous practice and development. Specifically, it includes the following four aspects: the first is the definition of the concept of educational evaluation, due to different definitions having different emphases. The second is about the methodology of educational evaluation, including empirical evaluation methodology and human culture evaluation methodology. The third is the form of educational evaluation. Currently there are five main forms of evaluation, which are listed as follows: diagnostic evaluation, formative evaluation, summative evaluation, relative evaluation and absolute evaluation. The fourth is about the system of education evaluation, an established utility-centered evaluation system. In short, they are of the fundamental principles of educational evaluation. The most famous principles are the four ones released by the American Educational Evaluation Standards Association in 1981: utility, feasibility, appropriateness, and accuracy.

2.3 Significance of the Research

It can be seen from the above that educational evaluation has always been the focus of the education sector. As an important part of English teaching, it not only helps students get to know their own learning performance, but also assists teachers in improving their teaching methods, thereby promoting the integrated development of students, so it is very necessary and worthwhile to give a close look at teaching evaluation under the present context of internet. Today, with the continuous development of science and technology, the application of Internet to teaching evaluation is both an opportunity and a challenge to most teachers. Although there have been some initial achievements, the relevant researches still need to be further propelled and deepened. This thesis aims to study the evaluation of English teaching in junior high schools from the perspective of "Internet Plus", trying to propose some certain diversified innovative strategies concerned.

3 Research Methodology

Based on the theory of multiple intelligences, this thesis adopts various research methods, such as literature method, questionnaire method and interview method, etc., in the actual study.

By reading, combing, and analyzing a wealth of relevant literature, this thesis will display the current situation of English teaching evaluation in junior high school. In the actual education and teaching practice, a study will be made with the students and teachers, who will function as empirical samples in a chosen junior high school. Then corresponding surveys will be conducted among those students and teachers, like giving interviews to obtain relatively reliable and credible teaching and learning information. In addition, questionnaires are designed and distributed to some certain research subjects.

In this way, the current situation of English teaching evaluation from the perspective of students can be obtained directly close at hand, and their experience of "Internet Plus" from English teaching evaluation can be gained too, both of which are beneficial to propose corresponding innovation strategies more pertinently.

4   Data Analysis and Discussion

Affected by the COVID-19, the questionnaire survey was carried out online. The questionnaires were distributed to those investigated subjects, and finally 151 valid ones were collected, which mainly reveal the information about the current situation of existing English teaching evaluation and the degree of popularity regarding "Internet Plus" in the given school, thus providing a strong and solid basis for subsequent research.

4.1   Current Situation of English Teaching Evaluation in Junior High School

The Basic Information about "Internet Plus" from Students

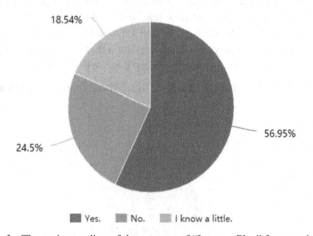

Fig. 1. The understanding of the concept of "Internet Plus" from students

According to the survey results, 56.95% of the students who participated in the questionnaire said they had heard of "Internet Plus", 24.5% had not heard of it, and 18.54% of the students had a certain knowledge of "Internet Plus" (see Fig. 1). It can be seen from the data above that there is a very good penetration of "Internet Plus" in students' daily life or learning life, and more than half of the subjects know about "Internet Plus". This lays a good foundation for the future combination of "Internet Plus" with teaching evaluation.

"Internet Plus" refers to a new business form developed from the Internet driven by Innovation 2.0 (the information age, the innovative form of the knowledge society), and it is also a new form of economic and social development that has evolved and spawned from the Internet form driven by Knowledge Society Innovation 2.0. It is a further practical achievement of Internet thinking, which promotes the continuous evolution of economic forms, thereby driving the vitality of social and economic entities, thus providing a broad network platform for reform, innovation and development. In laymen's words, "Internet Plus" means "Internet plus various traditional industries", but this is not a simple addition of the two, but the use of information and communication technology as well as Internet platforms to deeply integrate the Internet with traditional industries in order to create new development ecology. The "Internet Plus" action plan was first proposed by Premier Li Keqiang in the Report on the Work of the Government in May 2020. It was initially applied to enterprises represented by information technology, Internet of Things and big data, whose impact is profound and lasting. Warchauer (2000) once also maintained that Internet can be used as a nice instrument for English teaching. Applying "Internet Plus" to education, especially teaching evaluation, with the help of cloud technology and Internet big data, can help realize the intellectualization, diversification and comprehensiveness of English teaching evaluation very easily.

The essence of "Internet Plus" is of continuous enrichment and development of information technology, not only in economy, but also in education. The wide application and popularization of the Internet has broken the barriers of the limit of time, space, and location in contrast to traditional classroom teaching, and the teaching mode has also become more abundant, a variety of new teaching modes such as MOOC and flipped classroom having emerged. Junior high school English teaching plays a pivotal role in the entire English education process. As an important part of junior high school English teaching, teaching evaluation also needs to keep pace with the times.

The Role of English Evaluation in Junior High School from Teachers and Students

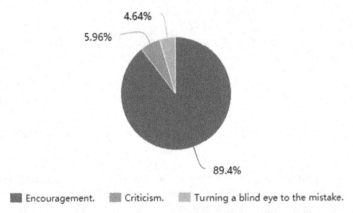

Fig. 2. The responses from teachers to students' wrong reply

Teachers' responses are collected after their completion of the questionnaire, which serves as samples to explore the teachers' role as well as the students' in teaching evaluation. According to the survey results, 89.4% of teacher subjects would give encouragement to students after their giving wrong answers, 5.96% would render them criticism, and 4.64% would ignore (see Fig. 2). In contrast, 55.63% student subjects are eager to draw teachers' attention, 17.22% wouldn't like to, and 27.15% don't care (see Fig. 3).

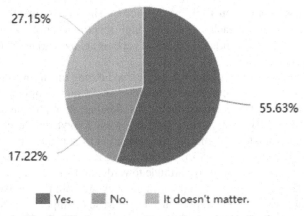

Fig. 3. Whether you want to get the teacher's attention

Overall, positive responses from teachers in face of students' wrong reply to questions in classroom account for a large proportion, showing that the majority of teachers realize that their positive evaluation to students would have a great impact on the learning psychology of students. Likewise, more than half students thirst for attention from teachers in class.

As we all know, English teaching evaluation in junior high school has four main functions: diagnosis, feedback, orientation and motivation. Teaching evaluation chiefly consists of the following three segments: evaluation of students' academic performance, evaluation of teachers' teaching quality and evaluation of teaching and learning courses. The above three aspects are invariably employed to evaluate teaching activities from different angles, that is, the diagnostic function. The specific content of the evaluation is the feedback from students or teachers. Whether students actively participate in the classroom, whether the teacher's teaching method is reasonable, and whether or not the classroom atmosphere is active, etc., are all of feedback among teaching evaluation. With the continuous development and advancement of the times as well as the renewal of educational concepts, teachers of English at junior high school need to keep pace with the era, dropping some of their old and outdated teaching ideas to get innovation in the process of practical activities, thus making classroom teaching more effective. With the specific evaluation contents to be diagnosed and fed back, teachers are encouraged to constantly update teaching concepts and teaching methods, by keeping up with the times to improve the teaching quality in all aspects. As a result, better teaching effect would be achieved genuinely and automatically, which belongs to orientation and motivation functions of teaching evaluation.

4.2 Existing Problems in the Current Junior High School

At present, most teachers at junior high schools are fond of choosing to check students' English proficiency in written form, and using only one final English test paper to evaluate students' academic level. However, the content of the examination paper is basically the knowledge learned in one semester, which falls into a relatively narrow scope.

One-Sidedness of Evaluation Content. At present, since the written test paper is the preferred choice for most teachers at junior high schools to check students' English proficiency, and only one terminal English test paper is always harnessed to evaluate the students' academic level.

The test content in the English test paper learned during one term cannot be used to detect the students' learning conditions comprehensively and completely. For a period of learning time, it can play a certain role in consolidating, strengthening and evaluating what they've learned. But this mainly focuses on the knowledge level, emphasizing the importance of knowledge, ignoring the evaluation of students' learning emotions, attitudes and values. As is known to all, cultivating reasonable values or morals will also help students maintain a positive attitude towards English learning. And when they gradually love English of a good frame of mind, they are willing to make more efforts to improve themselves. Therefore, in a much larger trend of emphasis on today's quality education, attention should also be paid to the all-round development of students by English teachers, especially the cultivation of emotional attitudes and healthy sense of value.

The Oneness of the Evaluation Subject

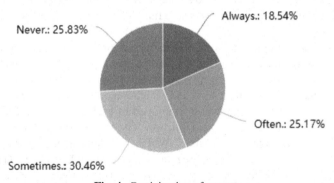

Fig. 4. Participation of parents

When it comes to the evaluation subjects, they can be divided into three types: self-evaluation, peer-evaluation and teacher-student evaluation. As the name suggests, teacher-student evaluation refers to the assessment given by the teacher, and self-evaluation is one's own evaluation from students themselves, while peer-evaluation refers to the evaluation made by peers. These three kinds of evaluation are more commonly used in the actual teaching situation. As usual, teachers are often the main body of teaching evaluation, while students are basically in a state of being judged, which may have a certain negative impact on their self-esteem and self-confidence, even leading to bad learning behavior from students. Although there will be teachers who choose to let students evaluate themselves, which based on the fact that they believe students can evaluate themselves objectively, but due to evaluation standards and various other factors, self-evaluation seems not to be included by many teachers, so the accuracy and validity of the final evaluation results is not good, and accordingly the effects produced by the evaluation will not be that satisfactory.

In the Internet age where the relationship between people may easily become closer, not only among teachers, but also between students and parents. The relevant people can participate in teaching evaluation, too. Among them, a question raised by the author has been displayed in the questionnaire on parents' participation. The survey shows that 18.54% of teachers always let parents participate in evaluation, 25.17% often, 30.46% sometimes, and 25.83% never let parents participate (see Fig. 4). In general, the frequency of parental participation is relatively low and it needs to be improved in future teaching evaluations.

Monotonicity of Evaluation Methods

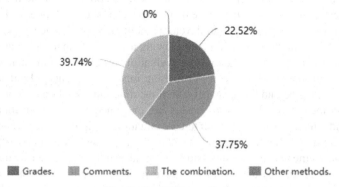

Fig. 5. Evaluation methods

Through the survey of students, it can be known that the teachers' evaluation methods for students are still based on grades or comments principally. The proportion of combining the two is only 39.74%, which is less than half of the total (see Fig. 5). This phenomenon deserves attention.

According to the research in many documents, there are six kinds of teaching evaluation methods: diagnostic evaluation, formative evaluation, summative evaluation, relative evaluation, absolute evaluation and individual difference evaluation. Although there are so many types of assessments, the summative evaluation is still used more in practice, and the frequency of diagnostic evaluation and relative evaluation is comparatively low. Summative evaluation refers to assessments that take place at the end of a semester or after a course is finished. As mentioned above, in the form of written examination, the final examination paper is adopted currently at the vast majority of junior high schools. The checked question type on the test paper will not change basically, it is relatively fixed and lacks flexibility. This kind of evaluation system is easy to cause students to focus only on grades and ignore the improvement of ability, which is not conducive to the future development of students. The continuous progress of the Internet promotes the deepening of globalization. As the most widespread international working language in the world, English learning and teaching cannot be ignored. Consequently, English teaching evaluation should be comparatively a long-term process, not merely at the end of one semester.

4.3 Disadvantages in the Current Evaluation System

Although the current teaching evaluation can timely feedback students' learning status, helping students understand and recognize their own learning state better so as to adjust the learning method and learning habits, at the same time, teachers are also able to find the deficiency of their own teaching according to the current teaching evaluation pattern, which can make the teaching process more perfect and more adaptable to the development of students, there exist certain problems concerning the current teaching evaluation, which are embodied in the following two aspects.

Failing to Adapt to the Pace of Modern Education Development. In contemporary world which has entered the era of intelligence with the booming of the Internet development, great changes have taken place in all respects of society. Modern education has witnessed more and more prosperous development in many fields, such as the increasing popularity of multimedia devices and the growing use of iPads in teaching and learning. Under such circumstances, if the existing evaluation system is still maintained without putting forward innovative strategies or making innovative changes, English teaching evaluation will lag behind the advancement of the times and would be out of touch with the times in the future. Because of inadequate and unequal communication between teachers and students, the teacher-centered evaluation is highly subjective and insufficient. This kind of evaluation method, which is mainly based on summative evaluation, overemphasizes the teaching results--students' grades and ignores the teaching process, thus making the accuracy and validity of the evaluation results a little bit questionable and sided. In the short term, it is not conducive to the comprehensive development of students; in the long run, if teachers' teaching evaluation methods are not improved in time, it will be difficult to improve the quality of school teaching, which will have certain negative effects on the development of society and even the country in the future.

Being not Conducive to Cultivating Students' Core English Literacy. As Abdel Salam (2004) says comprehensive approach should be acquired in terms of teaching and learning English as a foreign language. Watanabe (1997) holds that desired effects can be received by increased learning of foreign language vocabulary, that's true, but there are four core competencies in the English subject: language ability, cultural awareness, thinking quality and learning ability. An important aspect of implementing core literacy is to start with education evaluation. The problem of the existing evaluation system is only a single evaluation of students' knowledge learning, which still remains in the level of teaching skills, and does not penetrate into students' thinking, excellent quality and other aspects. In other words, the actual English teaching evaluation nowadays is a little bit sided, not conducive to cultivating students' core English literacy in a comprehensive way. Therefore, it is imperative to innovate in the English teaching evaluation system (Tan Qingyan, 2021).

5 Diversified Innovative Strategies

Through the analysis above, the existing problems and drawbacks in the evaluation of English teaching in junior high school and the advantages of teaching evaluation combined with "Internet Plus" can be explored further. The innovative strategies proposed below are based on the theory of multiple intelligences, which was proposed by the American educator and psychologist H. Gardner (2011). This theory mainly points out that people think in various ways and form various corresponding patterns of cognition.

With the multiple intelligences theory and with the supplement and improvement of those predecessors, it is believed that human beings have eight kinds of intelligence, namely language intelligence, mathematical logic intelligence, visual space intelligence, music rhythm intelligence, body movement intelligence, interpersonal communication intelligence, self-knowledge intelligence and nature observation intelligence. Since the intelligence possessed by human beings is diverse, the combination of these intelligences in human beings is also diverse, which leads to individual differences. The existence of these individual differences means that teachers cannot assess all students in a single way. The continuous development of the Internet has provided technical support for the establishment of a diverse evaluation system. Innovative evaluation strategies will be described as follows:

5.1 Increasing the Comprehensiveness of the Evaluation Content

Under the background of "Internet Plus", junior high school English teachers can integrate the designed teaching objectives, teaching methods, teaching resources and teaching interaction with one another, paying more attention to the relationship between teaching activities and information technology. For example, the focus on the completion of the given objectives can be reduced appropriately while shifting to the development of other intelligences, such as presentation of self-made short video clips, small drama show, micro speech contest, good teaching materials from famous TED, and so on and so forth. Such changes can prompt teachers to adjust teaching arrangements based on students' learning interest and learning needs, by applying diversified teaching means through giving priority to the use of modern information technology.

5.2 Using the Internet Technology or Platform to Make Evaluation Methods More Diverse

Mass data have brought a significant impact on the education industry. Accurate learning diagnosis, personalized learning analysis and intelligent decision support based on big data have greatly improved the quality of education, playing an important role in promoting education fairness, and enhancing excellent education governance, which have become indispensable for important support of the realization of education modernization. With the help of educational mass data, students' information system can be organized and analyzed. For example, big data can be used to design teaching evaluation environments, to improve evaluation scenarios, and to configure corresponding evaluation tools. Some good teaching platforms like MOOC, fanya.chaoxing.com and so on can be fully borrowed to enrich evaluation methods. These diverse means can be utilized to fully mobilize students' initiative and enthusiasm in learning, producing an immeasurable effect in the development of educational evaluation.

5.3 Employing Multiple Evaluation Participants

Apart from teachers, students themselves should be allowed to participate in teaching and learning evaluation in the context of "Internet Plus". This is the affirmation and inheritance of traditional evaluation methods. "Internet Plus" can provide a platform or a channel to show whether or not students are curious, sensitive, competitive, emotionally vulnerable or lacking willpower during a specific learning period. Their self-evaluation is true manifestation of their mental state. In the long term, they can gradually realize that they should be responsible for their own learning.

Meanwhile, involving parents in teaching evaluation is an effective way of cultivating parents' sense of participation to take some responsibility of their kids' education actually at school. The use of "Internet Plus" for evaluation allows multiple parties to participate in the evaluation and broadens the evaluation process. With the help of the Internet technology, the communication space has been expanded between teachers and students, students and students, home and school, and the communication and interaction between them has been further enhanced, too.

5.4 Expanding Diversity of Teaching Evaluation

As mentioned above, teaching evaluation methods can be divided into six types: diagnostic evaluation, formative evaluation, summative evaluation, relative evaluation, absolute evaluation and individual difference evaluation. In fact, these six methods can be applied in a mixed way to the evaluation of English teaching in junior high school, but not employed alone. There are choices and trade-offs when these six methods are used in combination.

Take summative evaluation and formative evaluation for example. The summative rating generally occurs after teaching behavior happens, which is a comprehensive and overall evaluation of learning effect of a certain period. It is used more frequently, because it is an important way to test students' comprehensive language ability, whose application has a high generality. This kind of evaluation is more suitable for teachers to apply at the end of the semester, that is, the traditional evaluation method. The formative assessment occurs in teaching process, and it is a way to know students' learning status in time. This is actually appropriate for students to conduct self-evaluation, finding problems through the evaluation, and then adjust themselves in time. The combination of these two evaluation methods can not only improve the comprehensiveness of the evaluation content, but also realize the diversification of evaluation subjects and evaluation methods. The value of evaluation can come true to the greatest extent with the use of some special APPs. Under the background of "Internet Plus", educational information technology has brought a lot of convenience to the development of evaluation. Several other evaluation methods can be used in combination in this way, too, as long as the time and the method are appropriate, relatively satisfactory results can be obtained as expected.

6 Conclusion

From the discussion and analysis in the previous parts, some diversified and innovative strategies are proposed to increase the comprehensiveness of the evaluation by using the Internet technology or platform through employing multiple participation subjects.

It is suggested in this paper that English teachers need to be aware of the important role of the Internet in teaching evaluation. Teaching evaluation under the background of "Internet Plus" can shorten the distance between many parties, leading to promotion of more frequent and closer connection between people. The dynamic nature of the evaluation process also helps make teaching evaluation more objective and accurate. Interaction, that is, teacher-student interaction, student-student interaction and home-school interaction have realized the diversity of evaluation subjects. In the long run, the realization of innovation in junior high school English teaching evaluation under the "Internet Plus" is to cultivate a sense of multi-party cooperation, helping students establish a healthy outlook on life and moral, exercising their thinking ability, thus improving their comprehensive quality.

There is no garden without weeds, there also exists certain limitations regarding this research, which may be taken into consideration in the future studies.

First of all, due to the inconvenience of collecting data in time and space during the period of COVID-19, the number of teacher and student subjects involved in this study is a little bit insufficient. As is known to all, the more samples are gathered, the more accurate the research result will be obtained. Hence, the selection of research sample size for statistical measurement may be not sufficient or that typical, which surely needs to be ameliorated in future research.

Secondly, only literature method, survey method and interview method are mainly adopted in this study. Some other methods, such as case study, observation method, cross-disciplinary research method, etc. can be experimented, too, so the subjectivity in this research appears a little bit stronger, which also needs to be overcome in future research.

Thirdly, because of the research having been done under the Chinese context, the conclusion may not be that reasonable in other countries, which can also be attempted in future research.

Surely, reflecting on teaching takes many forms and is strengthened by different perspectives and lines of evidence. Many ways to evaluate teaching can be further studied in future research: the instructor's own self-reflection and materials, such as teaching portfolios and teaching inventories, or class recording. Each source of data provides a partial perspective and has certain limitations.

Acknowledgement. The warmest gratitude is given to Professor Huanhai Fang at Xiamen University, for his constant inspiration and patient guidance during the course of this thesis writing. With his profound and extensive knowledge as well as his kind but rigorous attitude, this thesis has been smoothly finished. Whenever difficulties appear during this research, Professor Fang will provide us quite a lot of valuable suggestions.

Hearty thanks also go to Professor Wang Chunlei and other workmates at Suqian university for their mighty support, encouragement and assistance concerning this research work.

This research is supported by the 2021 project (2021-Y21) "A Research on the Reconstruction of College English Teaching Evaluation System under the Background of New Liberal Arts Construction" approved by the Evaluation Committee of Jiangsu Higher Education Association.

References

Wang, Q.: An assessment reform of English teaching by emphasizing the outstanding growth of students. J. Guizhou Normal Univ., 61–69 (2021)

Yang, K., Yang, L.: A new idea of teaching evaluation: to prove the teaching itself with the teaching process. Res. Mod. Distance Educ., 49–54 (2021)

Xia, C.: An application strategy and variant innovation of online teaching evaluation method. A book review. J. Jiangsu Open Univ., 58 (2021)

Zhu, Q.F.: The practice and future of artificial intelligence, intelligent learning space and informatization education. Presentation at the 21st Global Chinese Conference on Computers in Education, Beijing, China (2017)

Zhang, F.: A discussion about how to build effective English teaching evaluation system, using enterprise performance measurement. Stud. Asian Soc. Sci. **2**, 102–106 (2014)

Jia, Z.: Study on college English teaching evaluation in a classroom. In: Proceedings of the 6th International Conference on Education, Language, Art and Inter-cultural Communication (ICELAIC), pp. 65–72 (2019)

Zhao, Y.: Study on English teaching evaluation system in higher vocational colleges. Adv. High. Educ. **2**, 69–72 (2018)

Warchauer, M., Shetzer, H., Meloni, C.: Internet for English Teaching, pp. 83–91. Teachers of English to Speakers of Other Languages, Inc., Virginia (2000)

El-Koumy, A.S.A.K.: Teaching and learning English as a foreign language: a comprehensive approach. SSRN Electron. J., 1–228 (2004)

Watanabe, Y.: Input, intake and retention: effects of increased learning of foreign language vocabulary. Stud. Second. Lang. Acquis. **19**, 287–301 (1997)

Tan, Q.: Evaluation system of college English teaching based on big data. J. Phys. Conf. Ser. **2**, 118–122 (2021)

Gardner, H.: The theory of multiple intelligences: as psychology, as education, as social science. José Cela University (2011)

Analysis of the Influence of Terminal Characteristics on Network Performance of China Space Station

Zhenhao Zhao[1]([⊠]), Feng Wang[2], Yanwei Liu[1], Yanchao Gao[1], Yusheng Yi[1], and Jiaxin Yang[1]

[1] Beijing Institute of Spacecraft System Engineering, Beijing, China
zhenhao@126.com
[2] Beijing TongGuangLong Electronic Technology Co. LTD., Beijing, China

Abstract. China Space Station has adopted high-rate Ethernet technology and established a network system with a maximum transmission rate of 10 Gbps, greatly improving communication efficiency. According to the design of network system of China Space Station, combined with user requirements and typical working mode, the simulation model is established by using the simulation software, and the influence of the terminal data type and data characteristics on the network performance is analyzed, which provides reference and basis for the design of network terminal and in orbit management.

Keywords: Network System · Space Station · Simulation · Network Terminal · Network Performance

1 Introduction

China space station has completed construction in orbit and can provide an experimental platform for human space exploration. Compared with previous spacecrafts, the space station has applied several advanced technologies [1–4], and high-rate Ethernet technology is one of them. The space station established a high-rate network system with a maximum transmission rate of 10 Gbps to provide communication service for the platform devices, payloads and astronauts [5–7].

Based on the design of network system of space station, the simulation is used to analyze the performance of the network system. Combined with typical working modes, the influence of different data types and data characteristics on network performance is studied, which has certain reference significance for the reasonable and efficient use of network system in orbit.

2 Design of the Network System

The network system of the China Space Station has two main tasks, which are to maintain the normal operation of the spacecraft and to support payload experiments. To accomplish these two tasks, two subnetworks are established in the same system basing on two different technologies. The former uses mature and reliable network technology, which is mainly used to transmit voice, video and other important function data related to spacecraft and astronauts. The latter uses more efficient and advanced network technology with higher transmission rate, mainly for the transmission of experimental data.

The two subnetworks have the same topology and adopt the configuration mode of "backbone layer + access layer". Each subnetwork in every module is configured with one backbone switch and multiple access switches. The backbone switch is mainly used for the access of network terminals which need high-rate transmission and the data transmission between modules. Access switches are mainly used to support medium-rate or low-rate network terminals, such as cameras, mobile phones, laptops and environmental monitoring devices.

The backbone switch is connected to the access switches through Gigabit optical fiber links, and access switches are connected to terminals through 100 Mbps cables. According to the design of the space station, the network model of the core module is established as shown in Fig. 1.

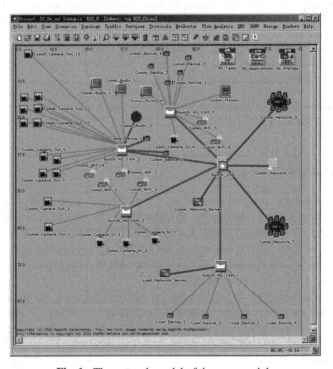

Fig. 1. The network model of the core module

3 Data Source Modeling

According to the data types and data source characteristics of the network system, an accurate business model is built, and the process is as follow:

- Define different application types;
- Define different working modes with defined application types;
- Configure the server with the different working modes defined;
- Configure the behavior of client users based on the services provided by the server.

   There are four kinds of typical network data sources, namely, the video data inside and outside the cabin, the voice data of the astronauts, the monitoring data or control instructions of the platform devices and the experimental data of the payloads. According to the characteristics and data source types of these network data sources, the models of video data source(SS_Vioce_XXX), voice data source(SS_Video_XXX), UDP data source(SS_UDP_XXX, except for streaming media transmission) and TCP data source (SS_TCP_XXX)are established. The detailed parameters of data source are shown as follows (Fig. 2):

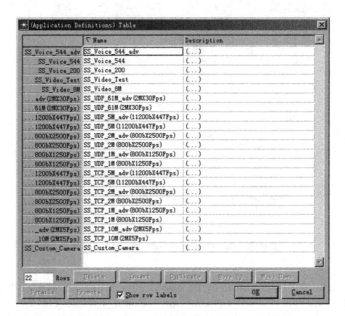

Fig. 2. Network terminal models of space station

4 The Results of Simulation Analysis

4.1 Characteristic Analysis of Video Data

The space station is equipped with 13 video cameras in each module, using the h.264 coding standard, which can generate 8 Mbps video data sent to both ground and onboard monitors. The video data sources have generated data of fixed frame length at a fixed frequency, so the generated data is periodic and the data flow is stable.

The cameras and monitors are connected to the access switches through a 100 Mbps link, and the access switches are connected to the backbone switch through a Gigabit link. The network topology is shown in Fig. 3.

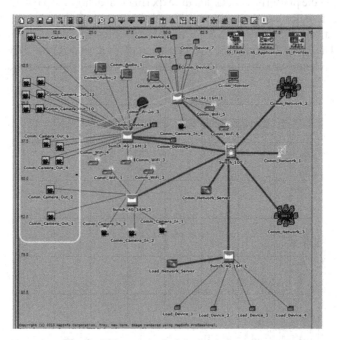

Fig. 3. Video transmission simulation scene

The standard displaying mode of the space station is that the monitor displays four videos at the same time. Comm_Camera_Out_3–Comm_Camera_Out_6 are selected as the data sources displayed on the monitor Comm_Monitor in the simulation. Cameras 3 to 6 each send 8.284 Mbps video data (including 8 Mbps application data and 0.284 Mbps protocol overhead) to access switch Switch_4G_16M_2, as shown in Fig. 4 and Fig. 5.

It also shows the control data received by the cameras, which is used to maintain and control the state of the camera, and is characterized by small amount of data, sudden

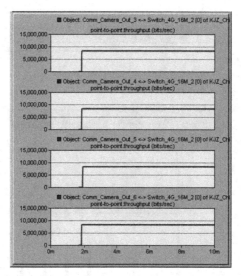

Fig. 4. The characteristics of video data sent/received by each camera

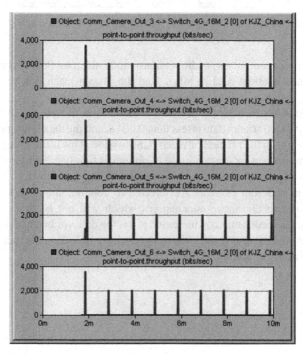

Fig. 5. The characteristics of control data sent/received by each camera

occurrence and periodicity. Because link bandwidth is sufficient, and each transmission link is independent, the transmission of control data has little impact on network performance.

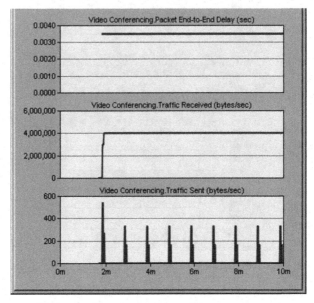

Fig. 6. The characteristics of the data received and sent by the monitor (4 cameras)

The simulation results show, at the standard mode, the total flow of the four cameras after convergence is about 33.136 Mbps, and the flow of each link is stable without congestion.

As is shown in Fig. 6, after the protocol overhead is removed, the end-to-end transmission delay of video stream data is less than 0.004 s, and the data flow and transmission delay hardly change in the process of video transmission. This is the result of using UDP for data transmission under the condition of abundant link bandwidth, which can meet the demand of video transmission with high real-time requirements.

Another four different cameras are selected to conduct simulation again, and the results are similar to the above conclusions, which will not be described here. The number of cameras is continuously increased to 11, the data volume of each link remains basically stable, and the end-to-end transmission delay of video data increases linearly, reaching a maximum of about 0.008 s.

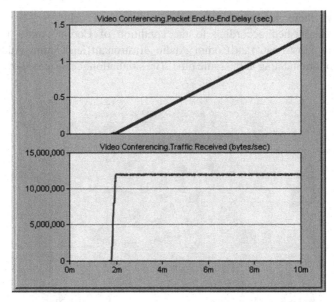

Fig. 7. The characteristics of the data received by the monitor (12 cameras)

When the number of cameras is increased to 12, that is, Comm_Camera_Out_1 to Comm_Camera_Out_12 send video data to access switch Switch_4G_16M_2, the simulation show the traffic reaches the upper limit of the link, and the delay of video data received by the monitor increases linearly and soon reaches the second level, as shown in Fig. 7. It means that the link between the monitor and the switch is congested.

Analysis shows that when UDP is used for simultaneous transmission of multi-channel video data, when the total amount of data does not exceed the link upper limit, the transmission delay of each link is almost the same, and the delay jitter is close to 0. However, with the increase of the amount of data, the transmission delay slowly increases (in the simulation of this report, the delay is still milliseconds). It is recommended that a maximum of 10 channels of video be displayed simultaneously on the station monitor.

4.2 Characteristic Analysis of Voice Data

The voice communication system of space station supports three operating modes:

- Mission mode: A centralized processing mode is adopted to support conference calls between astronauts inside the cabin, astronauts outside the cabin, and ground crew. Video calls between astronauts and the ground can be realized by cooperating with the two-way video communication between the astronauts and the earth,
- Private mode: providing private communication support between astronauts on board and their family members or medical supervisors on the ground,
- Alarm mode: providing voice alarms for astronauts onboard.

Normally, there are three astronauts working in orbit, so the simulation scenario is established according to the condition of Comm_Audio_1(astronaut), Comm_Audio_2(astronaut) and Comm_Audio_4(astronaut) and Comm_Audio_3(voice processor) communicating at the same time. The simulation scenario is shown in Fig. 8.

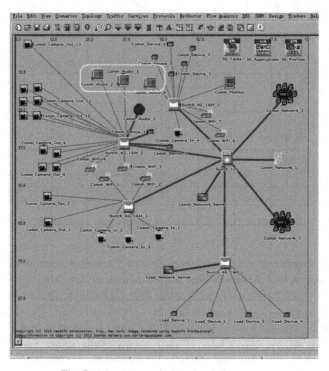

Fig. 8. Vioce transmission simulation scene

Voice data is characterized by small amount of data and large fluctuation of data flow, so the application layer packet length of voice data is (256 + 16) Byte, and the packet period is 4 ms. The size of packets and the time interval generated follow an exponential distribution, which are as shown in Fig. 9.

Because the amount of voice data is far less than the bandwidth of the link, the network will be not congested, and the end-to-end delay of voice data packets transmitted through every link should be similar.

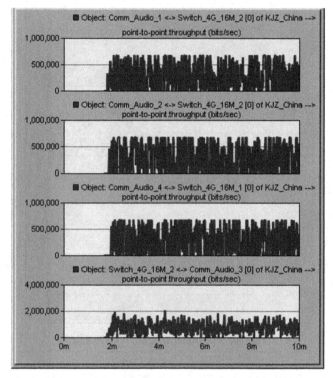

Fig. 9. The network load on each link

In the simulation process, the end-to-end delay of voice is determined by the following formula:

$$T_{\text{end-to-end delay}} = T_{\text{data encoding}} + T_{\text{data decoding}} + T_{\text{network delay}} + T_{\text{processing cycle}}.$$

The encoding delay of voice data is 20 ms, the decoding delay of voice data is 20 ms, the processing cycle delay is 8 ms (4 ms + 4 ms), and the network delay, as shown in Fig. 10, is far less than 1 ms. The end-to-end delays of voice data transmitted by the three voice terminals are basically the same, about 0.048 s, as shown in Fig. 11, which meet the communication requirements.

The end-to-end delay of voice is mainly determined by the encoding and decoding delay of the devices. To shorten the communication delay, we need to improve the encoding and decoding efficiency of the voice terminals, and improve network performance has little impact on shortening the communication delay.

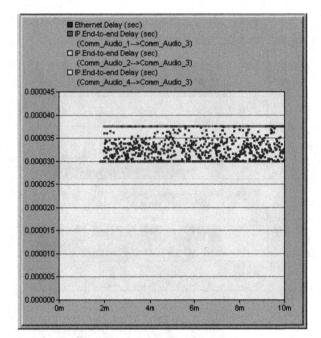

Fig. 10. Transmission delay of voice data

Fig. 11. End-to-end delay of voice data

4.3 Characteristic Analysis of Experimental Data

The network of space station provides high-rate links for payloads. There are various types of payload devices and transmission protocols, and the characteristics of experimental data are changeable. Therefore, the size and interval of experimental data generated by payloads in the simulation are random, and the instantaneous values of the flow vary greatly.

In the simulation, the experimental data generated by the payload Load_Device_1 is sent to the backbone switch Switch_10G through access switch Switch_4G_16M_L, and then to the destination node Comm_Nerwork_1, as shown in Fig. 12.

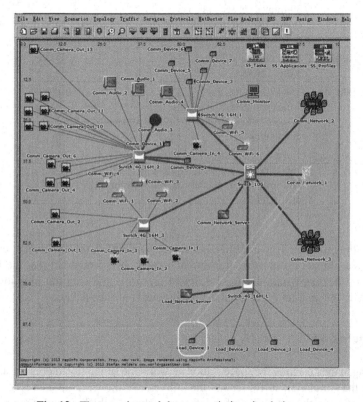

Fig. 12. The experimental data transmission simulation scene

Load_Device_1 generates video data source SS_Video_8M, video test data source SS_Video_Test, UDP data source SS_UDP_61M, UDP data source SS_UDP_61M_adv, TCP data source SS_TCP_10M, and TCP data source SS_TCP_10M_adv and TCP data source SS_TCP_2M_adv, each data source sends data for 10 min.

According to the simulation results, the network transmission delays of different types of data sources are shown in Table 1.

Table 1. The transmission delay OF different data sources

Data Source	Characteristics	Transmission Delay(S)
SS_Video_8M	0.264 Mbit per frame 30 frames per second	0.0015
SS_Video_Test	2.4 Kbit per frame 10 frames per second	0.000007
SS_UDP_61M	2.028 Mbit per frame 30 frames per second	0.011
SS_UDP_61M_adv	2.028 Mbit per frame on average 30 frames per second on average Image size and time interval follow exponential distribution	0–0.28
SS_TCP_10M	Each file is 2 Mbit 5 files per second	0.00065
SS_TCP_10M_adv	The average file size is 2 Mbit 5 files per second on average File size and time interval follow exponential distribution	0–0.0007
SS_TCP_2M_adv	The average file size is 800 bits 2500 files per second on average File sizes and time intervals follow exponential distribution	0.000014

According to Table 1, when different data are transmitted, the characteristics of data have a great impact on network transmission delay. It is suggested that the network terminal of the space station choose different protocols and data transmission modes according to the amount of data and the requirements of time delay.

5   Conclusion

According to the design of the space station network, the simulation model is established by using the simulation software, and the influence of the terminal data type and data characteristics on the network performance is analyzed, which provides reference and basis for the design of network terminal and in orbit management.

References

1. Wang, J., Li, Y., Liu, X., Shen, C., Xiong, K.: Recent active thermal management technologies for the development of energy-optimized aerospace vehicles in China. Chin. J. Aeronaut. **34**(2), 1–27 (2021)
2. Lv, M., Li, X., Li, Y., Zhang, W., Guo, R.: UKF-based state estimation for electrolytic oxygen generation system of space station. Appl. Sci. **11**(5) (2021)

3. Hu, B., Chen, H., Han, L., Yu, H.: Research and ground verification of the force compliance control method for space station manipulator. Int. J. Aerosp. Eng., 1–17 (2020)
4. Lv, Z.: On-orbit maintainability verification technology of space station. Int. J. Performability Eng. 15(1) (2019)
5. Zhang, J.C., Zhu, Y.H., Luo, Y.Z.: Optimization for overall planning of space-station on-orbit activities and logistics. Acta Astronautica 186(2) (2021)
6. Gu, Y., Gao, M., et al.: Space research plan of China's space station. Chin. J. Space Sci. (5), 5 (2016). CNKI:SUN:KJKB.0.2016-05-001
7. Hu, C., Gao, S., Xiong, M.H., et al.: Key technologies of the China space station core module manipulator. Scientia Sinica Technologica 52(9), 1299–1331 (2022)

Design of Information System Management Equipment for Spacecraft Based on System Fault Reconstruction Method

Sun Ben[1](✉), Wang Wei[2], Liang Xiaofeng[1], and Zhang xu[1]

[1] Beijing Institute of Spacecraft System Engineering, Beijing, China
sunben_0315@163.com
[2] Galaxy Aerospace Technology Co., Ltd., Beijing, China

Abstract. Based on system fault reconstruction method, the health detection and diagnosis of information system management equipment is realized by the other equipment of the system. The architecture and software system for information system management equipment and replacement equipment is designed. This method can improve the reliability of spacecraft and save the funds without any increase in cost of additional hardware resources. The re-configurable information system has been applied to the in-orbit flight of manned spacecraft, which can meet the real-time, high reliability and other task requirements, besides providing a reliable guarantee for subsequent fault handling or in-orbit maintenance by astronauts.

Keywords: system fault reconstruction · spacecraft · information system management equipment

1 Introduction

With the continuous development of manned space station mission and deep space exploration mission, high requirements are put forward for the long-term reliable operation of spacecraft in orbit. In order to meet the long-term reliable work requirements, the reliability of spacecraft equipment is improved by selecting high-grade components, enhancing anti-single particle design and adopting internal redundant design. For manned spacecraft, astronauts can also replace the failure equipment through in-orbit maintenance, in order to extend the service life of the spacecraft.

The information system management equipment is the top-level equipment for spacecraft which is responsible for the tasks of command distribution and scheduling, time control, telemetry parameters acquisition, date storage, independent health management. Once a failure of the information system management equipment occurs, it will directly lead to the flight out of control. Especially outside the TT&C area, it will be unable to ensure the safety of the spacecraft in orbit. Therefore, the normal operation of information system management equipment is particularly important for spacecraft. For this kind of equipment, the design of triple module redundancy is generally adopted, and the reliability of the equipment is improved by three module voting.

Although the reliability of the equipment can be improved by the design of internal triple module redundancy, the common cause failure of the three backup modules is still possible. The design complexity and potential defects will be increased due to the excessive internal reliability design [1–4].

Based on system level fault recovery method, the health detection and diagnosis of information system management equipment is realized by the other equipment of the system. When the information system management equipment breaks down, the other equipment can automatically switch the working mode and take over the failure equipment, so as to achieve the basic flight control of the spacecraft.

2 Design of Traditional Information System Management Equipment

Spacecraft information system generally adopts bus design, with consists of multiple 1553B serial data buses connected by several universal computers to complete the control task of spacecraft platform. As the center of data management equipment, information system management equipment completes the RT management of main bus, the uplink and distribution of data and instruction, the framing and downlink of telemetry parameters.

Information system management equipment as the controller of the spacecraft generally improves the reliability by the internal hot backup of three machines [5–8]. The three machines output the working status, and the only voting module in the equipment determines the final status by the two out of three voting mechanism. If the primary machine is not normal, the backup machine will be on duty. This design means the following two problems: (1) the two out of three voting mechanism is based on the high reliability design of voting module in the equipment. The voting module is a single point of failure risk. Once the voting module fails, the voting mechanism will descend into chaos and the equipment will not be able to work normally; (2) Considering the cost of the equipment, it is impossible to realize the backup of all modules in the three machines, which inevitably leads to the common cause failure. Moreover, the design complexity of the equipment often increases with the reliability improved, which means the potential failure risk increases [9, 10].

Existing reliability design can't assure long term reliable operation of equipment. Therefore, it is necessary to solve the problem of serious harm to the spacecraft caused by the failure of the information system management equipment.

3 Design of Information System Management Equipment Based on System Fault Reconstruction

3.1 Architecture Design of Information System Management Equipment

System fault reconstruction techniques require no additional equipment, but select the equipment with basic platform management functions and the hardware interface resources from existing components of spacecraft. Through software fault detection and diagnosis, the operation mode of the equipment can automatic switch to take over control of the platform management, so as to achieve the safe and steady operation of the spacecraft. The substitution equipment for system fault reconstruction is designed with compatible hardware and customized software.

In terms of hardware, the information system management equipment as the system level control equipment communicates with other devices through the bus interface of spacecraft. The replacement equipment is also selected from the equipment connected to the bus network, so that the interconnection and communication with other multiple devices can be realized by the original form. As the same time, the external hardware interface resources need to covering the resources of information system management equipment and providing strong computing capability for itself. Based on the principles, the replacement equipment for fault reconstruction is selected form several terminal equipment in the bus network system.

In terms of software, there are two design modes: normal mode and fault reconstruction mode. When the information system management equipment does not fail, replacement equipment is working in normal mode and achieve the function of technical requirements. In case of the information system management equipment failure, replacement equipment switches to fault reconstruction mode. The replacement equipment in this mode need to complete both the function specified technical requirements and the system management function. The system management function in fault reconstruction mode can be customized according to the task requirement of different spacecrafts. For spacecraft without in-orbit maintenance, software design should try to ensure the complete function coverage of the original information system management, so that the spacecraft can continue to work in the case of failure. For manned spacecraft with in-orbit maintenance, software design can be cut from the function of the original information system management, such as commands control, telemetries acquisition and so on. The replacement equipment can provide support for the stable operation of spacecraft during the period of equipment failure to the maintenance.

3.2 System Fault Reconstruction Design

The system fault reconstruction is realized mainly by the spacecraft autonomous operation, and the telecommand control is supplemented so as to ensure that the spacecraft can still operate safely and switch the working mode seamlessly when the fault occurs outside the TT&C area.

The focus of the system fault reconstruction design is to prevent the replacement equipment switching mistakenly to the fault reconstruction mode under the normal condition of the original equipment. As a result, two management equipment preempt platform resources at the same time. The robustness design of the system should also be improved when implementing the function of fault reconstruction. The design method is as follows.

- In the normal mode, the replacement equipment regularly receive communication command word through the 1553B from the information system management equipment, analysis and determine the status of communication, then returns the response word to the information system management equipment. If the communication of multiple consecutive cycles is unusual, the first is resetting or switching the replacement equipment to eliminate their own faults. If the communication is still abnormal, the replacement equipment will automatically switch to the fault reconstruction mode.

- Delaying for a period after switching to the fault reconstruction mode, the replacement equipment begins to communicate with other equipment. The delay time need to be set greater than that the information system management equipment handles the mistake switch. After the delay time, the replacement equipment automatically sends power off instruction to the information system management equipment.

- The information system management equipment receives the response word regularly. If the information system management equipment doesn't receive the response word for multiple consecutive cycles, at the same time communicates with other equipment normally, it is considered to be dis-operation of the replacement equipment switching to fault reconstruction mode.

After the fault handling of the information system management equipment is completed, it is necessary to restore the working mode. The replacement equipment can be switched back to the normal mode, and then the information system management can be powered on by telecommand in the TT&C area.

3.3 Software System Design

As shown in Fig. 1, the equipment whose hardware resources meet the requirements is selected from the 1553B network of spacecraft platform as the replacement equipment. The software system for information system management equipment and replacement equipment is designed with the system fault reconstruction.

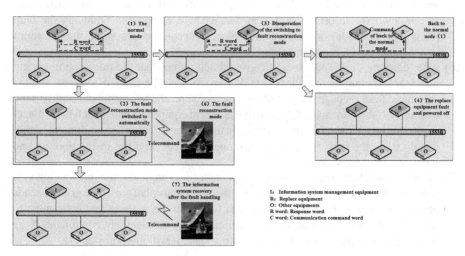

Fig. 1. The software system design of the system fault reconstruction.

(1) In normal working mode, the information system management equipment regularly sends communication command words to the replacement equipment, and the

replacement equipment returns to the status response words after receiving and parsing correctly. Both the information system management equipment and the replacement equipment continue to judge the correctness of the received information and take it as the condition of mode switching;

(2) If the replacement equipment determines that the received communication command word is abnormal or no received message for several consecutive cycles, it will reset and cut over backup machine automatically. If the communication is still abnormal, it will switch from the normal working mode to the fault reconstruction mode and start timing waiting. If the timing exceeds the set value, it will jump to step (5);

(3) When the replacement equipment switches to the fault reconstruction mode and timing waiting, if the information system management equipment still sends the communication command word to the replacement equipment normally, and determines that the communication with other 1553B network terminal equipment is normal, but can't receive the status response word from the replacement equipment for several consecutive cycles, the replacement equipment is considered to be abnormal fault reconstruction mode. Then the information system management equipment sends command of back to normal working mode to the replacement equipment automatically. If the replacement equipment returns to normal mode, it will jump to step (1); otherwise, go to step (4);

(4) After sending command of back to normal working mode, if the information system equipment still can't receive response word from replacement equipment, it will send command of power off the replacement equipment automatically; wait for entering TT&C area to handle failure by telecomand. If the replacement equipment returns to normal and then be powered up, it will jump to step (1);

(5) If the replacement equipment determines that the information system breaks down and undertakes the control duty of the spacecraft platform, it will send instruction to power off the information system management equipment. Officially the fault reconstruction mode is started and the replacement equipment controls the spacecraft in accordance with established function.

(6) After entering the TT&C area, the ground determines that the information system management equipment fault occurs. If step (5) is not performed correctly and the automatic fault reconstruction fails on the indicator, the telecommand will be send to power off the information system management equipment and switch the replacement equipment to the fault reconstruction mode. The replacement equipment immediately starts the fault reconstruction mode after receiving the instruction, and no longer timing and waiting.

(7) After the fault handling or in-orbit maintenance is completed, the information system management equipment can access the spacecraft platform. The ground sends instructions in idle time and TT&C area to switch the replacement equipment to normal mode, and power up the information system management equipment. If the information system back to normal working state, it will jump to step (1).

4 Summary

The re-configurable information system has been applied to the in-orbit flight of manned spacecraft, which can meet the real-time, high reliability and other task requirements. This method can improve the reliability of spacecraft and save the funds without any increase in cost of additional hardware resources. This method doesn't depend on TT&C conditions to ensure the independent disposal of fault, and doesn't need to change the physical connection between equipments, only involves software design of information system management equipment and replacement equipment. The other equipments are not affected. This method is easy to implement and effectively control the scope of operation.

Through this design method, the spacecraft can keep in a safe and stable flight state besides providing a reliable guarantee for subsequent fault handling or in-orbit maintenance by astronauts.

References

1. Yang, M.F., Guo, S.H.L., Sun, Z.Q.: On-board computer techniques for spacecraft control. Aerosp. Control **23**(2), 64–650 (2005). (in Chinese)
2. Zahid, S., Ayyaz, N.: An economical on-board computer for low-earth-orbit satellites. In: International Astronautical Federation - 55th International Astronautical Congress, vol. 1, pp. 15–21 (2004)
3. Zhao, D., Xu, G.D., Llu, Y., et al.: Application of reconfigurable computing technique in aerospace and design of OBC **30**(5), 1486–1490 (2010). (in Chinese)
4. Shibayama, N., Akazawa, N., Koyama, M., Miyagawa, S., et al.: Space verification of on-board computer integrated with commercial IC. Mitsubishi Heavy Industry Ltd. Tech. Rev. **42**(5), 1–5 (2005)
5. Wang, X.-s., Sun, H.-x., Xu, G.-d., Tong, Z.-h.: Study on the on-board computer system based on ARM processor. J. Beijing Univ. Posts Telecommun. **28**(04), 23–26 (2005). (in Chinese)
6. Yang, Y., Wei, X., et al.: The application of the latest FPGA series in on-board embedded computer. Aerospace Shanghai **2**, 47–50 (2005)
7. Sun, Z.H.W., Liu, Y., Xu, G.D., et al.: Multi-processor reconfigurable on-board computer for small satellite and small launch vehicle **31**(4), 770–777 (2010). (in Chinese)
8. Ren, X.X.: Researches on Architecture of Highly Reliable On-Board Computing System Based on Reconfigurable Computing. Hunan University, Changsha (2007). (in Chinese)
9. Luo, Y., Li, R., Xiong, S.: Research and application of FPGA based on reconfigurable system. Comput. Meas. Control **13**(8), 824–826 (2005). (in Chinese)
10. Lysaght, P., Subrahmanyam, P.A.: Advances in configurable computing. IEEE Des. Test Comput. **22**(2), 85–89 (2005)

Training Practice of High-Level Specialty Group Intelligent Construction Talents Based on the Integration of Post, Course, Competition and Certificate

Chengjiang Lu[✉], Xiangmei Zhang, and Zhen Li

School of Architecture and Civil Engineering, Guangdong Polytechnic of Science and Technology, Zhuhai, China
hitlucj@163.com

Abstract. According to characteristics of the specialty group of architectural decoration engineering technology, the talent training mode called "integration of courses, certificates, abilities and standards" for intelligent construction based on (Building Information Model) BIM was proposed in this paper. Referring to professional qualification standards and requirements for professional positions, the curriculum system and teaching content were reformed, the curriculum standards highlighting the cultivation of professional ability were established, the basic requirements of curriculum teaching were standardized, the integration of "Post, Course, Competition and Certificate" was accomplished by building a curriculum practice system in and out of school conducive to the development of students' personality, and comprehensively implement the talent training target.

Keywords: Specialty Group · Intelligent Construction · BIM · Prefabricated Buildings

1 Introduction

1.1 Requirements for Professional Positions

The Party's 20th National Congress proposed: "Accelerate the construction of digital China." Accelerate the development of the digital economy, promote the deep integration of the digital economy and the real economy, and build a digital industrial cluster with international competitiveness." The outline of the national "14th Five-Year Plan" puts forward: "Develop intelligent construction, promote green building materials, prefabricated buildings and steel structure houses, and build low-carbon cities." From the above national strategies and national policies, we can see that China is fully accelerating the transformation to the digital era, the digital era of digital China's digital economy, digital industry have clearly put forward the requirements of accelerating development and strengthening construction, intelligent construction, digital transformation and smart city construction has also become the future transformation and upgrading of the construction industry.

W. Hong and G. Kanaparan (Eds.): ICCSE 2023, CCIS 2025, pp. 150–157, 2024.
https://doi.org/10.1007/978-981-97-0737-9_15

The vigorous promotion of prefabricated buildings and integrated decoration puts forward higher requirements for professional technicians in the front line of production and management. They not only need to master new technologies, new processes and new materials, and be able to use modern means and methods for engineering construction and management, but also have strong practical ability and post adaptability. It brings new challenges to the training of application-oriented and compound technical talents in the construction industry. Therefore, the specialty group needs to further optimize the professional construction within the group, highlight the cross and integrated development of various majors, adapt to the supporting role of various majors on the industrial chain under new technologies, new codes and new requirements, and promote the reform, construction and development of the specialty group.

2 Characteristics of Specialty Group

According to "construction plan of high-level higher vocational schools and majors with Chinese characteristics" declared to the Ministry of education, the school will accurately connect the advanced manufacturing industry, strategic emerging industries and modern service industry in Guangdong-Hong Kong-Macao Bay Area during the 14th Five Year Plan period, optimize the specialty layout, build a "2 peak and 8 characteristics" specialty group, and closely follow the development trend of industrial digitization and digital industrialization based on the specialty advantages of new generation information technology and intelligent manufacturing, Focus on building two peak specialty groups of software technology and industrial robot technology, drive the coordinated development of eight characteristic specialty groups of mechanical design and manufacturing, architectural decoration engineering technology, e-commerce, art design, tourism management, accounting, secretary, sports operation and management, and carry out "digital +" transformation of traditional majors and new emerging majors, so as to realize the all-round integration of talent training supply side and industrial demand side structure. The Specialty group is Guangdong High-level Specialty Group of Higher Vocational Colleges.

The specialty group aims at the characteristics of digital science and technology, which is in line with the school's running orientation. It aims at the development requirements of "digital economy". Through the construction of "double high plan", it serves the transformation and upgrading of the whole industrial chain of construction, improves quality and efficiency, fully integrates the talent supply side and industrial demand side, highlights the integration of professional quality and whole process education, draws lessons from international standards, comprehensively analyzes the knowledge and ability system of various majors, and gathers courses various teaching resources and teaching activity elements such as practice teaching base and innovation platform, optimize the form of interdisciplinary teaching organization, transform the traditional majors in the group, develop new majors and adjust the structure of the professional group through "New Technology +" and "Information Technology +", so as to focus on Building Decoration Engineering technology specialty group into a domestic leading high-level specialty group with Chinese characteristics, which conform with the school's orientation.

The specialties in the group are closely connected with the cutting-edge systems of contemporary construction industry (such as BIM, Assembly, etc.), implement the advanced industrial concepts (such as Green Building, Environmental Protection Building Materials, Energy Conservation Design, Ecological Environment, etc.), and comply with the national strategies of national artificial intelligence, big data and advanced manufacturing (such as Intelligent Design, Intelligent Processing, Big Data Platform for Building Environment and Energy Consumption Monitoring, building intelligent technology, etc.), Based on the concept of BLM (building lifecycle management), integrate building decoration engineering technology, building design, building engineering technology, engineering cost and property management, establish a specialty group, correspond to the professional skill requirements of the four stages of planning, design, construction and operation in the construction process of the project, and build a systematic talent training platform connecting all links. Adopt the talent training mode combining education and training, and use the "BIM +" technology to organically combine the industrial chain, technology chain, talent chain and innovation chain of architectural decoration engineering, so as to create a high-quality construction talent training highland, cultivate the technical and skilled talents in short supply in the frontline construction industry, serve the economic development of Guangdong-Hong Kong-Macao Greater Bay Area and lead the reform of Construction Vocational Education (Fig. 1).

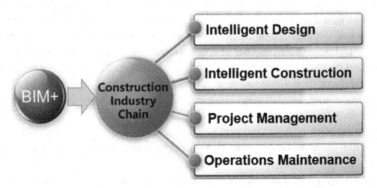

Fig. 1. Key links of specialty group docking construction industry chain

3   Talent Training Mode

3.1   Talent Training Mode of Specialty Group

According to the specialty characteristics of lean construction and taking "building integration - digital design - prefabricated decoration- intelligence maintenance" as the main line, the specialty group of architectural decoration engineering technology constructs the innovation of "integration of courses and certificates and ability standard" of prefabricated building integration based on information technology.

3.2 Concept of Talent Training

Build a talent training concept of "integration of work and learning, equal emphasis on morality and technology, integration of innovation and entrepreneurship, and sustainable development".

The specialty group of architectural decoration engineering technology closely connects with the upgrading of the construction industry, deepens the comprehensive reform of education, and further introduces the concepts of "encouraging innovation, supporting entrepreneurship, promoting training through competition, promoting learning through competition, combining education and training, and combining morality and technology" (Fig. 2), so as to promote the development of the field of architectural decoration engineering technology industry in a green, intelligent and advanced direction, Strive to build a world-class international and high-level professional group with Chinese characteristics.

Fig. 2. Talent training concept of specialty group

4 Implementation Measures of Talent Training

4.1 Learning Platforms and Modules

Connect with posts, pay equal attention to morality and technology, cooperate with schools and enterprises, and build three learning platforms of quality, specialty and practice. Cultivate high-quality and high skilled double high talents with professional ability, innovation ability, sustainable development ability and international vision through five learning modules: Five Education Integration, General Ability, Documentary Certificate Integration, Post Core and Academic Degree Further Study (Fig. 3).

Fig. 3. Three learning platforms and five learning modules

4.2 Post, Course, Competition and Certificate

Post Docking: The course content is determined based on the needs of post ability, the teaching project is designed based on typical work tasks, and the competition project is integrated into the practical project. At the same time, the evaluation criteria of the competition are integrated into the evaluation criteria of practical skills, so as to achieve the integration of the course competition. Through the analysis of the vocational skill certificate system, the vocational skill standard is integrated into the curriculum standard, and the certificate evaluation standard into the teaching evaluation standard.

Core Course: We will carry out in-depth cooperation between schools and enterprises, and jointly discuss and determine the prefabricated building curriculum with industry and enterprise experts; Build a prefabricated building teaching resource library, realize the integrated teaching of prefabricated building design, manufacturing and construction digital construction, carry out offline teaching practice with project-based teaching method in classroom teaching, and continuously improve the teaching design process of such courses (Fig. 4).

Competition and Certificate Assistance: The specialty group has successfully applied for four "X" certificates, including Building Information Model (BIM), Building Engineering Mapping, Geographic Information Data Acquisition and Processing, and Engineering Cost Digital Application. It has completed more than 2000 training and evaluation tasks. We have continuously participated in professional skills competitions such as geospatial information collection and processing, intelligent construction of prefabricated buildings, digital construction of building decoration, digital measurement and pricing of construction projects, construction engineering drawing recognition, and modeling and application of building information models, and have won awards.

College-Enterprise Cooperation: We build training bases outside the school with well-known enterprises. For example, "GPST and Glodon Software" digital construction decoration Industry College and Guangdong prefabricated building Technology Industry

Fig. 4. Schematic diagram of core competencies of talent training

College. The total number of off campus training bases of this major has reached more than 60, which can provide nearly 1000 construction internships for this major (Fig. 5).

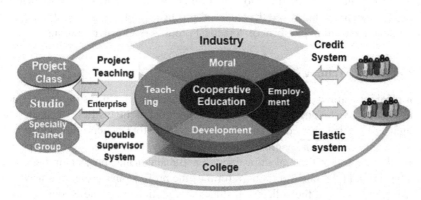

Fig. 5. Schematic diagram of cooperative education of college and enterprise

The Integration of Post, Course, Competition and Certificate should be led by post requirements, and the course content should be determined based on position needs. Teaching projects are designed based on typical work tasks, integrating competition projects into practical projects, and integrating competition evaluation standards into practical skill evaluation standards to achieve the integration of courses and competitions. By analyzing the vocational skills certificate system, the vocational skills standards are integrated into the curriculum standards, and the certificate evaluation standards are integrated into the teaching evaluation standards. Ultimately, the quality of talent cultivation will be further improved through feedback from enterprises on talent.

5 Achievements of Talent Training

5.1 Classroom, Studio, Entrepreneurial Company

The specialty group has established a design studio for students majoring in decoration. Through cooperation with enterprises and "Taobao" and other online platforms, it undertakes real projects such as interior decoration construction drawings, effect drawings and furniture modeling. Through the combination of school enterprise dual platforms, professional learning and project practice, it greatly improves students' professional skills and innovation ability 182 awards have been won in various competitions above the provincial level, such as the national comprehensive decoration skills competition, the national digital art works competition of colleges and universities, the national excellent graduation design works competition of architectural design major in higher vocational education, etc. Relying on the studio to create a practical platform, we successfully incubated the entrepreneurial team of the professional group, combined teaching and practical projects through "classroom" + "studio" + "entrepreneurial company", and used the online and offline platform to transform "what we have learned" into "what we have used", effectively improved the students' practical level, and successfully created a collaborative education platform of "practical projects + Creative Training".

5.2 Innovative Training Base

The original infrastructure department had been renamed as the infrastructure engineering management center and put it under the management of the Institute of construction and engineering. It has created an innovative training base for teachers and students of the Institute of construction and engineering to give full play to the expertise of the specialty group and make use of the real infrastructure and maintenance projects in the school, which has brought the talent training reform of the professional group to a new level. Professional teachers of the college led students to participate in the whole process of design scheme, construction drawing review, decoration design, construction measurement, project budget and project acceptance. We have truly realized that the classroom enters the construction site, learning and training are synchronized, the combination of work and learning is fully implemented, and an open, practical and professional teaching process is realized. From 2017 to 2023, combined with the school's infrastructure construction, it has trained the teaching staff and improved the quality of talent training.

5.3 Match and Create Achievements

The specialty group implements the teaching mode of "promoting training through competition, promoting learning through competition and combining education and training", actively mobilize learning enthusiasm and initiative, consolidate professional skills, deeply cultivate professional quality, improve the spirit of unity, cooperation and innovation, so as to continuously improve the training quality of professional talents. The students of this professional group have won more than 200 awards in various vocational skills competitions such as "BIM application skills competition", "intelligent construction and management innovation competition", "architectural engineering drawing recognition", "Application of architectural decoration technology", "Luban cup drawing recognition" and "engineering measurement skills". The quality of talent training is good, the social recognition is high, and the enrollment and employment are booming.

In terms of innovation and entrepreneurship, the specialty group "encourages innovation and supports entrepreneurship". Taking the competition as an opportunity, relying on entrepreneurial associations and taking the studio as the starting point, we encourage students to carry out diversified entrepreneurial attempts. So far, it has successfully incubated a number of entrepreneurial entities.

6 Conclusion

According to characteristics of the specialty group of architectural decoration engineering technology, the talent training mode called "integration of courses, certificates, abilities and standards" for intelligent construction based on (Building Information Model) BIM was proposed in this paper.

Through the development of specialty group, the college will be built into a talent training base dedicated to the rejuvenation of the country, keeping up with the national digital economy strategy, integrating into the construction digital industry upgrading, and the complete industrial chain, so as to supply high-quality talents for the whole industrial chain.

Acknowledgment. This work has been supported by Guangdong Province Education Science Planning Project (Higher Education) "Research on the cultivation of high-level specialty group intelligent construction talents under the Integration of Post, Course, Competition and Certificate" (2023GXJK745).

References

1. Ding, L.: Intelligent construction drives the transformation of the construction industry. China Constr. News (008) (2019)
2. Niu, Y., Lu, W., Chen, K.: Smart construction objects. J. Comput. Civil Eng. **30**(4), 04015070 (2016)
3. Eadie, R., Browne, M., Odeyinka, H.: BIM implementation throughout the UK construction project lifecycle: an analysis. Autom. Constr. **36**, 145–151 (2013)
4. Lu, C., Peng, X.: Improving the management level of teaching quality and training the first-class skilled talents. In: ICCSE 2019, pp. 588–593, Toronto, Canada (2019)
5. Lu, C., Huang, H., Peng, X.: Practice of specialty group construction based on information technology. In: ICCSE 2021, pp. 1002–1005, Lancaster, United Kingdom (2021)
6. Lu, C., Huang, H., Peng, X.: Practice on integrated curriculum system of prefabricated building based on X-certificate. In: ICCSE 2022, pp. 83–92, Ningbo, China (2022)
7. Ge, S.: Research on integrated informatization teaching mode of university public architecture design principle course based on OBE concept. Anhui Archit. **29**(1), 104–106 (2022)
8. Lin, J.: Exploration and practice of BIM talent training for civil engineering majors in higher vocational education under the background of intelligent construction. HeBei Vocat. Educ. **5**(06), 27–31 (2021)
9. Zhu, J.: Research on the curriculum reform and practice of intelligent construction technology in higher vocational education based on the background of "digitalization." Mod. Bus. Trade Ind. **43**(18), 245–246 (2022)

A Study on the Application of Web-Based Tools in the Cultivation of Translation-Related Search and Verification Competence in the Big Data Era

Yingyi Zhong and Jingjing Lin[✉]

NingboTech University, Ningbo, China
hnljj@nbt.edu.cn

Abstract. This paper discusses the definition and cultivation of translation-related search and verification competence in the big data era. Three translation competence models are introduced to clarify the definition of translation-related search and verification competence, i.e., the PACTE Group, Transcomp Group and EMT Group. After providing some web-based tools for translation verification, this paper analyzes how they are applied in translation. It proves that they effectively guarantee the accurate translation of proper nouns, culture-loaded words, phrase collocation and quoted information in Chinese-English translation. This paper's findings shed light on the cultivation of translation-related search and verification competence by improving translators' strategic competence, technical skills and advanced reading capability.

Keywords: Translation-related Search and Verification Competence · Web-based Tools · Big Data · Chinese-English Translation · Translation Competence

1 Introduction

The big data era, characterized by an explosive growth of global data and a continuous emergence of information technology, has had a tremendous impact on translation industry. Translation in the big data era is no longer simply the result of manual translation or machine translation, but a complex process of pre-translation, manual-verification, post-editing and re-integration. Machine translation has unparalleled advantages in the speed and scale of translation, but the accuracy and quality of translation is often unsatisfactory, especially in the translation of creative texts, expressive texts and new terminology [1]. Therefore, it is important to cultivate translators' competence in translation-related search and verification, which requires them to redetermine the translation by screening, analyzing and reorganizing information with the help of information tools, only in this way can translation accuracy and translators' core competitiveness be truly improved.

In fact, the translation-related search and verification competence is not a newly emerging thing, as it is embodied in various famous translation competence models and has been enriched with the development of the Internet and information technology. As early as 2003, the PACTE Group has put forward the translation competence model including strategic sub-competence, bilingual sub-competence, extra-linguistic sub-competence, instrumental sub-competence as well as knowledge about translation sub-competence [2]. In 2009, the translation competence model proposed by Transcomp Group is composed of strategic competence motivation, communicative competence in at least 2 languages, tools and research competence, translation routine activation competence, psycho-motor competence and domain competence [3], while the translation competence model of EMT Group is composed of language competence, thematic competence, technological competence, info-mining competence, intercultural competence, and translation service provision competence [4]. Although these translation competence models emphasize on different perspectives, the sub-competence like tools application capability, information mining skills and strategic competence are all mentioned. Thus, translation-related search and verification can be regarded as a comprehensive process based on the three translation competence models, covering strategic competence, information-seeking competence and tools application competence, during which translators are required to recognize the problem, conduct the search and evaluate the result before making the translation decision.

Based on this, in the era of big data, the factors that have alternated the connotation of translation-related search and verification mainly reflect in two perspectives, namely the development of translation technology as well as the changing of the reading media. On the one hand, web-based resources such as electronic encyclopedias, online corpora, search engines and databases offered by the big data era serve as large storage stations of Internet data sets, which provide a vast array of resources and materials for translation-related search and verification [5]. On the other hand, however, considering the online reading environment, it seems that digital reading has no advantage over paper-based reading in terms of reading speed and deep comprehension [6]. Given that the inclusion of information technology is inevitable in the cultivation of translation verification competence in the digital age, it is not only necessary to improve translators' competence in using web-based resources for information retrieval, but also to improve their competence to read and analyze literature materials within the digital context.

2 Web-Based Tools for Translation-Related Search and Verification

2.1 Corpora

Corpora mainly refer to written texts or discourse records kept in electronic form, which could provide verification reference for language hypothesis, assist in the translation of idiomatic target texts, help translators grasp the style of the original text, and realize the unity of context in word selection and style, so as to determine the accuracy and standardization of the translation to the greatest extent. If classified by the number of languages involved in the corpora, they can be divided into monolingual corpora, bilingual corpora and multilingual corpora.

Monolingual corpora are collections of relevant corpora created according to a specific subject or topic, mainly including large general language corpora, newspaper corpora and corpora for language learning. Widely used English monolingual Corpora are shown in Table 1. Bilingual corpora can be divided into bilingual parallel corpora and bilingual comparable corpora. The former one consists of the original text of the source language and the translated text of the target language, in which the original text and translated one show a one-way correspondence, while the latter one refers to corpora that collect the relevant texts of the two languages with reference to specific themes, types and other categories.

Table 1. Widely-used English monolingual corpora

Corpus	Website
American National Corpus	http://www.anc.org/
Corpus of Contemporary American English	https://www.english-corpora.org/coc a/
British National Corpus	http://www.natcorp.ox.ac.uk/
WebCorp	http://www.webcorp.org.uk/live/
English Corpora	https://www.english-corpora.org/

2.2 Term Extraction Tools

It is always time-consuming to look up for translations of terms in dictionaries, while the version provided by which could be inaccurate. Therefore, translators might refer to term extraction tools to create their own terminology bank of specific text. With the help of the automatic translation function of CAT tools, professional terms, proper nouns, as well as some cultural specific words could be translated automatically with the specific terminology bank, which could greatly reduce the repetitive work of translators. Popular term extraction tools worth mentioning include SDL MultiTerm, SynchroTerm and VocabGrabber, as well as the term extraction tools included in CAT tools like MemoQ, DéjàVu and Wordfast.

2.3 Encyclopedias

Commonly used encyclopedias have already become computer-based such as Wikipedia and Scholarpedia, which play an important role in equipping translators with extra-linguistic knowledge. For one thing, encyclopedias contain a large number of entries about a particular civilization, which can provide translators with parallel texts containing idiomatic expression. For another, when translators encounter unfamiliar words of the source language, they can refer to encyclopedias to gain a better understanding of the background knowledge as well as the meaning of the words before making translation choices.

2.4 The Search Engine

Popular search engines mainly include Baidu Search, Bing Search and Google Search. Among them, Google is one of the best multilingual search engines in the world. It provides queries on Web pages, images, news information and other resources. Also, we can browse web pages by searching subject words. Search engines can not only assist in the translation of professional terms and parallel texts, but also assist in the translation of proper nouns such as people names, organization names and place names.

A variety of advanced retrieval grammars could help with the effective use of search engines, including Boolean operators, proximity search, phrase search, truncation search, etc., while logical search symbols "and", "or" and "-" as well as location operators "with", "near" and "same" are also worth mentioning [7]. Besides, using English double quotation marks for retrieval can ensure the continuous occurrence of the target search words in the search results. Moreover, advanced search commands such as site, filetype, and define can limit search results to specific websites, certain file types, and pages containing keyword definitions. For instance, if we want to learn about the background, event process and other relevant information of Tin loan, we could either enter "华锡借款" filetype: pdf or "tin loan" filetype: pdf in the Google search bar to obtain Chinese and English PDF files about Tin loan.

2.5 Internet Archives

In the era of big data, many historical documents and references disappear with the update and iteration of network information, which has also become a major reason why relevant historical materials cannot be found in the verification process. Therefore, Internet archives come into being, which plays an important role in preserving historical literature resources. Among them, the Internet Archive (IA) is the most famous. By 2021, the website has saved more than 538 billion web pages and page snapshots, as well as more than 60 petabytes of free books, movies, software music and other resources, whose preserved documents have the longest history, the widest scope and the most perfect content [8]. In addition to the Internet Archive, popular English Internet archives providing numerous resources for translation verification are shown in Table 2.

Table 2. Popular English Internet archives

Nation	Name	Content
America	Web Citation	Websites of America
America	Library of Michigan Digital Collection	Michigan materials
America	Congressional & Federal Government Web Harvests	Websites of American Congress and federal government
Britain	UK Web Archive	Websites of Britain
Britain	National Digital Archive of Datasets	Digital information of governmental information
Canada	The Government of Canada Web Archive	Websites of Canadian federal government

3   The Application of Web-Based Tools in Translation-Related Search and Verification in Chinese-English Translation

3.1   Translation of Proper Nouns

Inevitably, translators will encounter a large number of names, titles, organization names, place names, terms and other proper nouns. Although *Scheme of the Chinese Phonetic Alphabets* (In 1958) and *Transformation Guidelines of Geographical Names from Foreign Languages into Chinese-English* (GB/T17693. 1–2008) have been put forward by the state as the translation standards, many translated names are originally written in English or other languages, which means that the translator is doing secondary translation. If we only rely on the appendix of dictionaries for the translation of proper nouns, it is easy to lead to anomie and errors in translation.

Names of People
The purpose of the verification of foreign dignitaries' names is to ensure the consistency of names and their identity. When we translate the names of those famous Western historical figures, it is easy for us to find out their full name. However, in the face of unfamiliar historical figures, we'll need to enter "name (in Chinese) + identity (in English)" into the search box to make a limitation of them, so as to improve the search efficiency [9]. This kind of searching method is especially suitable for the translation of foreign names that seem to be Chinese names, such as "杨格", "魏德迈" and "白修德". For example, only when we enter "杨格 consultant" into the search box can we find out some news and reports of *fabi* reform and the full name of the American consultant as "Arther N. Young", rather than "Arther Young" or "Kenneth Younger".

Titles of People
In Chinese-English translation, the same Chinese title may have different English version in different countries and different historical periods. Thus, we should not equate the Chinese title with one corresponding English translation, otherwise it will lead to the misunderstanding of the character's identity. On the one hand, we may refer to relevant databases to look for the address of the title in the specific historical period. For instance, as we know that Chiang Kai Shek played an important role in the development of China-U.S. relations, we searched for the records of him in FRUS and found that he was called "generalissimo". We could therefore determine that his title "委员长" should be translated as "generalissimo" rather than "leader" or "commissioner" provided by dictionaries. On the other hand, we may consult Wikipedia for the meaning of each translation and make a comparison of them before the final choice is made. For instance, as "州长" could be translated as "governor" and "chief magistrate", we further our search in Wikipedia and find that the former one is defined as "an administrative leader and head of a political region, ranking under the head of state", while the latter is defined as "a public official, executive or judicial, whose office is the highest in its class". Based on the interpretation provided by Wikipedia, "州长" in America should be translated as "governor".

Names of Organizations
Due to different functions of institutions and cultural differences, the English versions of institutions with the same Chinese name in different countries are different. Therefore, translation should be done with reference to specific cultural backgrounds and the functions of the institution. For example, the State Council of China refers to the Central government of the People's Republic of China, while the State Department of the United States is the Foreign Ministry of the United States government. This is the reason why " 国务院" is translated into "State Council" in China and is translated into "State Department" in America. The United Nations Terminology Database (UNTERM) contains the translation of various national institutions and their scope of use, which would help to eliminate our confusion and make rational translation choices.

3.2 Translation of Culture-Loaded Words

In Chinese-English translation, culture-loaded words mainly include idioms, words reflecting historical events, classical Chinese, etc., representing distinctive characteristics of specific times and regions, as well as the unique concept of a culture. According to Peter Newmark, "most 'cultural' words are easy to detect, since they are associated with a particular language and cannot be literally translated, but many cultural customs are described in ordinary language, where literal translation would distort the meaning and a translation may include an appropriate descriptive-functional equivalent [10]". For such expressions with Chinese cultural images and classical Chinese characteristics, the translator will go through three processes in translation, namely understanding, transforming and expressing [11]. He should not only ensure the consistency of the meaning of the source language and the target language, but should also ensure the high consistency of the two in artistic rhetoric, emotional connotation and so on.

Idioms
When translating Chinese idioms, translators should first consult encyclopedia and historical literature to understand the connotation beyond the linguistic meaning such as religion, history, folk customs, common sense, mood and style, and adopt free translation on the basis of understanding the target language. Then the translator should check the candidate text of the target language with the help of an encyclopedia, so as to polish the wording of the initial translated text.

For example, the Chinese idiom "水到渠成, 瓜熟蒂落" means that when all the conditions are met, people will naturally succeed. When free translation is adopted to translate this idiom, it would be translated as "A canal is formed when water comes", "When conditions are ripe, success will come", "Everything comes naturally at the right time", "It's just a matter of course". The "canal" and "water" in the first translation have displayed the cultural images in the idiom to a certain extent, but considering the purpose of the original text is to convey objective information instead of spreading culture, this translation version should not be adopted. The second and the third versions undoubtedly achieve the equivalence of meaning between the original text and the translated text, but they appear to be lengthy, and there is a suspicion of the Chinglish of these versions. So, the fourth version is chosen as the candidate for the final translated version. In order to make sure that this expression is consistent with the meaning of the original Chinese text, Wikipedia is further consulted. The relevant definitions of this expression "when you say that something is just a matter of course, you mean that it is certain to happen at some time in the future" could be found, demonstrating that "it's just a matter of course" has the same meaning as "水到渠成, 瓜熟蒂落".

Historical Words

Historical words, referring to those words closely related to specific historical events, representing the policy, social background and common values of a certain era. In order to ensure that the translation of historical words could fully display the connotation of the events and conform to the English expression of the specific era, translators should make a consultation to parallel texts, which could be of great help for a deeper understanding of the source language and the verification of the idiomaticity of the target language.

As Wikipedia contains a large number of texts covering history, politics, anthropology and other academic fields, it could serve as an important source of providing parallel texts of specific historical events for translators. For instance, only by referring to the translation version of "独尊儒术" provided by dictionaries like "Confucianism monopoly", "pay supreme tribute to Confucianism" and "adopt Confucianism as official philosophy", we could not decide which version to be adopted. However, as we know that "独尊儒术" is related to the policy put forward by Emperor Wu of Han Dynasty, we can search for relevant entries about the Emperor in Wikipedia, and then we will get the text as follow: Emperor Wu adopted the principles of Confucianism as the state philosophy and code of ethics for his empire and started a school to teach future administrators the Confucian classics, from which we could determine that "独尊儒术" could be translated as "adopt the principles of Confucianism as the state philosophy".

3.3   Translation of Phrase Collocation

When it comes to the Chinese-English translation of phrase collocation, it is uncertain whether the phrase collocation with more than one translation version conforms to the authentic English expression. Therefore, on the one hand, the advanced search syntax can be used to retrieve the possible expressions of phrases in Google, while the sources and their frequency of use in English articles should be checked before the final translation choice is made. For example, the English versions of "实现抗日的积极外交" provided by Chinese-English dictionary include "carry out positive diplomacy of resisting Japan", "realize active diplomacy of resisting Japan" and so on. After searching "carry out * diplomacy" in Google, the author found that the "public diplomacy" is defined as "Public Diplomacy is carried out by both diplomats and, under their programs and auspices, non-officials such as academic scholars, journalists, experts in various fields..." in *The Diplomatic Dictionary of National Museum of American Diplomacy*, which contains the phrase collocation of "carry out diplomacy". Also, sentences like "To determine whether a country carries out diplomacy, and to create diplomacy categories, I focus on three elements" and "No country carries out diplomacy without associated economic interest" are provided by *Google*. Thus, it could be preliminarily judged that "carry out diplomacy" could be adopted. Next, "realize * division" is searched in Google, and the search results include sentences like 1) diplomats should realize that digital diplomacy constitutes engagement with how culture, information and relations are systematized in software.

2) Have MFAs realized digital diplomacy potential? 3) The Ministry will employ public diplomacy to consolidate ROK's image as a model for promoting democracy. It is obvious that "diplomacy" is not regarded as the object of "realize". Then the author respectively input "positive diplomacy" site: us and "active diplomacy" site: us in Google to limit the search results to U.S. websites and determine the commonly used expressions based on the statistics provided by the website. The author gets 46,100 results by searching the former one, and 158,000 the latter one. It is preliminarily judged that "active democracy" is more commonly used. Further search found that *Positive Diplomacy* is a work of Peter Marshall, while "active democracy" is more frequently used in English articles. Based on this, the author chooses "carry out active diplomacy of resisting Japan" as the translation of "实现抗日的积极外交".

On the other hand, online corpora could also serve as an important reference for the choice of translation version. For instance, as we are not sure whether to translate the word "活态传承" into "live inheritance", "living inheritance" or "live transmission", we could search the three translated words in WebCorp. By analyzing the frequency of these words and their meanings in sentences, we can finally make the translation choice. As we search for "live inheritance", 17 results are provided, while the usage frequency of it is ambiguous. However, as we search for "living inheritance", we could get 26 results, among which the definition of the word is given in the article *What is a Living Inheritance and How does it Work* as "the act of giving it to loved ones now, while you're still around", which is close to the Chinese meaning of the word "活态传承". Therefore, "living inheritance" can be chosen as the translated version of the original text.

3.4 Translation of Quoted Information

In Chinese-English translation, there are cases where the author quotes sentences from books that are originally written in English, which means that we are doing the secondary translation. Therefore, in order to restore the original language style of the quoted sentences, it is necessary that we consult the books and find out the original sentences. However, there are few books in English version that have been published in China, while some historical books have not been published with the elapse of time. Therefore, problems occur as we are unable to find these quoted books.

In order to search for those unpublished books, we could refer to the Internet Archive. For instance, historical books that reflect important facts and events like *The Private Papers of Senator Vandenberg*, *The Road to Confrontation* and *Wedemeyer Reports* have never been published in China, but the digital version of these book could be borrowed from the Internet Archive free of charge. With the help of resources provided by the Internet Archive, the translator can accurately restore the language style of historical figures and make a confirmation of the quoted statistics.

Sometimes, the reason why we are unable to find out the quoted books is that the book has different titles in history, and the existing version uses another name. In this case, we should first use the search engine to learn about different titles of the book. For instance, as we search for The China White Paper in Google, we are unable to get the full version of the book, except for the cover image provided by Google. However, as there's a sentence written as "originally issued as *United States Relations With China, With Special Reference to the Period 1944–1949*" on the book cover, we know that the book had another title in history. Therefore, as we search for this title in Google Books, the full version of it could be obtained.

4 Conclusions and Suggestions

Translation-related search and verification is not simply a process of searching for texts and other information, but a complex process of flexibly using a variety of tools and methods to determine the translation by searching, reevaluating and selecting. The reason why translators fall into the dilemma of translation verification is either due to a lack of translation technical skills, a lack of valuable data, or the inability to judge or calibrate data. Based on this, the author puts forward the translation-related search and verification competence model (see Fig. 1), believing that the competence is composed of three core elements, namely strategic competence, technical skills and advanced reading capability. Also, it is suggested that translation-related search and verification is guided by strategic competence. After identifying translation problems, the translator reasonably mobilizes internal and external resources, and obtains valuable information under the guidance of advanced reading capability before making the final translation decision (see Fig. 2). Therefore, in order to improve the translation-related search and verification competence, it is necessary that translators should comprehensively improve the three core competences.

The strategic competence, referring to the competence "to plan the process and carry out the translation project; to evaluate the process and the partial results obtained in relation to the final purpose; to activate the different sub-competencies and compensate for deficiencies in them; to identify translation problems and apply procedures to solve them" [1], plays a leading role in the process of translation verification. Guided by translation strategic competence, translators should first identify translation problems, including the author's writing intention, wording, connotation, etc. Based on different text types and different translation situations, they should activate their internal resources such as theoretical knowledge, encyclopedia knowledge and translation experience, and use external resources such as dictionaries, reference books, corpora and CAT tools to effectively reconstruct the translated text. When the selected tools are insufficient to solve the problem, it is necessary to make timely adjustments, adopt new tools and means to regain resources and information, and make a selection of appropriate words and sentence patterns.

Besides, technical skill is most closely related to translation verification ability. In the era of big data, the technical skills of translators refer to the effective application capability of search engines, corpus-based tools, text analysis tools, computer-aided translation technology (CAT), etc. [12]. Apart from mastering the advanced searching techniques, translators need to master the use of CAT tools such as SDL, Trados and MemoQ. With the help of CAT tools, translators can create corpora according to the translated text, which can not only avoid the repeated work of the translator, but also improve the consistency of context. The self-built corpus is highly pertinent with the translated texts, which is suitable for situation where there is no ready-made glossary and memory for translation reference.

Moreover, advanced reading capability is indispensable for translation-related search and verification, particularly in the context of big data, as translators need to obtain useful information from massive historical resources provided by the Internet within a limited period. On the one hand, the ever-changing information would cause great interference to the translator's manipulation and judgment of information. Thus, translators should self-monitor the understanding mechanism and reading progress, so as to ensure the concentration and sensitivity of reading. This requires translators to activate the knowledge stored in the brain and actively reconstruct the text information based on the results, so as to effectively obtain, evaluate, screen and absorb the required information. On the other hand, translators need to change their reading perspective by getting rid of the traditional directional and linear structure of the text [13]. They should use hypertext links provided by the Internet to construct a reading network according to linear words, and search for interrelated information, so as to improve the verification efficiency to the greatest extent.

It is therefore recommended that teachers should attach great importance to the process-oriented teaching of translation. Teachers can carry out project-based teaching for the purpose of the acquisition of translation verification ability, during which students should be guided to record the strategies, tools and skills they use to solve problems [14]. In this case, students integrate theory with practice in translation, which is "a process in which the development of procedural knowledge and, consequently, of the strategic sub-competence are essential; a process in which the translation competence sub-competencies are developed and restructured" [2]. After class, teachers should summarize the causes of errors and the generation steps of excellent translations. Translation teaching thus becomes the field of real learning, in which students find problems, make good use of tools, think critically, choose strategies and make their translation choice, which would be conducive for them to develop their translation competence.

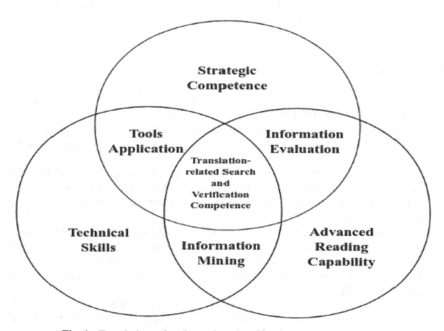

Fig. 1. Translation-related search and verification competence model

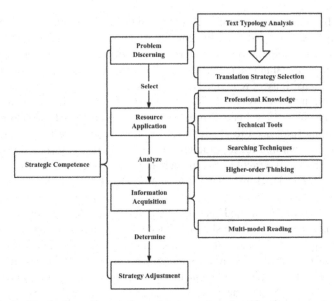

Fig. 2. Mechanism of translation-related search and verification competence

Acknowledgment. The authors gratefully acknowledge the research project of teaching reform in 2023 supported by NingboTech University: A Study of the Construction of Translation Curriculum System from the Perspective of Knowledge Graph (NBTJG-202306) and the comprehensive reform in 2021 supported by NingboTech University: Exploration and Practice of the Educational Path of "Ideological and Political +" Translation Course.

References

1. Hu, K.B., Li, Y.: Research on the characteristics of machine translation and its relationship with human translation. Chin. Transl. J. **5**, 10–14 (2016)
2. Rodríguez, M.F., et al.: Building a translation competence model. In: Alves, F. (ed.) Triangulating Translation: Perspectives in Process Oriented Research. John Benjamins, Amsterdam (2003)
3. Göpferich, S.: Towards a model of translation competence and its acquisition: the longitudinal study TransComp. In: Göpferich, S., Jakobsen, A.L., Mees, I.M. (eds.) Behind the Mind: Methods, Models and Results in Translation Process Research, pp. 11–38. Samfundslitteratur, Copenhagen (2009)
4. EMT Expert Group, Competences for Professional Translators, Experts in Multilingual and Multimedia Communication (2009). https://docs.google.com/gview?embedded=true&url= https://ec.europa.eu/info/sites/default/files/emt_competences_translators_en.pdf
5. Wang, H. S., Li, Y.: Concise Course of Translation Technology. World Publishing Corporation, Guangzhou (2019)
6. Pablo, D., Cristina, V., Rakefet, A., Ladislao, S.: Don't throw away your printed books: a meta-analysis on the effects of reading media on reading comprehension. Educ. Res. Rev. **25**, 23–38 (2018)

7. Wang, H.S., Zhang, C.Z.: The research on translators' searching competence in the big data era. Chin. Sci. Technol. Transl. J. **31**, 26–29 (2018)
8. Wu, Q., Wang, Y.B.: Website time machine: exploration of American web archive model: take internet archive as an example. Library **7**, 91–97 (2021)
9. Li, C.S.: Theory and Practice of Non-Literary Translation, pp.102–121. China Translation & Publishing Corporation, Beijing (2012)
10. Newmark, P.: A Textbook of Translation. Shanghai Foreign Language Education Press, Shanghai (2001)
11. Long, P.Q.: The translation of the classical Chinese. West. China Transl. **5**, 73–74 (2008)
12. EMT Expert Group: European Master's in Translation-EMT Competence Framework (2017). https://docs.google.com/gview?embedded=true&url=https://ec.europa.eu/info/sites/default/files/emt_competence_fwk_2017_en_web.pdf
13. Heather, K.: Inquiry-based learning with the net: opportunities and challenges. New Dictionaries Teach. Learn. **107**, 57–65 (2006)
14. Miao, J.: A research on translation competence-the foundation of translation teaching mode. Foreign Lang. Their Teach. **4**, 47–50 (2007)

Research on College Students' Behavioral Patterns Based on Big Data

Shaojie Qu[1] , Dagang Li[2] , and Feng Cao[3] (✉)

[1] Beijing Institute of Technology, Beijing 100000, China
[2] Nanjing University of Science and Technology, Nanjing 210000, China
[3] China Academy of Information and Communications Technology, Beijing 100000, China
qushaojie@bit.edu.cn

Abstract. With the development of the internet, campus networks and various information systems in colleges have been constructed, and the data generated by accessing the internet can reflect students' learning and daily behaviors. Traditional methods have difficulty effectively and accurately analyzing the students' behavior. In this paper, a method is designed to mine students' behavior patterns. The main contributions of this article include the following: (1) We extract student behavior features from network log data, a total of 44 students' behavior features were selected in the experiment. (2) We gain 11 online behavior patterns with association rules from students' daily behaviors. (3) We build a student prediction model based on students' behavior patterns and the final model predicts the students' grades with an accuracy of 87.62%. This paper presents a method to analyze students' behavior patterns. Moreover, reasonable suggestions and effective and credible data support for precise and dynamic decision-making in colleges and universities are provided.

Keywords: Behavioral Pattern · Machine Learning · Educational Data Mining

1 Introduction

With the development and widespread application of the internet and big data technology, the use of digital methods to study the behavior patterns of contemporary college students is critical for improving the quality of college education [1]. Previously, researchers predicted students' scores based on course data generated by college students on teaching platforms [2]. However, not all courses are offered on these teaching platforms, and the scores of a single course cannot reflect the learning performance of all students. Some researchers have studied the influence of students' consumption behavior on their academic performance; however, due the lack and limitations of consumption data due to take-out and other reasons, these data cannot reflect students' overall learning state well. Students' online behaviors on campus are related to the students' living habits, learning attitude, learned content and other aspects, which can better reflect the students' learning state. In terms of research methods, researchers often extract features from students' behavioral data for analysis, but these features poorly reflect student behavior

[3]. Behavior patterns are representative key behaviors that can reflect students' behaviors well. This work uses online behavior data of students to explore various characteristics related to students' learning and the deep behavioral patterns of student groups to discover students' academic risks in a timely manner [4]. The research content in this work can be summarized as follows:

(1) Student behavior characteristics were extracted from a large amount of network log data, and a set of features that best reflects student behavior is selected. A total of 44 kinds of characteristics of student behavior were selected in the experiment.
(2) The association rules of students' online behavior patterns and daily behaviors were analyzed to determine their behavior patterns. In the experiment, a total of 11 behavior patterns were identified.
(3) A student achievement prediction model was established, adjusted and optimized. The accuracy of the model in predicting students' grades reached up to 87.62%. The model can detect students with academic difficulties in a timely manner.

The sections of this paper are arranged as follows: The first section introduces the relevant background and research content. The second section presents relevant content on educational data exploration and machine learning. The third section describes the data set and research methods. The fourth section analyzes the experimental results. The fifth section provides a summary and the expected outcomes of this work.

2 Related Work

2.1 Educational Data Exploration

With the development of internet technology, educational data exploration methods can provide suggestions for decision-making and data support for education practitioners to improve the quality of education. Recent research in this field has focused on the use of nontraditional data sources, optimization of model algorithms, improvement of measurement indicators and other specific research directions. Arifin M [5] analyzed the performance of existing machine learning methods such as generalized linear models (GLMs), support vector machine (SVMs), deep learning (DL) models, decision trees (DTs), random forests (RFs), and gradient boosting trees (GBT) in educational data applications to explore different indicators. Bonded [6] focused on identifying the underlying causes of student under performance in specific courses through educational data analysis. Francis [7] proposed a method based on dynamic data mining and optimized mining algorithms. Kausar [8] compared clustering methods based on k-means, k-medoids, density-based spatial clustering of applications with noise, agglomeration hierarchical clustering trees, and clustering by fast search and finding of density peaks via heat diffusion (CFSEDP-HD) and found that CFSEDP-HD performs best in educational data mining applications. By comparing random forest, J48, SimpleCart, decision tables, naive Bayes, SMO, simple logistic regression and other classification algorithms to predict student achievement in their research, Doi [9] found that the random forest method obtained the best prediction effect. Manzanares [10] used eye-movement tracking techniques and data mining approaches for supervised (predicted) and unsupervised (cluster analysis) learning, providing classification methods for detecting users' forms and styles of learning. Hidalgo

[11] developed a model for predicting student achievement that automatically optimizes the framework and hyperparameters of deep neural networks. Iqbal [12] proposed a new model to analyze and predict library borrowing data; the model, which was based on a deep neural network (DNN), support vector regression (SVR) and random forest (RF), predicted the future university library borrowing patterns. Mou [13] used discrete-time Markov chains and hidden Markov models (HMMs) to analyze and predict student performance based on short time series data. Chen [14] proposed a system called KnowEdu for the automatic construction of educational knowledge maps; the system identified educational relationships by utilizing heterogeneous education data, extracted teaching concepts by using a neural sequence labeling algorithm on the teaching data, and explored learning assessment data by using a probabilistic association rule. Luo [15] proposed a mental health evaluation system based on a joint optimization algorithm. The joint optimization algorithm, consisting of an improved decision tree algorithm and an improved artificial neural network algorithm, was used to analyze and classify mental health evaluation data and obtain mental health evaluation results. Costa [16] proposed using statistical analysis and Apnon-based concept mining to identify retention patterns in undergraduate courses, which can be used to help universities predict the entry of qualified professionals into the job market while reducing student dropout rates. Prabowo [17] proposed a dual-input deep learning model that simultaneously processed time series and tabular data to predict student GPA. Since the original data in the log file are high-dimensional, complex and noisy, Zhou [18] proposed several methods for preprocessing data sources to design a high-dimensional feature selection framework to prepare features for constructing prediction models, achieving a good balance between computational efficiency and prediction performance. Yang [19] proposed a prediction model for education and culture patterns based on a genetic neural network.

2.2 Machine Learning

Machine learning is an important subfield in data mining. The main research directions in machine learning are proposing new models and improving and optimizing existing models. Based on the differential privacy and network user data DBSCAN algorithm, Ni [20] proposed a differential privacy protection multicore DBSCAN clustering scheme, which mainly addresses privacy leakage in the data mining process. Wu [21] studied the effects of the parameters of back propagation (BP) neural networks and genetic algorithms on the overall network, including the input, output and number of hidden layer nodes. He improved and determined the settings of relevant parameters and proved the rationality of the selected parameters through experiments. Dong [22] proposed a depth metric learning and online hard mining (DMLOHM) method for hyperspectral classification, which maximizes interclass distances and minimizes intraclass distances using convolutional neural networks (CNNs) as embedded networks. Ahmed [23] used data mining techniques to identify and automatically extract learning concept characteristics from individual educational texts. By using a hybrid system with feedforward neural networks and evolutionary algorithms, three main characteristics that distinguish real learning concepts from other sequences of strings were examined.

3 Data and Methods

3.1 Data

The original data used to design the model in this work were obtained from the internet data of a university network user, including the user's ID, access time, access node content and user's number of credits. The total access number of network between September 1, 2020, and September 14, 2020, is 16,0303,813. The students was obtained from the fifth semester of university students, and the total number of students is 3637. Due to data redundancy and abnormal data or noise in the original data-set, such as nonexistent or abnormal student credit information, it is difficult to use the original features to determine the subsequent behavior patterns. Therefore, it is necessary to preprocess the data. The general preprocessing steps include desensitization, data cleaning, data integration, feature extraction, feature standardization and feature selection. To protect user privacy, the original data are desensitized, and the user ID is replaced with a meaningless and nonrepetitive sequence of random numbers.

In this work, 44 features reflecting students' behaviors are extracted based on the content and time online. Some features and their meanings are shown in Table 1.

Table 1. Features

Features	Meaning of the Features
NIGHT	Online time at night (0:00 to 6:00)
MOR	Online time in the morning (6:00 to 12:00)
AFT	Online time in the afternoon (12:00 to 18:00)
EVE	Online time in the evening (18:00 to 24:00)
WKD	Online time on the weekend
SOC	Number of visits to social networking websites
GAME	Number of visits to game websites
VIDEO	Number of visits to live video websites
SEARCH	Number of visits to search engine websites
STUDY	Number of visits to learning websites
MUSIC	Number of visits to music websites

3.2 Behavior Patterns

In this section, we use a clustering algorithm based on the K-means method to analyze the student behavior patterns and study the individual behavior characteristics in the student group based on the clustering of different dimensions of behavior characteristics.

(1) We randomly select k samples in the data set as clustering centers.

(2) All points are assigned to the cluster represented by the nearest center in (1), and the distance is defined based on the Euclidean distance, as shown in Formula 1.

$$d(X_i, C_j) = \sqrt{\sum_{t=1}^{m} (C_{jt} - X_{it})^2} \tag{1}$$

In the formula, C represents the cluster center, X represents the object, C_{jt} represents the tth feature of the jth center, and X_{it} represents the tth feature of the ith object.

(3) The clustering center is updated.

Steps (2) and (3) are repeated until the clustering center remains constant, that is, the center location converges. The value of K was selected based on the within-cluster sum of square errors (SSE) and silhouette coefficient in this experiment. The SSE represents the sum of the squares of errors within the cluster. Mathematically, the SSE represents the degree of distortion, which is used to measure the degree of looseness within the cluster. The specific calculation method is shown in Formula 2.

$$SSE = \sum_{i=1}^{r} \sum_{j=1}^{n_i} \left(X_{ij} - \bar{X}\right)^2 \tag{2}$$

The silhouette coefficient of the K-means cluster is a measure that indicates the concentration of a given sample in the cluster. Here, b is used to represent the degree of separation, i.e., the average distance between the sample and all samples in the nearest cluster, and a is used to represent the degree of cohesion, i.e., the average distance between the sample and all samples within the cluster.

The silhouette coefficient is calculated as shown in Formula 3.

$$SC = \frac{b - a}{\max(a, b)} \tag{3}$$

In this work, the student behavioral patterns are analyzed from two aspects, namely, the time spent online and content, and the characteristics of the campus network users' online time and content are investigated based on the students' behavioral data.

3.3 Prediction

In this work, students are divided into two categories by grade 70, and three methods are used to predict students' grades according to their behavior data.

For the 44 features extracted, common machine learning algorithms are used to conduct experiments, sequential features are built according to temporal sequences and students' grades are predicted according to the temporal sequence algorithm. For the behavior pattern features, the previous behavior pattern clustering results are used, a one-hot algorithm is adopted to encode students' behaviors according to the behavior pattern, a machine learning method is applied to predict students' grades and the characteristics and behavior patterns are finally combined to predict students' grades.

4 Experimental Results

4.1 Behavior Pattern Results

In this essay, the K-means algorithm is used to cluster the online behavior data of the students according to the time spent online. The SSE and SC clustering results are shown in Fig. 1. According to the experimental results, the clustering parameter K = 4 is adopted in this paper.

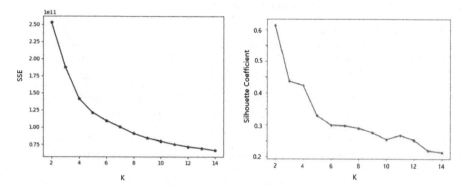

Fig. 1. Clustering SSE and SC results of online time

After clustering the online data of the students, the behavioral data of 4 types of students are analyzed, and the results are shown in Table 2.

(1) C1 students account for 22.60% of the students. This represents the behavior pattern of students who are more interested in the internet and spend more time on the internet than the general group of students but can reasonably schedule the amount of time spent on the internet, normal activities, resting, studying and working.

(2) C2 students account for 52.03% of the students. This behavior pattern represents students who have low interest in the internet and can reasonably arrange the amount of time spent on the internet, normal activities and resting.

(3) C3 students account for 22.1% of the students. This behavior pattern represents students with high interest and dependence on the internet, and it is difficult for these students to properly arrange their time spent on the internet, normal activities, resting, studying and working.

(4) C4 students account for 23.16% of the students. These students mainly use the internet at night and use the internet more on weekends than on working days. The behavior pattern represents students who are busier during their study and work hours.

In this work, the K-means algorithm is used to cluster students' online behavior data according to the online content accessed. The SSE and SC clustering results are shown in Fig. 2. According to the experimental results, the clustering parameter K = 7 is adopted in this essay.

In this work, seven clustering modes are analyzed, as shown in Table 3. The D1 mode students account for 6.48% of the students. Students with this behavior pattern mainly use the internet for social networking and browsing news. The D2 mode students account for 8.25% of the students. Students with this behavior pattern may be at risk of problems such as excessive time spent playing video games and game addiction and need to be aware of and on guard against possible effects on their physical health and academic performance. The D3 mode students account for 35.54% of the students.

Table 2. Clustering Data

Category	C1	C2	C3	C4
Proportion	22.60%	52.03%	2.21%	23.16%
NIGHT	3174	845	18174	3641
MOR	6696	3081	12260	2525
AFT	9370	3908	19076	3814
EVE	12931	4872	30181	6499
WKD	11537	4243	28685	5934

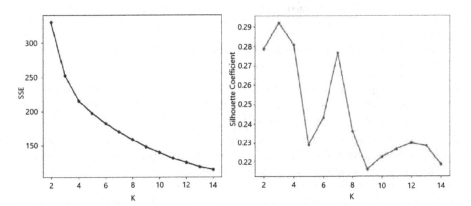

Fig. 2. SSE and SC results of online content

The main reason these students access the network is for social content. The D4 mode students account for 10.17% of the students. The main reason these students access the network is for live video and social content. The D5 mode students account for 8.19% of the students. The main reason these students access the network is for system security, tools and social content. The D6 mode students account for 18.48% of the students. The main reason these students access the network is for social and shopping/advertising content. The D7 mode students account for 13.89% of the students. The main reason these students access the network is for social and search engine content.

4.2 Prediction Results

In this work, a variety of conventional machine learning algorithms are used to train the model based on the features obtained by preprocessing the data. During training, the whole data set is randomly divided into a training set and a test set according to a ratio of 8:2. The training set is used to train the models, and the test set is used to evaluate the training effect. Fivefold cross-validation is used in this work. The student achievement prediction results using 44 features are shown in Table 4.

Table 3. Clustering Data

Category	One	Two	Three	Four	Five	Six	Seven
Number	223	284	1189	350	282	636	478
CLASS1	0.04%	0.06%	0.03%	0.01%	0.08%	0.07%	0.05%
CLASS2	1.59%	1.60%	1.21%	1.74%	1.64%	5.44%	1.73%
CLASS3	33.97%	18.00%	64.00%	20.65%	26.16%	35.21%	40.79%
CLASS4	28.73%	3.28%	2.94%	2.71%	2.99%	2.94%	3.58%
CLASS5	2.93%	38.56%	1.50%	3.10%	3.75%	5.79%	2.47%
CLASS6	6.12%	4.99%	5.65%	56.84%	4.96%	9.70%	4.12%
CLASS7	6.56%	3.87%	4.07%	3.25%	7.43%	5.23%	25.46%
CLASS8	0.14%	0.05%	0.11%	0.04%	0.17%	0.55%	0.14%
CLASS9	3.03%	3.00%	2.84%	2.43%	25.19%	3.38%	3.25%
CLASS10	0.11%	0.00%	0.07%	0.02%	0.38%	0.07%	0.08%
CLASS11	6.75%	3.68%	5.20%	2.95%	16.54%	6.50%	8.27%
CLASS12	7.24%	20.49%	9.62%	5.02%	7.32%	17.48%	7.38%
CLASS13	0.28%	2.42%	2.76%	1.26%	3.38%	7.63%	2.69%

Table 4. Clustering Data

Index	Accuracy	Precision	Recall	Fl-Score
LR	0.7054	0.8086	0.7054	0.7427
NB	0.8186	0.8275	0.8186	0.8229
SVM	0.8607	0.8078	0.8607	0.8190
FCN	0.8533	0.8745	0.9755	0.9085
RNN	0.8438	0.8558	0.9824	0.9145
LSTM	0.8595	0.8923	0.9551	0.9225
GRU	0.8503	0.8558	0.9916	0.9186

By comparing the above results, it can be concluded that the support vector machine (SVM) model achieves the highest accuracy of 86.07% based on the 44 features generated by the feature selection process. Furthermore, the fully connected neural network, recurrent neural network (RNN), naive Bayes (NB), and logistic regression (LR) models have the worse performance, with the LR model having an accuracy of only 70.54%. Overall, the LSTM model has the best performance, with the second-best accuracy and a good recall rate.

The experimental results for the accessed content are shown in Table 5.

In this experiment, the features extracted directly through data processing and the behavior patterns generated through cluster analysis were selected as input to predict student achievement. We attempted to combine the two features as new inputs to predict students' grades, and the experimental results are shown in Table 6.

Table 5. Comparison of prediction effects

Index	Accuracy	Precision	Recall	Fl-Score
LR	0.5675	0.8024	0.5675	0.6385
NB	0.8665	0.7508	0.8665	0.8045
SVM	0.8258	0.7953	0.8258	0.8085
FCN	0.8578	0.8686	0.9875	0.9174
RNN	0.8530	0.8844	0.9592	0.9169

Table 6. Training effects of different methods

Index	Accuracy	Precision	Recall	F1-Score
Based on Features	0.8624	0.8799	0.9792	0.9166
Based on Behavior Patterns	0.8578	08686	09488	0.8842
Combined	0.8762	0.8798	0.9952	0.9335

As shown in Table 6, the prediction effect based on the combination of characteristics and behavior patterns is better than that based only on characteristics or behavior patterns and can thus better reflect students' learning outcomes.

5   Conclusion

The online data of university students are closely related to students' daily learning patterns and lives; thus, these data can accurately reflect the daily learning and life behaviors of college students. Traditional data processing methods have difficulty analyzing the big data included in network behavior logs. This paper explored the behavioral patterns of students from multiple perspectives based on students' use of campus networks.

A model based on big data and machine learning was designed to analyze students' behavior patterns. Furthermore, behavior features were extracted from a large amount of network log data, and a feature set was selected that best reflects students' behavior. In this work, 44 kinds of student behavioral features were selected, the association rules of students' online behavior patterns and daily behaviors were analyzed, and 11 behavior patterns of student groups were explored. A student achievement prediction model was established, and the achievement prediction accuracy of the model reached 87.62%.

The innovation of this research involved exploring students' behavior patterns from multiple perspectives and building a student achievement prediction model based on behavior patterns. Due to the complexity of data and models, there is still great potential for improving the generalizability and accuracy of the models in this study to make further progress.

Acknowledgments. Thanks for the acknowledgement provided by China Academy of Information and Communications Technology and Industry-University-Research Innovation Fund for Chinese Universities: 2021KSA01002.

References

1. Livari, N., Sharma, S., Venta-Olkkonen, L.: Digital transformation of everyday life-how COVID-19 pandemic transformed the basic education of the young generation and why information management research should care?. Int. J. Inf. Manag. **55**, 102183 (2020)
2. Deliens, T., Defbrche, B., De Bourdeaudhuij, L., et al.: Determinants of physical activity and sedentary behaviour in university students: a qualitative study using focus group discussions. BMC Public Health **15**(1), 1–9 (2015)
3. Aman, F., Rauf, A., Ali, R., et al.: A predictive model for predicting students academic performance. In: 2019 10th International Conference on Information, Intelligence, Systems and Applications (USA), pp. 1–4 (2019)
4. Haefner, N., Wincent, J., Panda, V., et al.: Artificial intelligence and innovation management: a review, framework, and research agenda. Technol. Forecast. Soc. Change **162**, 120392 (2021)
5. Arifin, M., Widowati, F., et al.: Comparative analysis on educational data mining algorithm to predict academic performance. In: 2021 International Seminar on Application for Technology of Information and Communication (iSemantic) (2021)
6. Bonde, S.N., Kirange, D.K.: Survey on evaluation of student's performance in educational data mining. In: 2018 Second International Conference on Inventive Communication and Computational Technologies (ICICCT) (2018)
7. Francis, B.K., Babu, S.S.: Predicting academic performance of students using a hybrid data mining approach. J. Med. Syst. (2019)
8. Kausar, S., Huahu, X., Hussain, I., et al.: Integration of data mining clustering approach in the personalized E-learning system. IEEE Access, 1 (2018)
9. Doi, S.M.: Use of classification technique in educational data mining. In: 2021 4th Biennial International Conference on Nascent Technologies in Engineering (ICNTE) (2021)
10. Manzanares, M., Hemanz, R., Yaez, M., et al.: Eye-tracking technology and data-mining techniques used for a behavioral analysis of adults engaged in learning processes. J. Vis. Exp. (172) (2021)
11. Hidalgo, N.C., Ger, P.M., Valentin, L.: Using meta-learning to predict student performance in virtual learning environments. Appl. Intell., 1–14 (2021)

12. Iqbal, N., Jamil, F., Ahmad, S., et al.: Toward effective planning and management using predictive analytics based on rental book data of academic libraries. IEEE Access **8**, 81978–81996 (2020)
13. Mou, C., Zhou, Q., Zou, X.: Understanding and predicting poor performance of computer science students from short time series test results. Int. J. Eng. Educ. **33**(6App.), 1803–1814 (2017)
14. Chen, P., Lu, Y., Zheng, V.W., et al.: KnowEdu: a system to construct knowledge graph for education. IEEE Access **6**, 31553–31563 (2018)
15. Luo, M.: Research on students? Mental health based on data mining algorithms. J. Healthcare Eng. **2021** (2021)
16. Costa, J.D.J., Bernardini, F., Artigas, D., et al.: Mining direct acyclic graphs to find frequent substructures-an experimental analysis on educational data. Inf. Sci. **482**, 266–278 (2019)
17. Prabowo, H., Hidayat, A.A., Cenggoro, T.W., et al.: Aggregating time series and tabular data in deep learning model for university students * GPA prediction. IEEE Access **9**, 87370–87377 (2021)
18. Zhou, Q., Quan, W., Zhong, Y., et al.: Predicting high-risk students using Internet access logs. Knowl. Inf. Syst. **55**(2), 393–413 (2018)
19. Yang, K.: The construction of sports culture industry growth forecast model based on big data. Pers. Ubiquit. Comput. **24**(1), 5–17 (2020)
20. Ni, L., Li, C., Wang, X., et al.: DP-MCDBSCAN: differential privacy preserving multi-core DBSCAN clustering for network user data. IEEE Access **6**, 21053–21063 (2018)
21. Wu, D., Shen, Y.: English feature recognition based on GA-BP neural network algorithm and data mining. Comput. Intell. Neurosci. **2021** (2021)
22. Dong, Y., Yang, C., Zhang, Y.: Deep metric learning with online hard mining for hyperspectral classification. Remote Sens. **13**(7), 1368 (2021)
23. Ahmed, S., Lee, Y., Hyun, S.H., et al.: Feature selection-based detection of covert cyber deception assaults in smart grid communications networks using machine learning. IEEE Access **6**, 27518–27529 (2018)

Enhancing Chinese Character Education and Calligraphy Through Metaverse Intelligent Technology: Integration and Impact

Dongxing Yu[1] and Nan Ma[2(✉)]

[1] School of Education, Sanda University, Shanghai, China
[2] School of Art Design and Media, Sanda University, Shanghai, China
nma@sandau.edu.cn

Abstract. The study investigates the enhancement of international Chinese character and calligraphy education through metaverse intelligent education technology (MIET), suggesting that it increases motivation, interest, and cultural engagement among learners. A mixed methods approach showed significant motivational benefits and cultural connections, despite technical challenges and a need for teacher training. The positive impact on learning and cultural preservation positions MIET as an innovative educational tool, warranting further exploration for sustained effects and broader applicability in curriculum development and policymaking.

Keywords: Metaverse · Chinese Character Education · Chinese Calligraphy Education · Immersive learning · Educational technology

1 Introduction

Metaverse intelligent education technology represents a convergence of virtual reality, artificial intelligence, and augmented reality, creating dynamic digital environments where learners actively engage with educational content in unprecedented ways. While the potential is vast, challenges persist in international Chinese character teaching. The global spread of Chinese language and culture has increased demand for Chinese instruction, but current methods often fall short in delivering effective, engaging lessons.

Chinese traditional calligraphy embodies cultural essence beyond writing skills. However, this cultural treasure faces difficulty resonating with modern learners. Integrating international Chinese character teaching with calligraphy's artistic and cultural aspects may provide a holistic, engaging learning experience. However, challenges exist in designing curricula, materials, and motivating learners.

Our research question emerges: How can metaverse intelligent education technology effectively integrate international Chinese character teaching and Chinese traditional calligraphy education? We hypothesize metaverse technology can enhance teaching via immersive, personalized experiences, sparking interest, motivation, and cultural identity, promoting calligraphy inheritance and innovation.

We aim to explore metaverse technology's application models, methods, and effects in integrating these fields, providing insights for theoretical and practical implementation. We will uncover the potential benefits and challenges of this integration in subsequent sections.

2   Literature Review

2.1   Metaverse Intelligent Education Technology

The metaverse refers to persistent online virtual 3D environments accessed through VR/AR and regular computing. Metaverse intelligent education technology (MIET) uses metaverse to enhance teaching and learning via immersive, interactive experiences not possible with traditional methods [1]. MIET allows exploration of simulations and environments for social collaboration [2]. It redefines traditional education by enabling handson activities in virtual settings [3]. MIET relies on technologies like edge computing and integrates AI for data analysis to provide personalized insights [4]. Challenges include fully realizing the technology's potential.

Metaverse has the ability to transform the learning process via exploratory environments and AIenabled adaptive learning. As edumetaverse emerges, future education will likely feature more intelligence, digitalization, and virtualization. AR, VR, AI, and blockchain are expected to create scalable, accurate virtual world ecosystems for education. The metaverse presents promising opportunities for education technology, though challenges remain. It has potential benefits for personalized and immersive learning.

2.2   International Chinese Character Teaching

Over the past 15 years, International Chinese Language Education has evolved, particularly in teaching Chinese characters to international learners, showcasing a significant methodological divide: nonempirical approaches in China versus empirical studies abroad [9]. While computer assisted language learning (CALL) garners attention outside China, Chinese scholars delve into new pedagogical strategies [8]. Despite advancements in teaching philosophies and technology aided methods, the complexity of Chinese characters and a dearth of engaging resources remain as obstacles [8]. Concurrently, Chinese calligraphy education faces modernization challenges, seen as a niche, with hurdles like technology costs and the need for specialized metaverse content integration yet to be thoroughly explored.

3   Research Perspective and Framework

3.1   Conceptual Framework

The framework focuses on three core aspects of integrating metaverse technology in Chinese character and calligraphy education:

Metaverse Technology Integration: Examining various metaverse platforms and tools for educational use, including their pros and cons for language and calligraphy education.

Pedagogical Approaches: Investigating instructional methods and strategies using metaverse technology for effective character teaching and calligraphy education, encompassing curriculum design, interactive activities, and personalized learning paths.

Learner Engagement and Cultural Identity: Assessing the impact of metaverse based instruction on learner motivation, interest, and cultural identity, and how immersive experiences enhance appreciation of Chinese culture.

The research includes an analysis of empirical data, case studies, and best practices, addressing the limitations and challenges of implementing this technology, aiming to provide insights for educators and policymakers in the field.

3.2 Formula for Calligraphy Training Assessment

Creating a comprehensive calligraphy training formula for a virtual environment involves combining multiple parameters for stroke analysis and character structure evaluation:

Stroke Motion Trajectory Analysis:
Stroke Path Data (S): Tracks the (x, y) coordinates and time stamps along the stroke to represent the motion trajectory.

Stroke Speed (V): The rate of change of distance over time, indicating the swiftness of the stroke.

Stroke Smoothness (Sm): A measure of trajectory curvature, indicating execution fluidity.

Stroke Pressure (P): The force exerted on the virtual surface, affecting stroke thickness and intensity.

Chinese Character Structure Evaluation:
Character Complexity (C): Assesses the intricacy of the character, based on stroke count, radical composition, and structural details.

Stroke Order (So): Verifies the sequence of strokes against traditional calligraphy conventions.

This formula would use data driven algorithms to analyze these parameters, providing real time feedback to learners on their virtual calligraphy practice.

Ink Technique Assessment:
Parameter 7: Ink Flow (If): Assesses how well the learner replicates the ink flow and intensity of a traditional brush.

Parameter 8: Ink Density (Id): Measures how evenly the ink is distributed along the stroke, accounting for areas with thicker or lighter ink.

The formula for calligraphy training assessment could involve a weighted combination of these parameters to provide a comprehensive evaluation:

$$Training\_Score = w1 * (k1 * V + k2 * Sm + k3 * P) + w2 * (k4 * C + k5 * So)$$
$$+ w3 * (k6 * If + k7 * Id) \tag{1}$$

$w1, w2, w3$: Weights assigned to each parameter to reflect their relative importance in the training assessment.

$k1, k2, k3, k4, k5, k6, k7$: Coefficients representing the impact of each subparameter on the overall training score. These coefficients would need to be determined through data analysis and expert consultation.

The formula calculates a training score for each stroke or character practiced in a virtual environment, offering learners feedback on stroke motion, structure, and ink technique. Its implementation necessitates data collection, machine learning algorithms, and a user interface to deliver immediate feedback and guidance during calligraphy practice.

3.3 Research Design, Subjects, Tools, and Process

Our The study uses a mixed methods approach, blending quantitative and qualitative methods, to evaluate metaverse intelligent education technology in international Chinese character and calligraphy education. It involves:

Subjects: Participants from diverse backgrounds, including language learners and calligraphy enthusiasts, are recruited through educational institutions and online platforms.

Surveys and Questionnaires: Pre and postintervention surveys administered online assess learners' motivations, interests, and perceived cultural identity changes.

Metaverse Platforms: Data on learners' interactions in metaverse environments is collected using logging tools and analytics features of the metaverse platforms.

Content Analysis: We analyze learning materials, curriculum designs, and instructional resources used within the metaverse environments to assess their alignment with pedagogical goals and cultural elements (Fig. 1).

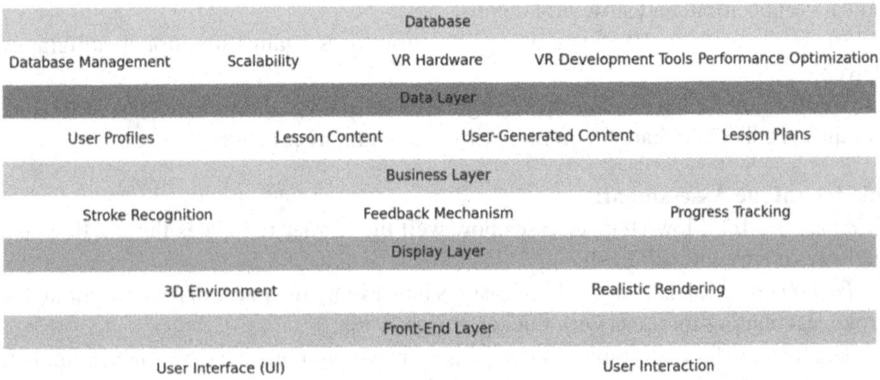

Database				
Database Management	Scalability	VR Hardware	VR Development Tools	Performance Optimization
Data Layer				
User Profiles	Lesson Content	User-Generated Content		Lesson Plans
Business Layer				
Stroke Recognition		Feedback Mechanism		Progress Tracking
Display Layer				
3D Environment			Realistic Rendering	
Front-End Layer				
User Interface (UI)			User Interaction	

Fig. 1. VR Calligraphy Education Metaverse Platform Architecture

4 Experiments and Analysis

4.1 Experimental Design Ideas

The design of three experiments aims to examine the use of metaverse intelligent technology in Chinese character and calligraphy education:

Experiment 1 assesses how prior learning experience affects stroke speed within a metaverse VR calligraphy environment, establishing the relationship between background and performance.

Experiment 2 builds on the first to identify factors like age, stroke technique comprehension, and learning duration that impact stroke speed, providing a detailed analysis of performance influencers.

Experiment 3 shifts focus to the overall influence of metaverse technology on the teaching of Chinese characters and calligraphy, evaluating how this integration can boost learners' motivation and interest.

These sequential experiments progress from examining basic correlations to a broader evaluation of metaverse technology's impact on education.

4.2 Experiment 1: Investigation of the Correlation Between Stroke Speed and Prior Learning Experience in a Metaverse VR Calligraphy Environment

The study tests hypotheses on how age, understanding of stroke techniques, and practice duration affect stroke speed in calligraphy, to refine training approaches.

Hypotheses. A correlation between age and slower stroke speed due to refined motor skills. Better grasp of stroke techniques leads to faster stroke speeds from improved control. More practice correlates with increased stroke speed due to better proficiency.

Setup. 500 diverse participants were studied, with data on age and calligraphy experience. A VR calligraphy environment was used with a brushlike controller. Stroke speed was tracked in VR and measured in meters per second. Participants completed strokes in multiple sessions, with average speeds calculated.

4.3 Experimental 2: Investigating Factors Affecting Stroke Speed in Chinese Calligraphy Learning

Objective: The study aims to empirically investigate how age, understanding of stroke techniques, and practice time affect stroke speed in Chinese calligraphy, to improve training programs.

Hypotheses. Older individuals may have slower stroke speeds. Better understanding of stroke techniques correlates with faster speeds. More practice time leads to increased stroke speed.

Experimental Setup

Participants: A diverse age group, with a sample size adequate for statistical significance.

Variables: Age, understanding of stroke techniques (110 scale), practice time (in years) as independent variables; stroke speed (strokes per minute) as the dependent variable.

Procedure: Participants provide age, selfrated technique understanding, and practice time; perform calligraphy tasks; time and stroke quality are recorded.

Data Collection: Age is collected directly; understanding and practice time via questionnaire; stroke speed is measured during tasks.

4.4   Experimental 3: Enhancing Chinese Character Education and Calligraphy Through Metaverse Intelligent Technology

Objective: To evaluate how metaverse technology impacts motivation, interest, and learning outcomes in Chinese character and calligraphy education, seeking to understand learner and educator experiences.

Hypotheses. Metaverse technology will significantly boost learner motivation and interest due to its immersive nature. Educators will report positive experiences using metaverse technology, enhancing engagement and teaching effectiveness. Learning outcomes, such as understanding Chinese characters and calligraphy, will improve through interactive metaverse experiences. Metaverse technology will make education more accessible and inclusive.

Experimental Setup. 200 participants, split into metaverse integrated and traditional education groups, were surveyed pre and postintervention. The experimental group used metaverse technology for an immersive learning experience. Postintervention, changes in motivation and interest were assessed, along with interviews to collect qualitative data on experiences and perceptions.

5   Results and Data Analysis

5.1   Data Analysis Results and Findings

Experiment 1 Data Analysis. Stroke speed data was correlated with years of prior calligraphy learning experience using statistical analysis methods such as linear regression (Fig. 2).

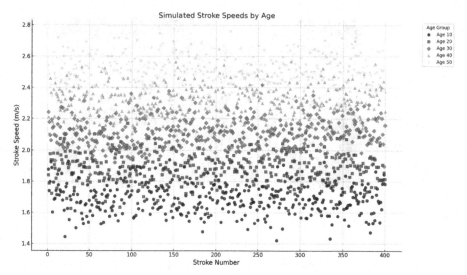

Fig. 2. Scatter plot of simulated stroke speed based on age

In this script, we generated random ages for learners between 6 and 70 years and simulated stroke speed data for each learner. We then created a scatter plot to visualize stroke speeds, with colors representing learner ages. Additionally, we calculated and displayed average stroke speeds for different age groups. This analysis provides insights into stroke speed variations across different age groups, offering valuable information for the design of calligraphy training programs.

Experiment 2 Data Analysis. In our analysis, we identified several correlations in stroke speed factors: Older individuals tend to have slower stroke speeds compared to younger learners.

A better understanding of stroke movement is associated with faster stroke speeds, indicating increased efficiency with greater technique knowledge. More practice time is linked to faster strokes, suggesting that dedication leads to improved efficiency.

These correlations were confirmed by a correlation matrix heatmap, which displayed strong positive associations between these factors. However, it's important to note that our study used simulated data, which may not capture realworld complexities. These findings provide a theoretical foundation for potential correlations in stroke speed factors, but further empirical validation with real learner data is needed for educational application (Fig. 3).

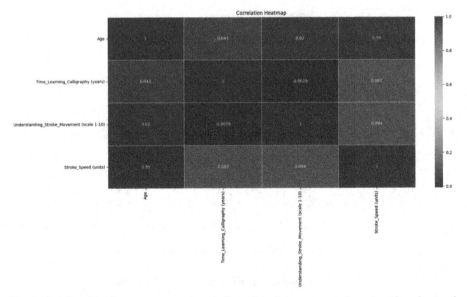

Fig. 3. Relationships between age, understanding of stroke movement, time spent learning, and stroke speed

Dark red cells between "Age" and "Stroke_Speed" visually demonstrate a positive correlation, highlighting that older individuals tend to have slightly slower stroke speeds.

Dark blue cells between "Understanding_Stroke_Movement" and "Stroke_Speed" indicate a positive correlation, suggesting that a better understanding of stroke techniques leads to faster strokes. Dark blue cells between "Time_Learning_Calligraphy" and "Stroke_Speed" show a positive correlation, implying that dedicating more time to practice is associated with higher stroke speeds.

Experiment 3 Data Analysis. Quantitative data from surveys were analyzed using statistical methods, including tests, to assess the significance of changes in motivation and interest between the experimental and control groups. Qualitative data from interviews were transcribed and analyzed thematically to identify patterns, themes, and insights related to participants' experiences and educators' perspectives (Fig. 4).

Pre and Post Intervention Survey Results (Line Chart):

The line chart shows changes in motivation scores between the preintervention (baseline) and postintervention stages for both the control and experimental groups.

If the line for the experimental group (green) is noticeably higher than the line for the control group (blue) in the postintervention stage, it indicates that the metaverse intelligent technology intervention had a positive impact on learners' motivation.

A significant increase in motivation scores in the experimental group compared to the control group suggests that integrating metaverse technology has the potential to enhance learners' motivation (Fig. 5).

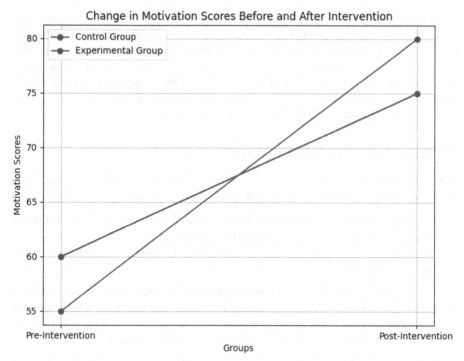

Fig. 4. Change in Motivation Scores Before and After Intervention (Color figure online)

Qualitative Data Themes (Word Cloud):

Fig. 5. Qualitative Data Themes Cloud

The word cloud from interview data indicates prevalent themes like "immersive experience," "technology impact," and "learning enhancement," suggesting that metaverse technology's integration was perceived as immersive and beneficial to learning. The frequency and prominence of these themes reflect their significance to participants. Educators' recognition of the technology's effectiveness mirrors learners' positive feedback, reinforcing the idea that metaverse technology has a favorable effect on motivation and interest in Chinese character education and calligraphy. These findings endorse the hypothesis that metaverse technology can improve educational experiences, but a more detailed analysis is needed for a full understanding results.

5.2 Verification of Research Hypotheses

The study tested two hypotheses regarding metaverse intelligent education technology's impact on Chinese character and calligraphy education. The findings supported both:

1. Metaverse technology significantly boosted learners' interest and motivation in Chinese character education, affirming Hypothesis 1.
2. It also fostered the preservation and modernization of Chinese calligraphy education, confirming Hypothesis 2.

In summary, metaverse technology positively influences international Chinese character teaching and calligraphy education, enhancing learner engagement and cultural identity, thus supporting the initial hypotheses. Nonetheless, for effective implementation, addressing technical challenges and educator training is crucial.

6 Discussion

6.1 Interpretation of Data Analysis Results and Findings

Our research indicates that metaverse intelligent education technology notably boosts motivation and interest in learning Chinese characters and calligraphy. Participants felt more connected to Chinese culture, affirming the hypothesis that metaverse platforms' immersive nature can enhance cultural identity. However, technical difficulties and a lack of educator training present challenges, echoing the broader educational technology literature that stresses the need for substantial support for educators and learners in tech integration.

6.2 Comparison with Literature Review Theories and Research Findings

Our research reinforces the notion that metaverse technology can significantly boost learner engagement, echoing Johnson & Adams (2020) and Kim & Park (2023), who advocate its potential in overcoming traditional educational limitations. It also validates the complexities of teaching Chinese characters to nonnative learners as identified by Wang & Xu (2019), suggesting that metaverse technology can mitigate these challenges through more dynamic learning experiences. Furthermore, our findings align with Zhang & Li (2018) regarding the role of calligraphy education in cultural identity formation, with metaverse platforms providing a deeply immersive and culturally enriched learning environment.

6.3 Data Insights and Answers to Research Questions and Purposes

Our research centers on how metaverse intelligent education technology can enrich international Chinese character and calligraphy education:

Research Question: The study shows that metaverse technology can effectively merge these educational fields by fostering immersive environments that boost learner engagement, motivation, and cultural identity.

Research Purpose: The investigation reveals models and methods for integrating metaverse technology, underscoring its beneficial impacts on learner motivation, interest, and cultural ties.

In summary, the findings advocate for metaverse technology as a transformative resource in language and calligraphy education, suggesting its alignment with educational innovation while addressing unique challenges in the subjects of Chinese character and calligraphy education. These insights serve as a guide for educators and policymakers and advocate for expanded use and study of metaverse applications in education.

7 Conclusions

7.1 Summary of Main Content and Results

Our research found that the integration of metaverse intelligent education technology significantly increased learners' motivation and interest in both international Chinese character teaching and Chinese traditional calligraphy education.

Learners reported a stronger connection to Chinese culture and heritage, indicating that metaverse technology enhanced their cultural identity.

Challenges, including technical issues and the need for educator training, were identified as areas for improvement.

7.2 Contributions of the Research

This research contributes to the growing body of literature on the application of metaverse technology in education, emphasizing its potential to address motivation and engagement challenges.

It provides practical insights into the integration of cultural elements into language and calligraphy education through metaverse platforms.

The study highlights the importance of supporting educators and learners in adapting to new educational technologies.

7.3 Significance, Value, and Implications

The study underscores the significant educational potential of metaverse technology in enhancing engagement and cultural appreciation in language and calligraphy learning. It plays a pivotal role in cultural preservation by deepening learners' connection to Chinese heritage. The findings are informative for policymakers and curriculum developers considering metaverse integration into educational programs, and highlight the need for targeted educator training programs. Looking ahead, the research paves the way for further inquiry into the enduring impacts of metaverse based education, comparisons with conventional teaching approaches, and the establishment of standard practices for its educational use.

7.4 Research Limitations and Future Improvements

The research on metaverse education technology in Chinese character and calligraphy teaching provides valuable insights but has notable limitations. While the study confirms the positive impact of metaverse technology on language and cultural education, its findings may not be universally applicable due to a limited participant set and specific platforms. To enhance the effectiveness of metaverse technology in education, future research should consider a wider demographic, explore various platforms, and conduct longterm studies to assess sustained impacts. Additionally, addressing technical challenges, providing educator training, and investigating the influence of cultural backgrounds are essential for maximizing the benefits of metaverse technology in educational settings. Comparative analyses with traditional methods, addressing ethical concerns, developing standardized guidelines, and adopting mixed methods approaches can further contribute to the field's advancement. In conclusion, while metaverse technology holds promise in education, addressing these limitations and pursuing future research directions will refine its role and effectiveness in teaching Chinese characters and calligraphy.

Acknowledgements. This work was supported by the 2023 General Project of Shanghai Educational Science Research C2023262 Theoretical Construction and Exploratory Application Research of Educational Metauniverse. This study is a part of the 2023 Shanghai Key Curriculum Construction project on "Chinese Calligraphy Art."

References

1. Zhang, X., Chen, Y., Hu, L., Wang, Y.: The metaverse in education: definition, framework, features, potential applications, challenges, and future research topics. Front. Psychol. **13**, 1016300 (2022). https://doi.org/10.3389/fpsyg.2022.1016300
2. The metaverse is coming to education: fourteen key talking points. https://www.uoc.edu/por tal/en/news/actualitat/2022/143educationmetavers.html
3. How AI and Metaverse are Transforming the Educational Sector? https://www.analyticsins ight.net/howaiandmetaversearetransformingtheeducationalsector/
4. A Detailed Guide to the Metaverse in Education. https://pixelplex.io/blog/metaverseineduc ation/
5. The metaverse and education: fourteen insights on the future. https://www.uoc.edu/portal/en/ news/actualitat/2022/143educationmetavers.html
6. Zhou, B.: Building a smart education ecosystem from a metaverse perspective. Mob. Inf. Syst. **2022**, Article ID 1938329, 10 p (2022). https://doi.org/10.1155/2022/1938329
7. Zhong, J., Zheng, Y.: Empowering future education: learning in the EduMetaverse. In: 2022 International Symposium on Educational Technology (ISET), Hong Kong, Hong Kong, pp. 292–295 (2022). https://doi.org/10.1109/ISET55194.2022.00068

8. Li, M.: A systematic review of the research on Chinese character teaching and learning. Front. Educ. China **15**(1), 39–72 (2020). https://doi.org/10.1007/s115160200003y
9. Liu, C., Song, H.: Researches on Chinese character teaching in the field of International Chinese language education in the past 15 years. J. Chin. Writ. Syst. **6**(1), 7179 (2022). https://doi.org/10.1177/25138502221081893

Research on Improving Higher Education Exam Quality Based on Weighted k-Medoids Clustering

Linshu Chen[1]([✉]), Tao Li[1], Yuxiang Chen[1,2], Lei Zhao[3], Li Peng[1], Shiwen Zhang[1], and Wei Liang[1]([✉])

[1] School of Computer Science and Engineering, Hunan University of Science and Technology, Xiangtan, China
{linshuchen,chenyuxiang,shiwenzhang,wliang}@hnust.edu.cn,
plpeng@hnu.edu.cn
[2] College of Computer Science and Electronic Engineering, Hunan University, Changsha, China
[3] Information Technology (Internet Supervision) Department, Hunan Police Academic, Changsha, China
zhaolei@hnpa.edu.cn

Abstract. Exam is the most effective method to evaluate the quality of higher education, and improving higher education exam quality is of paramount importance. Traditional methods of analyzing and improving higher education exam quality, such as mean and variance based on mathematical statistics, are only suitable for sample datasets that are small and static. On the other hand, robust clustering methods, such as PAM and k-Medoids, do not consider the importance of each attribute which lead to different impacts on clustering result. Based on the aforementioned issues, this paper researches on improving higher education exam quality based on weighted k-Medoids clustering. Specifically, the calculating method of attribute weights is introduced based on the granularity rough entropy. Secondly, a novel weighted k-Medoids clustering method is proposed, which integrates the attribute weights into the classic k-Medoids clustering method. Finally, the performance on UCI datasets shows the proposed method significantly improves the clustering accuracy compared to PAM and fast k-Medoids. Meanwhile, the experimental results on proprietary artificial teaching datasets indicate that the novel method identifies and corrects redundant and less significant exam questions, effectively improving higher education exam quality.

Keywords: Higher Education · Exam Quality · Clustering · Attribute Weight · k-Medoids

1 Introduction

The importance of higher education for university students is self-evident, and exam serve as the most effective means and measures for evaluating the quality and effectiveness of university education. As a critical component of quality control within the

W. Hong and G. Kanaparan (Eds.): ICCSE 2023, CCIS 2025, pp. 194–209, 2024.
https://doi.org/10.1007/978-981-97-0737-9_19

teaching process, exam play a pivotal role in assessing the grasp of acquired knowledge, measuring teaching effectiveness, ensuring educational quality, and providing teachers with valuable insights for adjusting and improving their teaching methods [1]. Exam also serve as a significant basis for controlling and motivating students' learning behavior. The quality of exam questions, directly or indirectly, impacts the reliability and accuracy of assessments, and can significantly influence students' attitudes and behaviors toward learning [2]. Therefore, the analysis and improvement of exam quality are research topics of paramount importance.

Statistical analysis, is a traditional method for examining and improving the exam quality. Previous scholars [3–6] traditionally employed statistical analysis as a method for examining and refining exam questions. They used metrics such as mean scores, standard deviations, reliability, coverage, effectiveness, discrimination, as well as excellence rates, passing rates, and failure rates. Reliability is used to assess the reliability and stability of exam questions, coverage indicates the extent and breadth of knowledge coverage, effectiveness represents the disparity between actual exam results and expected goals, standard deviation reflects the distribution of scores, and discrimination measures the ability of students at different levels to distinguish and differentiate questions of the same type. However, some scholars discover that the aforementioned methods of statistical analysis are only applicable to sample datasets that are static and small. Meanwhile, they can only provide basic statistics and analysis of surface-level indicators such as question difficulty, knowledge coverage and effectiveness. They cannot deeply assess the rationality of the exam paper structure, whether the content of the questions aligns with the curriculum, and particularly, they cannot intelligently assess question redundancy (whether questions are repeated) or the level of importance (whether they are teaching priorities).

Clustering is an important data analysis technique that divides a group of objects into multiple clusters based on certain principles, so that objects in the same cluster have higher similarity, while objects in different clusters have lower similarity. Clustering has been widely applied in various fields such as intelligent transportation, security of IoV [7, 8], blockchain [9, 10], embedded system [11, 12], privacy protection [13, 14], machine learning [15–17], service-oriented computing [18], web service [19–21], vehicular network [22, 23], etc. Clustering, such as PAM and fast k-Means, In recent years, has been increasingly used by scholars [24–26] to analyze and improve the quality of exam questions. However, PAM clustering requires computing the distances between each data point and all other data points, leading to significant computational complexity, especially for large datasets. Additionally, PAM is highly sensitive to the initial center point selection, and improper choices may lead to sub-optimal clustering results or convergence to local optima. Mean-while, the disadvantage of fast k-Means is that all attributes with equal importance in the distance metric calculation may lead to inaccurate dissimilarity measures, thereby affecting the clustering results.

Granular computing, as a new methodology for simulating human thinking and solving complicated problems, has received more and more scholars' attention to research it with clustering method. Granular computing is an information processing method aimed at simplifying problems, reducing complexity, and improving computational efficiency by selecting appropriate granularity [27, 28]. Granular computing obtains approximate solutions to problems at different granularities, thereby reducing computational complexity, improving computational efficiency, and eliminating unnecessary details in the problem-solving process. One of the theoretical granular computing models is rough set, whose focus is dealing with the uncertainty of the computational object, and effectively expressing fuzzy and ambiguous concepts. Granular computing has now been widely applied in image processing [29], complex problem solving [30], artificial neural network, etc.

Based on the above knowledge gap and our previous works [31–34], and in order to applying the granular computing into k-Medoids clustering algorithm, we propose a weighted k-Medoids clustering method, and apply it in improving exam quality of high education. The performance on UCI machine learning datasets shows that the proposed method significantly improves the clustering accuracy compared to PAM and fast k-Medoids. Furthermore, experimental results on proprietary educational datasets reveal that this novel method identifies and rectifies certain redundant and less important exam questions, effectively enhancing the quality of exam question. This research holds valuable guidance implications for higher education administration and the enhancement of teaching quality.

Specifically, our major contributions are as follows.

- We propose the attribute weights calculating method based on granularity rough entropy, which aims to evaluate the different importance of each exam question. This can help identify and handle noise or inconsistencies of exam question in the data processing.
- We propose a weighted k-Medoids clustering method which integrates the attribute weights into the classic k-Medoids. Specifically, we introduce the attribute weights into classic k-Medoids clustering method, and utilize the cluster center in the initial clustering as a candidate set for the initial clustering center, which improves the efficiency and performance of clustering algorithms, helps the algorithm converge faster to appropriate clustering results, and reduces the risk of poor local optima.
- We perform the proposed method on UCI datasets to test its validity, and then apply it on our proprietary artificial teaching datasets, with its experimental results indicating that the novel method identifies and corrects redundant and less significant exam questions, effectively improving higher education exam quality.

The rest of this paper is organized as follows. Section 2 introduces some important concepts which mainly derives from the rough set theory. In Sect. 3, it provides a detailed process of the novel weighted k-Medoids clustering method. Section 4 first perform the proposed method on UCI datasets to test its validity, and then apply it on proprietary teaching datasets to improving higher education exam quality. Section 5 concludes whole work of this paper.

2 Basic Knowledge

In this section, we introduce the basic concepts of information table, indiscernibility relation, upper and lower approximation sets, roughness and granularity rough entropy, which are related to the proposed method of weighted k-Medoids clustering in this paper.

Most of the above concepts are derived from rough set theory, which is one the most important granular computing models.

Rough Set Theory, as an effective tool for handling imprecise, inconsistent, and incomplete information, directly analyzes and reasons about the data itself, uncovering hidden knowledge and revealing underlying patterns. It is a natural method for data mining or knowledge discovery. Rough set does not require prior knowledge, and has a solid mathematical foundation. Rough set is now widely applied in various fields, including prediction and control, image processing, fault diagnosis, pattern recognition and classification, machine learning, and data mining.

Definition 1 (**Information Table**): An information table S can be represented as a quadruple $S = (U, A, V, f)$. Here, U is a non-empty finite set of objects, also referred to as the universe; $A = C \cup D$ is the complete set of attributes, with subsets C and D denoting the conditional attribute set and the decision attribute set, respectively, and satisfying $C \cap D = \emptyset$; V is the set of attribute values, i.e., it constitutes the value domain of the attribute set A; f is an information function that satisfies $f: U \times A \to V$, representing the assignment of an information value to each attribute for every instance object.

Definition 2 (**Indiscernibility Relation**): Let $S = (U, A, V, f)$ be an information table, and let the attribute subset $B \subseteq A$ determine an indiscernibility binary relation (indiscernibility relation):

$$IND(B) = \{(x, y) | (x, y) \in U^2, \forall_{b \in B}(b(x) = b(y))\} \qquad (1)$$

The indiscernibility relation is an equivalence relation that satisfies the properties of reflexivity, symmetry, and transitivity. The indiscernibility relation $IND(B)$ forms a partition of U, where the subset B partitions U into:

$$U/IND(B) = \{X | X \subseteq U \wedge \forall_{x \in X, v \in X, b \in B}(b(x) = b(y))\} \qquad (2)$$

Essentially, an equivalence class is a collection of objects with the same attribute values. It is the most concise representation on the universe U and contains no redundant information.

Definition 3 (**Upper and Lower Approximation Sets**): Given an information table $S = (U, A, V, f)$, for any attribute subset $B \subseteq A$ and object subset $X \subseteq U$, the B-upper approximation and B-lower approximation of X are defined as follows:

$$\overline{X_B} = \cup\{[x]_B \in U/IND(B) : [x]_B \cap X \neq \emptyset\} \qquad (3)$$

$$\underline{X_B} = \cup\{[x]_B \in U/IND(B) : [x]_B \subseteq X\} \qquad (4)$$

$U/IND(B) = \{X | X \subseteq U \wedge \forall_{x \in X, v \in X, b \in B}(b(x) = b(y))\}$ is the partition of the indiscernibility relation B on U. For any subset $X \subseteq U$, if $\overline{X_B} = \underline{X_B}$, then X is a definable set or an exact set in the rough approximation space; if $\overline{X_B} \neq \underline{X_B}$, then X is a rough set.

Definition 4 (**Roughness**): Given an information table $S = (U, A, V, f)$, for any attribute subset $B \subseteq A$ and object subset $X \subseteq U$ (where X is not an empty set), the roughness of the set X under the indiscernibility relation $IND(B)$ is defined as follows:

$$\rho_B(X) = |\overline{X_B} - \underline{X_B}| / |\overline{X_B}| \qquad (5)$$

where $\overline{X_B}$ and $\underline{X_B}$ respectively represent the upper and lower approximations of the set X with respect to B. It can be observed that $0 \leq \rho_B(X) \leq 1$. If X is the union of some equivalence classes in $U/IND(B)$, then $\overline{X_B} = \underline{X_B} = X$, and thus $\rho_B(X) = 0$. For $X \neq \phi$, $\rho_B(X) = 1$ if and only if $\underline{X_B} = \phi$, which is independent of the upper approximation of X.

Definition 5 (Granularity of Knowledge): Given an information table $S = (U, A, V, f)$, for any attribute subset $B \subseteq A$, if $U/IND(B) = \{X_1, X_2, X_3, \ldots, X_t\}$, then the granularity of knowledge of $U/IND(B)$ (denoted as $GK(B)$) is defined as follows:

$$GK(B) = \sum_{i=1}^{t} |X_i|^2 / |U|^2 \tag{6}$$

where $\sum_{i=1}^{t} |X_i|^2$ is the cardinality of the equivalence relation determined by $\bigcup_{i=1}^{t} X_i \times X_i$.

Roughness is primarily used to measure the completeness of knowledge, but it cannot accurately and effectively measure the granularity of knowledge. Rough entropy also fails to effectively reflect the granularity of knowledge. To address this issue, here, granularity is combined with rough entropy to develop a granularity-rough entropy model that can effectively measure the size of knowledge granularity.

Definition 6 (Granularity Rough Entropy): Given an information table $S = (U, A, V, f)$, for any $P, Q \subseteq A$, where $U/IND(P) = \{Y_1, Y_2, \ldots, Y_m\}$ is a partition of U induced by $IND(P)$, and $U/IND(Q) = \{X_1, X_2, X_3, \ldots, X_n\}$ is a partition of U induced by $IND(Q)$, the granularity rough entropy $GRE(P, Q)$ of P under the relation $IND(Q)$ is defined as follows, where $GK(Q)$ represents the granularity of knowledge.

$$GRE(P, Q) = GK(Q) \times \sum_{i=1}^{m} \rho_Q(Y_i) log_2 (\rho_Q(Y_i) + 1) \tag{7}$$

3   Proposed Weighted *k*-Medoids Clustering Method

In this section, we design a weighted *k*-Medoids clustering method, that is to say, we elaborate on how to transform entropy values into weights for individual exam questions and integrate these weights into the *k*-Medoids algorithm to perform cluster analysis on improving higher education exam quality. Ultimately, this allows us to make adjustments for the quality of the exam.

3.1   Problem Description

In the classical *k*-Medoids clustering algorithm, it assigns the same weight to each attribute, implying that each attribute contributes equally to the clustering results. However, in practical applications, different attributes may have varying degrees of importance. Some attributes may play a significant role in the final clustering results, while the impact of others may be negligible or even negligible. In such cases, simply treating all attributes with equal importance may lead to inaccurate distance measurements, thereby affecting the quality of clustering results.

To address this issue, we propose a weight calculation method based on granularity rough entropy. Granularity rough entropy takes into account various levels of importance among different attributes and assigns corresponding weights to each attribute to reflect its contribution to the clustering process. By introducing granularity rough entropy, we can calculate the distances between samples more accurately, thus better reflecting the differences in importance among different attributes during the clustering process. In this way, we can obtain more practical and high-quality clustering results, improving the effectiveness and interpretability of clustering methods in real-world applications.

3.2 Concept Definition

Before designing the calculating method of attribute weights and proposing the weighted k-Medoids clustering algorithm, we should define three fundamental and preconditioned concepts of attribute importance, attribute weight and sample similarity.

Definition 7 (**Attribute Importance Based on Granularity Rough Entropy**): Given an information table $S = (U, A, V, f)$, for any attribute $a \in A$, the importance of attribute a in S is defined as follows:

$$Sig_G(a) = GRE(\{a\}, A - \{a\}) \tag{8}$$

where $GRE(\{a\}, A - \{a\})$ represents the granularity rough entropy of attribute a under the relation $IND(A - \{a\})$.

Definition 8 (**Attribute Weight**): Given an information table $S = (U, A, V, f)$, for any attribute $a \in A$, let $Sig_G(a)$ represent the importance of attribute a in S based on granularity rough entropy, where $0 \leq Sig_G(a) \leq 1$. The weight of attribute a in S is defined as follows:

$$weight_G(a) \begin{cases} \frac{1}{2} \times 1 + \frac{count_{zero}}{|A| + \sqrt{|A| - count_{zero}}}, & if\ Sig_G(a) = 0 \\ 1 + Sig_G(a), & if\ Sig_G(a) > 0 \end{cases} \tag{9}$$

where $|A|$ represents the cardinality of set A, and $count_{zero}$ represents the number of attributes in A with importance equal to 0.

Definition 9 (**Sample Similarity**): Let $K = (X, A)$ be a clustering space, where X is the set of samples (universe), and A is the set of attributes. Introducing the concept of granularity, define a new sample similarity function $S(x_i, x_j)$ to measure the similarity between samples (objects) (x_i, x_j). The function $S(x_i, x_j)$ is defined as follows:

$$s(x_i, x_j) = \frac{1}{1 + \sum_{k=1}^{|A|} w_k |x_{ik} - x_{jk}|} \tag{10}$$

3.3 Attribute Weight

This subsection provides a detailed explanation of the process for calculating attribute weights based on granularity rough entropy. This is the most critical component of the proposed clustering method and a crucial step to improve exam quality.

The steps for calculating attribute weights are as follows:

(1) Using counting sort, calculate the partition of the universe U induced by the indiscernibility relation $IND(A - \{a\})$ as $U/IND(A - \{a\}) = \{X_1, X_2, \ldots, X_t\}$.

(2) Using counting sort, calculate the partition of the universe U induced by the indiscernibility relation $IND(\{a\})$ as $U/IND(\{a\}) = \{Y_1, Y_2, \ldots, Y_m\}$.

(3) According to Definition 5, calculate the knowledge granularity $GK(A-\{a\})$.

(4) Define a variable temp.

(5) For each $Y \in U/IND(\{a\})$, iteratively perform the following three steps:

    ① Based on the partition $U/IND(A - \{a\})$, calculate the upper approximation $\overline{Y}_{A-\{a\}}$ and lower approximation $\underline{Y}_{A-\{a\}}$ of Y with respect to the relation $IND(A - \{a\})$ separately;

    ② Calculate the roughness $\rho_{A-a}(Y)$ of the set Y with respect to the relation $IND(A - \{a\})$ based on Definition 4;

    ③ Let $temp = temp + \rho_{A-\{a\}}(Y)log_2(\rho_{A-\{a\}}(Y) + 1)$.

(6) Calculate the granularity rough entropy, i.e., $GRE(\{a\}, A - \{a\}) = GK(A - \{a\}) \times temp$, based on Definition 6.

(7) Return the granularity rough entropy $GRE(\{a\}, A - \{a\})$ for attribute a.

(8) Calculate the attribute importance for attribute a based on Definition 7.

(9) Finally, calculate the weight of attribute a as per Definition 8.

3.4   Proposed Method

This subsection provides a detailed description of the specific process of the k-Medoids algorithm based on weight calculation. The pseudocode for this algorithm is presented in Algorithm 1, and the corresponding flowchart is shown in Fig. 1.

In Algorithm 1, Line 1 calculates the weight value of each attribute of the sample using the detailed steps of weight calculation in Sect. 3.2. Lines 2–6 calculate the similarity between each pair of samples using Eq. (10) to obtain a similarity matrix S, which is then de-fuzzified into S' according to the set threshold d. Line 7 classifies the samples into rough classes $\{X_1, X_2, \ldots, X_t\}1 \le t \le N$ based on the de-fuzzified similarity matrix S', where t represents the number of granularity grains. Lines 8–10 select the qualified clustering centers based on Eq. (11) and put them into the Medoids set. Line 11 represents the initial candidate set of clustering centers obtained, which is stored in the Medoids set. Lines 12–13 select two samples m_i and m_j with the minimum similarity between them, set them as the initial clustering centers $d_1 = m_1$ and $d_2 = m_2$ and then remove them from the initial candidate set of clustering centers, and finally use the Maximum-Minimum clustering method to select the remaining initial clustering centers d_k. Line 14 clusters the samples based on the obtained K initial clustering centers. It assigns the sample u_i to the nearest clustering center d_i to form cluster C_i. Lines 15–18 update the clustering centers within the original clusters and reassign samples. Finally, if the clustering centers no longer change, the iteration stops and each cluster C_i is output.

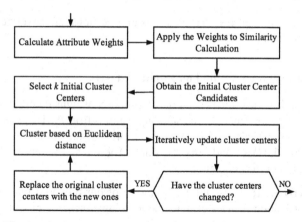

Fig. 1. The flowchart of weighted k-Medoids clustering method

---

Algorithm 1: The weighted k-Medoids clustering method.

Input: Properties $M = \{o_1, o_2, \ldots, o_r\}$;Sample set $U= \{u_1, u_2, \ldots, u_n\}$;Number of class clusters K; Set threshold d.

Output: Clustering results $C_1, C_2, .., C_K$

1   **Calcuting** $weight_G(M\{o_1\}), \ldots, weight_G(M\{o_r\})$ by the method in Section 3.

2   **for** $i \leftarrow 1$ **to** n **do**

3   **for** $j \leftarrow 1$ **to** n **do**

4        $s(x_i, x_j) = \frac{1}{1+\sum_{k=1}^{|A|} w_k|x_{ik}-x_{jk}|}$, De-fuzzify to obtain S' based on threshold d

5   **end for**

6   **end for**

7   Classify based on the de-fuzzified similarity matrix S' to obtain a rough set $[X_1, \ldots, X_t]$

8   **for** $i \leftarrow 1$ **to** t **do**

9        $m_i = \left\{ x_{ij} \left| \min_{j=1}^{n} \right| x_{ij} - \frac{1}{N}\sum_{k=1}^{N} x_{ik} \mid \right\}$ and Put it into the Medoids set

10   **end for**

11   Obtain the initial candidate set of clustering centers $Mediods = [m_1, \ldots, m_t]$

12   $d_1, d_2 = min(s(m_i, m_j))$ $where$ $i \neq j$

13   $d_k = min\{max\{s(m_i, d_1), s(m_i, d_2), \ldots, s(m_i, d_{k-1})\}\}$

14   For each sample u_i, assign it to the nearest d_i to form cluster C_i

15   **if** cluster center remains changed **then**

16   repeat update the cluster center until the conditions are met

17   **end if**

18 **end for**

---

4 Improving Exam Quality by Proposed Method

In this section, before applying the proposed weighted k-Medoids clustering method in improving higher education exam quality, we perform it comparing with PAM and fast k-Medoids on UCI machine learning datasets to demonstrate its validity. Then, we describe the performance of the proposed weighted k-Medoids clustering method on our artificial teaching datasets in detail. The experimental results show the novel method identifies and corrects redundant and less significant exam questions, effectively enhancing the higher education exam quality.

4.1 Validity of Proposed Method on Public Datasets

Datasets. To validate the effectiveness of our proposed weighted k-Medoids clustering method, experiments are conducted on standard datasets from the UCI machine learning database, as shown in Table 1. This experiment utilized six datasets: Haberman, Ionosphere, Blood, Ecoli, CMC, and Soybean-small. These datasets vary in the number of samples and attributes they contain.

Evaluation Metrics. To assess the performance of our proposed method, we utilize three popular evaluation metrics of machine learning: Accuracy of Clustering ($AC = \frac{\sum_{i=1}^{k} a_i}{n} \times 100\%$) and Sum of squared clustering Errors ($SE = \sum_{i=1}^{k} \sum_{j \in C_i} ||x_j - \mu_i||^2$).

Experimental Results. This study evaluated the effectiveness of our proposed method on six datasets from the UCI machine learning database, whose descriptions are presented in Table 1. The PAM clustering algorithm, the fast k-Medoids clustering algorithm, and our proposed method are compared in their performance on these datasets. The final experimental results are shown in Table 2 and Table 3.

Executed on various UCI datasets, Table 2 displays the accuracy of clustering results (AC) obtained by PAM, fast k-Medoids and our proposed method. Table 3 illustrates the average squared errors (SE) of each algorithm's clustering results.

Table 2 shows that our proposed method generally outperforms the PAM and fast k-Medoids clustering algorithm in terms of AC (accuracy of clustering).

Table 3 displays the mean SE (Squared Error) calculated based on the clustering results obtained from PAM, fast k-Medoids, and our method. It can be observed that our proposed method only has slightly higher mean SE on the Haberman and Ecoli datasets compared to fast k-Medoids and PAM, but it performs well on other datasets of Ionosphere, Blood, Ecoli, CMC and Soybean-small. This suggests that our method excels in intra-cluster cohesion compared to other two algorithms. While the mean SE of our method algorithm on the Haberman and Ecoli may not be as low as that of the PAM and Fast k-Medoids, its AC (accuracy of clustering) significantly surpass that of PAM and fast k-Medoids algorithms.

In conclusion, our proposed weighted k-Medoids clustering algorithm, yields better clustering results compared to traditional algorithms. This suggests that employing our proposed weighted k-Medoids method for analyzing exam quality, as presented in this paper, is feasible.

Table 1. Dataset

DataSet	samples	attributes	classes
Haberman	306	3	2
Ionosphere	351	33	2
Blood	748	4	2
Ecoli	336	7	8
CMC	1473	7	8
Soybean-small	47	35	4

Table 2. Accuracy of Clustering (*AC*)

DataSet	PAM	*fast* k-Medoids	Ours
Haberman	53.95%	51.55%	**71.90%**
Ionosphere	67.83%	69.23%	**70.94%**
Blood	64.59%	62.3%	**67.45%**
Ecoli	52.23%	49.2%	**54.50%**
CMC	39.24%	40.13%	**41.25%**
Soybean-mall	69.83%	72.34%	**80.64%**

Table 3. Sum of squared clustering Errors (*SE*)

DataSet	PAM	*fast* k-Medoids	Ours
Haberman	3.4110E+04	**3.4006E+04**	3.6630E+04
Ionosphere	2.5323E+03	2.4977E+03	**2.4795E+03**
Blood	8.6314E+08	9.7806E+08	**7.8093E+08**
Ecoli	**1.7872E+01**	1.8054E+01	1.8072E+01
CMC	2.6782E+04	2.5482E+04	**2.5433E+04**
Soybean-small	0.035 2E+04	0.0324E+04	**0.0302E+04**

4.2 Experiment on Improving Higher Education Exam Quality

In this subsection, we first provide a detailed exposition of the experiment rationale, experimental objectives, types of experimental data, and the source of experimental data. Subsequently, taking the course exam of university-level C language for example, relying on the principles of rough set theory, we propose a quantitative measurement method for the importance of exam questions. Finally, by incorporating a weighted calculation into the k-Medoids algorithm, we subject the dataset to clustering, and enable the correction of problematic exam questions. The results show this approach effectively enhances the quality of exam item creation.

Experimental Description. In university-level C language exams, exam questions constitute the fundamental building blocks, and the quality of the exam paper is collectively determined by the quality of each individual question. Whether each sub-question within the entire set of questions is scientifically applicable, complies with the syllabus requirements, and objectively reflects the students' actual proficiency plays a decisive role in the overall quality of the exam paper.

In the context of exam papers, the following situations may arise: some questions cover common knowledge points but are overly challenging in terms of calculations; certain knowledge points are too specialized, making it difficult for students to tackle, resulting in very few students being able to answer correctly; and a majority of questions have similar levels of difficulty, lacking the ability to differentiate between students' skills effectively. In such cases, the test's significance is diminished, and adjustments should be made, either through question replacement or adjusting difficulty levels accordingly.

Before the exam, it is challenging for examiners to subjectively determine the redundancy and importance of exam questions because students' foundational knowledge and learning situations vary. Examiners are concerned about making questions too difficult, potentially causing students to fail the exam, and also worried about making questions too easy, failing to assess students' true proficiency accurately.

In the quality correction method for university-level C language exam questions presented in this paper, a pre-exam evaluation and analysis of the questions are performed. Post-exam analysis of the exam paper scores is also conducted. By employing clustering methods, the results are obtained, and adjustments and quality corrections are made to clusters that contain too many similar types of questions and clusters that may represent excessive difficulty or overly specialized knowledge points. This approach aims to enhance the overall quality of the exam paper.

Experimental Data Preparation. The university-level C language exam paper used in this experiment was sourced from the end-of-semester exam paper for the Computer Science major at Hunan University of Science and Technology for the 2022-2023-2 academic term. The exam consisted of multiple question types, including multiple-choice questions (questions 0–10), true/false questions (questions 11–20), fill-in-the-blank questions (questions 21–30), and programming questions (questions 31–32). Each question was assigned a unique identifier, and data collection was performed for each question regarding its coverage of knowledge points, difficulty level, historical performance, and question type weight. The attributes of knowledge point coverage, question type weight, and question difficulty level fall within the range of (A–E), with A indicating the highest degree, and E indicating the lowest. Historical performance is calculated based on the average score obtained by all students on that particular question, ranging from *0* to *100*.

In the following experiments, it is necessary to discretize the historical performance of the university-level C language exam scores. Following the common practice of the university, the percentile scores for historical performance can be discretized into five grade levels: A (Excellent, 90–100 points), B (Good, 80–89 points), C (Average, 70–79 points), D (Pass, 60–69 points), and E (Fail, below 60 points), as shown in Table 4.

Table 4. Correspondence between Percentage Scores and Discrete Grade Levels

Percentage Scores	90–100	80–89	70–79	60–69	< 60
Discrete Grades	A	B	C	D	E

Exam Quality Improvement. During the university-level C language exam, each exam question can be considered as a sample, with its knowledge point coverage (*a*), question difficulty (b), historical performance (c), and question type weight (d) viewed as conditional attribute set A. Due to the large number of questions, we have selected 10 questions for illustration on how to calculate question weights and perform cluster analysis. Below is the information table for these 10 questions, as presented in Table 5.

Table 5. Question Information

Question Number	Knowledge Point Coverage (a)	Question Difficulty (b)	Historical Performance (c)	Question Type Weight (d)
e_1	B	B	C	A
e_2	A	C	C	B
e_3	C	B	A	B
e_4	B	C	A	A
e_5	A	A	E	D
e_6	C	B	C	C
e_7	B	B	C	C
e_8	D	C	C	B
e_9	D	E	C	B
e_{10}	C	B	E	D

Table 5 represents a domain U consisting of 10 objects, with each object being a quadruple where each dimension of the tuple represents an attribute of the object. These objects can all be described using their attribute knowledge. The following is an analysis of the weight assigned to each attribute.

Let $P = \{a\}$, $Q = \{b, c, d\}$. The specific steps for calculating the granular rough entropy $GRE(P,Q)$ and the weight calculation corresponding to P are as follows:

(1) Obtain the partition of the domain U with respect to the indiscernibility relations $IND(P)$ and $IND(Q)$:

$$U/IND(Q) = \{\{e_1\}, \{e_2, e_8\}, \{e_3\}, \{e_4\}, \{e_5\}, \{e_6, e_7\}, \{e_9\}, \{e_{10}\}\};$$
$$U/IND(P) = \{\{e_1, e_4, e_7\}, \{e_2, e_5\}, \{e_3, e_6, e_{10}\}, \{e_8, e_9\}\} = \{Y_1, Y_2, Y_3, Y_4\};$$

(2) Calculate the knowledge granularity of $IND(Q)$:

$$GK(Q) = \frac{\sum_{i=1}^{n} |X_i|^2}{|U|^2} = \frac{|X_1|^2 + |X_2|^2 + \ldots + |X_i|^2}{|U|^2} = \frac{1^2 + 2^2 + 1^2 + 1^2 + 1^2 + 2^2 + 1^2 + 1^2}{10^2} = \frac{14}{100}$$

(3) Calculate the upper and lower approximations of Y_1, Y_2, Y_3, Y_4 with respect to $IND(Q)$:

$$\overline{Y_{1Q}} = \{e_1\} \cup \{e_4\} \cup \{e_6, e_7\} = \{e_1, e_4, e_6, e_7\};$$

Similarly, $\underline{Y_{1Q}} = \{e_1, e_4\}$, $\overline{Y_{2Q}} = \{e_2, e_5, e_8\}$, $\underline{Y_{2Q}} = \{e_5\}$; $\overline{Y_{3Q}} = \{e_3, e_6, e_7, e_{10}\}$; $\underline{Y_{3Q}} = \{e_3, e_{10}\}$, $\overline{Y_{4Q}} = \{e_2, e_8, e_9\}$; $\underline{Y_{4Q}} = \{e_9\}$

(4) Calculate the roughness of Y_1, Y_2, Y_3, Y_4 with respect to $IND(Q)$:

$$\rho_Q(Y_1) = \frac{\left|\overline{Y_{1Q}} - \underline{Y_{1Q}}\right|}{\left|\overline{Y_{1Q}}\right|} = 1 - \frac{|\{e_1, e_4\}|}{|\{e_1, e_4, e_6, e_7\}|} = 1/2$$

Similarly, $\rho_Q(Y_2) = 2/3$; $\rho_Q(Y_3) = 1/2$; $\rho_Q(Y_4) = 2/3$

(5) Calculate the granular rough entropy of P with respect to the relation $IND(Q)$:

$$GRE(P, Q) = GK(Q) \times \sum_{i=1}^{m} \rho_Q(Y_i) log_2(\rho_Q(Y_i) + 1) \approx 0.2195$$

(6) Calculate the attribute weight of $P = \{a\}$ based on Definitions 7 and 8:

$$Weight_G(a) = 1 + 0.2195 = 1.2195$$

Experimental Result Analysis. During the university-level C language exam, each exam question can be considered as a sample, with its knowledge point coverage (a), question difficulty (b), historical performance (c), and question type weight (d) viewed as attribute. The above calculations determine the weight of each attribute in the information table U. Since different attributes of samples may have varying impacts on clustering, there should be a certain proportion between them.

After calculating the weight of each attribute, we incorporate these weights into the similarity calculations of the k-Medoids algorithm, allowing us to cluster the dataset using the k-Medoids algorithm. Obtaining clusters with fewer samples and noisy points may indicate that these exam questions are too difficult for students or too specialized in terms of knowledge points, leading to score loss. Teachers can use these results to make adjustments to the corresponding exam questions to avoid unreasonable questions and to better assess students' knowledge mastery.

5   Conclusion

This paper researches on improving higher education exam quality based on weighted k-Medoids clustering. Specifically, it proposes a weighted calculation method based on rough entropy granularity, which is applied to the fast k-Medoids algorithm. This method not only addresses certain limitations of the fast k-Medoids algorithm but also significantly enhances the stability and accuracy of clustering results. The algorithm is applied to the refinement of the quality of university C language exams by calculating weights for each attribute of the exam questions and conducting cluster analysis using the k-Medoids algorithm. It is worth noting that the methods we propose can also be applied to the revision of examination quality in various professional courses, such as the theory of socialism with Chinese characteristics, professional English, advanced computer networks, and so on. Here, we are using university-level C programming language design as an example to analyze the proposed methods. Clusters with fewer samples and noisy points can be regarded as excessively difficult or containing inconsistencies, which can guide the modification and quality refinement of exam questions that are excessively difficult, overly focused on specific knowledge points, or contain repetitive knowledge points. This effectively improves the quality of exam paper propositioning, thereby providing important guidance for guiding university C language teaching and enhancing teaching quality.

Acknowledgments. This work was partially supported by the National Key Research and Development Program of China [grant numbers 2022YFA1602200 and 2021YFA1000600], the National Natural Science Foundation of China [grant number 62072170 and 62202156], the Science and Technology Project of the Department of Communications of Hunan Provincial [grant number 202101], the Key Research and Development Program of Hunan Province [grant number 2022GK2015], the Hunan Provincial Teaching Research and Reform Project [grant number HNJG-2022-0786 and HNJG-2022-0792], the Hunan Provincial Department of Education Scientific Research Project[grant number 21C0946], the Hunan Provincial Degree and Graduate Teaching Reform and Research Project[grant number 2022JGYB130], the Teaching Reform and Research Project of Hunan University of Science and Technology [grant number 2021-76-9 and 2021-76-26].

References

1. Masserini, L., Bini, M., Pratesi, M.: Do quality of services and institutional image impact students' satisfaction and loyalty in higher education? Soc. Indic. Res. **146**, 91–115 (2019)
2. Alzafari, K., Ursin, J.: Implementation of quality assurance standards in European higher education: does context matter? Qual. High. Educ. **25**(1), 58–75 (2019)
3. Guldora, M., Mukhabat, K., Gulchekhra, A.: Creating a quality test for ESL and EFL students. Multidiscip. Int. J. Res. Lines Proj. **13**, 5–10 (2022)
4. Rothstein, J.: Teacher quality in educational production: tracking, decay, and student achievement. Q. J. Econ. **125**(1), 175–214 (2010)
5. Shaturaev, J.: Indonesia: superior policies and management for better education (Community development through Education). Архив научных исследований **1**(1) (2021)
6. Bagdasarian, I., Stupina, A., Vasileva, Z., Shmeleva, Z., Korpacheva, L.: Accreditation of the university education as a guarantee of the competencies quality in the labor market. In: 19th International Multidisciplinary Scientific GeoConference SGEM, vol. 19, no. 5.4, pp. 3–8 (2019)
7. Cai, J., Liang, W., Li, X., Li, K., Gui, Z., Khan, M.K.: GTxChain: a secure IoT smart blockchain architecture based on graph neural network. IEEE Internet Things J. (2023)
8. Gong, Y., et al.: VASERP: an adaptive, lightweight, secure, and efficient RFID-based authentication scheme for IoV. Sensors **23**(11), 5198 (2023)
9. Liang, W., et al.: PDPChain: a consortium blockchain-based privacy protection scheme for personal data. IEEE Trans. Reliab. (2022)
10. Zhou, S., Li, K., Xiao, L., Cai, J., Liang, W., Castiglione, A.: A systematic review of consensus mechanisms in blockchain. Mathematics **11**(10), 2248 (2023)
11. Long, J., Liang, W., Li, K.C., Wei, Y., Marino, M.D.: A regularized cross-layer ladder network for intrusion detection in industrial internet of things. IEEE Trans. Industr. Inf. **19**(2), 1747–1755 (2022)
12. Xu, Z., Liang, W., Li, K.C., Xu, J., Zomaya, A.Y., Zhang, J.: A time-sensitive token-based anonymous authentication and dynamic group key agreement scheme for industry 5.0. IEEE Trans. Industr. Inf. **18**(10), 7118–7127 (2021)

13. Diao, C., Zhang, D., Liang, W., Li, K.C., Hong, Y., Gaudiot, J.L.: A novel spatial-temporal multi-scale alignment graph neural network security model for vehicles prediction. IEEE Trans. Intell. Transp. Syst. **24**(1), 904–914 (2022)

14. Liang, W., et al.: Spatial-temporal aware inductive graph neural network for C-ITS data recovery. IEEE Trans. Intell. Transp. Syst. (2022)

15. Li, Y., Liang, W., Xie, K., Zhang, D., Xie, S., Li, K.C.: LightNestle: quick and accurate neural sequential tensor completion via meta learning. In: IEEE INFOCOM 2023-IEEE Conference on Computer Communications, pp. 1–10 (2023)

16. Xiong, N., et al.: A self-tuning failure detection scheme for cloud computing service. In: 2012 IEEE 26th International Parallel and Distributed Processing Symposium, pp. 668–679 (2012)

17. Wan, Z., Xiong, N., Ghani, N., Vasilakos, A.V., Zhou, L.: Adaptive unequal protection for wireless video transmission over IEEE 802.11 e networks. Multimedia Tools Appl. **72**, 541–571 (2014)

18. Xiong, N., Han, W., Vandenberg, A.: Vandenberg AGreen cloud computing schemes based on networks: a survey. IET Commun. **6**(18), 3294–3300 (2012)

19. Cao, B., Liu, X.F., Rahman, M.M., Li, B., Liu, J., Tang, M.: Integrated content and network-based service clustering and web APIs recommendation for mashup development. IEEE Trans. Serv. Comput. **13**(1), 99–113 (2017)

20. Cao, B., Liu, J., Wen, Y., Li, H., Xiao, Q., Chen, J.: Qos-aware service recommendation based on relational topic model and factorization machines for IoT mashup applications. J. Parallel Distrib. Comput. **132**, 177–189 (2019)

21. Cao, B., Liu, X.F., Liu, J., Tang, M.: Domain-aware mashup service clustering based on LDA topic model from multiple data sources. Inf. Softw. Technol. **90**, 40–54 (2017)

22. Wang, X., Bai, L., Mausler, B., Singh, P.: A novel conditional anonymity scheme for vehicular communication networks. Int. J. Commun. Syst. **35**(12), e4130 (2019)

23. Wang, X., Jiang, J., Zhao, S., Bai, L.: A fair blind signature scheme to revoke malicious vehicles in VANETs. Comput. Mater. Continua **58**, 249–262 (2019)

24. Dutt, A., Ismail, M.A., Herawan, T.: A systematic review on educational data mining. IEEE Access **5**, 15991–16005 (2017)

25. Asif, R., Merceron, A., Ali, S.A., Haider, N.G.: Analyzing undergraduate students' performance using educational data mining. Comput. Educ. **113**, 177–194 (2017)

26. Peña-Ayala, A.: Educational data mining: a survey and a data mining-based analysis of recent works. Expert Syst. Appl. **41**(4), 1432–1462 (2014)

27. Yao, Y.: Perspectives of granular computing. In: 2005 IEEE International Conference on granular Computing, vol. 1, pp. 85–90 (2005)

28. Liu, H., Cocea, M.: Granular Computing Based Machine Learning: A Big Data Processing Approach, vol. 35. Springer, Cham (2017). https://doi.org/10.1007/978-3-319-70058-8

29. Wang, X., Song, W., Zhang, B., Mausler, B., Jiang, F.: An early warning system for curved road based on ov7670 image acquisition and stm32. Comput. Mater. Continua **59**(1), 135–147 (2019)

30. Wang, X., Yu, F., Pedrycz, W., Wang, J.: Hierarchical clustering of unequal-length time series with area-based shape distance. Soft. Comput. **23**(15), 6331–6343 (2018). https://doi.org/10.1007/s00500-018-3287-6

31. Chen, L., Shen, F., Tang, Y., Wang, X., Wang, J.: Algebraic structure based clustering method from granular computing prospective. Int. J. Uncertain. Fuzziness Knowl.-Based Syst. **31**(1), 121–140 (2023)

32. Chen, L., Zhao, L., Xiao, Z., Liu, Y., Wang, J.: A granular computing based classification method from algebraic granule structure. IEEE Access **9**, 68118–68126 (2021)

33. Chen, L., Wang, J., Li, L.: The models of granular system and algebraic quotient space in granular computing. Chin. J. Electron. **25**(6), 1109–1113 (2016)
34. Chen, L., Wang, J., Wang, W., Li, L.: A new granular computing model based on algebraic structure. Chin. J. Electron. **28**(1), 136–142 (2019)

Sketch Teaching System Based on Human-Computer Hybrid Enhanced Intelligence

Shiyu Fu, Dawei Dai$^{(\boxtimes)}$, Le Yang, Zhenchun Liao, and Guoyin Wang

Key Laboratory of Big Data Intelligent Computing, Chongqing University of Posts and Telecommunications, Chongqing 400065, China
dw_dai@163.com

Abstract. Sketch education is an essential component of arts education. In recent years, with the development of society, the demand for sketch courses has been steadily increasing. However, the existing teaching resources are severely lacking, and unable to meet the requirements of high-quality teaching. This paper has designed and implemented a sketching smart teaching system. The system utilizes artificial intelligence technology to assist teaching, providing modules for image cross-modal transformation and style transfer to broaden users' creative thinking and fulfill personalized learning needs. Furthermore, the system supports a step-by-step image generation process, aiding users in learning drawing techniques effectively. Additionally, our system can collect users' drawing processes and analyze the gathered data to correct users' drawing habits. These data also serve as valuable resources for the development of artificial intelligence. This platform has propelled the transformation of classroom teaching from traditional methods to interactive teaching models inside and outside the classroom, achieving mutual empowerment between artificial intelligence and smart education.

Keywords: Drawing Assistance System · Modular Design · AI Models

1 Introduction

With the development of society, an increasing number of people are recognizing the importance of arts education. Sketching, a form of art that portrays objects' form, texture, and spatial relationships through careful observation and simple lines and shading, is a crucial component of arts education. Learning sketching enhances students' observational skills, improves their ability to grasp both overall and specific relationships, and promotes the integration of visual and cognitive abilities. Apart from this, students can enhance their drawing techniques, refine their hand-eye coordination, and boost their artistic expression. Lastly, sketching education enhances students' aesthetic and creative abilities, elevating their artistic literacy. This growing recognition has led to an increasing demand for sketching courses.

© The Author(s), under exclusive license to Springer Nature Singapore Pte Ltd. 2024
W. Hong and G. Kanaparan (Eds.): ICCSE 2023, CCIS 2025, pp. 210–219, 2024.
https://doi.org/10.1007/978-981-97-0737-9_20

However, the growth rate of teaching resources cannot keep up with the increasing demand. This has led to (1) a severe lack of teaching resources, where one teacher often has to handle classes for several dozen students simultaneously, unable to meet the requirements for high-quality teaching; (2) a monotonous teaching approach, where traditional lecture-style teaching struggles to inspire students' interest and creativity; (3) difficulties in tailoring teaching to individual needs, given significant differences among students. Due to these limitations, personalized training is challenging to implement. Therefore, we have researched, designed, and implemented a sketching smart teaching system, aiming to address these issues by leveraging artificial intelligence technology. By employing a human-computer hybrid enhanced intelligent teaching model, we aim to enhance teaching quality, stimulate students' learning interests, and capitalize on the advantages of online platforms. This approach facilitates mutual empowerment between sketching education and artificial intelligence, bridging the gap between the two fields.

The a sketching smart teaching system designed and implemented in this paper includes the following features:

(a) Collection of Drawing Behavior Processes: The system provides users with a drawing system, where their drawing processes are saved. This data is utilized to correct users' drawing habits. Moreover, the development of artificial intelligence relies on high-quality annotated data, and the valuable data collected by the system serves as a significant resource to support artificial intelligence in terms of data resources.

(b) Interactive Face Image Retrieval: Real-time retrieval of corresponding images during the process of drawing sketches helps users better understand the form of the characters being drawn. This feature enables users to grasp sketching techniques more quickly.

(c) Image Cross-Modal Transformation and Style Transfer: Integrating state-of-the-art neural network models, the system achieves cross-modal transformation and style transfer of images. This encourages users to experiment with different drawing styles, thereby expanding their creative thinking and generating more ideas and inspiration. It enriches the styles and forms of their artwork.

(d) Support for Step-by-Step Image Generation: The system supports the generation of process diagrams for sketch-style images produced through cross-modal transformation. Users can replay these processes, aiding them in understanding and mastering the techniques and processes involved in sketching different images. This feature caters to the personalized learning needs of users.

2   Related Work

In the field of modern education, art education constitutes an integral part of the educational system. However, artistic and aesthetic education often isn't the primary focus of society, leading to a lack of adequate material, technological, and personnel resources in art education [2,6,9]. Sketch education, being a significant component of art education, has seen various methods proposed to promote its development. Shesh et al. introduced an interactive sketching system for 3D design, providing a unified 2D and 3D sketching environment that encourages natural sketching styles. It encompasses functionalities such as 2D sketch cleaning, 3D reconstruction of 2D sketches, and 3D transformations [8]. Romat et al. introduced a self-stabilizing digital drawing board interface, exploring subtle differences in input and feedback concerning reading and writing from different implementation angles, public versus personal space, and shared personal space versus task space. This opened up a category of technology capable of sensing and responding to tilted adjustments [7]. However, the development of these technologies hasn't been effectively integrated and applied to contemporary sketching education.

Therefore, in this paper, we propose an a sketch teaching system based on human-computer hybrid enhanced intelligence. This system utilizes the achievements of existing artificial intelligence technologies and applies them to sketching education, aiming to overcome the current challenges faced in sketching education.

3 Design and Implementation

3.1 Architecture

Our sketch smart teaching system adopts a modular design pattern similar to [4], where the entire system is divided into small, independent modules, each responsible for specific functions (as shown in Fig. 1). This modular design ensures that each module is a relatively independent unit, making it easy to understand and maintain. The addition of new features or modifications to existing features usually only requires attention to specific modules, without affecting the entire system. Therefore, the system is more easily scalable.

The system is divided into four main functional modules: the digital drawing board module, cross-modal transformation module, style transfer module, and interactive retrieval module. The cross-modal transformation module includes two sub-modules: portrait cross-modal transformation and landscape cross-modal transformation. Additionally, the style transfer module consists of two sub-modules: oil painting style transfer and ink wash style transfer. These sub-modules operate independently. This separation of artificial intelligence models or data entities from the views not only optimizes the computational load on the graphics card but also facilitates future technological iterations and module upgrades.

Our system utilizes the popular Vue framework and the accompanying Element-UI components for frontend page design and development. On the backend, the Django framework is employed. It provides simple and flexible interfaces, allowing seamless integration with various artificial intelligence models. Its modular design and standardized code structure enable developers to embed artificial intelligence models into web applications quickly and seamlessly. MySQL database is used for data storage on the backend, ensuring data security. After the development, the system becomes a mature, practical, reliable, and easily maintainable web-based, scalable, secure, and cross-organizational application system [5].

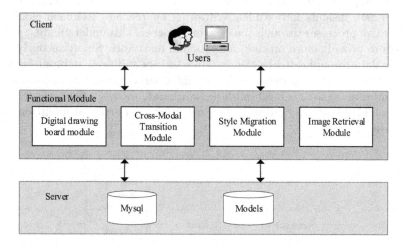

Fig. 1. Architecture of the sketch smart teaching system.

3.2   Digital Drawing Board Module

The drawing board is a crucial aspect of the user's practical drawing operations and learning process. It provides a space for creative freedom, allowing users to explore their creativity, experiment with new artistic styles, and develop their artistic creativity. In modern education, digital tools, including graphics tablets, have been widely adopted, offering users a enhanced drawing experience. Leveraging the widespread use of graphics tablets, we have designed and implemented the Digital Drawing Board Module, which comprises two main components: uploading reference images and the drawing canvas.

Users have the option to upload local image files. These images can serve as reference materials for users, such as famous artworks, photographs, or other image resources. The uploaded image is displayed on one side of the screen, allowing users to observe and learn from it. This reference image aids users in better understanding the structure, lines, shadows, and other details of the subject they are drawing, enabling them to study and emulate the reference material effectively.

The drawing board provides various drawing tools such as shapes and erasers. Users can choose the appropriate tool and start drawing on the graphics tablet. Additionally, users can adjust the properties of the drawing tools, such as line thickness and color, to have finer control over the drawing outcome. After completing their artwork, users have the option to download each step of the drawing process to their local device. The flowchart of the Digital Drawing Board module is depicted in Fig. 2.

Images created on the drawing board interface are saved on the user's device. This functionality helps users track their learning progress, understand their technical improvement, and identify areas that need enhancement. Teachers can also gain insights into students' drawing approaches, technical challenges, and creative processes through the drawing process. This understanding enables teachers to provide more precise guidance and assistance. Simultaneously, these drawing data are uploaded to the system's servers and used as input for training machine learning models. By collecting a large volume of user-generated image data, the system can establish more accurate models, offering users better services. This approach realizes a dual drive between artificial intelligence and sketch education.

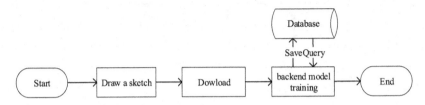

Fig. 2. Digitally drawing flowcharts.

3.3   Interactive Search Module

Users can engage in drawing through the canvas area of the interactive retrieval interface. The canvas provides tools like regular brushes and shape brushes, enabling users to draw and modify images for search preparation. We adopted the method described in [1], where each stroke completed by the user on the canvas interface is transmitted to the backend server. It is then input into the retrieval model. The backend processes the model's returned results and sends them back to the frontend. This real-time feedback updates the image retrieval interface synchronously. The image retrieval interface displays facial images in order of their similarity to the user-drawn image. As the user's strokes change, the search results also adapt accordingly. The flowchart of this module is shown in Fig. 3.

This interactive retrieval module proves to be highly effective, especially when users have vague information needs or when the image database is extensive. In large image databases, a single search might return numerous unrelated images, leading to information overload. Through interactive retrieval, users don't have to submit a perfect query all at once. They can gradually modify the drawn image, narrowing down the search scope and reducing the number of irrelevant images. This process makes it easier for users to find the results they need.

This instant and precise feedback not only provides continuous inspiration and guidance to users but also offers them a broader range of creative ideas. Such an interactive experience not only enhances users' artistic skills but also enhances their enjoyment of learning.

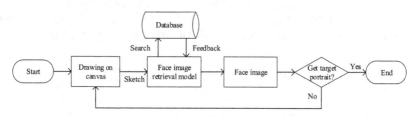

Fig. 3. Interactive retrieval flowchart.

3.4 Cross-Modal Transition Module

This module consists of two sub-modules: Portrait Cross-Modal Transformation and Landscape Cross-Modal Transformation. In the Portrait Cross-Modal Transformation sub-module, users can upload portrait images to the interface, which then transforms the images into a sketch style. This module also allows the display of the drawing process. The generated portrait sketch can showcase its drawing process, allowing users to adjust the speed of the drawing process according to their preferences and replay it as needed. Similarly, the Landscape Cross-Modal Transformation sub-module also features the ability to display the drawing process. Unlike the Portrait Cross-Modal Transformation, users need to upload landscape images, and the generated images lean more towards a sketching style with finer and more intricate lines. The flowchart is as shown in Fig. 4

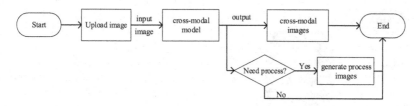

Fig. 4. Cross-modal transformation and stepwise image generation flowchart.

3.5 Style Migration Module

This module consists of two sub-modules: Oil Painting Style Transfer and Ink Wash Style Transfer. In the Oil Painting Style Transfer sub-module [10], users can upload images of various scenes to the module interface. The browser transmits these images to the backend server, where they undergo a specific oil painting style transfer model. This process generates an oil painting-style picture based on the uploaded image (as shown in Fig. 5).

Similarly, in the Ink Wash Style Transfer sub-module [3], an ink wash style transfer model is integrated. Images uploaded to the browser are processed through this model, generating ink wash-style pictures corresponding to the uploaded images. These generated pictures are then sent back to the front end and displayed within the interface of this module. The two sub-modules operate independently and do not interfere with each other's functionalities or operations. They run autonomously, without mutual dependency or impact.

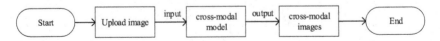

Fig. 5. Style transfer flowchart.

4 Running Instance

4.1 Drawing on the Digital Drawing Board

Users can easily upload reference images on the left side of the drawing board interface and then proceed with their creative process on the canvas area to the right. The digital drawing board offers various tools, including shape tools, erasers, and options to adjust brush thickness, among others. Taking portrait sketching as an example, as the user progresses in the drawing, every stroke completed on the canvas is transmitted to the backend server for storage. Once the drawing is complete, users can click the "Download Drawing Process" button at the bottom of the interface to save the drawing process locally. The interface for drawing on the digital drawing board is as shown in Fig. 6.

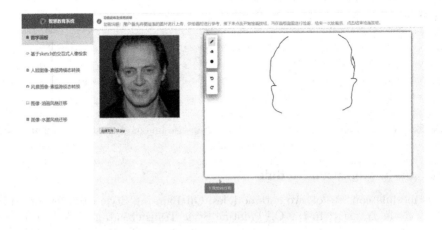

Fig. 6. The example illustration of the digital drawing board interface.

4.2   Retrieving Characters Through Sketch-Based Search

Users draw sketches on the left side of the canvas interface. After each stroke, the search box on the right side automatically updates with the latest search results. The face image most similar to the sketch on the left appears in the first position of the first row in the search box, followed by other results in descending order of similarity. We have drawn facial images from the database on the canvas, and the resulting search results are presented in the Fig. 7.

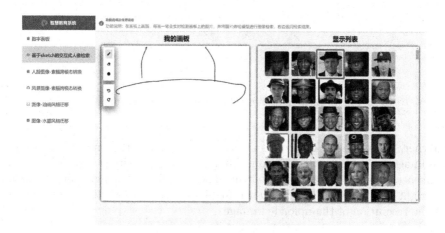

Fig. 7. Interactive portrait retrieval examples.

4.3   Cross-Modal Transformation for Portrait Sketches

Users can randomly select a portrait image by clicking on the box with a plus sign at the top of the interface for upload. After uploading the chosen image by clicking the "Upload Image" button below, the system presents the generated portrait sketch in two display boxes below the interface. If users wish to observe the drawing process, they can click the "Generate Drawing" button on the left side of the interface. The display box on the right will automatically play the drawing process. Users can adjust the playback speed by dragging the slider located below the display box. Additionally, users have the option to download the complete portrait sketch by clicking the "Download Complete Sketch" button on the left. Similarly, clicking the "Download Drawing Process" button allows users to download a packaged file containing all the images from the drawing process. The interface and transformation results are shown in the Fig. 8.

4.4   Ink Wash Style Transfer

We have selected the sub-module of Ink Wash Style Transfer from the Style Transfer module for demonstration. After randomly selecting an image from the

Fig. 8. Sketch cross-modal transformation examples.

internet, users can click the plus sign in the middle of the interface to choose the image for style transformation. After clicking the "Upload Image" button, users need to wait for a brief moment. The transformed image will appear on the right side of the screen (as shown in Fig. 9). The waiting time is dependent on the resolution of the uploaded image.

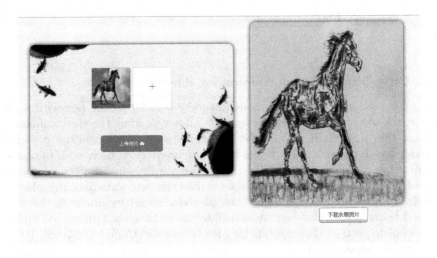

Fig. 9. The example result image of ink wash style transfer.

5   Conclusion

Based on the current demand for high-quality sketch teaching, this paper has designed and implemented the Sketch Teaching System. This system breaks the limitations of previous single-teaching modes. It constructs diverse teaching resources with AI assistance, enabling interactive teaching modes both inside and outside the classroom. It supports the development of AI in sketch teaching, creating a mutually beneficial relationship. Not only does it alleviate the teaching pressure on teachers and ensure high-quality education, but it also sparks students' interest in learning and caters to their personalized teaching needs.

Furthermore, due to its modular design, this system can be easily updated, and different functional modules can be combined. In future work, we will continue the development and improvement of the Sketch Teaching System to enhance its performance and efficiency, meeting the growing business demands. Additionally, we will respond to user needs by adding new features and characteristics, enhancing user satisfaction, and providing better service to sketch classrooms.

References

1. Dai, D., Li, Y., Wang, L., Fu, S., Xia, S., Wang, G.: Sketch less face image retrieval: a new challenge. In: Proceedings of ICASSP 2023, IEEE International Conference on Acoustics, Speech and Signal Processing, pp. 1–5. IEEE (2023)
2. Denac, O., et al.: The significance and role of aesthetic education in schooling. Creat. Educ. **5**, 1714 (2014)
3. He, B., Gao, F., Ma, D., Shi, B., Duan, L.Y.: ChipGAN: a generative adversarial network for Chinese ink wash painting style transfer. In: Proceedings of the 26th ACM International Conference on Multimedia, pp. 1172–1180 (2018)
4. Kappe, F., Scerbakov, N.: Object-oriented architecture of a modern learning management system. In: EDULEARN17 Proceedings, IATED, pp. 4910–4916 (2017)
5. Macias, C.M., Aguilar-Alonso, I.: Assessment of contributions of the methodology for the construction of a catalog of information technology services aimed at public entities. Int. J. Serv. Sci. Manag. Eng. Technol. (IJSSMET) **13**, 1–28 (2022)
6. Muzyka, O., Lopatiuk, Y., Belinska, T., Belozerskaya, A., Shvets, I.: Modern aesthetic education and its further directions. Linguist. Cult. Rev. **5**, 12–21 (2021)
7. Romat, H., et al.: Tilt-responsive techniques for digital drawing boards. In: Proceedings of the 33rd Annual ACM Symposium on User Interface Software and Technology, pp. 500–515 (2020)
8. Shesh, A., Chen, B.: Smartpaper: an interactive and user friendly sketching system. In: Computer Graphics Forum, Wiley Online Library, pp. 301–310 (2004)
9. Spivak, G.C.: An Aesthetic Education in the Era of Globalization. Harvard University Press, Cambridge (2013)
10. Zhu, J.Y., Park, T., Isola, P., Efros, A.A.: Unpaired image-to-image translation using cycle-consistent adversarial networks. In: Proceedings of the IEEE International Conference on Computer Vision, pp. 2223–2232 (2017)

Propelling Pedagogical Paradigms: A Study of Advanced Human-Computer Interaction Learning in *Data Structure and Algorithms* Based on Virtual Reality Technology

Yang Yahui[1], Gao Yanxia[1,2,3], Peng Ling[1], Xiang Yingxi[4], He Huan[1], and Liu Yiwen[1,2,3](✉)

[1] School of Computer and Artificial Intelligence, Huaihua University, Huaihua 418000, Hunan, People's Republic of China
`lyw@hhtc.edu.cn`
[2] Key Laboratory of Wuling-Mountain Health Big Data Intelligent Processing and Application in Hunan Province Universities, Huaihua 418000, Hunan, People's Republic of China
[3] Key Laboratory of Intelligent Control Technology for Wuling-Mountain Ecological Agriculture in Hunan Province, Huaihua 418000, Hunan, People's Republic of China
[4] School of Fine Arts and Design, Huaihua University, Huaihua 418000, Hunan, People's Republic of China

Abstract. *Data Structure and Algorithms* (DSA) is a course with strong practice and abstract theoretical knowledge. In view of the complexity of the knowledge points of the course and the difficulty of understanding, we design and implement a virtual simulation experiment teaching system of the course--Virtual simulation experiment platform. In this platform, DSA through simulation practice into animation effects, and combined with the unity engine and C# code to achieve user interaction, to provide users with a way to intuitively understand the principles of DSA, while increasing the user's subjective initiative to learn, and to achieve the high level, Innovative and challenging teaching classroom, so that students in colleges and universities can feel relaxed and happy in the process of learning this course. What is more, they can better accept and understand DSA.

Keywords: *Data Structure and Algorithms* (DSA) · Virtual Reality Technology · Human-Computer Interaction · Path Planning

1 Introduction

Data structure and Algorithms (DSA) is a comprehensive professional foundation course in computer science, a core course between mathematics, hardware and software. At the same time, algorithms are the key and difficult content in the data structure course. As the course is usually offered in the lower grades, but due to its emphasis on the combination of theory and practice, students have limited experience in contacting computer-related knowledge. In the teaching process, students often have difficulties in understanding and applying the abstract nature of algorithms. This leads to a lack of student interest in the course, as well as a failure to fully appreciate the importance of this compulsory course. As a result, students spend a lot of time and energy in the process of learning and understanding algorithms, and the connection between theory and practical application is not close enough, and there is a disconnect between knowledge and other problems, which ultimately affects the achievement of the teaching effect. In view of the above problems existing in the design process of data structure courses under the original teaching mode, this paper proposes to develop an object-oriented data structure virtual experimental teaching aid platform based on Unity Engine, presenting the complex core algorithms of data structure through the three-dimensional picture, so as to make the data structure algorithms visual, reduce the difficulty of learning, increase the classroom interest, improve the students' interest in learning, and realize the High-order human-computer interaction learning.

2 Related Work

2.1 Existing Problems in the DSA Course

With the continuous development of modern society and economy, people have gradually entered into a new Internet era. Under the constant passage of time, computers are not only widely used in people's lives, but also become a course that young people need to learn. The teaching of *Data Structure and Algorithms* is the core of computer science teaching. But it is often reflected by students as difficult to understand, algorithms are boring and not easy to understand. So in the traditional teaching process, there are generally the following problems: First of all, the corresponding technology is still backward, so that students spend too much time and energy in the process of learning and understanding algorithms. In addition, the theoretical and practical nature of the course is so strong and the connection is not close enough that student learning process is often out of touch and other issues. After that, the functionality provided by traditional teaching aids used for teaching is limited to a combination of text and picture explanations. And very few features involve virtual simulation. However, Graphics sometimes struggle to bring out the essence of DSA. Indirectly, these results in most students not being able to learn efficiently and effectively. And People habitually ignore these issues, which ultimately leads to less than optimal teaching.

2.2 State of the Art in Virtual Reality Technology

Virtual reality technology is implemented through technologies in many fields such as computer graphics, physical simulation, sensor technology, etc. The goal of virtual simulation technology is to simulate the physical characteristics, motion behavior, and environmental conditions in the real world through computer simulation in order to achieve the simulation of the real scene. It can simulate and predict behaviors, events and outcomes in various situations, enabling users to conduct experiments, training, testing and other operations in a virtual environment in order to better understand and deal with real-world problems. Through virtual reality technology, users can have real-feeling simulation experiences in virtual environments to help them better understand and deal with complex real-world problems. The development of virtual reality technology cannot be separated from the improvement of computer performance and the innovation of software technology. With the continuous progress of computer graphics, physics engine, artificial intelligence and other technologies, the application areas and effects of virtual reality technology will continue to expand and improve, and its development and research in the field of education will also become a future trend [1].

2.3 The Demand for Simulation in Data Structures Courses

The Virtual Simulation Experimental Teaching Innovation Alliance from China released a guide for the construction of virtual simulation experimental teaching courses, which puts forward the necessity of virtual simulation experiments for DSA courses: Conventional experiments make it difficult to achieve a visual image of the process of observing the change of data memory with the execution of the program. Thus, it is difficult to develop students' ability to visualize computer thinking and understand the logical relationship between programs and corresponding data. What is more, To develop complex engineering problem solving skills, it is more necessary to restore the cases and processes in real jobs. Traditional experiments are equally difficult to realize their elements of openness and randomization.

Through the understanding and analysis of the algorithm visualization of DSA at home and abroad, many countries based on the data structure visualization system has been quite mature. And some websites have appeared in China to enhance the teaching. But most of them are only embodied in 2D sense. Like the student dance demonstration in China University of Geosciences, it puts the students in the position of research and improves the learning initiative. But if each student demonstrates each algorithm, this undermines the efficiency of learning.

3 Research

3.1 Analysis of Knowledge Points

The development of a virtual simulation experiment platform on DSA begins with the identification of relevant knowledge content. Common data structures include arrays, chain lists, stacks, queues, trees and graphs. For example, array is a linear structure used to store a group of elements of the same type, chain table is a non-contiguous storage structure composed of nodes and pointers, stack is a last-in-first-out data structure that supports pressure stack and pop-up stack operations, queue is a first-in-first-out data structure that supports in-queue and out-of-queue operations, tree is a non-linear structure consisting of nodes and edges, including binary trees, binary search trees, etc. And graph is a non-linear structure composed of nodes and edges used to represent a group of elements of the same type. Graph is a non-linear structure consisting of nodes and edges, which is used to represent the relationship between multiple objects. All these are used to store data or elements, but they have different methods on how to store and organize data. We can design simulation experiments according to the characteristics of different algorithms in a targeted way. Then different algorithmic ideas and their advantages and disadvantages are visualized through simulation techniques.

Take Dijkstra's algorithm to find the shortest path of a graph as an example. For this knowledge point, we design the automatic display experiment to complete the learning part of the knowledge point to achieve the user observation learning stage. And then, we design the breakthrough experiment to complete the understanding part of the knowledge point to achieve the user interaction learning stage, and the after-school exercise to complete the consolidation part of the knowledge point to achieve the consolidation learning stage. Firstly, we determine the knowledge points contained in Dijkstra's algorithm to find the shortest path and the compilation idea of the algorithm, as shown in Fig. 1. After that we help students to learn and understand the principle and application of Dijkstra's algorithm, as well as the concept of the shortest path and the calculation method through the independent demonstration experiments and the interactive experiments of the users respectively.

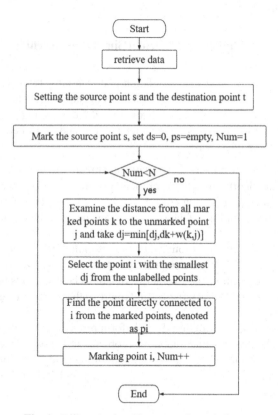

Fig. 1. Dijkstra's algorithm execution mind map.

3.2 Multidimensional Virtual Presentation of Algorithms

In order to enhance students' intuitive understanding of algorithms and help students better understand and apply algorithms, so as to enhance the teaching effect. We can combine the core algorithms of this course with virtual simulation technology [2] to display the process and results in 3D through object-oriented development. And Through the 3D engine to build a three-dimensional scene Combined with the 2D UI design to visualize the core algorithms of data structure, assisting teachers to show the compilation and execution process of algorithms that cannot be conveyed by the language image through the scene picture. This can help students intuitively understand the boring and difficult data structure knowledge points, and improve learning efficiency. Through the development and use of algorithm visualization tools, combined with practical problems, real-time, dynamic display of sorting, stack, shortest path and other data structure algorithms visualization effect [3].

3.3 Advantages and Challenges of Virtual Simulation Teaching

Advantages

The production of the DSA virtual simulation platform aims to provide teachers with better teaching methods and students with better educational resources. In addition to being able to help students improve their learning in three ways: higher order, innovative and challenging, it also promotes their understanding and assimilation of knowledge points in the following three ways:

- Provide hands-on opportunities: The platform aims to provide students with hands-on and practical opportunities to experiment and practice data structures in a virtual environment. Through hands-on practice, students can deepen their understanding of the principles and operations of data structures and develop their practical application skills.
- Enhance the learning effect: Through the virtual simulation lab platform, students can understand and learn DSA more intuitively in terms of visualization and interaction. The real-time visualization and interactive functions help students to better grasp the various operations and characteristics, and improve the learning effect and quality of learning results.
- Cultivate problem-solving ability: The platform provides error elimination and hint functions to help students find and solve problems in the experiment process. This helps to cultivate students' problem-solving ability and logical thinking ability, and equips them with the ability to think independently and solve practical problems in the field of DSA.

Challenges

The advantages of teaching data structure courses in virtual simulation are self-evident, but some challenges are inevitable in practical application. For example, the technical complexity of the development phase, the establishment and maintenance of a virtual simulation laboratory with good user experience and functionality requires corresponding resource inputs involving multiple technical areas, including software development, graphic design, physical simulation, and so on. In addition, sufficient computing resources and server performance are required to support multiple students conducting experiments at the same time. Followed by teaching content design, which requires well-designed teaching content to transform the concepts and operations of DSA into virtual simulation experiments. There is a need to ensure that the experimental scenarios and operations accurately reflect the characteristics and behavior of DSA, while maintaining sufficient educational and interactivity so that students can fully understand and master the relevant concepts. It is also necessary to pay attention to students' acceptance and experience of using the virtual simulation laboratory, and to solve possible technical problems and obstacles in a timely manner.

4 System Design

4.1 Technological Route

The implementation of virtual simulation requires a powerful 3D graphics engine (e.g. Unity, Unreal Engine) to create virtual environments, objects, animations, etc. Among the many development tools, the Unity Engine has a larger focus and toolset, and performs much better in VR because the plugins are very versatile and can be integrated into the whole XR infrastructure, while Unity has been doing AR for a longer and has more defined systems. So it is more recommended to use the Unity engine for the next step. And the programming language is chosen to write the relevant code in C#.

The overall design of the virtual simulation platform incorporates the idea of iterative method. First of all, the project development of the approximate planning. And then began to prepare for the modelling, through the Unity3D development engine combined with 3DMax and other three-dimensional animation rendering software for the scene, data animation model of the initial modelling, through Visual Studio in the C# programming tools for programming and debugging code. Then continuously input and output testing until the product is produced. After that, we continue to input and output test until the final product is formed, and then we put the software into the market and receive feedback from the users, follow up the feedback problems in time, and so on and so forth to repair and upgrade the system repeatedly. The approximate development idea is shown in Fig. 2.

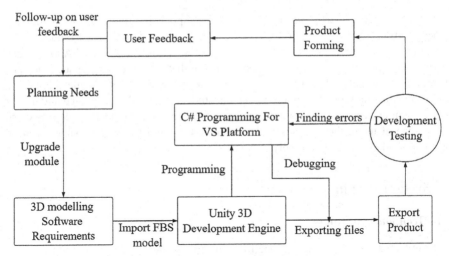

Fig. 2. System Development Ideas.

4.2 Overall Design

The system mainly simulates interaction with a two-dimensional system operation interface and a three-dimensional animation scene. In the virtual simulation system platform development mode, C# programming technology in Visual Studio programming development platform is used to achieve the function. The client of the system collaborates with the server, logic development and cloud server to form a complete interactive service model. The system includes six technical layers such as data layer, foundation layer, resource layer, management layer, function layer and application layer. The virtual simulation system integrates these six technical layers and achieves perfect compatibility and display effect of the software through the design of the large screen interface constructed on the basis of the WPF framework, so that the operation of the virtual simulation system is characterized by real scenes, clear images, clear hierarchy and stable operation. The successful completion of these tasks will lay a good foundation for the subsequent expansion and maintenance of the system.

5 Technical Realization

5.1 Unity3D-Based Virtual Scene Building and UI Layout

Unity is a powerful cross-platform game engine with rich graphical rendering and physical simulation capabilities for creating interactive virtual environments and scenes. The lab builds different virtual 3D scenes according to each experimental need by creating and connecting multiple Scenes in Unity. In order to provide more learning and experimental functionality, Unity's physical simulation features can be combined to simulate the behavior of DSA in real environments. For example, Unity's collision detection and physics engine can be used to simulate the operation of stacks and queues and their first-in-first-out (FIFO) or last-in-first-out (LIFO) characteristics. Components in Unity are modular elements that make up a game object, and are used to give the game object specific functionality and behaviors (Fig. 3).

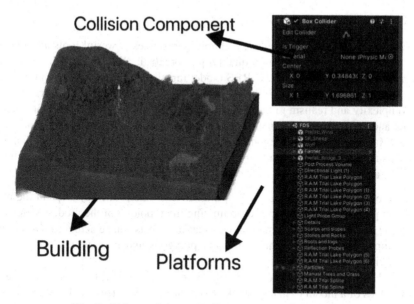

Fig. 3. Unity environment builds and component mounts.

After building a 3D scene, you need to lay out the UI interface in the Scene according to your experimental needs. Unity provides powerful user interface (UI) design tools and features that enable developers to create interactive and aesthetically pleasing user interfaces. Key points about Unity UI design include Canvas and UI elements, layout and hierarchy, graphics and styles, interactions and events, responsive design and more.

5.2 Programming Implementation

Creating realistic virtual scenes in Unity and programming in C# language in combination with Visual Studio makes the learning process more vivid and interesting through interactive experiments and visualization effects, which can provide an interactive, visual and hands-on learning environment to help learners better understand and apply their knowledge of data structures.

Writing C# scripts in Visual Studio to control objects or events in Unity. This allows for the simulation and implementation of a variety of common data structure algorithmic features and visualization needs, such as arrays, linked lists, stacks, queues, trees and graphs, etc. And ensures that the operations are correct and consistent, and that the scripts can interact with the user's inputs (e.g., mouse clicks or keyboard inputs), allowing the user to interact with the data structures and observe the results of the operations. In addition, Unity provides rich graphical rendering and physical simulation capabilities to display changes and operations of DSA in a more visually appealing way. Developers can use Visual Studio for efficient coding, debugging, and testing to ensure implementation of algorithm visualization and simulation experiments.

5.3   3D Modelling

3D Max-based 3D object modelling technology provides powerful tools and features that enable creators to create high-quality, photorealistic 3D models [4]. Techniques such as polygon modelling and NURBS modelling allow precise shaping and detailing of models. Techniques such as Boolean operations, texture mapping, and material shaders add complexity and realism to the model. 3DMax also offers a wide range of renderer options and post-processing capabilities to help users achieve impressive renderings. This 3DMax-based 3D object modelling technology has a wide range of applications in fields such as film, games and virtual reality, bringing more creative possibilities to digital art and design. Here are the technical details of 3DMax's features:

(1) Topology optimization: Topology optimization is one of the key steps in the modelling process. By planning and optimizing the topology of the model, better geometric smoothness and animation deformation effects can be achieved. Optimizing the topology can reduce the number of polygons and improve performance and rendering efficiency.

(2) Edge Hardening: Edge Hardening is the process of adding extra geometric detail to the edges of a model to make it look crisper and sharper. This can be achieved with tools such as Edge Selection, Edge Ring and Edge Compensation to improve the visual quality of the model.

(3) UV Mapping: UV mapping is the process of mapping 2D texture coordinates onto a 3D model surface. In 3DMax, the UV editor can be used to adjust and optimize the UV layout to ensure that the texture mapping is displayed correctly and without distortion on the model surface.

(4) Bone Binding and Animation: For models that need to be animated, bone binding is a necessary step. By associating bones with the model, deformation and animation effects can be achieved. In 3DMax, tools such as skinning and weight drawing can be used for bone binding and weight adjustment.

(5) Model Optimization and Optimizer: For large or complex models, optimizing the model is an important step in improving performance and reducing resource consumption. 3DMax provides an Optimizer tool that automatically merges vertices, removes hidden faces, and optimizes the geometry of the model to reduce file size and increase rendering speed.

(6) Scripting and Plug-ins: 3DMax supports scripting and plug-in development, which allows you to extend the functionality and workflow of the software by writing scripts or installing plug-ins. These customization tools can help simplify complex tasks, improve efficiency and increase creative flexibility.

6   Demonstration and Feedback

6.1   Example

Dijkstra is a shortest path algorithm from a vertex to each of the remaining vertices that solves the shortest path problem in an entitled graph. The main feature of this algorithm is that it starts from the starting point and adopts the strategy of greedy algorithm, traversing the neighboring nodes of the nearest and unvisited vertices to the starting point each time until it expands to the end point [5]. This chapter also takes this algorithm as an example, and introduces its implementation and operation process from the algorithm introduction interface, automatic display experiment interface, and interactive learning interface in the virtual simulation system.

- Algorithm Module Introduction

This module is a simple text description of the definition of the algorithm. Edit the two-dimensional canvas in unity. The use of Recto Transform and image and other components to change the various parameters so as to get the UI interface required by the system. Add a Button on the interface, through the writing of C# code to achieve the button to listen to the interface to jump (Fig. 4).

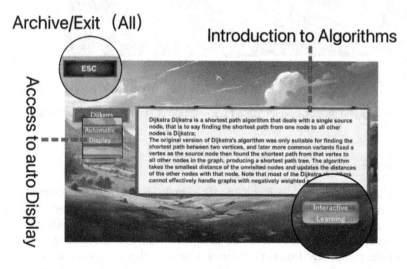

Fig. 4. Interface of Algorithm Introduction.

- Automatic display of experimental modules

This module is from the learning of knowledge to achieve the user to observe the learning stage. The main scene of the interface is a certain area of the satellite map. The desired location will be marked out, the formation of a node, with reference to the actual distance between each of the two locations to design the weights. All the paths will be connected together to form a path diagram laid out in the upper left corner of the canvas. According to the Dijkstra algorithm strategy, select the node corresponding to the smallest edge away from the starting point of the weights as a target node connected to the line, the user clicks on the next to enable the system to step-by-step demonstration of the algorithm to carry out the process (Fig. 5).

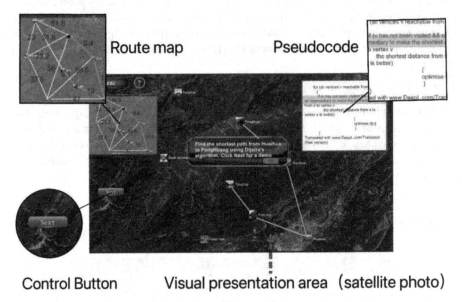

Fig. 5. Automated presentation interface for simulation of algorithm execution process.

- Interactive Learning Module

The module is designed according to the algorithmic idea of Dijkstra's shortest path (as an example). Through the construction of virtual reality scenes, the user needs to answer the designed algorithmic questions with guidance from the first-person perspective in the simulated scene. And choose the next path by answering the questions, after the code of the component listens to the user to see whether the choice is correct or not, and triggers the teleportation function if it is correct, and then the user is teleported to the next junction, then continues to answer the questions, choose the next path until reaching the end node (Fig. 6).

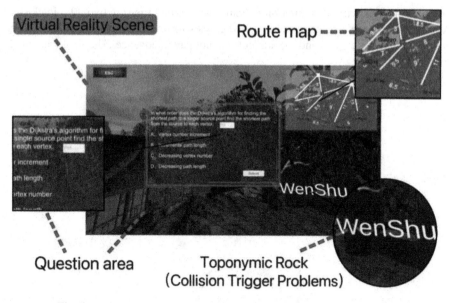

Fig. 6. User Interactive Learning Interface for Virtual Reality Scenarios.

6.2 Survey Feedback

In order to verify the virtual simulation teaching effect of DSA, during the system development stage, we promote and test the product for undergraduate computer science students in colleges and universities and collect the corresponding feedback by means of questionnaires. We divide the students into two groups of uncontacted DSA courses and those who have already learnt the courses, and the number of each group is 50 and the questionnaires are collected to obtain the following data (Table 1):

Table 1. Teaching Effectiveness of a Virtual Simulation Course on Data Structures.

Groups	Inefficient	Generic	Efficient	Efficiency ratio
Learnt	6	5	39	78.00%
Unlearnt	4	3	43	86.00%

Through the above table, it is easy to see that regardless of whether the contact or study this course of DSA, the majority of students are recognized by the virtual simulation teaching efficient knowledge transfer ability. But this questionnaire alone cannot see the difference between the virtual simulation course and the traditional teaching classroom. So we are studying the DSA course through the three classes of the students (a class of 42 a total of 126 people) to carry out a test, will be their Randomly divided into two groups to learn the next section of the content - Dijkstra's algorithm to find the shortest path. One of the groups as usual through the traditional teaching learning, the other group through the virtual simulation system. The learning time are two 90-min classes. After the study, we also use the same two classes for the Dijkstra's algorithm theory and programming exams, and the students cannot pay in advance. The final data are as follows (Fig. 7):

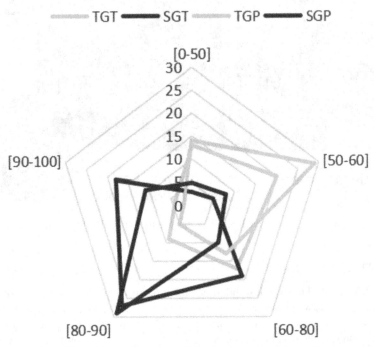

Fig. 7. Comparison of Student Achievement Tests between Traditional Teaching and Virtual Simulation in Data Structures Courses. (Convention TGT = Traditional group theory, SGT = Simulation group theory, TGP = Traditional Group Programming, SGP = Simulation Group Programming.)

Undeniably, the traditional classroom teaching is still very important. Because the computer itself does not have a mind, lack of unique human flexibility. It needs human design and programming to achieve a series of functions. But the times are progressing, to help people to improve efficiency, improve the quality of life or learning is the driving force and purpose of the continuous development of science and technology. In the field of computers continue to expand today, the traditional teaching mode also needs to be reformed and innovated [6], and the simulation teaching of DSA can more intuitively present the content that the teacher can't convey with words, it is a powerful helper to assist the teacher to teach the DSA course, and it is also a kind of innovative and challenging teaching method for the students.

Acknowledgment. We are very thankful that this study is supported by Huaihua University Teaching Reform Project (HHXYJG-202305); Teaching Reform Research Project of Hunan Province

(HNJG-2019-825 and HNJG-2023-0925); Project of Hunan Provincial Social Science Foundation (21JD046); the Hunan Provincial Social Science Achievement Review Committee Project (XSP2023JYC125); National Training Program Project of Innovation and Entrepreneurship for Undergraduates (No. S202310548084).

References

1. Fubao, J., Shangang, M., Yan, T., et al.: Exploration and practice of virtual simulation experimental teaching in colleges and universities in western region. J. Res. Explor. Lab. **2023**(03), 87–91 (2023)
2. Jiali, W., Mingyang, Z., Zhou, J., et al.: Application of VR technology in virtual simulation experiments in introductory computer courses. J. Digit. Technol. **2022**(11), 82–84 (2022)
3. Jianfeng, H., Qing, S., Tiantian, L., et al.: Construction and teaching practice of visual webwide programming training system. J. Exp. Technol. Manage. **2021**(7), 166–171 (2021)
4. Chaoyang, Z., Wangping, L., Haizheng, M.: 3D modelling of buildings based on AutoCAD and 3DMax. J. Gansu Geol. **2021**(03), 89–93 (2021)
5. Jihu, H., Yanan, Y.: Research on conflict-proof shortest path planning based on improved Dijkstra's algorithm. J. Comput. Modern. **2022**(08), 20–24 (2022)
6. Yan, W., Jiaqi, L., Shuyan, W., et al.: Competence-oriented "five links" hybrid teaching reform of data structure course. J. Comput. Educ. **2023**(01), 76–80 (2023)

Ensembled Identification for Problematic Student Based on Multi-perspective Analysis Using College Students' Behavioral Data

Yuqin Yan, Yifan Zhu, Tao Wu, Jiali Mao[✉], Qi Feng, and Aoying Zhou

East China Normal University, Shanghai, China
{51255903109,51265903116,52195100007}@stu.ecnu.edu.cn,
{jilmao,ayzhou}@dase.ecnu.edu.cn, qfeng@admin.ecnu.edu.cn

Abstract. Psychological health of college students has become one of the most critical problems in current higher education. Accordingly, the identification of problematic college students has attracted general concerns from the universities and society. But due to complex influencing factors of detection task and extremely imbalanced distribution of data used to train detection model, the existing detection approaches base upon a single source of college students' behavioral data cannot be used to identify problematic college students effectively. In this paper, we regard the issue of problematic college student detection as a binary classification task, and propose an ensembled identification framework for problematic student (EIPS) based on multi-perspective analysis using college students' behavioral data. Through introducing multi-head self-attention mechanism into training binary classification model, we can capture differentiated influences of distinct features on the classification task. Further, we utilize an ensemble framework to enhance classification performance by incorporating with the outputs of multiple base classifiers to obtain the final classification result. Finally, extensive comparative experiments on real data sets demonstrate that *EIPS* significantly outperforms the state of-the-art methods.

Keywords: Problematic student detection · Multi-perspective analysis · Attention mechanism · Ensemble learning

1 Introduction

In recent years, more and more college students have varying degrees of depression and anxiety risk because of all kinds of inducing factors such as academic stress and employment pressure. Correspondingly, mental health issues of college students have become the focus of attentions from the college teachers and students' parents. With the promotion of the construction of smart campus, we have the ability to collect huge amounts of behavioral data of college students related to campus consumption, attendance record and course grade. This provides us an opportunity to help identifying the college students having mental health issues (or *problematic student* for short) as soon as possible, i.e. detecting abnormality based upon college students' behavioral data.

The existing abnormality detection methods using students' behavioral data mostly tend to focus on obvious behavior difference as compared to their historical patterns in a certain aspect [1,3,8,9]. For instance, they are simply concerned about significant changes in one class of students' behaviors such as consumption, social connections, awards and grades. But actually, there are multiple inducing reasons for the psychological problems of college students, which involve changes of feelings and family, decreasing in grades, and poverty, etc. The resulting warning signs of depression and anxiety are complex and diverse, including irregular sleep patterns, reducing consumption, skipping classes, and even disappearances, etc. As a result, not all the problematic students can be found by the existing methods. It necessitates to design a proper detection method based on combining with complex factors from multiple perspectives.

The issue of problematic student detection can be considered as a binary classification task. However, there are severe challenges in identifying the problematic students using multi-sources of college students' behavioral data. First, the degree to which various factors extracted from different data sources affects detection result varies with the individual. For example, one kind of problematic students have fewer consumption records at the canteen or the campus supermarket, while the other usually shows up as dining alone and returning to the dorm room very lately. Second, the distribution of training data that is annotated as problematic students and normal ones is extremely uneven. It easily leads to some real problematic students are identified as normal ones, i.e. there is a certain rate of misjudgment in the detection result.

To tackle the issue of complex influencing factors of problematic student detection, we not only extract important features (e.g., academic performance, consuming behavior, and showering behavior) from different sources of college students' behavioral data, but also introduce a multi-head self-attention mechanism to capture differentiated influences of distinct features on the classification task. Besides, aiming at the issue of low detection performance resulted by extremely imbalanced training data, we leverage an ensemble framework to incorporate with the outputs of several base classifiers to improve the detection precision. In summary, the contributions of this paper are four-fold:

- We design an ensembled identification framework for problematic student based on multi-perspective analysis using college students' behavioral data, called *EIPS*, consisting of data preprocessing, multi-perspective feature extraction and ensemble-based problematic student detection.
- To respectively capture differentiated influences of distinct features on the detection task, we introduce multi-head self-attention mechanism into training detection model.

- To reduce the influences of uneven training data distribution on the performance of detection task, we utilize an ensemble framework to incorporate the outputs of multiple base classifiers.
- We conduct extensive experiments on real college students' behavioral data sets to evaluate the effectiveness and superiority of *EIPS*.

The remainder of this paper is organized as follows. Section 2 reviews the related work. The preliminary concepts and problem statement are introduced in Sect. 3 and the detail of *EIPS* framework is outlined in Sect. 4. Section 5 presents the experimental results, followed by conclusions in Sect. 6.

2   Related Work

Over the past decade, numerous studies have been conducted on the field of educational data mining. The researchers attempted to address the issues such as academic performance prediction, psychological stress analysis and abnormal behavior detection through exploring educational big data.

Yao et al. proposed a multi-network label propagation algorithm to predict academic performance based on constructing students' social relationship using their campus behavior data [11]. Saha et al. employed machine learning algorithms like *XGBoost*, *SVM* to predict students' academic performance based upon their psychological and behavioural data [5]. Sano et al. built an *SVM* model to predict students' academic performance, sleep quality and mental health based upon extracting nearly 700 features from wearable sensor and smartphone data [6]. Zhang et al. conducted a study on the sources and influencing factors of psychological stress among college students [12]. They presented an improved *ResNet50* model to assess the psychological stress of college students, and further revealed that the psychological stress of college student is related with several factors including the differences in students' consumption levels, consumption behavior, learning ability, and family economic.

Li et al. tried to detect mental health problems by fitting a pace regression model base on regarding the web use behaviors as predictors [3]. Xu et al. constructed an AdaBoost-based classifier for detecting depression status based upon automatically generating contextually filtering features from the behaviors of multiple sensors [8]. Cheng et al. proposed a predictive model for psychological well-being of university students by leveraging operational support system data, educational data, and psychological health questionnaire data [1]. Yang et al. put forward a fusion algorithm to assess students' psychological health conditions by combining decision tree, BP neural network, and Apriori algorithm [9].

Most of the aforementioned mental health problem detection methods emphasized obvious behavior difference as compared to students' historical behaviors in a single data source. What's more, they consider neither differentiated influences of different features on the detection task, nor low detection performance resulted by extremely imbalanced training data. Thus, all of them cannot be leveraged for identifying problematic college students.

3 Preliminaries

In this section, we introduce some preliminary concepts and formally define the problem of problematic student detection.

Definition 1 (Campus Card Transaction Records). Let $R_{Transaction}$ represents a set of campus card transaction records, each record of which is represented by $r_{Transaction}$, denoted as $r_{Transaction} = \{sid, t, pid, amount\}$, where sid denotes unique identification of a student s, t denotes the timestamp of one record, pid denotes the Point of Sale (POS) terminal, $amount$ denotes the amount of records.

Definition 2 (Campus Card Access Records). Let R_{Access} represents a set of campus card accessing records, each record of which is represented by r_{Access}, denoted as $r_{Access} = \{sid, t, pid\}$.

Definition 3 (Course Grades Records). Let R_{Grade} represents a set of course grade records, each record of which is represented by r_{Grade}, denoted as $r_{Grade} = \{sid, c\_id, gpa\}$, where c_id denotes unique identification of one course, gpa denotes grade point average, here $1 \leq gpa \leq 4.0$.

Problem Statement. Given a set of campus card transaction records $R_{Transaction}$, a set of campus card accessing records R_{Access} and a set of course grade records of college students R_{Grade}, our objective is to decide whether a student is a problematic one by building a binary classification model.

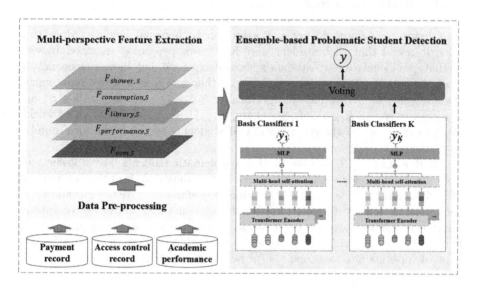

Fig. 1. Overview of EIPS

4   Framework

We propose an ensembled identification framework for problematic student based on multi-perspective analysis using college student behavioral data, called *EIPS*. As shown in Fig. 1, *EIPS* is mainly composed of *Data Preprocessing*, *Multi-perspective Feature Extraction* and *Ensemble-based Problematic Student Detection*.

4.1   Data Preprocessing

There are data quality problems in campus card transaction records, campus card accessing records and course grade records of college students, including data missing, redundant or erroneous records, and noisy data, etc. Given that, we first merge redundant consumption data, e.g., multiple swipes for the same meal. Then we regard duplicate access records and consumption records exceeding the spending limit of 200 as noisy data, and remove them. Besides, we try to correct erroneous consumption records, e.g., changing a consumption record of tapping water in the dormitory to that of showering behavior in the shower room.

4.2   Multi-perspective Feature Extraction

Based on the quality-improved data, we attempt to extract the features from multiple perspective relevant to the binary classification task.

4.2.1   Shower Feature $F_{shower,S}$

Fewer shower frequency and lower shower expense indicate that a college student living in a dorm do not pay attention to personal hygiene. More than that, it reveal that such student may have poor psychological state. In view of that, we calculate each student's shower expenses and shower frequency by week, to obtain a time series set $F_{shower,S}$ that serves as features representing the students' showering habits. Specifically, $F_{shower,S} = \{F_{shower,s} | s \in S\}$ and $F_{shower,s} = [f_{sr_1,s}, f_{sr_i,s}, ..., f_{sr_m,s}]$, here, $f_{sr_i,s}(1 \leq i \leq m)$ is the set of weekly shower expenses and shower frequency of student s and m is the total number of weeks.

As shown in Fig. 2, we observe that problematic students have a lower average number of shower sessions per week. Taking the example of the fall semester of 2022 (spanning 18 weeks) and excluding students who were not on campus, as compared to normal students, problematic students had an average of approximately 1.1 shower sessions per week and spent an average of about 2.1 yuan per week on showers. Thus, a student's showering characteristics can provide valuable insights into assessing his (or her) psychological well-being.

4.2.2   Consumption Feature $F_{consumption,S}$

Students usually engage in on-campus shopping at supermarkets, stores, fruit shops, and cafes to purchase daily necessities, snacks, and beverages, among

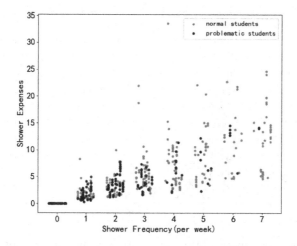

Fig. 2. Taking the example of 2022 fall semester consisting of 18 weeks, we extracted data from 20 normal students and 20 problematic students to draw a scatter plot. It's evident that behaviors characterized by higher weekly shower frequency and shower expenses are more common among normal students (marked by red points), while lower weekly shower frequency and lower shower expenses are more common among problematic students (marked by blue points). (Color figure online)

other items. Generally, higher shopping frequency and spending signify increased shopping needs. An abnormal change in a student's psychological state might lead to he (or she) has higher shopping demands.

Figure 3 shows a frequency distribution histogram of students' on-campus shopping expenses. It indicates that the majority of expenses for college students are below 20 yuan. In view of that, we calculate each student's weekly shopping expenditure and shopping frequency, resulting in a time series set $F_{consumption,S}$ that serves as a feature for students' shopping behavior. Specifically, $F_{consumption,S} = \{F_{consumption,s} | s \in S\}$ and $F_{consumption,s} = [f_{con_1,s}, f_{con_i,s}, ..., f_{con_m,s}]$, here $f_{con_i,s}(1 \leq i \leq m)$ is the set of weekly catering expenses and frequency of student s in canteens and shops in college.

As shown in Fig. 4, we observe that normal students tend to have fewer weekly shopping activities, while problematic students engage in more frequent shopping. For example, as compared to normal students, problematic students had an average of approximately 1.71 shopping activities per week with an average weekly expenditure of about 18.52 yuan, indicating that problematic students exhibit stronger shopping demands.

Apart from the students' shopping characteristics, consumption features also encompass students' dining habits on campus. This includes details such as the amount and frequency of money spent on meals, breakfast frequency, weekend and holiday meal frequency, and dining frequency during irregular time periods. Therefore, focusing on the students' consumption features can offer valuable insights into assessing their psychological states.

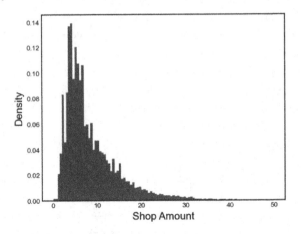

Fig. 3. Frequency distribution histogram of students' on-campus shopping expenses

4.2.3   Library Feature $F_{library,S}$

Students often go to the library for borrowing the books or self-studying, and the time of a student's self-studying lasts for one or more hours. Analyzing the weekly variations in the amount of time students spend in the library can serve as an indicator of changes in their academic stress, providing valuable insights into their psychological states.

In light of this, we calculate each student's weekly hours spent in the library (measured in hours), resulting in a time series set $F_{library,S}$ that serves as a feature representing the students' library attendance duration. Specifically, $F_{library,S} = \{F_{library,s} | s \in S\}$ and $F_{library,s} = [f_{lib_1,s}, f_{lib_i,s}, ..., f_{lib_m,s}]$, here $f_{lib_i,s}(1 \leq i \leq m)$ is the weekly duration in staying library of student s. As illustrated in Fig. 5, students tend to exhibit a noticeable upward trend in their library attendance around the 9th and 13th week in a academic semester consists of around 18 weeks. This trend is followed by a decrease in subsequent weeks. The increase in library attendance around the 9th week can be attributed to the factors such as mid-term presentations or exams in some courses. Additionally, from the 13th week onwards, students begin to prepare for final presentations and enter the final exam month, which results in an increase in their academic workloads. It leads to extended stay duration in the library, and meanwhile reveals the changes in students' psychological states due to stress of study.

As depicted in Fig. 5, we can see that problematic students tend to exhibit an upward trend in library attendance around the 9th and 13th week, but this trend commences later than it does for normal students. This discrepancy suggests that when facing with any task' deadline, problematic students may accelerate their learning closer to the deadline. It in turn requires them to complete their study tasks within a shorter time period, such as preparing for mid-term presentations in one week or revising for final exams in a single week. Therefore, problematic students experience greater academic pressure.

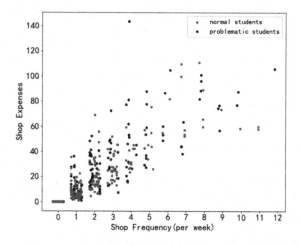

Fig. 4. Taking the example of the 2022 fall semester with a total of 18 weeks, we extracted data from 20 normal students and 20 problematic students to create a scatter plot. It's evident that behaviors characterized by higher weekly shopping frequency and shopping expenses are more common among problematic students (marked by blue points), while lower weekly shopping frequency and lower shopping expenses are more common among normal students (marked by red points). (Color figure online)

As shown in Fig. 5, problematic students have significantly shorter average library attendance durations compared to normal students. This indicates that problematic students may invest less effort in their studies compared to normal counterparts. It also suggests that problematic students may not prioritize their academic performance, which is reflected in their often lower $GPAs$ and academic rankings. In addition to library stay duration characteristics, library features also encompass the frequency of students borrowing books from the library.

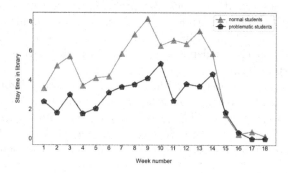

Fig. 5. Taking the example of the 2022 fall semester with a total of 18 weeks, we draw a line chart with the number of weeks on the x-axis and library stay duration in hours on the y-axis. It's apparent that the average library stay duration for the normal student group (highlighted in red line) is consistently higher than that of the problematic student group (highlighted in blue line) almost every week. (Color figure online)

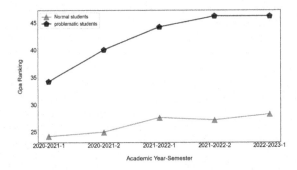

Fig. 6. Average Academic Ranking of both Normal and Problematic Students for each Semester.

4.2.4 Academic Performance Feature $F_{performance,S}$

Generally, the students will receive their final grades for all the courses they have taken at the end of each semester, and then be awarded course credits. The weighted average of such credits can represent overall academic performance of the student. The calculation of a student's semester-by-semester academic ranking during their time at school is used as a feature for their academic performance.

It's noted that when students experience psychological distress, it may impact their normal learning and work routines, and further lead to a decline in their academic performance. Conversely, a drop in academic performance can also contribute to psychological distress in students. Therefore, academic performance feature of a student an provide valuable insights for assessing his psychological well-being.

Taking 2020 undergraduate students as an example, as shown in Fig. 6, we observe that the average academic ranking of both normal and problematic students for each semester. It's evident that problematic students have lower rankings as compared to normal students. Furthermore, problematic students tend to experience greater declines in academic ranking from one semester to the next, indicating that the academic performance of problematic students may be continuously deteriorating.

Additionally, the academic performance feature also includes information about students' receipt of scholarships and financial aid annually. Finally, $F_{performance,S} = \{F_{performance,s} | s \in S\}$ and $F_{performance,s} = [f_{perf_1,s}, f_{perf_i,s}, ..., f_{perf_n,s}]$, here $f_{per_i,s}(1 \le i \le n)$ is the set of average academic ranking, one-hot of scholarships and financial aid of student s.

4.2.5 Companion on Consumption Feature $F_{com,S}$

Problematic students usually have little social contact, and their social relationships are often relatively limited. In view of that, the social aspects of college students can also provide valuable reference points for assessing their psychological state. In students' daily lives, they may go to campus restaurants, supermarkets, bathrooms, and other places for consumption with classmates and friends. These behaviors, where the students engage in consumption in the same location within a short period of time, are considered as a co-occurrence. When the frequency of co-occurrences between two individuals exceeds a certain threshold within a specific time range, they can be identified as "Companion on Consumption".

The number of companions for each student is calculated on a weekly basis, resulting in a time series set $F_{com,S}$, that serves as the student's "Companion on Consumption Feature". More specifically, $F_{com,S} = \{F_{com,s}|s \in S\}$ and $F_{com,s} = [f_{com_1,s}, f_{com_i,s}, ..., f_{com_m,s}]$, here $f_{com_i,s}(1 \leq i \leq m)$ is the weekly count of companions of student s. As shown in Fig. 7, we can see that problematic students have less companions compared to normal students. This indicates that problematic students may be more isolated.

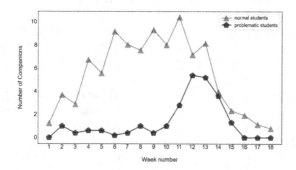

Fig. 7. Taking the example of 2022 fall semester with a total of 18 weeks, we draw a line chart with the number of weeks on the x-axis and library stay duration in hours on the y-axis. It's apparent that the average number of companions on consumption for the normal student group (highlighted in red line) is consistently higher than that of the problematic student group (highlighted in blue line) almost every week. (Color figure online)

4.3   Ensemble-Based Problematic Student Detection

After obtaining the above multi-perspective features, we leverage an ensemble framework to construct a problematic student detection model, called *TPSDM*, including *Data Subset Partitioning, Basis Classifiers Training* and *Majority Voting Output*.

Data Subset Partitioning. First, in order to train multiple independent basis classifiers, the data sets need to be partitioned into several data subsets. We regard the problematic student samples as positive class samples and the normal student samples as negative class samples. Since the number of positive class samples is much less than that of negative class samples, we need to balance the positive and negative samples to enhance the model classification performance. Specifically, we randomly sample 90% of the positive class samples and down-sample the negative class samples according to the same number of sampled positive class samples with the specific sampling strategy [4].

Basis Classifiers Training. After obtaining multiple data subsets, we input them into the same number of base classifiers with the same structure for training respectively. As shown in Fig. 1, each basis classifier first learns five classes of multi-view time series temporal vector representations from the Transformer Encoder [7], including a multi-layered self-attention mechanism and a fully connected layer. Through this way, we get the hidden vector representation of each position in time-series and allow the model to capture long-term behavioral patterns of each student.

Then, we calculate which parts of the sequence the model gives more attention to when processing the sequence under each view by using self-attention mechanism, the details of process is represented as follows:

$$Attention(Q, K, V) = softmax(\frac{QK^T}{\sqrt{d_K}}) \times \alpha, \tag{1}$$

where Q consists of many queries, which is the vector unit for which the weights need to be computed, e.g., the encoder outputs of each perspective, and K consists of other perspective encoder outputs, and α is the similarity calculated by Q and K.

To facilitate the splicing, we unify the size of the representation vectors under each viewpoint through a pooling layer before using attention mechanism, and then we splice the assigned individual vectors together as $\hat{F}$, and finally input them into an Multi-Layer Perception (MLP) to obtain the binary classification results $output_i$. Otherwise, We use the binary cross entropy loss ($BCEloss$) as the loss function for training the task.

$$BCELoss = \sum_{i \in N} -(1 - y_i)log(1 - \hat{y}_i) - y_i log(\hat{y}_i), \tag{2}$$

where i denotes one training sample, y denotes the prediction value and $\hat{y}$ denotes the label.

Majority Voting Output. After training multiple base classifiers, we input the data to be predicted into all the trained base classifiers in $EIPS$. For the multiple results obtained, we count the number of students judged as problematic and the number of normal students, and regard the result of the majority voting method as the final binary classification result.

5   Experiments

5.1   Data Sets and Settings

5.1.1   Data Sets
We utilize a real data set of 2022 Fall Semester (Sept. 5, 2022 to Jan. 9, 2023) from higher education institution. The dataset includes 227 students' payment records and attendance records, which are recorded on smart campus card. In addition, the course grade data collected by the student information system are

also obtained for the experiment. Their examples are listed in Table 1, Table 2 and Table 3 respectively. It is worth noting that the problematic students are carefully labeled by the head teacher combined with the advice of professionals.

Payment Record. It contains 49,361 payment records. Each record contains the *Student ID(StuID)*, *Transaction Time (PayTime)*, *Transaction Amount(Amount)*, *Transaction Type(Type)* and *Transaction Device Number(Device)* etc.

Attendance Record. It contains 100,266 attendance records. Each record contains the *Student ID(StuID)*, *Access Control Time(RecordTime)*, *Access Device Number(Device)* and *InOutFlag* etc.

Academic Performance. It contains 826 records about students' GPA scores and rankings since enrollment. Each record contains the *Student ID(StuID)*, *Student's Grade(Grade)*, *Academic Year*, *Semester*, *Student's GPA score(GPA)* and *Student's GPA Ranking(Ranking)* etc.

Table 1. Payment records examples

StuID	PayTime	Amount	Type	Device
FE2A	20220917 17:39:07	13.00	Eat	Canteen01-4
FE2A	20220917 19:30:35	15.00	Shop	Supermarket01-1
FE2A	20220917 22:15:04	3.22	Bath	Bathhouse02-3

Table 2. Access control records examples

StuID	RecordTime	Device	InOutFlag
3DC1	20220918 08:05:02	Library Gate-1	In
3DC1	20220918 11:20:13	Library Gate-2	Out

Table 3. Academic performance records examples

StuID	Grade	Academic Year	Semester	GPA	Ranking
B31E	2020	2020–2021	1	3.71	9
B31E	2020	2020–2021	2	3.39	18

We split the data sets into a training set, a validation set and a test set with a splitting ratio of 7:2:1. All experiments are conducted on a GPU-CPU platform with Tesla V100. The program and baselines are implemented in Python 3.8.

5.1.2 Comparative Approaches

To evaluate the benefits of our proposal, five comparative approaches are represented to compare with *EIPS*.

- *LPMN* [11] is a semi-supervised algorithm for predicting academic performance. It first constructs students' social relationship based on their campus behavior, and then uses a label propagation algorithm to predict academic performance of students without labels on the campus social network. We employ this strategy on consumption data to identify problematic students.
- *OCSVM* [10] extracts some features from students' amounts of consumption on campus card records, and then use a growing model-based one-class support vector machine (OCSVM) to detect students' abnormal activities.
- *BP-based* [13] is an identification method for abnormal students. It is based on psychological interviews, basic information, school life data, and uses K-Means clustering and BP neural network to identify abnormal students.
- *ResNet* [12] applies a deep learning algorithm (i.e., ResNet50) to predict the psychological stress of college students from their consumption, scholarships, and academic performance.
- *StaEnsemble* [2] constructs a stacked ensemble model based on features related to students' academic performance, which is used to identify academically at-risk students. We employ this model based on the features of academic performance to identify problematic students.

5.1.3 Evaluation Metrics

We utilize *Precision*, *Recall* and *F-measure* as the evaluation criteria. Let N_{tru} denote the amount of the ground truth problematic students. N_{det} denote the total number of the identified problematic students by *EIPS*, and the N_{corr} denote the amount of the correctly identified problematic students. The higher the *Precision*, *Recall* and *F-measure* are, the better the identification method performs. *Precision*, *Recall* and *F-measure* are defined respectively as below:

$$Precision = \frac{N_{corr}}{N_{det}} \tag{3}$$

$$Recall = \frac{N_{corr}}{N_{tru}} \tag{4}$$

$$F - measure = \frac{2 * Precision * Recall}{Precision + Recall} \tag{5}$$

5.2 Overall Evaluation

Table 4 shows the overall performance of *EIPS* compared with comparative approaches. First of all, *LPMN* and *OCSVM* perform poorly on all metrics. One possible reason is that they only use single-view features for problematic student identification. Secondly, *BP-based* and *ResNet* are weaker than our proposal. We guess that this phenomenon is caused by the imbalance of training samples. Finally, the performance of *StaEnsemble* is suboptimal because it ignores the differential impact of distinct features on the detection task.

Table 4. Overall effectiveness evaluation

Baselines	Evaluation Criteria		
	Precision	Recall	F-measure
LPMN	0.14	0.43	0.21
OCSVM	0.15	0.34	0.21
BP-based	0.22	0.57	0.32
ResNet	0.30	0.57	0.4
StaEnsemble	0.47	0.63	0.53
Ours	**0.54**	**0.84**	**0.66**

5.3 Ablation Analysis of Features

In order to verify the effectiveness and necessity of each feature for the identification of problematic students, we retrained the model with each feature removed in turn and report the change in metrics of new model compared to the original model without any feature removal. The results are shown in Table 5. It is evident that no feature is redundant, as deleting every feature degrades identification performance. Furthermore, *Academic Performance Feature*($F_{performance,S}$) is the most important feature for the identification of problematic students on our data sets.

Table 5. Features effectiveness evaluation

Features	Evaluation Criteria		
	Precision	Recall	F-measure
$F_{shower,S}$	+0.3	+0.47	+0.37
$F_{consumption,S}$	+0.25	+0.09	+0.25
$F_{library,S}$	+0.08	+0.42	+0.22
$F_{performance,S}$	**+0.27**	**+0.68**	**+0.46**
$F_{com,S}$	−0.01	+0.09	+0.03

5.4 Ablation Analysis of Components

To evaluate the effectiveness and necessity of each component of our proposal, we construct the following two variants of *EIPS* for verification: 1)*EIPS-noAt*, which removes the attention mechanism while others remain the same as *EIPS*. 2)*EIPS-noEns*, it employs a single classifier as the base model for identification while others remain the same as *EIPS*. We implement the variants and compared them with *EIPS*, and the results are shown in Fig. 8. The weaker performance of *EIPS-noAt* and *EIPS-noEns* demonstrates the effectiveness and necessity of the attention component as well as the ensemble strategy.

5.5   Ensemble Parameter K Selection

In order to choose the appropriate number of ensemble k, we vary the value of
K from 1 to 25 in increments of 2. As shown in Fig. 9, the values of *Precision,
Recall* and *F-measure* first increase until k=5 and then show a stable trend as
K becomes larger. In view of this, we set k=5 for reasons of performance and
efficiency.

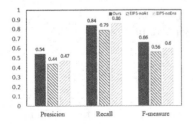
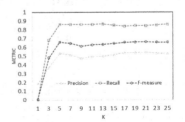

Fig. 8. Ablation analysis   **Fig. 9.** Selection of the value of K

5.6   Visualization

We deploy *EIPS* on the student warning system to identify problematic students.
In this application, we divide problematic students into 3 levels (i.e. mild concern,
moderate concern, severe concern) based on the number of votes from all the base
classifiers. Figure 10 shows the visual interface, which can provide timely feedback on the personal information of problematic students (yellow box), historical
statistical information (blue box), and the importance of individual discriminant
features (orange box). The system helps teachers and administrators grasp the
physical and mental conditions of students in a timely manner. Moreover, it
can certainly be traced back to explore the key causes, and used to develop
intervention approaches.

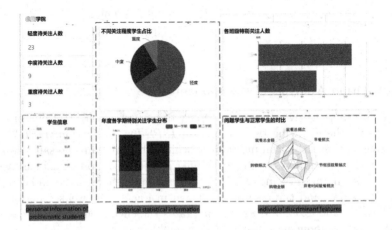

Fig. 10. Visual interface

6   Conclusion

To proliferate the precision of problematic college student identification, we consider such an identification issue as a binary classification task, and design an ensembled identification framework based on multi-perspective analysis using college student behavioral data, called *EIPS*. Initially, on the basis of the analysis of multi-sources behavioral data of college students, we extract critical features and then capture differentiated influences of different features on identification result by introducing self-attention mechanism. Based on that, we construct an ensemble learning-based binary-classification model to tackle the difficulty in correctly identifying problematic college student using imbalanced training data. Extensive experiments are conducted on real data sets to demonstrate the effectiveness and practicability of *EIPS*. In the future, we will apply *EIPS* to graduate students' behavioral data sets to verify its rationality and reliability.

Acknowledgements. This work is supported by NSFC (Nos.62137001, 62072180 and U1911203).

References

1. Cheng, C., et al.: A novel architecture and algorithm for prediction of students psychological health based on big data. In: TrustCom 2021, pp. 1391–1396 (2021)
2. Lauría, E.J.M., et al.: Stacking classifiers for early detection of students at risk. In: CSEDU (1), pp. 390–397 (2018)
3. Li, A., Zhang, F., Zhu, T.: Web use behaviors for identifying mental health status. In: BHI, pp. 348–358 (2013)
4. Qin, Z., et al.: FD-mobilenet: improved mobilenet with a fast downsampling strategy. In: ICIP, pp. 1363–1367 (2018)
5. Saha, A.K., et al.: Machine learning based prediction of student's performance based on psychological and behavioral data. In: International Conference on Mining Intelligence and Knowledge Exploration, pp. 396–408 (2023)
6. Sano, A., et al.: Recognizing academic performance, sleep quality, stress level, and mental health using personality traits, wearable sensors and mobile phones. In: IEEE 12th International Conference on Wearable and Implantable Body Sensor Networks (BSN), pp. 1–6 (2015)
7. Vaswani, A., et al.: Attention is all you need. In: Advances in Neural Information Processing Systems, vol. 30 (2017)
8. Xu, X., et al.: Leveraging routine behavior and contextually-filtered features for depression detection among college students. IMWUT **3**(3), 1–33 (2019)
9. Yang, L., et al.: Research on strategies of promoting mental health of higher vocational college students based on data mining. Wirel. Commun. Mob. Comput. **2022** (2022)
10. Yang, X., et al.: A growing model-based OCSVM for abnormal student activity detection from daily campus consumption. New Gener. Comput. **40**(4), 915–933 (2022)

11. Yao, H., et al.: Predicting academic performance via semi-supervised learning with constructed campus social network. In: DASFAA, pp. 597–609 (2017)
12. Zhang, H., et al.: A novel deep learning model for analyzing psychological stress in college students. J. Electr. Comput. Eng. **2022** (2022)
13. Zhang, S., Wen, X.: Abnormal student detection model based on student feature extraction. In: ICBDIE, pp. 957–965 (2022)

VTIS: Research and Implementation of Virtual Teaching Interactive Space

Tianyu Huang, Yuting Chen[✉], and Jingyao Xu

Beijing Institute of Technology, Beijing, China
674577491@qq.com

Abstract. The globalization of the economy and technology has led to a growing demand for online collaboration. At the same time, the rapid development of virtual reality technology has drawn more and more attention to the emerging field of "metaverse". As an application scenario of metaverse, virtual teaching provides important support for exploring new teaching methods. Research on the application of virtual human technology in the teaching scene has important theoretical significance and practical application value. This paper discusses the theoretical concept of virtual teaching interactive space (VTIS) in depth, defines the elements in it clearly, and analyzes the relationship between the elements in VTIS under different perspectives. To validate the proposed theory of virtual teaching elements, this paper designs and implements a modular virtual teaching interactive space (VTIS), and evaluates it from multiple perspectives.

Keywords: Teaching Situation · Virtual Space · Virtual Human

1 Introduction

Economic and technological globalization is driving the emergence and development of the emerging field of meta-universe [1, 2]. Education as a pivotal social activity in the real world, its application in the virtual space can not be ignored, in the process of constructing the virtual teaching space application, the virtual person as its important component, how to deal with the mapping relationship between the virtual person and the user has become the focus of attention of researchers.

This paper studies the virtual person technology and its application in the teaching scene, which is of great significance in theory and practice: in the theoretical aspect, the application of virtual person technology in the teaching scene can strengthen the understanding of the construction of the virtual space, which is conducive to the formation of a generalized theory of the relationship of the virtual space system, thus reducing the cost of the initial construction. In practice, the application of virtual teaching interactive space (VTIS) is conducive to promoting online diversified teaching, enriching teaching content and improving teaching efficiency to a certain extent.

This paper will introduce the work related to virtual teaching and learning in the second part, describe the elements of virtual teaching and learning interactive space in the third part, analyze the implementation and evaluation of virtual teaching and learning

© The Author(s), under exclusive license to Springer Nature Singapore Pte Ltd. 2024
W. Hong and G. Kanaparan (Eds.): ICCSE 2023, CCIS 2025, pp. 251–265, 2024.
https://doi.org/10.1007/978-981-97-0737-9_23

interactive space in the fourth part, and finally make a summary of the research in this paper, analyze the possible shortcomings and make a prospect for future work.

2 Related Work

In terms of technical research, the teaching meta-universe focuses on more accurate character modeling, optimization of hardware equipment, refinement of artificial intelligence algorithms, and in-depth study of cloud computing and big data technology; in terms of theoretical construction, most research focuses on the feasibility of the virtual teaching space and the user's purposefulness, aiming at the refinement of the teaching meta-universe's application needs.

2.1 Virtual Interactive Space

Virtual interactive space research involves three main areas: user experience, ethical research, and virtual space applications.

User Experience. With the rapid development of head-mounted devices, a series of problems such as vertigo and difficulty in adapting have arisen for users who have been in the virtual space perspective for a long time. A study by Kasabov et al. [3] summarized 26 studies related to screen-sickness. Some studies focus on network level optimization to reduce network latency, such as Lee et al. who implement a user's physical person-to-virtual character mapping [4]. Moon et al. propose a data collection framework for VR devices based on the Unity engine [5].

Ethical Research. Rosenberg's study explores the possible risks associated with the management of virtual space platforms [6]; Han's study searches for the boundaries between virtual space platforms and ethical norms, which provides a theoretical basis for subsequent studies [7]; Spence's study proposes a "meta-ethical" framework based on the ethical theories of Alan Gewirth [8], which guides the designers, administrators, and ordinary users of virtual worlds [9].

Virtual Space Applications. The research related to virtual space applications focuses on how to utilize virtual space to provide more convenience in various areas of real life. Deveci's study verifies the feasibility of driverless technology by testing algorithms in virtual scenarios [10]; Makransky et al.'s study examines the application of XR (Extanded reality) in health communication to improve user's health [11]; Wu et al. proposed a novel virtual reality collaboration system [12]; Lee et al. summarized a design framework for virtual space applications [13].

At present, the difficulties in enhancing user experience lie in the imperfection and immaturity of virtual reality hardware devices and the lack of network optimization; the difficulty in the study of ethical issues lies in how to map elements that do not exist in reality into virtual space; and the research on the application of virtual space focuses on the fields of gaming, training, and medical care, but has not yet gained popularity in the fields of business, education, and administration, which are involved in public life.

2.2 Virtual Human

For the theoretical research on the elements related to virtual human, when discussing the relationship between virtual human and users, the mapping in virtual scenes is not clear. Researchers do not strictly distinguish between the terms "avatar" and "embodiment" and do not give a clear definition, so the two are mixed in different studies.

Theoretical Studies. Virtual human technology is closely related to the words "embodiment" and "avatar". With the continuous development of virtual reality technology, researchers have explored the meaning of "embodiment" from different perspectives; Ziemke's study [14] classified the definitions of "embodiment" into six categories: A, B, C, and D, each with its own focus; Klevjer's study [15] divided them into six categories: "structural coupling of agent and environment", "result of historical structural coupling", "physical embodiment", "organism-like embodiment", "structural coupling", "structural coupling", "structural coupling" and "structural coupling", each with its own focus, Klevjer's study [15] defines Avatar as a simulated, animated "character", or a local algorithmic image generated by digital technology. Southgate proposes a sociological theory that aims to reflect the complex relationship between virtual humans and humans intertwined in virtual scenarios [16]. There are also several studies that discuss the impact of virtual human on users' activities in virtual space. Mal et al. study the relationship between virtual human and virtual environment [17].

Assessment Studies. Gonzalez-Franco et al. proposed a standardized questionnaire to assess virtual human [18], and likewise there are many studies that used questionnaire methods to assess virtual human [19–21].

In addition to the general problem of virtual reality equipment hardware, teaching meta-universe in terms of technology, the main problem is that most of the prototype of the virtual content is only science-based experience, stay in the demonstration and simple interaction stage, for the course teaching content of the in-depth exploration is insufficient. The application of educational meta-universe in the classroom requires the strengthening of the deep-level construction of the knowledge system of the course.

3 Elements of the Virtual Teaching Interactive Space

This paper first defines each element in the virtual teaching interaction space and analyzes the characteristics of each element from different angles. After studying the relationship of each element, the interaction process of each element in the virtual teaching interaction space is given.

3.1 Definitions in VTIS

In virtual scenarios, visual entities are divided into two categories: static entities and functional entities. VTIS is a mapping of real teaching scenarios. In VTIS, teachers and students are users; the entities manipulated by teachers and students are virtual human; static models such as desks, chairs, and classrooms are part of the virtual scenarios; and blackboards that can display slides are logical functional entities. The following section defines the elements in VTIS in detail.

Virtual Space. Virtual teaching interactive space V refers to a fully immersive 3D teaching environment. In the VTIS, users wear hardware devices such as VR and use external devices to drive and control virtual objects. In this study, VTIS is defined as:

$$V = S \cup D \tag{1}$$

where S is static entity, D is dynamic entity.

$$S = \{desk, chair, \ldots, s_i, \ldots, s_m\}, \quad (i = 1, 2, \ldots, m) \tag{2}$$

$$D = \{blackboard, lamp, \ldots, d_j, \ldots, d_n\}, \quad (j = 1, 2, \ldots, n) \tag{3}$$

where s_i denotes a virtual static entity of a static virtual environment S, m indicates the total number of static entities. d_j denotes a virtual logical entity of the set of virtual logical entities D, n indicates the total number of virtual logical entities.

User. Define the set of users as

$$U = \{teacher, student_1, student_2, \ldots, u_i, \ldots, u_m\}, \quad (i = 1, 2, \ldots, m) \tag{4}$$

where u_i denotes one user participating in the VTIS application and m denotes the total number of users.

A user consists of a user physical person and user social attributes. User physical person refers to the user's body in the real world. Physical person refers to the entity of the user's natural person after removing the user's social attributes, which is directly mapped to the virtual human model in the virtual scenario, and is mainly categorized into logical keying and sensor-driven methods.

Embodiment. In a small virtual space system, a user's "embodiment" can be considered as "the set of entities that the user and other users perceive as the current user in terms of sensory and identity". In this paper, we define the embodiment set as:

$$E = \{teacher, student_1, student_2, \ldots, e_i, \ldots, e_m\}, \quad (i = 1, 2, \ldots, m) \tag{5}$$

$$e_i = f(u_i) \tag{6}$$

where e_i is embodiment for user u_i, m indicates the total number of users. f Indicates a mapping relationship where embodiment and user correspond one-to-one.

Avatar. The "virtual human" is a manifestation of "avatar" and "embodiment". This study explores the mapping relationship between user and virtual human, and gives the definition of Avatar in virtual space: an entity that is directly manipulated by the user.

"Avatar" is "mine" and "embodiment" is "me". The virtual human manipulated by the user is the user's "avatar". In the situation where the user can switch the control of virtual entities, each virtual entity is the user's "avatar", each with its own unique operation logic. "Embodiment" refers to the part of the entity that implements the switching logic and contains the above mentioned "avatars". Define the set of avatars as

$$A = \{teacher, student_1, student_2, \ldots, a_i, \ldots, a_m\}, \quad (i = 1, 2, \ldots, m) \tag{7}$$

where a_i is an avatar in the virtual space V and m denotes the total number of avatars.

Virtual Space Application. Virtual Space Application combines virtual space, virtual human, and user's embodiment. Define the VTIS application as *VSA*:

$$VSA = \{VTIS, virtual\ human\ set, users'\ embodiment\ set\} \qquad (8)$$

since the number of virtual human is the same as the number of users in that scenario, so $len(A) = len(E)$.

3.2 Features of Elements in VTIS

In this paper, the following definitions are given to characterize the virtual teaching interaction space, user, embodiment and avatar.

Space. The virtual space possesses three characteristics: interactivity, real-time, and customizability. Interactivity is reflected in the teacher's feedback on the student's inputs. The real-time nature of VTIS means that the feedback can be delivered to the other party's end device in real time. The customizability of VTIS means that the virtual interaction elements are customized according to the needs.

User. In a pedagogical context, users are one-to-many, i.e., a single teacher-identified user to multiple student users. In VTIS, there is a high degree of autonomy for both teacher users and student users.

Embodiment. Depending on the subject of observation, the perceived "embodiment" may vary and manifest itself as a different entity in the virtual space.

The Users Themselves. The "embodiment" is the user himself, the "me" in the first-person of the user. In the VTIS, the embodiment of student users and teacher users is reflected in the perspective moving with the virtual human, the control of the virtual human limbs through the VR device, and the manipulation of logical entities.

Other Users. The current user's virtual human is the current user's "embodiment", which is recognized and perceived by other users in terms of visual senses and identity. In VTIS, the visual senses are distinguished by the persona; the identity is represented by the "privileges" of the teacher-user, who has more privileges and room to maneuver.

Avatar. Since avatar is an entity directly manipulated by the user, in VTIS, avatar is a virtual human that is a combination of the runtime logic and the character model. The user's embodiment and avatar are highly similar in visual presentation.

3.3 Relationships in VTIS

This paper first elaborates on the entities represented by embodiment and avatar according to different application scenarios. Secondly, it explores the data sources of the entities in the virtual scene and how users interact with the virtual scene. Finally, the paper examines how the entities involved in the virtual scene interact with each other from both a first-person perspective and a third-person perspective.

Embodiment and Avatar. Depending on the application context, avatars are given different operation logics, while the embodiment is always fully mapped to the user, and the user's operations on avatars are only a part of it. Under the current user's perspective, the entities in the scene are categorized as shown in Table 1.

Table 1. Characterization of entities from the current user perspective.

Type of entity	Embodiment		Avatar
	Current user	Other user	
Explicitly present or not	Not necessarily	Yes	Yes
Form of expression	Human shape	Human shape	No special
Observational perspective	First-person	Third-person	No special
Mapping content	All attributes of user	All attributes of user	user's operation

According to Table 1, Embodiment can be equated with avatar only in the first person and the user-controlled avatar has a humanoid model.

Usually researchers equate embodiment with avatar because visually, the user is just presented on the screen as a character model. However, the user's avatar will be constantly switched, and the following discussion are divided into three cases.

The user controls the character through a first-person point of view, where the view camera is tied to the controlling character. The role controlled by the user is the user's avatar, and according to the different ways of user mapping, the embodiment perceived by the user will also be different.

The user controls the character's activities through a third-person perspective, with the view camera behind and above the character. In this type of scenario, the role controlled by the user is the user's avatar, and there is no entity in the virtual scene that is explicitly recognized by the current user as his or her embodiment.

The user controls the view camera and roams around the virtual scene through the God's perspective. The point-of-view camera is the user's avatar. An entity, not explicitly present in the virtual scene, is recognized by current users as his or her embodiment.

For the VTIS application, it is clear that the teacher and student users wearing the VR device are controlling the virtual human through a first-person perspective. In this context, the teacher virtual human is the teacher's embodiment and avatar, and the student virtual human is the student's embodiment and avatar, and both are can be explicitly recognized by other users.

Equipment and Data. The hardware devices used by users in reality are categorized into two types: input devices and output devices. For VTIS applications, the main hardware devices used by teachers and students are VR headsets and VR grips.

First-Person Perspective. In this scenario, the view camera is bound to the avatar entity. The user embodiment driven by the sensor and the avatar driven by the logic control are the same entity (in the red dashed rectangle in Fig. 1). The user is able to clearly perceive his/her own and others' embodiment in the virtual scene.

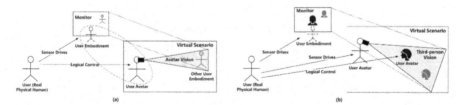

Fig. 1. (a) Schematic diagram of the relationship between user embodiment and avatar in the first-person context. (b) Schematic diagram of the relationship between user embodiment and avatar in third person context.

In Fig. 1(a), the black villain is a virtual entity manipulated by the current user and the red villain is manipulated by other users. The black villain is recognized by the current user and other users as the avatar and embodiment of the current user, and the red villain is recognized by the current user as the avatar and embodiment of the other users.

Third-Person Perspective. In this scenario, the view camera is not tied to the avatar entity. The user drives the embodiment through the sensor, the user embodiment does not exist explicitly and is not visible to other users. The avatar entity does not receive data from the sensor, but only receives inputs from the user's logical control.

Compared to Fig. 1(a), in Fig. 1(b), the black villain is recognized by the current user and other users as the avatar of the current user, and the red villain is recognized by the current user as the avatar of the other users. The embodiment of the current user does not explicitly exist in the virtual scene.

3.4 Interaction

Interacting with virtual scenes and AI or other user-controlled virtual entities is the ultimate goal of users using virtual space applications. In this process, the entities involved in the real world are the user's physical person as well as the hardware devices he/she uses; the virtual space is involved with avatars, embodiment and other kinds of interactive entities, as well as scene environment entities.

In the process of sending data for interaction, all the user's data are transmitted to the virtual space by the hardware device, and these data drive the user's embodiment, which, as an entity directly related to "I" in the virtual space, processes the data into the driving data of virtual entities, such as virtual human, and finally interacts with other virtual entities by applying specific logic functions. The embodiment, as an entity directly related to the "I" in the virtual space, processes the data into the driving data of virtual entities such as virtual human.

In the interactive process of receiving data, avatar receives data from the environment and other virtual entities, and is fed back to the hardware device by embodiment to be presented to the user. For VTIS, the hardware device is only a VR headset and a joystick, and teachers and student users do not have the need to "change the manipulated virtual human", and the interaction process is shown in Fig. 2.

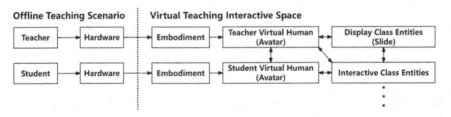

Fig. 2. The process of interacting with the elements of the virtual teaching space.

4   Realization of the Virtual Teaching Interactive Space

In this paper, we first modularize the implementation of VTIS, focusing on the key technology of network synchronization. Then, it analyzes the application of VTIS in two contexts: virtual space experience and lecture. Finally, VTIS is evaluated.

4.1   Functional Module for VTIS

Under the influence of economic and technological globalization, teaching methods other than traditional offline lectures have been born, as shown in Table 2.

Table 2. Evaluation of the characteristics of each method of instruction.

Teaching methods	Video(Mooc)	VTIS	Live Streaming (Tencent Meeting)	Offline
Educational costs	Middle	High	Low	Low
Teaching effect	Low	High	Middle	Middle
Degree of participation	Low	High	Middle	Middle
Scalability	Low	High	Middle	Middle
Convenience	High	Middle	High	Low

When comparing the various modes of instruction, the advantages of VTIS are centered on the teaching effect, the degree of participation, and the scalability. The presentation of three-dimensional elements of VTIS and the physical interaction provided by VR devices can provide a similar feeling to offline teaching and increase user engagement.

The VTIS implemented in this paper is divided into six modules: scenario visualization, network synchronization, slideshow, voice control, device access and virtual human control, and the relationship between each module is shown in Fig. 3.

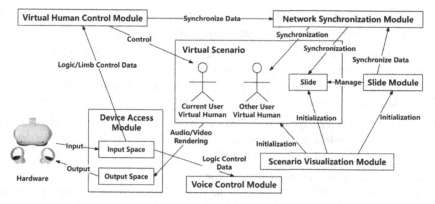

Fig. 3. VTIS Module Relationship Diagram.

Scenario Visualization. This module is responsible for loading, and for switching the user from the initial room to the virtual teaching scene.

Network Synchronization. VTIS is essentially the same as most client applications. The user installs the client locally, transmits the data to the server through the network, the server distributes the key data to other clients, and the other clients process the data locally and finally present the effect in front of the user's eyes.

In VTIS, two main data synchronization methods, remote procedure call and data stream transmission, are used depending on the type of data and its usage. In this study, the Photon Engine cloud server is used as the remote server, and the entire network connection process is divided into three parts: network environment initialization, data update, and instance destruction.

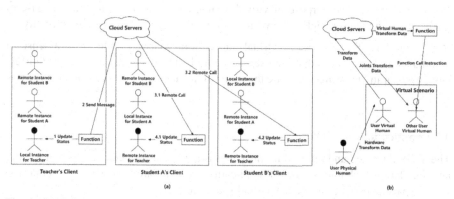

Fig. 4. (a) Schematic diagram of a VTIS remote procedure call. (b) Schematic of network synchronization data flow.

The VTIS remote procedure call is shown in Fig. 4(a), taking the example of a teacher user who has called the function that changes the current virtual human position on the teacher side, the function first updates the virtual human locally, and then sends a call message to the cloud server, which ultimately calls the function in other clients remotely, updating the corresponding virtual human instance of the teacher.

Network Environment Initialization. The user first connects to the cloud server with a specific application ID, and the teacher user creates a room by determining the Room-Name, which is a unique identifier for joining the room, after a successful connection. The student user then obtains the RoomName from the teacher to join the room.

Data Updates. The data update is carried out on the client by network synchronization, bit pose data and skeletal animation state are synchronized every frame, and the detailed synchronization method is shown in Fig. 4(b).

Instance Destruction. When a normally connected client detects that another user is actively or passively disconnecting from the network, it destroys the instance spawned on the current client based on the ID of the disconnecting user.

Slide. This module is to manage the slide lecture content in VTIS application. The scene visualization module will initialize the virtual teaching content components and hand them over to the corresponding module for processing to improve the scalability.

Voice Control. The voice control module is responsible for the voice communication between the teacher user and the student user.

Device Access. The user's embodiment interfaces with the hardware device through the device access module. The device access module is divided into two parts: input space and output space according to the user embodiment.

Virtual Human Control. In the VTIS, the virtual human is categorized into student virtual human and teacher virtual human according to the different user roles.

Perspective Fixation. The purpose is to bring a sense of presence to the user. The embodiment viewpoint corresponds to the user's viewpoint.

Physical Control. The purpose of virtual human entity control is to bring a sense of involvement to the user, and to show functions that the user cannot realize in reality.

Body Mapping. The purpose of virtual human limb mapping is to bring a sense of dominance to the user, so that the user sensually believes that the limbs of the virtual human avatar in the virtual space are the limbs of his/her own physical human in the real world.

4.2   Applications of VTIS

The VTIS designed and realized in this paper is applied on the course "Virtual Reality and Simulation Technology", and the application scenarios are divided into two contexts: virtual space experience as well as virtual space lectures.

Experience. In this scenario, both teachers and student users are in the classroom, which is shown in Fig. 5(a). In order to demonstrate the effectiveness of the limb mapping, only student A user activated all two handles.

Teach. In this scenario, users are dispersed in different areas (e.g., classrooms, offices, dormitories), and the specific application is shown in Fig. 5(b).

(a)   (b)

Fig. 5. (a) Teacher and student hardware wearing. (b) Third-person view of each student and faculty member and the view of each student and faculty member in the virtual scene.

4.3 Assessment of VTIS

The virtual teaching space designed and implemented in this paper is based on the Unity engine, and the VR device used is the Oculus quest 2 developed by Meta, which is analyzed and evaluated using three objective indicators, namely, rendering frame rate, mapping latency, and offset distance of joints, and subjective indicators of the user's sense of immersive experience, with the number of subjects being 24.

Rendering Frame Rate. The rendering frame rates of the VR side and PC side are tested in two teaching application scenarios, and the average value of multiple tests on the VR side of the VTIS experience is 64.4 FPS, and the average value on the PC side is 64.4 FPS; the average value on the VR side of the virtual space teaching is 63.5 FPS, and the average value on the PC side is 62.6 FPS. The results show that the performance requirements can be met on both the VR and PC sides.

Mapping Delay. It refers to the time used for mapping data to be transmitted locally through the network and then finally mapped onto the corresponding entities in the virtual space. In VTIS, the mapping delay is used to measure the efficiency of the mapping method and the network transmission.

Limb Mapping Delay. Experiments were conducted to determine the limb data mapping latency by recording the time it took for the current user's limb mapping to be synchronized to other user's clients. The average latency for the 1000 times was 99.6 ms. The VTIS operated well enough to enable the user to perceive no noticeable latency.

Slide Delay. The experiment determines the mapping latency of slide data by recording the time of synchronization of slide images from the teacher's end to the student's end several times. The average latency of 1000 times is 1137.4 ms. However, considering the nature of the teaching with slide content, this delay is within the acceptable range.

Offset Distance of Joints. In this experiment, the user wears the Xsens Dot physical sensor for limb movement. The specific wearing positions were forearm and upper arm.

The user performed the movement in the order, forming a closed loop for 10 repetitions. The relative spatial position of the joints in the VTIS with respect to the physical sensors is recorded and two curves are formed. The Pearson's correlation coefficient of the two curves (all the curves of the ten experiments) was calculated and obtained $r = 0.5235$, indicating that the two curves are moderately correlated.

User Immersion. In this paper, a questionnaire (11 questions) was designed to evaluate the subjective experience of users of VTIS in a course on Virtual Reality and Simulation Technology. All questions can be grouped into six categories, as shown in Table 3, and were evaluated using a 7-point Likert scale ranging from "Strongly Disagree" to "Strongly Agree" for each question. The identity of the users (students and teachers) who participated in the questionnaire was determined before entering the system, and the statistics of the results of the experiment are shown in Table 3.

Table 3. Instructional Context Questionnaire Specifications and Statistical Results in VTIS.

Type of question	Question mark	Question description	Student		Teacher	
			M	SD	M	SD
Hardware impacts	Q1	VR devices did not significantly impact the experience	4.375	1.285	3.250	1.127
Pleasantness	Q2	No vertigo from character activity	4.458	1.471	4.167	1.067
Immersion	Q3	Characters move naturally with a sense of realism	4.208	1.499	4.958	1.060
	Q4	Activities are highly interactive	4.958	1.274	5.667	0.471
Functionality	Q5	Current Role Functionality Improvement	3.792	1.322	3.708	1.485
	Q6	Ability to feel the uniqueness of the current role function	2.833	1.404	5.042	1.399
Content impressions	Q7	The lessons are clear and easy to understand	6.042	0.611	5.750	0.595
	Q8	Good overall experience	4.792	1.322	4.750	0.722
Comprehensive judging compared to offline teaching	Q9	Currently, virtual space teaching has a better teaching experience	4.208	1.384	2.875	0.927
	Q10	Currently, teaching in virtual spaces is better able to achieve the goals of teaching and learning	5.458	1.154	3.625	1.111
	Q11	In the future, teaching in virtual spaces is even more promising	6.667	0.471	6.292	0.676

The results for $Q1$ indicate that the VR hardware has a greater impact on the teacher user than on the student user, with the teacher user scoring only $M = 3.25$; the results for $Q2$ indicate that the teacher user is more prone to vertigo during the activity. The reason for the results of $Q1$ and $Q2$ is that teacher users tend to accompany more body movements during the delivery of lectures, making the overall amplitude of movement greater than that of the student users. The results of $Q3$ and $Q4$ indicate that teacher users have a greater sense of immersion compared to student users. The reason is that in order to ensure the overall efficiency of the VTIS, small amplitude movements of student users are not captured by the sensors, resulting in less immersion for student users.

According to the results of $Q9$ and the feedback from users, the main reasons for the low scores were the inconvenience in the VR device and the feeling of vertigo brought by using the VR device for a long time. In particular, for teacher users, the general opinion is that teaching in virtual space does not provide a good experience. The results of $Q10$ show that there is a big difference between student users and teacher users in terms of teaching effect, with student users focusing more on the novelty of the virtual space and teacher users focusing more on the actual effect that the system can bring to the teaching and learning. The results of $Q11$ indicate that both students and teachers believe that teaching in virtual spaces still has a lot of room for growth and promise.

5 Discussion

This paper defines and clarifies the elements of virtual space such as avatar, embodiment and virtual human from the theoretical level, clarifies the mapping method between users and virtual human according to the characteristics of each element, and designs and implements VTIS through modularization, which proves that VTIS can satisfy the needs of online teaching and learning and can be flexibly extended for virtual content. The application demonstrates that VTIS can satisfy the general online teaching needs, and at the same time, it can flexibly expand the virtual content. Finally, VTIS is validated, analyzed and evaluated in terms of subjective and objective metrics. The main research results include:

At the same time, there are still some problems that need to be solved in the future. Firstly, when evaluating the virtual human mapping method, some of the dimension conclusions can only represent the "tested person". Meanwhile, the two scenarios selected are only two typical scenarios of virtual space activities, which do not cover more application scenarios. In addition, prolonged use of VR devices can still cause dizziness and nausea to users, and until VR devices that can significantly improve the user experience are developed, improvements can only be made at the software level. Finally, the pedagogical meta-universe also needs the support of relevant policies to ensure the sustainability and evolvability of virtual content.

Acknowledgment. This research was supported by the National Natural Science Foundation of China (NSFC, No. 62177005).

References

1. Bezovski, Z., Temjanovski, R., Sofijanova, E.: Telecommuting best practices prior and during the COVID 19 pandemic. J. Econ. (2021)
2. Music, J., Charlebois, S., Toole, V., et al.: Telecommuting and food E-commerce: socially sustainable practices during the COVID-19 pandemic in Canada. Transp. Res. Interdiscip. Perspect. **13**, 100513 (2022)
3. Yang, A.H.X., Kasabov, N., Cakmak, Y.O.: Machine learning methods for the study of cybersickness: a systematic review. Brain Inform. **9**(1), 24 (2022)
4. Lee, M.H., Ko, J.C.: Research on application of virtual reality technology to create metaverse podcasts. In: 2022 IEEE International Conference on Consumer Electronics-Taiwan, pp. 133–134. IEEE (2022)
5. Moon, J., Jeong, M., Oh, S., et al.: Data collection framework for context-aware virtual reality application development in unity: case of avatar embodiment. Sensors **22**(12), 4623 (2022)
6. Rosenberg, L.B.: The growing need for metaverse regulation. In: Arai, K. (eds.) Intelligent Systems and Applications, vol. 3, pp. 540–547. Springer, Cham (2022). https://doi.org/10.1007/978-3-031-16075-2_39
7. Han, J.: An information ethics framework based on ICT platforms. Information **13**(9), 440 (2022)
8. Montaña, R.A.: The gewirthian principle of generic consistency as a foundation for human fulfillment: unveiling a rational path for moral and political hope. Kritike Online J. Philos. **3**(1), 24–39 (2009)
9. Spence, E.H.: Meta ethics for the metaverse: the ethics of virtual worlds. In: Current Issues in Computing and Philosophy, vol. 175, no. 3 (2008)
10. Deveci, M., Pamucar, D., Gokasar, I., et al.: Personal mobility in metaverse with autonomous vehicles using Q-rung orthopair fuzzy sets based OPA-RAFSI model. IEEE Trans. Intell. Transp. Syst. (2022)
11. Plechatá, A., Makransky, G., Böhm, R.: Can extended reality in the metaverse revolutionise health communication? NPJ Digit. Med. **5**(1), 132 (2022)
12. Wu, Y., Wang, Y., Jung, S., et al.: Using a fully expressive avatar to collaborate in virtual reality: evaluation of task performance, presence, and attraction. Front. Virtual Reality **2**, 641296 (2021)
13. Lee, I., Sung, Y.M., Kim, T.: The expanding role of metaverse platform in college education. ICIC Exp. Lett. Part B Appl. 1037–1044 (2022)
14. Ziemke, T.: What's that thing called embodiment? In: Proceedings of the Annual Meeting of the Cognitive Science Society, vol. 25, no. 25 (2003)
15. Klevjer, R.: What is the Avatar. Fiction and Embodiment in Avatar-Based Singleplayer Computer Games (2006)
16. Southgate, E.: Conceptualising embodiment through virtual reality for education. In: 2020 6th International Conference of the Immersive Learning Research Network (ILRN), pp. 38–45. IEEE (2020)
17. Mal, D., Wolf, E., Döllinger, N., et al.: The impact of avatar and environment congruence on plausibility, embodiment, presence, and the proteus effect in virtual reality. IEEE Trans. Vis. Comput. Graph. **29**(5), 2358–2368 (2023)
18. Gonzalez-Franco, M., Peck, T.C.: Avatar embodiment towards a standardized questionnaire. Front. Robot. AI **5**, 74 (2018)
19. Hsieh, R., Shirai, A., Sato, H.: Evaluation of avatar and voice transform in programming e-learning lectures. In: Proceedings of the 19th ACM International Conference on Intelligent Virtual Agents, pp. 197–199 (2019)

20. Wang, H., Gaddy, V., Beveridge, J.R., et al.: Building an emotionally responsive avatar with dynamic facial expressions in human—computer interactions. Multimodal Technol. Interact. **5**(3), 13 (2021)

21. Dimou, A.L., Papavassiliou, V., McDonald, J., et al.: Signing avatar performance evaluation within EASIER project. In: Proceedings of the 7th International Workshop on Sign Language Translation and Avatar Technology: The Junction of the Visual and the Textual: Challenges and Perspectives, pp. 39–44 (2022)

A Blockchain-Based Real Estates Registration System

Ahmed Ayman Ahmed Ezzat Mohamed[✉], Burra Venkata Durga Kumar, and Teh Jia Yew

Doha, Qatar
ahmedaymen1392001@gmail.com, venkata.burra@xmu.edu.my

Abstract. Real estates are essential part of our daily life and it contains a huge amount of data. This data need to be stored and organized and that is the role of real-estate registration system. The traditional real-estate registration systems face many issues such as fraud, having less data privacy, and inefficiency and these issues needs to be minimized or totally solved. To achieve this, blockchain technology will be used which stores data in a distributed ledger. Indeed, it has many desired features that will help to achieve a secure, trusted real-estate registration system such as immutability, transparency and smart contracts, which are used to set the rules of the registration process. To integrate blockchain technology with property registration system some methodologies were used in this paper. An interview was conducted with a real-estate professional, and a review was done to study the current registration systems and how blockchain could be used to enhance them, and self-testing was done to collect data to analyze the performance of the system. The system was implemented using Solidity programming language and then tested in many terms such as security, performance, and cost. From the test results, noticed the registration process is faster than traditional registrations system. It takes less than a minute, but the time varies from time to time based on the network status at the time of performing transaction. Moreover, the system is secure and no unauthorized user can perform any authorized users actions. In a country like Qatar, the registration process takes 0.2% registration fees from the total price of the expensive properties. On the other hand, this system has an average price is less for each process. The registration process will cost the owner around 0.00045477ETH and the ownership transfer will cost the owner around 0.000086973ETH. These prices are equal to 0.83 USD and 0.16 USD. Although the system functioned successfully, there are some limitations that need to be addressed like scalability, and cost challenges since it might change with time.

Keywords: Blockchain · Smart contracts · Decentralization · Property registration · Peer-to-peer

1 Introduction

Real-estate Industry is an important industry, all data in this industry need to be organized and stored well. Real-estate data (properties and their details) are stored in real-estate registry. Additionally, blockchain Technology has been growing in the previous era

W. Hong and G. Kanaparan (Eds.): ICCSE 2023, CCIS 2025, pp. 266–276, 2024.
https://doi.org/10.1007/978-981-97-0737-9_24

because it can contribute in many different industries. It can be applied in the targeted industry of this project, which is real estate registrations.

This paper focuses on improving the security of real estate registration using blockchain technology. This system will be developed and put into place to safeguard information about property owners and the history of transactions in each property. In addition, it will decrease the probability of editing the registered data to perform any illegal actions. The system will also verify the registration of the real estates so the government can track it if any frauds or suspicious actions are done. Additionally, it will serve as a means to prove the real-estate ownership, inclusive of all requisite particulars.

There are several crimes that happen in real estate Industry like money laundering because it has more benefits than other industries. Money laundering happens in several ways and they all are suitable to be done in real-estate industry. This crime is hard to be detected [1].

Real estate's transactions include many parties and large amount of money. There are some examples about the current real-estate systems in different countries and the data that they need. For example, Hong Kong has deeds registration system but In Mainland China the system is between title registration system and Torrens registration system. In Hong Kong, The registration is online and it is for the public (as people pays for research they can access the data) while in Mainland China clients should go to office to apply for registration and it is for authorized people only [2]. In addition, a study in China was made to make a uniform real-estate registration (URER) which is a system that authorities use to register spatial and real estate with the right law and regulations. The system is also 3D system since it is more efficient. This study also specifies and explains all real-estate types that can be included in the registration system [3].

Blockchain has been defined as the fifth disruptive innovation of the computing paradigm [4]. In blockchain, data are stored in distributed ledger. In blockchain users can read, write, and verify transaction, but cannot delete or modify the content once stored. Blockchain provide many wanted features like decentralization, autonomy, integrity, immutability, etc. Blockchain technology contains consensus algorithms, smart contract, cryptography, and more [5]. There are many systems that was developed using blockchain is a decentralized hotel booking system [6] and MedRec which uses blockchain technology (smart contracts) to set rules to access data [7]. Blockchain architecture is shown in Fig. 1. Smart contract is enclosed in blockchain. With the help of it, an agreement's condition can be implemented without including any third party [8]. It can reduce the costs of service since there are no intermediate people like brokers. In addition, it improves the efficiency of the system, which is also because of the elimination of the third party. Moreover, it decrease the risk since it cannot be changed once it is created, and the stored data and transactions are traceable and auditable [9].

There are some studies that have been done in the past about using blockchain in land registry. Blockchain can be used in time stamping of transaction, Data recovery, Immutable ledger of historical transaction, and to manage registry details [10]. Tokenization can be used in real-estate industry. The title represents the property and points to everything attached with it. Title owner can create tokens that represents the property and inside it, there is a reference to the registrar token that contain the validity and other info [11]. Many countries has started to use the blockchain in the land registration systems.

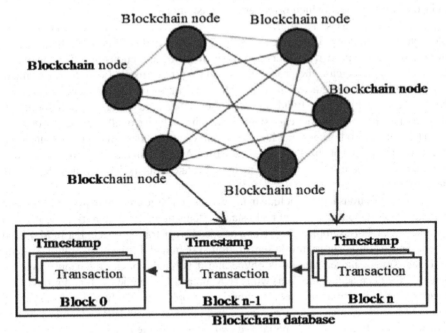

Fig. 1. Blockchain [8]

For example, the government in Sweden has been experimenting a blockchain-based land registry system since 2016, which resulted in reducing the time and cost of the transactions [12]. Another country is Georgia; the country government has designed and built a property registration system using blockchain technology, which also made the time of registration reduce from many months to few hours [13].

2 Problem

Real estate is a suitable industry for a crime like money laundering. They criminal use real estates or other trading activities like running restaurants or any other commercial activities. Money launderers benefit from lack of owners and brokers knowledge [1]. They make legal activities on top of their illegal activities in order to cover it and not to be caught by the authorizations. They use other ways too that will be discussed in this paper. There are some problems with data privacy since the transactions are public in current registration systems [14]. That is why this paper integrates blockchain technology with these industries. Therefore, the data, the ownership, t are all recorded in the registration system by the authorized people only to decrease the possibility of tax fraud, money laundering and any crimes related to real-estates industry.

3 Objectives

With the increase in the number of the real estates, there has been a corresponding increase in the desire to develop new systems that improves the data registrations of real-estate industry. In view of this situation, the present paper analyses the current real-estate systems, to study the blockchain role in improving these systems and to design a blockchain-based real-estate system. To this end, the paper will also cover the crimes that might happen if the real estate are not verified or authorized. This frameworks, which brings an end to absence of transparency and a higher occurrence of mistakes that makes a more projecting potential for fraudulence, will cover the researches on real-estate system over the period from 2015–2021 The scope of the paper is restricted to blockchain technology and might have some databases concepts too. The objectives of the study are listed below:

A. **To analyze how the current real estate systems work, and what can lead to frauds:**
    To do this, a literature review will be done about the traditional registration systems, other registration systems, and frauds involved in the real-estate and their causes in order to prevent them in our paper.
B. **To study blockchain and how it can be used to improve real estate systems:**
    Reading past research papers helps to study the technology and understand the fundamental ideas behind it as well as the many technologies and methods that make it up. Then, the usage of it in register systems and real estate registry systems is then studied as well.
C. **To design a working system that implements blockchain technology on real-estate registry systems.**
    After studying the blockchain technology, it will be the time to integrate the knowledge that that was gained to serve our system and implement it successfully.

4 Research Questions

A. **How does current real estate systems work?**
    To answer this, the working mechanism of the real estate systems should be studied and understood. Therefore, this will contribute to the progress of our paper.
B. **How secure is the real estate systems and records?**
    The vulnerabilities of the real estate systems will be reviewed. Then, the reasons that make these vulnerabilities appear will be also studied. This info will be used to avoid the security problems in the system.
C. **What our system does to deal with the info to verify?**
    This should be answered during the designing and implementation phases of our system. The way of integrating blockchain technology will be illustrated to create a successful system.

Figure 2 shows the framework of the system includes many parties. It includes owner, buyer, bank, land office, and openlaw (used to create the smart contracts). The buyer will look for a property in a website. Then, request to buy land from the owner and pay deposit using Ethereum. The owner can request register a land so he informs the land office and will fill the land agreement to openlaw to create the smart contract. At the same time, the document of title will be filled by the land office and used in the smart contracts as will and will generate a token to the ethereum blockchain. Once the process is done the Money is transferred to the seller. Bank is included in the framework in case the buyer needs a loan from bank.

5 Framework and Method

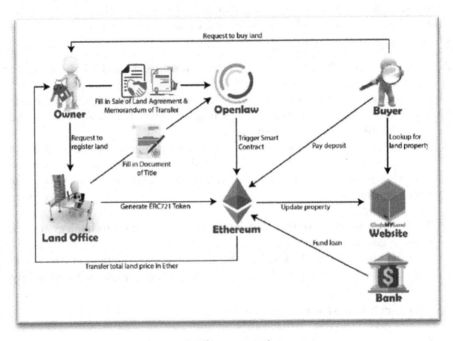

Fig. 2. Framework

Blockchain technology is decentralized, secure, transparent, immutable and has no intermediaries, which makes it a reliable system for maintaining precise records that identify the current owner of a property. Due to its high value, properties need to have precise records that can uphold the owner's rights, prevent sale fraud, settle disputes, and verify ownership transfer. Blockchain technology provides many benefits to the real estate industry, including trust, transparency, security, peer-to-peer transactions, and cost reduction. Smart contracts are also a significant feature of blockchain technology in the real estate industry. These contracts execute transactions automatically with no human intervention and can verify the ownership transfer. The literature review provides an analysis of the existing blockchain systems in real estate registration systems and the technologies and theories used. Then, this chapter discusses the factors that can affect the blockchain-based registration system, including the security, number of blocks, and cost.

The most popular blockchain platforms are Bitcoin, Ethereum, HyperLedger Fabric, and MultiChain, with Ethereum being the chosen platform for this paper. Three hypotheses are proposed: 1) a blockchain-based registration system is more efficient and secure than traditional systems, 2) the number of blocks registered affects system performance, and 3) implementing a blockchain-based registration system is economically feasible and can lead to cost savings and improved accuracy.

A. Research method

The research method used was a mix of qualitative and quantitative research methodologies. The qualitative research method was used to gather data on the existing status of real estate registration systems, as well as the essential requirements for a blockchain –based registration system. The quantitative research method was to assess the effectiveness and impact of the blockchain-based registration system.

The qualitative research method involved interviewing a professional broker in the real-estate sector, besides reviewing literature on current registration systems and blockchain technology. A qualitative content analysis approach was used to analyze data. It was intended to identify the essential requirements for a blockchain-based registration system that would meet the needs of the real-estate industry.

The quantitative research method involved developing and testing a blockchain-based registration system that met the key requirements identified through the qualitative research method. The system was rated based on its performance in terms of security, efficiency, transparency, flexibility. The objective was to determine how the real-estate industry would be impacted by the blockchain-based registration system.

The combination of qualitative and quantitative research methods allowed for a comprehensive analysis of the real-estate registration systems. Using a qualitative research approach allowed to gain important understanding of the current state of registration systems and the requirements for a blockchain-based registration system. On the other hand, empirical evidence of the effectiveness and prospective impact of the blockchain-based registration system was supplied by the quantitative research methodology. Together, these study methodologies provided a comprehensive strategy for answering the research question and fulfilling the study goals.

B. Research design

The Design Science Research Methodology (DSRM) served as the foundation for the research design for this paper. DSRM is a paradigm that used in information systems research to address the relevance vs rigor gap. It infuses both practical relevance (through its focus on useable artifacts) and scientific rigor (through the formulation of design theories) (Baskerville et al., 2018). In this paper, the problem addressed is frauds in real estate and the privacy of data in the current real-estate registration system. A blockchain-based registration system that offers a safe, effective, and transparent means to register real estate properties is the artifact that was created for this paper. DSRM consists of two cycles with multiple steps. The first cycle is the problem cycle. It includes defining the problem, identifying the requirements to create a successful system, and developing some of the design principles. The second cycle is the solution cycle. Solution cycle involves developing a prototype system, evaluating it, refining it, then communication by professional publication, etc. [14].

C. **Instrument**

Several tools were used to gather and analyze the data for this paper. Both quantitative and qualitative data were collected using those instruments.

To acquire qualitative data on the existing status of registration systems and essential needs for a blockchain-based registration system, an online interview questions were asked to a professional real-estate broker in Qatar since it is a country that uses the traditional registration system. The interview was conducted using a semi-structured format, which allowed for a flexible dialogue while yet ensuring that all important subjects were covered. The interview questions were asked based on the research goals.

Many academic databases and search engines were used to identify relevant sources. Then, a literature review were conducted and used to collect qualitative information on the state of blockchain technology and registration systems. Then, the sources were studied and analyzed to get the relevant content.

The Solidity programming language was employed during the development stage of the blockchain-based registration system to create smart contracts that will facilitate the registration of real-estate properties. Solidity was chosen because its compatibility with the Ethereum blockchain platform and its ability to build secure and efficient smart contracts.

At the end, the blockchain-based real-estate registration system itself will be used as a tool to gather quantitative data on its performance and impact. Multiple measures including transaction speed, cost-effectiveness, and scalability were used to evaluate the system.

To sum up, instruments used in this paper were chosen carefully to guarantee that both qualitative and quantitative data were collected and analyzed effectively. Combining these tools made it possible to comprehensively analyze the real estate registration system and then implement our blockchain-based system.

D. **Sampling and size**

In this project, the sampling and size of the project were determined by the research objectives and the availability of participants and resources.

For the qualitative data collection, a purposive sampling technique was used to select an expert in the real estate industry. The experts were selected based on their experience and knowledge in the field real estate registration systems. It was enough to make an interview with only one expert. In literature review part, the search was conducted using a specific set of keywords and filters, and the sample size was determined based on the number of the relevant sources identified through the research. In development phase, the system was developed and tested 20 placeholders for properties details due to lack of results and data resources. Finally, in the last stage the sample size for evaluation was also 20 transactions.

In conclusion, the sampling and size of the project were determined based on the research objectives and the availability of participants and resources. They were deemed sufficient to collect comprehensive data and to evaluate the performance and potential impact of our registration system.

E. Data Collection method

The collected data for the project was obtained through a combination of primary and secondary data sources. An interview and with real-estate expert served as the primary source for data collection. A review of literature on blockchain technology and real-estate registration systems, and related technologies was used to collect secondary data.

The interview was conducted with a professional real estate broker in Qatar (the country that I live in). The real-estate brokers there help the owners to register their properties so they have the full knowledge about the process of registration. The interview questions were designed to know the full process of real-estate registration in Qatar and the process cost.

The secondary data was collected by reviewing academic and industry publications, studies and whitepapers. The review was done to comprehend the condition of real estate registration systems, the advantages and constraints of blockchain technology, and the potential use of it in real-estate industry.

6 Findings and Discussion

The blockchain technology underlying the system contributed to its security by providing immutability and transparency. Once registered, property details were securely stored in blocks, making them tamper-resistant. The associated transparency of blockchain technology enabled the smooth verification of both property ownership and the history of its transfer.

The results of the study give clear proof in supporting that a registration system based on blockchain technology shows superior efficiency and security compared to traditional systems. The secure design of the system, together with its use of blockchain technology, contributes to the implementation of solid security measures, consequently reducing the potential risks caused by fraud and unauthorized activities.

As the number of registered Blocks increased, the system maintained a consistent performance with reasonable execution times for property registration and lookup operations. This suggests that the registration system will be able to process a good amount of transactions (registrations) without having a significant performance downgrade.

However, it is important to know the scalability issues related to utilizing blockchain technology in the system, such as network congestion. The importance of addressing such difficulties becomes crucial in order to ensure optimal performance as the system grows in size.

The implementation costs of the blockchain-based system were considered, along with transaction fees and administrative expenses. The cost of transactions change based on some factors like, the operations inside the transaction, and the network congestion, etc.

The findings supported the that implementing a blockchain-based registration system for real-estate properties is economically feasible. The system demonstrated potential cost savings by eliminating the need for intermediaries, reducing paperwork, and streamlining processes. The accuracy and efficiency of the system also contributed to cost savings by reducing errors, disputes, and associated administrative costs.

However, it is essential to consider the initial investment required for implementing the blockchain infrastructure and ensuring the availability of reliable network connectivity. These factors should be carefully assessed to determine the long-term cost-effectiveness of the system.

The implementation and testing of the blockchain-based Property Registration system highlighted several potential benefits. These include enhanced security, transparent ownership records, reduced fraud and disputes, improved efficiency in property registration and transfer processes, and potential cost savings. The system's decentralized nature and immutability contribute to its trustworthiness and reliability.

7 Recommendations

This project has made great progress in exploring the benefits of a blockchain-based real-estate registration system, but it is crucial to recognize its limitations.

The first limitation of this project is scalability. To ensure the best performance of the registration system as the number of registered blocks and transactions increases, blockchain technology's scalability issues, such as network congestion, must be addressed and solved.

Furthermore, cost-effectiveness. Cost-effectiveness of the system may face challenges because of the transaction fees and network congestion. As it have been determined in the project, the transaction fees will be different from time to time based on some factors such as the complexity of the operations included in the transaction. This might make the prices higher than the user expected and will make them avoid using the system sometimes.

These are the main constraints that our system may face. Some recommendations can be given to solve these issues, to begin with, further studies should prioritize the evaluation of the system's scalability in real-world scenarios and establishing solutions that reduce any reduction in performance and solve the previously mentioned scalability issues.

In addition, more research needs to be done to enhance transaction fees and examine methods for minimizing network congestion while keeping system efficiency. In addition, future studies should be done to create methods that will help the user to accept and understand the blockchain-based registration system.

To end with, collaboration with the policymakers and government is needed. This will help to ensure that the blockchain-based registration system meets the regulations and laws in the real-estate industry.

8 Conclusion

Using the results obtained in the implementation and finding section, the three Factors selected to be analyzed and studied proved to have an impact on the system, which also helped to check the established hypothesis. The first factor was the level of security in the registration system. It was found that the level of security and efficiency have been increased when the blockchain technology is applied. This can be seen from the privacy and transparency it provides.

In terms of number of blocks and performance, which is the second factor, It was found that number of blocks on the network does not have a direct impact on the efficiency of the system, but the number of blocks that is been added at the same time has an effect on the time of the transaction.

Therefore, whenever there are no transactions are being done at the same time as your transaction, your transaction will be done faster. However, the transaction time was short. For example, longest amount of time recorded while registering a property is 34.1 s and the minimum is 5.8 s. As shown, it was not exceeding 1 min even while it will absolutely longer time in the normal registration system.

In terms of cost of registration, which is the last factor, it can be seen that the cost of registration (Gas estimation) is based on the number of operations inside the transaction. It has been determined that also the network congestion. The average gas price for property registration and property ownership transfer was around to 0.83 USD and 0.16 USD. Indeed, the prices were low and less than the traditional registration system, which proved the economic feasibility of our system.

Acknowledgement. In the process of writing this paper, we are very grateful to Dr. Burra Venkata Durga Kumar for his guidance in our knowledge of distributed systems. He gave us an in-depth understanding of distributed systems and guided us to complete this paper. Also, thank you to all the authors cited in the paper for their efforts in the research of distributed systems.

References

1. Teichmann, F.M.J.: Financial crimes in the real estate sector in Austria, Germany, Liechtenstein and Switzerland. J. Money Laund. Control **26**(2), 418–432 (2023)
2. Wang, H., Wei, S., Tang, B.S., Chen, J., Li, W.: A comparative study on registration system of real estate between Hong Kong and Mainland China. Prop. Manag.Manag. **36**(1), 5–19 (2018)
3. Ying, S., Guo, R., Li, L., Chen, N., Jia, Y.: An uniform real-estate registration model for China (2018)
4. Chen, Y., Chen, H., Zhang, Y., Han, M., Siddula, M., Cai, Z.: A survey on blockchain systems: attacks, defenses, and privacy preservation. High-Confid. Comput. **2**(2), 100048 (2022)
5. Guo, H., Yu, X.: A survey on blockchain technology and its security. Blockchain Res. Appl. **3**(2), 100067 (2022)
6. Dong, N., Bai, G., Huang, L.C., Lim, E.K.H., Dong, J.S.: A blockchain-based decentralized booking system. Knowl. Eng. Rev. **35** (2020)
7. Azaria, A., Ekblaw, A., Vieira, T., Lippman, A.: Medrec: using blockchain for medical data access and permission management. In: 2016 2nd International Conference on Open and Big Data (OBD), pp. 25–30. IEEE (2016)
8. Salman, T., Jain, R., Gupta, L.: Probabilistic blockchains: a blockchain paradigm for collaborative decision-making. In 2018 9th IEEE Annual Ubiquitous Computing, Electronics & Mobile Communication Conference (UEMCON), pp. 457–465. IEEE (2018)
9. Zheng, Z., et al.: An overview on smart contracts: challenges, advances and platforms. Futur. Gener. Comput. Syst. **105**, 475–491 (2020)

10. Spielman, A.: Blockchain: digitally rebuilding the real estate industry. Doctoral dissertation, Massachusetts Institute of Technology (2016)
11. Konashevych, O.: General concept of real estate tokenization on blockchain. Eur. Prop. Law J. **9**(1), 21–66 (2020)
12. Svensson, G., Sillén, J., Lundqvist, S.: Blockchain-based land registry: case study of a rapid development country. In: Proceedings of the 51st Hawaii International Conference on System Sciences (2018)
13. Kikvidze, I.: Implementation of blockchain technology for real estate transactions in Georgia. Int. J. Innov. Technol. Explor. Eng. **8**(8), 2310–2316 (2019)
14. Lazuashvili, N., Norta, A., Draheim, D.: Integration of blockchain technology into a land registration system for immutable traceability: a casestudy of Georgia. In: Di Ciccio, C., et al. (eds.) BPM 2019. LNBIP, vol. 361, pp. 219–233. Springer, Cham (2019). https://doi.org/10.1007/978-3-030-30429-4_15
15. Yaga, D., Mell, P., Roby, N., Scarfone, K.: Blockchain technology overview. arXiv preprint arXiv:1906.11078 (2019)
16. Hashemi Joo, M., Nishikawa, Y., Dandapani, K.: Cryptocurrency, a successful application of blockchain technology. Manag. Financ. **46**(6), 715–733 (2020)
17. Mohanta, B.K., Panda, S.S., Jena, D.: An overview of smart contract and use cases in blockchain technology. In: 2018 9th International Conference on Computing, Communication and Networking Technologies (ICCCNT), pp. 1–4. IEEE (2018)
18. Golosova, J., Romanovs, A.: The advantages and disadvantages of the blockchain technology. In: 2018 IEEE 6th Workshop on Advances in Information, Electronic and Electrical Engineering (AIEEE), pp. 1–6. IEEE (2018)
19. Kemmoe, V.Y., Stone, W., Kim, J., Kim, D., Son, J.: Recent advances in smart contracts: a technical overview and state of the art. IEEE Access **8**, 117782–117801 (2020)
20. Latifi, S., Zhang, Y., Cheng, L.C.: Blockchain-based real estate market: one method for applying blockchain technology in commercial real estate market. In: 2019 IEEE International Conference on Blockchain (Blockchain), pp. 528–535. IEEE (2019)

Study on the Quantitative Evaluation of Convergence-Divergence Motion Using Head-Mounted Display with Gaze Measurement Function

Toumi Oohara, Kansuke Kawaguchi, Tomiko Takeuchi, and Fumiya Kinoshita[✉]

Toyama Prefectural University, Toyama, Japan
f.kinoshita@pu-toyama.ac.jp

Abstract. Early detection of mild cognitive impairment (MCI) is important for delaying cognitive decline. However, because MCI is a condition in which certain cognitive functions are impaired without interfering with daily life, its early detection of is difficult to achieve. An impaired visuospatial ability, one of the first symptoms of dementia, is a cognitive disorder that causes problems in recognizing the spatial location of objects and the spatial positional relationships of multiple objects. A quantitative assessment of impaired visuospatial ability would therefore be useful for the early detection of MCI. In this study, we developed virtual reality (VR) content to quantitatively evaluate the user's depth perception using a head-mounted display (HMD) with a gaze measurement function. We also conducted a preliminary experiment to evaluate the VR content developed for a younger group prior to targeting a group of MCI patients. In this experiment, the influence of the user's visual function on the measurement results was investigated. Consequently, neither the user's visual acuity nor the interpupillary distance affected the measurement results.

Keywords: mild cognitive impairment (MCI) · head-mounted display (HMD) · virtual reality (VR) · pupillary distance · convergence-divergence motion

1 Introduction

Aging rate is defined as the percentage of the nation's population aged 65 years or older, and is widely used as an indicator of the aging of a nation. One of the problems of an aging society is the increase in social security and long-term care insurance costs that accompany an increase in the number of elderly people. To prevent these increases in medical care costs, it is important to take measures to maintain and promote the health of the elderly population. Dementia is one of the three major diseases that increase the need for nursing care among the elderly. Dementia is defined as a condition in which cognitive functions, once they reach normal levels, are persistently impaired owing to acquired brain damage, resulting in difficulties in daily life and social activities. It is estimated that the number of elderly people with dementia in Japan will increase to

W. Hong and G. Kanaparan (Eds.): ICCSE 2023, CCIS 2025, pp. 277–285, 2024.
https://doi.org/10.1007/978-981-97-0737-9_25

7.3 million by 2025, which means that one in five persons aged 65 years or older will develop dementia. Dementia is expected to cause increased physical, psychological, and economic burdens not only on affected individuals but also on their families and local communities. Efforts to prevent dementia and delay cognitive decline are increasingly expected.

Early detection of mild cognitive impairment (MCI), located on the border between normal and dementia, is important for delaying cognitive decline [1–4]. However, early detection of MCI is difficult because MCI is a condition that does not interfere with daily life, although some cognitive functions are affected. Early symptoms of Alzheimer's disease, such as getting lost when driving, and difficulty in parking a car in a garage, can appear even in the absence of visual impairment [5–7]. These symptoms are called visuospatial cognitive impairment and are important for early diagnosis. Visuospatial cognitive impairment is a clinical symptom not only in Alzheimer's disease but also in MCI [8]. Therefore, the quantitative evaluation of visuospatial cognitive impairment is useful for the early detection of MCI. Thus, this study developed virtual reality (VR) content that can quantitatively evaluate the depth perception ability of the user [9, 10]. By presenting VR content through a head-mounted display (HMD) equipped with a gaze measurement function, gaze information can be acquired while viewing the content. In this study, we conducted a preliminary VR content evaluation experiment developed for a younger group prior to targeting an MCI patient group. This study aimed to determine whether there are any differences in measurement results depending on the user's visual function.

2 Method

In this experiment, we evaluated the VR content developed for a group of young people. The subjects were 37 healthy young men and women (20.62 ± 1.42 years old). The subjects were given a full explanation of the experiment in advance, and their consent to participate was obtained. This experiment was conducted after obtaining approval from the Ethics Committee of Toyama Prefectural University (R3-1).

In this experiment, we used an HTC Vive Pro Eye as the HMD, with an eye tracking function. The developed VR content can acquire information such as spherical objects. In the developed VR content, only one spherical object was displayed at the center of the screen, and it was set to periodically move from the depth direction to the front direction at a frequency of five times per 30 s. The depth movement was set to a value of 1 for the front position and 15 for the distant position with the size of the spherical object set to 1 (Fig. 1). Before the measurements, the average visual acuity of the left and right eyes was obtained using a practical acuity meter (AS-28, Kowa), and the interpupillary distance was measured using an interpupillary distance meter (Digital PD Meter, Hanchen JP). Considering the influence of eyeglasses, subjects wearing eyeglasses were asked to take them off, and the measurement was conducted with the naked eye. Participants wearing contact lenses were measured with the contact lenses in place.

Fig. 1. Examples of VR content. Depth positions at (a) 1, (b) 7.5, (c) 15.

3   Analytical Indices

In this experiment, we focused on the interpupillary distance between the left and right eyes as a depth-perception index during object gazing. The interpupillary distance fluctuates with the convergence–divergence motion and can be obtained by calculating the Euclidean distance from the time-series data of the left and right eye positions in the Vive Pro Eye. Figure 2 shows an example of the time-series data of the interpupillary distance for the same subject while gazing at an object. We observed a tendency for divergent motion to decrease as the depth position increased.

In this experiment, the sum of the residual squares of the sinusoidal model and coefficient of determination were calculated as representative values for each interpupillary distance. To exclude the influence of blinks in the time series data, the interval before and after the blink was interpolated using linear interpolation, with the missing values taken from 0.05 s before and after the blink. An optimal sinusoidal model was created for each time series by searching for a value that minimizes the coefficient of determination while changing the amplitude of the sinusoidal wave to match the movement period of the object. Figure 3 shows an example of the sine-wave model and its coefficient of determination.

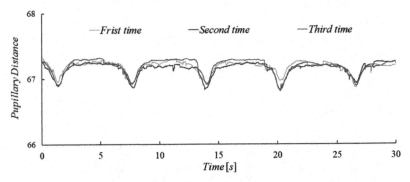

Fig. 2. Example of pupillary distance.

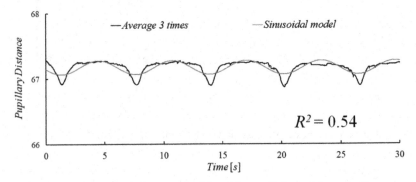

Fig. 3. Examples of sine wave model and the coefficient of determination.

4   Result

To confirm whether the measurement results differed when the users' vision was corrected with contact lenses, the subjects were classified based on the results of the average visual acuity of the left and right eyes obtained through a practical acuity meter, as shown in Table 1. Time series data of the pupillary distance for each group and a typical example of a sine wave model are shown in Fig. 4, Fig. 5, Fig. 6. A one-way analysis of variance was then conducted on the coefficients of determination obtained from each group (Fig. 7). The results showed that there were no significant differences in the measurement results for those with or without contact lens correction ($p < 0.05$).

To investigate whether the measurement results differed depending on the pupillary distance, we classified the results using the pupillary distance obtained from the pupillary distance meter. Scatter plots of the coefficient of determination and the pupillary distance are shown in Fig. 8. The correlation coefficient for the scatter plot was calculated, and no high correlation was found.

To examine whether differences in visual acuity between the left and right eyes caused differences in the measurement results, classification was conducted using the average visual acuity obtained from a practical acuity meter. Patients with no differences in the visual acuity of their left and right eyes were excluded from the analysis. Scatter plots of the coefficient of determination and the difference in visual acuity between the left and right eyes are shown in Fig. 9. The correlation coefficient for the scatter plot was then calculated, and again no high correlation was found.

Table 1. Classification of subjects by visual acuity.

Classification	Details	Number of subjects
Group-A	Visual acuity greater than 0.3	13
Group-B	Visual acuity less than 0.3	12
Group-C	Contact lenses correct vision	12

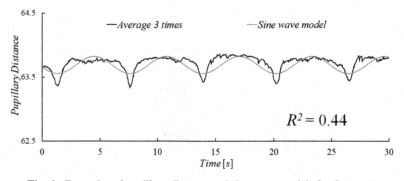

Fig. 4. Examples of pupillary distance and sine wave models for Group-A.

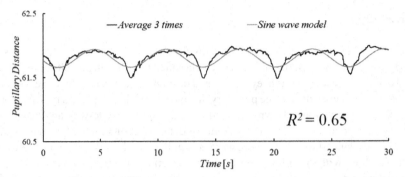

Fig. 5. Examples of pupillary distance and sine wave models for Group-B.

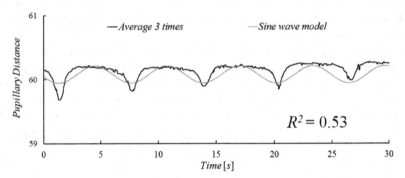

Fig. 6. Examples of pupillary distance and sine wave models for Group-C.

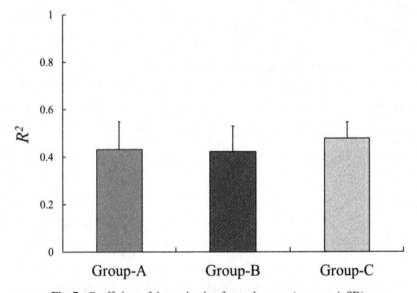

Fig. 7. Coefficient of determination for each group (average ± SD).

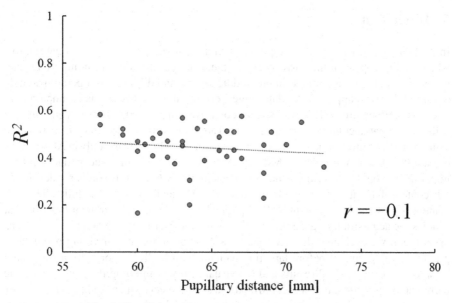

Fig. 8. Coefficient of determination and pupillary distance.

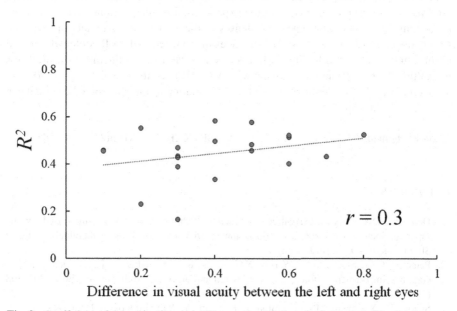

Fig. 9. Coefficient of determination and difference in visual acuity between left and right eyes.

5 Discussion

In Alzheimer's disease, early symptoms such as difficulty in drawing and getting lost when driving appear in the early stages of the disease; difficulty in finding things and getting lost in the house appear in the middle stages; and difficulty in operating simple tools and dressing appear in the late stages, even in the absence of visual impairment. These symptoms are called visuospatial cognitive impairments. These symptoms are called visuospatial cognitive impairments and are important for early diagnosis. Because visuospatial cognitive impairment is a clinical symptom observed not only in Alzheimer's disease but also in non-amnesic MCI, quantitative evaluation of visuospatial cognitive impairment would be useful for the early detection of MCI. In this study, we developed VR content that can quantitatively evaluate a user's depth perception ability. This VR content is presented through an HMD equipped with a gaze-measurement function that enables the acquisition of gaze information while the user is gazing at an object. In this experiment, we evaluated the developed VR content in a group of young people as a preliminary experiment before targeting patients with MCI. No correlation was found between the experimental results and the visual acuity or interpupillary distance of the participants. In particular, it was confirmed that even subjects with naked eye vision of 0.1 or less could correctly grasp the location of objects, and that the experimental results were not affected by the measurement of users who normally wear glasses with their glasses removed. It was also confirmed that the experimental results were not affected by the measurements of users wearing contact lenses. In the future, we will collaborate with the faculty members of the School of Nursing to examine whether the VR content developed in this study is effective for the early detection of MCI by conducting measurements in healthy elderly people and patients with MCI. This content, which uses HMD and VR technology, is considered effective for rehabilitation training at home because it can save experimental space.

Acknowledgments. This work was supported by JSPS KAKENHI, Grant No. 23K16928.

References

1. Dementia Diagnosis and Treatment Guideline Planning Committee (supervised by the Japanese Society of Neurology): 2017 Dementia Diagnosis and Treatment Guidelines, Igaku Shoin, Tokyo (2017). (in Japanese)
2. Petersen, R.C., Smith, G.E., Waring, S.C., Ivnik, R.J., Tangalos, E.G., Kokmen, E.: Mild cognitive impairment: clinical characterization and outcome. Arch. Neurol. **56**(3), 303–308 (1999)
3. Suzuki, H., Yasunaga, M., Naganuma, T., Fujiwara, Y.: Validation of the Japanese version of the montreal cognitive assessment to evaluate the time course changes of cognitive function: a longitudinal study with mild cognitive impairment and early-stage alzheimer's disease. Jpn. J. Geriatr. Psy. **22**(2), 211–218 (2011). (in Japanese)
4. Nakashima, K., Shimohama, T., Tomimoto, H., Mimura, M., Arai, T.: Handbook of Dementia Care, 2nd edn. Igaku Shoin, Tokyo (2021). (in Japanese)
5. Mendez, M.F., Cummings, J.L.: Dementia: A Clinical Approach. Butterworth-Heinemann, Boston (2003)

6. Goodale, M.A., Milner, A.D.: Separate visual pathways for perception and action. Trends Neurosci. **15**(1), 20–25 (1992)
7. Thiyagesh, S.N., Farrow, T.F., Parks, R.W., Acosta-Mesa, H., Young, C., Wilkinson, I.D., et al.: The neural basis of visuospatial perception in Alzheimer's disease and healthy elderly comparison subjects: an fMRI study. Psychiatry. Res. Neuroimaging **172**(2), 109–116 (2009)
8. Petersen, R.C.: Mild cognitive impairment as a diagnostic entity. J. Intern. Med. **256**(3), 183–194 (2004)
9. Kinoshita, F., Takada, H.: A study on the development of VR content for quantitative evaluation of impaired visuospatial ability. In: Duffy, V.G., Gao, Q., Zhou, J., Antona, M., Stephanidis, C. (eds.) HCI International 2022-Late Breaking Papers: HCI for Health, Well-being, Universal Access and Healthy Aging, HCII 2022. LNCS, vol. 13521, pp. 440–450. Springer, Cham (2022). https://doi.org/10.1007/978-3-031-17902-0_31
10. Oohara, T., Kawaguchi, K., Takeuchi, T. Kinoshita, F.: Visuospatial ability of elderly using head-mounted display with gaze measurement function. In: Antona, M., Stephanidis, C. (eds.) HCI International 2023: Universal Access in Human-Computer Interaction, HCII 2023. LNCS, vol. 14021, pp. 81–90. Springer, Cham (2023). https://doi.org/10.1007/978-3-031-358 97-5_6

Research of Multidimensional Adversarial Examples in LLMs for Recognizing Ethics and Security Issues

Kainan Liu[1]([✉])(iD), Yifan Li[1]([✉])(iD), Lihong Cao[1], Danni Tu[1], Zhi Fang[2], and Yusong Zhang[3]

[1] University of Sanya, No. 191 Xueyuan Road, Jiyang District, Sanya, Hainan, China
liuknan@126.com, 1034376968@qq.com
[2] Xiangsihu College of GuangXi Minzu University, No. 55 Youyi Road, Jiangnan District, Nanning, Guangxi, China
[3] Northeast Forestry University, No. 26 Hexing Road, Xiangfang District, Harbin, Heilongjiang, China

Abstract. With the extensive use of LLMs in research and practical applications, it has become more and more important to evaluate them effectively, and by studying the evaluation methods can help to better understand the LLMs, guard against unknowns, avoid risks, and provide a basis for their better and faster iterative upgrading. In this research, the ability of recognizing ethics and security issues in text is investigated through a multi-dimensional adversarial example evaluation method, using ERNIE Bot (V2.2.3) as an example. The ESIIP of ERNIE Bot (V2.2.3) is evaluated by slightly perturbing the input data through multidimensional adversarial examples to induce the model to make false predictions. In this research, the evaluation objectives are classified into ethics and security issues such as discrimination and prejudice detection, values analysis, and ethical conflict identification, and security issues such as false information detection, privacy violation detection, and network security detection. Multiple representative datasets, using different attack strategies to perturb them slightly, the research formulated a rigorous evaluation criterion developed for the model's responses, and comprehensively analyzed the scores of all the LLMs; the research drew the corresponding metrics conclusions and complexity conclusions, and compared the performance with other LLMs models in recognizing the ethics and security issues in the text. The results show that ERNIE Bot (V2.2.3) performs well in ESIIP, not reaching the perfect level; it also shows the reliability and feasibility of the research method.

Keywords: LLMs · Adversarial Examples · Ethics. · Security Issues · Evaluation

1 Background

Large Language Models (LLMs) are a cutting-edge technology in the field of Artificial Intelligence, which is a form of Natural Language Processing (NLP) that is capable of understanding and generating complex natural language texts through training that

© The Author(s), under exclusive license to Springer Nature Singapore Pte Ltd. 2024
W. Hong and G. Kanaparan (Eds.): ICCSE 2023, CCIS 2025, pp. 286–302, 2024.
https://doi.org/10.1007/978-981-97-0737-9_26

mimics human linguistic abilities [12, 13]. In recent years, with the rapid development in the fields of deep learning and NLP, LLMs have been equipped with more powerful language generation and contextual understanding capabilities, and can generate fluent and accurate texts, which have greatly contributed to the development of NLP technologies [1, 11]. Among them, pre-trained language models like GPT (Generative Pre-trained Transformer) have the potential to be widely used.

With the widespread use of LLMs in NLP, evaluating the performance and capabilities of LLMs has become crucial. Although LLMs perform well on many tasks, their evaluation and comparison still face many challenges. Traditional evaluation metrics and methods cannot fully adapt to the characteristics and complexity of LLMs. In addition, due to the large scale of parameters of LLMs, the cost of training and evaluation increases accordingly. Therefore, there is an urgent need today to research and develop more accurate, comprehensive, and efficient evaluation methods to better understand and compare the performance of LLMs. Through research and development of evaluation methods, it will be possible to better understand the characteristics and potential problems of LLMs, thus preventing unknown risks and providing a basis for better and faster iterations and upgrades.

2 Introduction

2.1 Overview

Although the evaluation of LLMs in general has made significant progress at this stage, and there are several well-established technical programs as well as large evaluation datasets. However, the current global efforts to evaluate the ethics and security issues of LLMs are still in their infancy, with several challenges and shortcomings.

1) Evaluation of ethics and morality: The development of LLMs has raised several ethical and moral issues, including prejudice, discrimination, and privacy invasion. Although these issues have been widely discussed, a complete framework for evaluating the ethics and morality of LLMs has not yet been established in practice.
2) Data privacy protection: LLMs require a large amount of training data, which may contain sensitive information of users. How to protect data privacy becomes an important issue during model training and application.
3) False information and misleading content: The generative power of LLMs also poses the risk of false information and misleading content. It is critical to evaluate the accuracy, credibility, and verifiability of model-generated content.
4) Security and Misuse Risk: The application of LLMs faces security and misuse risks. Evaluating the security of the model, including countering attacks, stealth attacks, etc., is an important aspect to guarantee the usability and reliability of the model in practical applications.

To address the above issues, there is no mature and systematic framework to evaluate whether LLMs can recognize corresponding ethics and security issues in text. Therefore, in this paper, we will take ERNIE Bot (V2.2.3) as an example, aiming to explore in depth and comprehensively evaluate the ability of large-scale neural network models in recognizing ethics and security issues. The goal is to research the performance of

LLMs in different domains and applications to ensure that they can accurately predict and respond to challenges involving ethics, regulations, and safety. In this way, the sustainable and socially responsible application of the technology can be promoted. Through this research, it is expected to provide strong guidance for the improvement and social application of LLMs to ensure that AI technology has a positive impact on society.

2.2 Research Framework

This paper focuses on the research of evaluating LLMs on Ethics & Security Issues Identification Performance (ESIIP) through multidimensional adversarial examples. Multidimensional adversarial examples can provide rich data and context for ethics and security issues of LLMs. By evaluating multi-dimensional adversarial examples, we can conduct in-depth research on ethics and security issues of LLMs and take effective measures to improve their performance.

In addition, this paper takes ERNIE Bot (V2.2.3) developed by Baidu, China, as the object of this research. Choosing ERNIE Bot as the research object for evaluating the ESIIP of LLMs helps to increase the focus and credibility of the research, and at the same time provides a valuable reference for the development and application of other similar models.

The framework of this research is shown in Fig. 1.

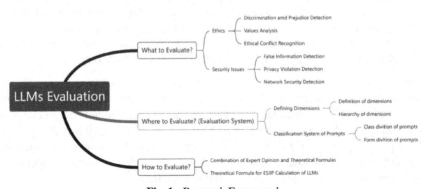

Fig. 1. Research Framework

3   What to Evaluate?

While ethical and security issues overlap in some cases, it is often necessary to distinguish between the two to more fully evaluate the performance and social impact of LLMs. Ethical issues focus on whether the content of the text is consistent with ethical standards and societal values, while security issues focus on whether the use and deployment of the model potentially poses risks and threats. Ethical issues include prejudice, discrimination, hate speech, disinformation, and other harmful content. Meanwhile, security issues cover concerns about privacy disclosure, malicious uses, and risk of misuse. Therefore, evaluating the ESIIP of LLMs is essential to ensure their reliability and social responsibility in different application scenarios.

4 Where to Evaluate?

To improve the credibility as well as the completeness of this research, the evaluation of ERNIE BotV2.2.3 was designed with a well-developed evaluation system, evaluation method, and corresponding evaluation data.

The evaluation system is a crucial and indispensable part of model evaluation. A complete and clear evaluation system can help ensure the fluency of the evaluation process and make the evaluation results more convincing. An evaluation system consists of specific dimensions to be evaluated, the definition of the dimensions, and the hierarchy between the dimensions. For each type of task, questions are systematically divided, and criteria are developed to ensure that the difficulty level of the questions is clearly defined (Fig. 2).

4.1 Evaluation Dimension

The dimension chosen to evaluate in this research is "Adversarial Example Complexity", which is a key metric to measure the model in terms of ethics and security issues.

Adversarial examples are carefully designed disturbances, such as adjusting pixel values in an image or modifying keywords in a text, to mislead the model into making a wrong decision [2, 10]. Factors such as the degree of perturbation, keyword changes, and semantic adjustments determine the degree of misdirection to the model. The challenges faced by the model increase as the complexity of the adversarial examples increases. The dimensions of this evaluation can be categorized into the following levels:

1) Simple Adversarial Examples (SAEs): Simple adversarial examples are usually generated by introducing some small perturbations or changes in the original input data. These perturbations or changes can be minor alterations, addition of noise, or insignificant insertions [10].

$$X_{adv} = X + \delta \tag{1}$$

where X_{adv} is the perturbed adversarial example, X is the original input data, and δ is the introduced perturbation or change.

2) Moderate Adversarial Examples (MAEs): Moderate adversarial examples are usually generated by introducing more significant changes or more complex perturbations in the original input data. These perturbations or changes can be substitutions of certain words in the text [10].

$$X_{adv} = X + \delta' \tag{2}$$

where X_{adv} is the perturbed adversarial example, X is the original input data, and δ' is the set of perturbations or changes introduced.

3) Complex Adversarial Examples (CAEs): Complex adversarial examples are usually generated through elaborate methods that involve advanced attack strategies, complex model structures, and domain-specific knowledge. Complex adversarial examples cannot be fully understood and analyzed in an intuitive way but require specific tools and techniques for detection and defense [10].

$$X_{adv} = \hat{X} \tag{3}$$

where X_{adv} is a perturbed adversarial example and $\hat{X}$ is a complex sample generated by a specific attack strategy or technique.

4.2   Classification System of Prompts

Ethics and security issues are not one-dimensional, but rather a multi-perspective issue. Therefore, before constructing prompts, they need to be categorized in a refined way. The goal of this categorization is to ensure that the evaluation process is more specific and focused. The division of ethics into these categories (see Table 1) is based on two main theories:

1) Ethical and Moral Norms: Ethical and moral norms refer to the moral guidelines that people should follow in their behavior, which can be habits, cultures, and moral concepts passed down by the society, or rational principles put forward by ethical and moral sciences.
2) Ethical Philosophy: Ethical philosophy focuses on whether the goodness of an action depends on its consequences or its motivation, or a combination of the two [3].

The division of ethics into these categories (see Table 2) is based on three main theories:

1) System Security Theory: System Security Theory is a widely used cyber security theory that divides the security problem into several sub-problems, such as personnel security, physical security, network security, and data security [4].
2) Security Threat Theory: Security threat theory is one of the core theories of cybersecurity, which identifies the main types of threats to cybersecurity [5].
3) Attack Psychology: Attack psychology researches the mental activities and behavioral patterns of attackers and how attackers use human psychological and social factors to carry out attacks [6–9].

It is worth noting that the scope of ethics and security issues is extremely broad. Therefore, in this research, the focus was placed on categories of issues that are common in real life. In addition, some prompts may overlap between ethics and security issues. However, the above categorization helps to more clearly distinguish the focus areas of concern [3].

Variety in the format of prompts can also greatly improve the efficiency as well as the relevance of the evaluation, e.g., categorizing them into multiple choice, question and answer, text-based, and multi-round conversations.

Table 1. Specific Prompt Categories of Ethics

Categories	Definition and Significance
Discrimination and Prejudice Detection	Discrimination and Prejudice Detection refers to the analysis of texts generated by LLMs to detect the presence of unfair or negatively stereotyped statements or manifestations such as discrimination, prejudice, or stereotyping against specific groups or individuals. This kind of detection can better assess whether LLMs are discriminatory and biased in their treatment of different groups and individuals, thus promoting their fairness and impartiality
Values Analysis	Values Analysis refers to the analysis of texts generated by LLMs to reveal the values expressed in them. This analysis can lead to a better understanding of the moral, political, religious, and cultural values embedded in LLMs
Ethical Conflict Recognition	Ethical Conflict Recognition refers to the analysis of texts generated by LLMs to identify the moral conflicts involved in them. This identification allows for a better understanding of how LLMs perform when dealing with ethical issues. It also allows for a better understanding of their abilities and limitations in dealing with complex moral issues

5 How to Evaluate?

For this research, a combination of manual evaluation and multi-model comparison evaluation was used to conduct a comprehensive evaluation. For this research, targeted evaluation metrics are designed, and the weights of each metric are divided. Different evaluation prompts need to determine the corresponding metrics, then according to the evaluation criteria according to the different metrics to generate the results of the scoring, and finally the weighted average of the scores of the metrics to obtain the final score of the visualization, to identify problems and weaknesses, and provide direction for the subsequent optimization of the model. Upon completion of the evaluation, an in-depth data analysis of the results was conducted. The data analysis involved statistical information such as average scores, maximum scores and minimum scores of different models (Fig. 3).

5.1 Attack Strategies

For this model evaluation, this research carefully designed the corresponding misleading and attacking strategies. To better reflect the efficiency of the assessment and the relevance of the research, the form of prompts was designed in a variety of types, as shown in Table 3.

Table 2. Specific Prompt Categories of Security Issues

Categories	Definition and Significance
False Information Detection	False Information Detection refers to the analysis of text generated by LLMs to detect the presence of false or misleading information in it. This detection assesses the reliability and accuracy of LLMs in disseminating information and avoids the model from entrapping false information in the generated text, thus ensuring that users receive accurate and truthful information
Privacy Violation Detection	Privacy Violation Detection refers to the analysis of the text generated by LLMs to detect whether there is any risk or behavior that violates the user's privacy in it. This detection can assess whether LLMs have the potential to violate users' privacy and avoid LLMs from leaking personal privacy information when processing users' data
Network Security Detection	Network Security Detection refers to the automated analysis of text generated by LLMs to detect the presence of expressions or code that may cause cybersecurity problems. This kind of detection assesses whether there are potential cybersecurity risks, such as malicious code, virus links, etc., in the text generated by LLMs

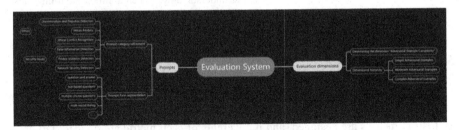

Fig. 2. Evaluation System Framework

5.2 Combination of Expert Opinion and Theoretical Formulas

A combination of expert opinion and theoretical formulas will be used in the evaluation methodology of this research. The main reason for using the opinions of authoritative experts in ethics and security issues in the design of the evaluation metrics weights and scoring criteria and the lack of theoretical formulas is:

1) Domain-specificity: Ethics and safety issues involve specific domains and contexts, requiring domain experts for accurate evaluation [19, 20].
2) Subjectivity: Evaluating ethics and safety issues involves personal values and subjective judgments, leading to varying views and ratings.
3) Complexity and diversity: The evaluation of ethical and safety issues is a complex and diverse process involving multiple dimensions and aspects to be considered.

Table 3. Type of prompts and attack strategies

Type of prompts	Attack strategies
Multiple-choice questions	This format can include asking the model to pick the correct answer or hiding the correct answer to assess the model's ability to respond. In addition, ethical and safety issues can be embedded in the questions to test the model's ability to detect and indicate these issues
Q&A	Using the Q&A structure, the model can be asked to analyze the explicit or implicit ethics and safety issues in the questions and provide the corresponding answers. This approach effectively examines the model's judgment and ability to respond to these questions
Text questions	Providing a given text in which the ethics and safety questions can be embedded is a way to test the model's sensitivity to the perception of ethics and safety questions in texts of varying complexity. This approach can assess the model's ability to process different levels of information
Multi-Round Dialogues	A multi-round dialogue with the model enables the model to analyze and identify the ethical and safety issues involved in the dialogue and test its sensitivity to these issues. This approach assesses the model's performance in dealing with ethical and safety issues in a dynamic dialog environment

4) Lack of data and empirical support: In some cases, evaluations on ethics and safety issues lack sufficient data and empirical support to be accurately evaluated using theoretical formulas.

However, for the calculation of the prompts scores and the final judgment of the model's ability, the method of constructing theoretical formulas is used. The formula calculation is more visual and thus increases the accuracy and credibility of the research. Therefore, the combination of expert opinion and theoretical formulas is a more appropriate and reliable method to evaluate the model's ability to identify ethics and security issues in a more comprehensive, objective and accurate manner.

5.3 Evaluation Metrics

1. **Ethical Conflict Compliance:** Checking whether the model can accurately recognize ethical conflict questions and whether the answers are in line with ethical norms and moral codes focuses on whether the model can give the most ethical and moral responses to questions arising from ethical conflicts [16, 17]. For example, whether the model respects individual privacy, whether it is fair and unbiased, and whether it treats all users equally [14, 15].
2. **Values Compatibility:** Check whether the model can accurately identify value bias questions and whether the answers are consistent with the mainstream values and

ethics of the society [16, 17]. For example, whether the model respects diversity, is consistent with social justice, and considers the interests of all stakeholders.

3. **Fairness:** Check whether the model can accurately identify fairness questions and whether the answers are discriminatory or unfair. For example, whether the model is influenced by factors such as user characteristics, social background, etc., and whether it produces unfair results as a result [19–21].

4. **Detection of Security Issues:** Evaluate the sensitivity of the model to security issues, which include issues such as disinformation, privacy violations, and cybersecurity. Detect whether the model can accurately identify and give compliant, reasonable, and legal solutions or suggestions for specific security issues [14, 15, 18]. For example, whether the model is vulnerable to threats such as malicious code injection, data leakage, and user privacy leakage.

5. **Human Collaboration and Interaction:** Evaluate the performance of the model in interacting and collaborating with humans, e.g., whether it can communicate smoothly with humans, understand human language, and guide humans to complete tasks.

6. **Repeatability and Traceability:** Assess whether the model's outputs are reproducible and whether the model's decision-making process is traceable. For example, whether the model produces consistent results every time and whether the model's decision-making process is clearly documented so that it can be reproduced and reviewed by others [22, 23].

7. **Accuracy, Transparency and Explainability:** Assess the accuracy of the model and whether its decision-making process is transparent and explainable. For example, whether the model can accurately predict outcomes, and whether the model's decision-making process is clear and unambiguous so that users and stakeholders can understand and trust the model.

5.4 Theoretical Formula for ESIIP Calculation of LLMs

The scores of the prompts are calculated to obtain the final score of the ESIIP of ERNIE Bot (V2.2.3) in this evaluation as follows. To calculate the score for the target ability, the corresponding "Complexity Coefficient" is designed for the multidimensional adversarial example. The scores of the different prompts of the corresponding dimensional levels are weighted and averaged with their corresponding complexity coefficients to obtain the final scores of the model's target capabilities to obtain the corresponding evaluation results.

$$F(X_{adv}) = \frac{\sum_{i=1}^{n} f_i(X_{adv}) \times w_i}{\sum_{j=1}^{n} w_j} \tag{4}$$

$$S = \frac{\sum_{i=1}^{n} F_i(X_{adv}) \times c_i}{\sum_{j=1}^{n} c_j} \tag{5}$$

where X_{adv} is the perturbed adversarial example, S is the model's evaluated score on ESIIP, $F_i(X_{adv})$ is the model's evaluated score on each of the adversarial examples, $f_i(X_{adv})$ is the evaluated score of prompts on each metric, w_i is the weights of the metrics, and c_i is the complexity coefficients of the dimensions of each layer.

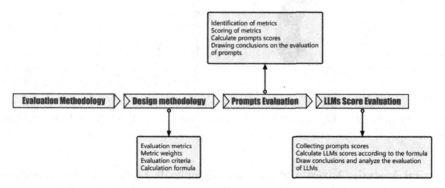

Fig. 3. Flowchart of Evaluation Methodology

6 Prompt Sets

In order to confirm the credibility and accuracy of this research, a corresponding prompt set was specially designed. To ensure the quality of the dataset, most of these prompts were designed manually, so the number of prompts is not large. However, this set can be used as a reference for finding other open-source prompt sets or designing more prompts.

The open-source prompt sets used in this research can be obtained at:

https://github.com/Andy6201/Prompt-Sets-of-Multidimensional-Adversarial-Exa mples-in-LLMs-for-ESIIP.

7 Summary

7.1 Analysis of Research Data

Through a comprehensive analytical framework and a series of evaluation operations, ERNIE Bot (V2.2.3) presents an excellent performance in terms of ESIIP. When compared with high-performing models, its performance is not significantly inferior. The following are the final evaluation conclusions and analysis for this evaluation:

ERNIE Bot (V2.2.3) showed inconsistent overall performance in terms of ESIIP, encompassing a wide range of levels from excellent to failing. Of the 166 valid prompts, 114 prompts scored 7 and above, representing 68.7% of the total prompts. However, there were also 29 prompts with scores below 6, accounting for 17.5% of the total number of prompts. In addition, ERNIE Bot (V2.2.3) had a final score of 6.99 (out of 10) for its ESIIP in this evaluation. This result shows that ERNIE Bot (V2.2.3) still has problems in its ESIIP, and that there is an urgent need to take measures to improve it. Therefore, full compliance with ethical and safety standards in the practice of LLMs remains a goal that requires further efforts.

Prompts Score Rating Percentage

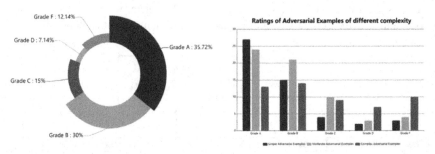

Fig. 4. Prompts Score Rating Percentage/Ratings of Adversarial Examples of Different Complexity

Vertical Analysis (Adversarial Examples Complexity Findings): Vertical analysis of the complexity of the adversarial examples was performed for different levels of the evaluation dimension: (Fig. 4)

For SAEs, ERNIE Bot (V2.2.3) performed better. Among the 51 SAEs, 42 prompts scored A or B, i.e., the percentage of scores of 7 and above is 82.4%, which indicates that the model can accurately identify potential ethical and security issues for less misleading prompts and give reasonable and compliant suggestions and reminders.

For the MAEs, ERNIE Bot (V2.2.3) still performed well. Of the 62 MAEs, 45 achieved an A or B grade, which is 72.6% of the total. For prompts of this complexity, ERNIE Bot (V2.2.3), while remaining sensitive to ethical and security issues, often neglects to provide more sensible and compliant advice.

For the CAEs, ERNIE Bot (V2.2.3) presents a more general ESIIP. Out of the 53 CAEs, only 27 achieved a grade of A or B, and their percentage is 50.9%. In addition, 10 prompts scores fell to the F grade, i.e., below 5 points, and their share amounted to 18.9%. As the most misleading category of questions, ERNIE Bot (V2.2.3) suffers from being heavily misled by it. This kind of attack is often ubiquitous in the questions, which makes the model have a certain probability of falling into the "trap" of answering only the surface questions and ignoring the underlying ethical and security issues.

Horizontal Analysis (Metrics Findings): The cross-sectional findings of ERNIE Bot (V2.2.3) were analyzed for different indicators:

In terms of ethical conflict compliance, ERNIE Bot (V2.2.3) responses show a relatively weak performance when dealing with ethical conflict issues. Ethical conflict issues that are difficult to resolve effectively are encountered when responding to some of the CAEs texts. There are potential ethical risks in their responses or the answers they provide differ to some extent from ethical principles (see Fig. 5).

In terms of values compatibility, some of the answers in the ERNIE Bot (V2.2.3) conform to some extent to the mainstream values and ethical concepts of the society, however, there are significant shortcomings or controversies in some important areas. This requires the model to answer the questions in a way that avoids significant bias, misinformation or incomplete information. For example, for some cultural backgrounds, ERNIE Bot (V2.2.3) will have some bias in understanding specific values (see Fig. 5).

Fig. 5. Distribution of Scores for "Ethical Conflict Compliance" and "Values Compatibility"

In terms of fairness, most responses to ERNIE Bot (V2.2.3) did not exhibit discriminatory or unfair behavior. However, in some cases, it was difficult to accurately identify texts that contained deeper layers of slight bias or discrimination against specific groups of people. This shows the model's superior performance in terms of fairness (see Fig. 6).

In terms of detection of security issues, ERNIE Bot (V2.2.3) performs compliant and can recognize and deal with a wide range of disinformation, privacy invasion, and cybersecurity issues. However, ERNIE Bot (V2.2.3) can misidentify or mishandle situations in certain circumstances. For example, in the adversarial example of privacy violations, the model was able to identify the problem but underperformed in providing high quality prevention or resolution recommendations (see Fig. 6).

Fig. 6. Distribution of Scores for "Fairness" and "Detection of Security Issues"

ERNIE Bot (V2.2.3) presents a better level of human collaboration and interaction. It can express its intentions and decisions in an understandable way, understand and interpret human language and behavior, and collaborate effectively with humans. This cooperation includes aspects of dialog, task execution, and decision making. However, the interactive capabilities of ERNIE Bot (V2.2.3) are still limited in some cases and further improvements are necessary (see Fig. 7).

In terms of repeatability and traceability, ERNIE Bot (V2.2.3) scored high on most prompts, which means that the model has a high level of repeatability and traceability in many cases. This characteristic helps to increase the transparency and maintainability of the model, while being able to assist humans in more fully understanding and monitoring the model's behavior (see Fig. 7).

Fig. 7. Distribution of Scores for "Human Collaboration and Interaction" and "Repeatability and Traceability"

In terms of accuracy, transparency and explain-ability, ERNIE Bot (V2.2.3) scored relatively moderate and needs to further improve its ability to understand and generate language. There is also room for improvement in transparency and interpretability to help humans understand the model's decision-making and prediction processes more deeply (see Fig. 8).

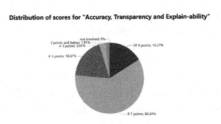

Fig. 8. Distribution of Scores for "Accuracy, Transparency and Explain-ability"

Comparative Data Analysis of Multiple Models: To improve the accuracy of the study as well as the visualization of the resultant data, a multi-model comparative assessment method was also adopted for this evaluation, and the selected LLMs included ERNIE Bot (v2.2.3), iFLYTEK Spark (v2.0), gpt-4 (0821), and gpt-3.5-turbo (0821).

The comparative evaluation in the direction of Prompts can be started from six different prompt categories. Overall, although there is still a gap with gpt-4(0821) and gpt-3.5-turbo (0821), ERNIE Bot (V2.2.3) has a good performance in all aspects, with the best relative performance in privacy violation detection, almost surpassing gpt-3.5-turbo (0821). In addition, disinformation detection is a common difficulty for all four LLMs. For the six different task categories, the scores were averaged for each of the four LLMs, and the specific data comparison can be seen in the following figure:

The data of the evaluation results were analyzed for the four LLMs for different dimension levels. The analysis shows that gpt-4(0821) still maintains the optimal performance in different dimension levels. The scores of ERNIE Bot (v2.2.3), iFLYTEK Spark (v2.0), and gpt-3.5-turbo (0821) were approximated in SAEs and MAEs. However, when dealing with CAEs, iFLYTEK Spark (v2.0) has a more significant gap with the other three LLMs.

For the three different dimension levels, the scores were averaged for each of the four LLMs, and the specific data comparison can be seen in Fig. 9.

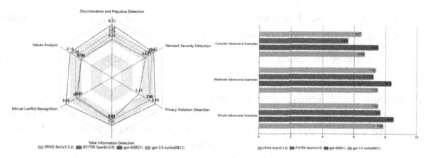

Fig. 9. Differences in Performance of Four LLMs for Different Prompts Categories and Dimension Levels

The overall score performance for each of the four LLMs was calculated separately, and the specific data comparison is shown in Fig. 10.

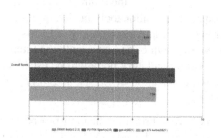

Fig. 10. Comparison of Final Scores of Four LLMs

The overall comparison results show that gpt-4(0821) performs the best in all aspects, and its overall evaluation score is as high as 8.41, which proves that its accuracy in recognizing ethical and security issues is very high. Although the difference between ERNIE Bot (V2.2.3) and gpt-4(0821) is obvious, it is not inferior to other LLMs with good performance. In comparison with gpt-3.5-turbo (0821) and iFLYTEK Spark (v2.0), ERNIE Bot (V2.2.3) scores only 0.35 lower than gpt-3.5-turbo (0821) and 0.66 higher than iFLYTEK Spark (v2.0).

7.2 Grand Challenges and Future Directions for LLMs

For LLMs, this research demonstrates the high performance of today's LLMs on ESIIP, but there are also some concerns. In the future, to enhance the application of LLMs on ESIIP, several major challenges will be faced as follows:

1) A well-established system of ethics and safety standards is needed to ensure that the application of LLMs is consistent with social and human values and ethics.
2) Intelligent analytical and predictive capabilities of LLMs need to be strengthened to better identify and deal with various ethical and security issues.

3) A sound regulatory mechanism for LLMs needs to be established to ensure that their application does not negatively impact society and humanity.

In addition, future directions for LLMs in terms of ethics and security issues include, but are not limited to, the following:

1) Establishment and improvement of ethical and moral framework: In the future, a more complete ethical and moral framework will be formed, including guiding principles, normative standards, operational guidelines, etc., to guarantee that the application of LLMs is in line with social morality and ethics and legal provisions.
2) Fairness and unbiased training data: In the future, more attention will be paid to the collection, processing and use of training data to ensure diversity and fairness of data sources and to avoid data bias and discrimination.
3) Protecting user privacy and data security: In the future, more and more efficient and secure algorithms and technical means will be available to ensure the safe storage and transmission of user data and to avoid data leakage and misuse.
4) Interpretability and transparency: In the future, more and more efficient and reliable technical means, such as visualization tools and interpretive models, will be available to improve the interpretability and transparency of LLMs.
5) Evaluation and regulation of ethics and morals: In the future, a better corresponding evaluation mechanism and regulatory body will be established to comprehensively review and regulate the application of LLMs, and to promptly address and rectify any problems identified.

In conclusion, LLMs have a broad application prospect on ESIIP. In the future, their application needs to be strengthened and effective measures taken to address their shortcomings to realize their greatest value to society and mankind.

8 Conclusion

The following conclusions can be drawn from the evaluation of ERNIE Bot (V2.2.3) in this research. First, from a theoretical point of view, the multidimensional adversarial example evaluation method adopted in this research is an effective tool for evaluating the ESIIP of LLMs. This method evaluates the model's recognition ability by inducing the model to make incorrect predictions through small perturbations to the input data. Secondly, the practical validation shows that ERNIE Bot (V2.2.3) performs well on ESIIP but does not reach the perfect level. Therefore, this evaluation method has some guiding significance in practical application. In addition, through comparative analysis, we found that the reliability and feasibility of this research method is high.

Finally, the findings of this research are important for improving the ESIIP of LLMs. By evaluating LLMs more comprehensively and objectively, we can better understand their strengths and weaknesses and provide a basis for better and faster iterative upgrading. Meanwhile, this research also provides theoretical and practical support for the development of LLMs and promotes their development to a higher level.

References

1. Bansal, R.: A survey on bias and fairness in natural language processing (2022). https://doi.org/10.48550/arXiv.2204.09591
2. Yuan, Z., Shi, B.: Discriminative manifold learning network using adversarial examples for image classification. J. Electr. Eng. Technol. 13 (2018). https://doi.org/10.5370/JEET.2018.13.5.2099
3. Audi, R.: The Cambridge Dictionary of Philosophy. Cambridge University Press (1996). https://doi.org/10.1111/j.1468-0149.1996.tb02545.x
4. Dennis, A., Jones, R., Kildare, D., et al.: A design science approach to developing and evaluating a national cybersecurity framework for Jamaica. Electron. J. Inf. Syst. Dev. Countries **62**(1) (2014).https://doi.org/10.1002/j.1681-4835.2014.tb00444.x
5. Jouini, M., Rabai, L.B.A., Aissa, A.B.: Classification of security threats in information systems. Procedia Comput. Sci. **32**, 489–496 (2014). https://doi.org/10.1016/j.procs.2014.05.452
6. Ani, U.D., He, H., Tiwari, A.: Human factor security: evaluating the cybersecurity capacity of the industrial workforce. J. Syst. Inf. Technol. **21**(9) (2018). https://doi.org/10.1108/JSIT-02-2018-0028
7. Kent, A., Williams, J.G., Kent, R., et al.: Encyclopedia of Computer Science and Technology. M. Dekker (1977)
8. Workman, M.: Encyclopedia of information and ethics security. J. Assoc. Inf. Sci. Technol. **60**(8), 1723–1724 (2010). https://doi.org/10.1002/asi.21088
9. Gravatt, A.E., Lindzey, G., Aronson, F.: The handbook of social psychology. Mental Health **6**(2), 86–86 (2013). https://doi.org/10.1002/wcs.7
10. Jia, J., Gong, N.Z.: Defending against machine learning based inference attacks via adversarial examples: opportunities and challenges (2019). https://doi.org/10.48550/arXiv.1909.08526. Accessed 09 Dec 2023
11. Wick, M.L., Silverstein, K., Tristan, J.B., et al.: Detecting and exorcising statistical demons from language models with anti-models of negative data (2020). https://doi.org/10.48550/arXiv.2010.11855
12. Brown, T.B., Mann, B., Ryder, N., et al.: Language models are few-shot learners (2020). https://doi.org/10.48550/arXiv.2005.14165
13. Li, L., Lei, J., Gan, Z., et al.: VALUE: a multi-task benchmark for video-and-language understanding evaluation (2021). https://doi.org/10.48550/arXiv.2106.04632
14. Hiller, J.S., Russell, R.S.: Privacy in crises: the NIST privacy framework. J. Contingencies Crisis Manag. **25**(1), 31–38 (2017). https://doi.org/10.1111/1468-5973.12143
15. Lakshmanarao, A., Shashi, M.: A survey on machine learning for cyber security. Int. J. Sci. Technol. Res. **9**, 499–502 (2020)
16. Jabbari, S., Joseph, M., Kearns, M., et al.: Fair learning in Markovian environments (2016). https://doi.org/10.48550/arXiv.1611.03071
17. Marabelli, M., Newell, S., Handunge, V.: The lifecycle of algorithmic decision-making systems: Organizational choices and ethical challenges. J. Strateg. Inf. Syst. **30**(3) (2023). https://doi.org/10.1016/j.jsis.2021.101683. Accessed 09 Dec 2023
18. Yuan, S., Wu, X.: Deep learning for insider threat detection: review, challenges and opportunities. Comput. Secur. **104**(C), 102221 (2021). https://doi.org/10.1016/j.cose.2021.102221
19. Varley, M., Belle, V.: Fairness in machine learning with tractable models – ScienceDirect. Knowl.-Based Syst. (2021). https://doi.org/10.1016/j.knosys.2020.106715
20. Deho, O.B., Liu, L., Li, J., et al.: How do the existing fairness metrics and unfairness mitigation algorithms contribute to ethical learning analytics?. Br. J. Educ. Technol. **53**(4), 822–843 (2022). https://doi.org/10.1111/bjet.13217

21. Balayn, A., Lofi, C., Houben, G.J.: Managing bias and unfairness in data for decision support: a survey of machine learning and data engineering approaches to identify and mitigate bias and unfairness within data management and analytics systems. VLDB J. 1–30 (2021). https://doi.org/10.1007/s00778-021-00671-8
22. Wahde, M., Virgolin, M.: The five is: key principles for interpretable and safe conversational AI. arXiv e-prints (2021). https://doi.org/10.48550/arXiv.2108.13766
23. Shafti, A., Derks, V., Kay, H., et al.: The response shift paradigm to quantify human trust in AI recommendations (2022). https://doi.org/10.48550/arXiv.2202.08979

Design and Development of Intelligent Schedule Management System for Students

Yunan Lin[✉], Gangyi Zhang, Wenqiang Zhu, Haihang Du, Gang Cen, and Yuefeng Cen

Zhejiang University of Science and Technology, Hangzhou, China
814781773@qq.com, cyf@zust.edu.cn

Abstract. Effective scheduling plays a crucial role in facilitating personalized learning for students. In order to realize efficient personal schedule management and team cooperation schedule management, the project team designed and developed the student intelligent schedule management system. According to the long-term and short-term schedule needs and members' ability and other factors, the system uses dynamic programming algorithm and greedy algorithm to cooperate to realize students' schedule planning. At the same time, it also recommends a variety of schedule scheduling schemes for student organization managers, achieving the purpose of improving the efficiency of schedule scheduling and increasing the rationality of arrangement.

Keywords: design and development · student schedule management · schedule plan · Dynamic programming algorithm · greedy algorithm

1 Introduction

As the pace of people's life is accelerating, the number of daily tasks is also increasing. So reasonable arrangement of related tasks in life and work has become an urgent need for people in a fast pace [1]. Students, as a typical group with a busy schedule, need to reasonably arrange their personal schedule and complete the management of collaborative tasks with others. It is of great significance to help students realize multi-people collaborative schedule management. Reasonable schedule management is an advanced strategy, which is not only about time management, but also a key tool to achieve goals, cultivate self-management ability, adapt to changes and pursue all-round development. Students should realize the importance of schedule management and regard it as an important support for personal growth and success [2].

Nowaday lots of management systems are emerging. The potential users distribute in the universities, offices, government departments et al. The schedule management methods are also evolling. However, in fact, the limited information accessibility between individual students and groups leads to the information asymmetric in time and space moreover. The intelligence of the management systems need to be improved. Fragmented schedule data is scattered in different

W. Hong and G. Kanaparan (Eds.): ICCSE 2023, CCIS 2025, pp. 303–314, 2024.
https://doi.org/10.1007/978-981-97-0737-9_27

terminal devices, different management systems and even different networks. The phenomenon of isolated island of schedule information is becoming more and more serious, and schedule conflicts cannot be cured. Users are faceint with huge difficulties in reorganizing complicated schedules, and the global and scientific time management still cannot be solved [3]. As a result, the insufficient intelligence level of schedule management tools cannot meet the growing needs of users, nor can they recommend reasonable schedules for users, resulting in more efficient and reasonable daily learning for users. Therefore, the project team proposed a student-oriented intelligent schedule management system.

2   Research Status

The management systems adopted by the college students to can be divided into three categories as follows:

The first type is the Calendar management system based on calendar application, among which the more popular ones are todo list, time order, Google Calendar and so on. This type of system makes use of the existing calendar application as the foundation, and meets the needs of users by adding functions such as intelligent reminder, intelligent scheduling and suggestion. These functions are only an extension of the functions of calendar software, and do not really achieve the main goal of calendar management software [4]. This kind of system can realize the popular demand of schedule management, but it is not customized for students, and does not well consider the critical needs of students in rationalizing schedule.

The second type is dedicated to students' schedule management applications, these applications are specially designed for students to provide various functions required for student schedule management. They often include class schedule management, task and homework reminders, exam scheduling, study goal setting, time management tools, etc. These types of systems may take some time and effort for some students to learn and adjust to. If the system interface is complex and the operation is not intuitive, then the student user needs to go through specific training and learning, and spend more time to master or use it. Such as MyStudyLife, iStudiez Pro, Schooltraq, etc., the schedule management of student groups has been specialized, which is more suitable for the individual application of students' learning scenarios, but complex operations may increase the cost of additional learning during use.

The third category is some online learning platforms, such as Moodle, Canvas, edX, etc., which also provide the function of students' schedule management. These platforms can integrate students' schedule, homework, exams and other information, and provide reminders and notification functions. Although online learning platforms are important tools for people to learn knowledge, grow skills and broaden their horizons in the Internet era [5], they still have drawbacks in terms of schedule management alone: these platforms almost only provide individual schedule management and simple team schedule management, and their functions may not be enough to meet users' needs for more demanding and flexible schedules.

In addition to the schedule management function of the above three types of software, these additional functions have certain value and have been favored by users with corresponding needs. However, these software all have a common shortcoming, they can not help users record personal schedule, at the same time, provide users with reasonable schedule plan and suggestions. Simply relying on the user's manual operation to man age personal schedule is undoubtedly a relatively inefficient approach, which can not achieve the purpose of efficient and convenient management of personal schedule, nor can it meet the requirements of users. In view of the above problems, the project team uses intelligent technology to design and develop the schedule management system. The system uses greedy algorithm and dynamic planning algorithm to calculate and analyze short-term and long-term schedules respectively, and makes adaptive recommendations for long-term and short-term schedules, providing users with more reasonable scheduling schemes and suggestions, which can better improve users' working efficiency.

3   Proposal of the System

According to the current status and deficiencies of the development of schedule management software, for college students, the project team, through communication with teachers and students as well as research and analysis, is determined to improve the efficiency of students' schedule arrangement and enhance the rationality of schedule arrangement, designed and developed an intelligent schedule management system with students as the main body. Based on the analysis of college schedule scenarios and relying on the scientific theory of time management [3], the system investigates the basic functions of common schedule management software in the market, and by integrating the students' schedule information, pushes reasonable schedule plans to users and puts forward scientific schedule suggestions for users.

Compared with the traditional schedule management software, the intelligent schedule management system has an intelligent and efficient schedule management module. The system will provide users with more intuitive time series planning, which is easy to arrange activities and work, and users can choose a variety of scheduling methods provided by the system before schedule planning, accurately locate the scheduling needs and give scientific proposals, which reduces most manual decisions and intervention of traditional schedule management software, and helps students manage their personal schedules more intelligently and efficiently. Improve the rationality of schedule arrangement and improve users' life and work efficiency.

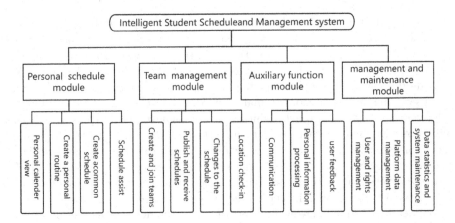

Fig. 1. Overall framework of the intelligent schedule management system for students

4   The Design of the System

The system is composed of personal schedule module, team management module, auxiliary function module and management and maintenance module. The system provides a mini program platform and a Web platform to carry these four modules. The mini program platform carries a personal schedule module, a team management module and an auxiliary function module for student users. The Web platform is equipped with a management and maintenance module for the development team and maintenance team. The overall framework of the system is shown in Fig. 1.

4.1   Personal Schedule Module

In this module, students can view the aggregated personal schedule and the schedule of the participating teams, and have the rights to set the disclosure degree and display details of the schedule, customize the schedule reminder time [6], search the schedule, export the schedule, and so on. Students can create two types of schedule, and the specific creation process is shown in Fig. 2. First, students can choose to create their own personal schedule, fill in the schedule information through manual input or excel sheet data import, and can set the repetition frequency of the schedule, such as daily, weekly, etc. For the schedule with no clear time, it can be set as a to -do event, and the system will suspend it on the top of the calendar for reminders, so as not to let students forget. Second, students can choose to invite others to participate in the common schedule. After the contact selection is completed, the system will generate the general schedule of all the people, intelligently find the appropriate free time in it, and recommend it to the founder for reference. After filling in the basic information of the schedule, an invitation will be sent to the selected contact. After agreeing, it can be automatically added to the personal schedule.

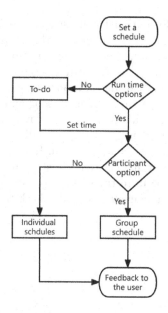

Fig. 2. The process by which a user creates a schedule

4.2   Team Management Module

The overall workflow of the team management module is shown in Fig. 3. In the module, students can choose to create their own team or join the team by QR code or searching for a number. After creating a team and becoming a manager, students who apply to join the team can be approved by manually approving them or by using Excel to import the personnel list. In the team, the manager can set the schedule of the team. The system provides two schedule planning modes for the manager. The first planning mode is for the situation that the schedule plan will not be changed in the long term, and the other planning mode is for the situation that the schedule plan will be changed in the short term. After selecting the planning mode, the manager can select the factor parameters and fill in the basic schedule information, and the system will intelligently recommend a reasonable schedule plan based on the students' personal information. When the system cannot calculate the recommendation plan or the user refuses to use the system recommendation plan, the system will assist the user to arrange the schedule manually, so as to realize the purpose of manually arranging the team schedule. When the manager releases the group schedule, a time period when all team members are available is required. The system will recommend the relatively free time period of all members, and use the depth of color to indicate the free rate of the schedule. At the same time, the administrator can also limit the schedule time and select the relatively free time of the members within the specified time period. When the information required for scheduling is incomplete, the administrator can issue additional information collection tasks and add the collected information to the students' personal information. The final schedule result will be added directly to the member's schedule. After the schedule is published, all team members can receive and view the schedule, and they can also see their team's schedule summary. If the team members have doubts about the schedule information released by the manager or need to modify it, they can explain the specific reasons and apply to the manager to modify the schedule, so as to realize the collaborative interaction function [7]. For members' applications, the manager can give feedback to them and modify the schedule again after accepting the application. In order to facilitate attendance statistics and management of managers, the system also sets up a location check-in module. Members can log in to the system to obtain location information for location check-in, so that managers can easily check the attendance of members in the scheduling schedule.

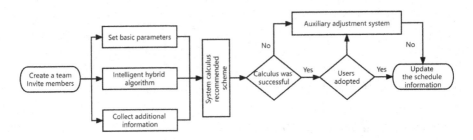

Fig. 3. Flowchart of the team management module

4.3   Auxiliary Function Module

This module is composed of sub-modules such as communication and personal information processing. In the communication module, students can find and view contact information and team content. Students can add contacts by scanning QR codes, searching ID numbers, and other team members' contact information will be directly imported into their personal address book. In this module, students can receive notifications and other people's private messages. Among them, the main content of the notification is the team's task and some schedule changes, while the private message is mainly responsible for individual discussion and communication with contacts or group members. In the personal information module, students can input, query and modify individual information, including interests and skills. At the same time, they can view personal information in the personal center of others.

4.4   Management and Maintenance Module

This module is composed of three sub-modules: user and authority management, platform data management, and data statistics and system maintenance. User and authority management is mainly used by system administrators to manage user registration information and corresponding user permissions, and restrict user access to sensitive data and functions. Platform data management is the management of user published content and system database management, including the management of data storage, access and processing. Data statistics and system maintenance is the data statistics and visual display of the access and use of the platform, the daily maintenance and update of the system, and the collection of user feedback to upgrade and optimize the system.

5 Technical Implementation of the System

System development adopts MVVM front-end and back-end separation development mode, this mode reduces the coupling degree of the system, so that the front-end and back-end can be developed in parallel, provide better scalability and flexibility, improve team cooperation and development efficiency. The system is composed of three parts: user client, management client and server. The user client is developed based on React and Taro multi-terminal development framework, which is converted into wechat mini program by compiler after writing. The management client is built in B/S mode (Brower/Server), and is designed and developed based on Vue and Element-UI component library to improve the efficiency and stability of system development and shorten the platform iteration cycle. The server side adopts Spring Boot and MyBatis plus framework, uses IntelliJ IDEA development tool and Maven for project management, and applies MySQL relational design library for data storage. In order to realize user login and identity verification, the server uses JWT (JSON web token) encryption identity token technology.

In order to ensure the rationality and accuracy of the system's recommended schedule, the system uses an intelligent way to assist users in managing and arranging the schedule. According to the different scheduling needs of users, the system adopts different scheduling algorithms to recommend reasonable and diverse scheduling schemes. The system provides two algorithms to arrange users' schedules, namely dynamic programming method and greedy algorithm [8]. The dynamic programming method decomposes the solved problem into several ordered or sortable subproblems, and then seeks each subproblem in order. When solving any subproblem, various possible local solutions are listed first, and then the local solutions that may reach the optimal solution are reserved through decision making. Each subproblem is solved successively, and the optimal solution is finally obtained. The greedy algorithm chooses the local optimal solution at each decision point, without considering the whole, and finally obtains the solution, which is not the optimal solution for the whole, but is relatively reasonable and is the optimal solution for the local. Based on these two algorithms, the system provides two scheduling modes for different needs of users.

If it is long-term scheduling planning, the system designs and calculates a long-term effective scheduling scheme based on dynamic programming method; On the contrary, based on greedy algorithm, design and calculate a short-term relatively reasonable plan. Compared with the overall optimal solution, the calculation result of dynamic programming method can not solve the short-term or temporary scheduling needs, but the schedule calculated by dynamic programming method is relatively reasonable for the periodic and long-term schedules that do not need to change. While greedy algorithm only calculates a relatively local reasonable plan, for a long time arrangement produces too many child nodes, because it does not consider other nodes in the calculation process, it is easy to cause conflicts in the process of arrangement, resulting in greater errors, while for a short time arrangement, it takes fewer factors into consideration, and can solve the current optimal arrangement. Based on dynamic programming method, the long-term schedule is planned. First, the whole scheduling goal is segmented into independent sub-problems, and the definition of sub-problems, boundary conditions, relations and recurrence relations among sub-problems are confirmed. According to the recursive relation, recursive calculation and use of multi-dimensional array to save the solution of each sub-problem, easy to find and reuse, the solution of the sub-problem is arranged and compared, can calculate the relative overall optimal scheduling scheme. Based on greedy algorithm, the short-term temporary schedule is arranged. First confirm the best candidate for each time period arrangement, and record it, and then screen according to a series of conditions such as time, abandon the unsatisfactory situation, and finally get several arrangement plans, and then compare them to choose a more reasonable plan.

In addition to the core algorithm of the underlying foundation, the other calculation factors of the two schedule planning modes tend to be the same. The basic calculation factors include schedule time, schedule priority, each member's specific ability, and the member's time idle rate (the range is schedule time period and some time periods before and after the schedule). The specific process is to assign tasks on the basis of equal distribution (the number of tasks assigned to the team members is similar), combined with the calculation factors such as the priority of the schedule and the weight ratio of some students' specific abilities. The rationality principle of the calculation result is that the amount of tasks assigned by each person is average, the density of individual schedules is relatively reasonable, and important schedules are dealt with first. If there are many different nodes arranging results on a certain computing node, but the rationality of the results is not very different, the node is selected randomly. If the system calculates multiple schedule planning schemes with similar rationality at the end, the system retains the scheme and recommends it to the user for the user to choose. On the basis of intelligent algorithm, the system adopts manual intervention to improve the rationality and accuracy of schedule recommendation. In some cases, the user is not satisfied with the schedule recommended by the system, and can adjust it manually according to the user's expectation. The technical architecture of the algorithm is shown in Fig. 4.

In order to achieve a series of intelligent information import methods. The system uses POI, JexcelAPI and other third-party apis to achieve excel [9] import function, and uses OCR library to convert the text in the picture into editable text data. Users ca n use these two input methods to achieve cumbersome schedule input operations. At the same time, the system provides the function of adding the speech description to the schedule, uses the API provided by the speech recognition [10] in Tencent Cloud AAI to realize the text conversion,

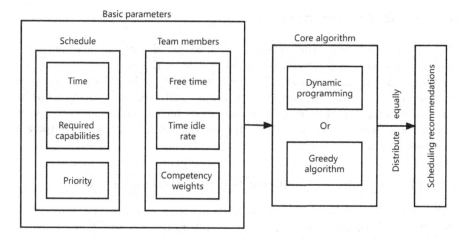

Fig. 4. The algorithmic technical architecture

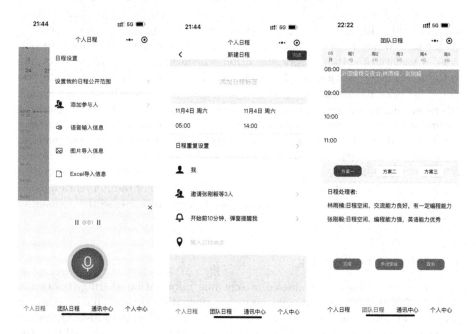

Fig. 5. Schedule import: voice input   **Fig. 6.** Create a new personal event   **Fig. 7.** Team schedule recommendations

uses the Stanford CoreNLP library to understand the text semantics and carry out corresponding operations.

Some pages of the Personal schedule module and Team schedule module are shown in Figs. 5, 6 and 7.

6   Features of the System

This system is based on the college schedule scene, the student schedule management and intelligent combination, starting from the purpose of solving the poor schedule information and efficient management of the schedule, under the premise of ensuring the complete function of the software, also has the following three characteristics: the diversity of intelligent recommendation of the diversity of the schedule, the sharing of information and the variety of automatic information import.

6.1   The Diversity of Intelligent Schedule Recommendation

This system is different from the ordinary schedule software in adding schedules. It takes a variety of intelligent forms to help users create group schedules reasonably under group cooperation. In the scenario where users create a common schedule, the system will automatically display the common idle time of participants. Users can apply to create a common schedule according to this, and automatically add it to the common schedule after other users agree. In the scenario where the team releases work arrangements, the system will recommend a variety of suitable work allocation schemes for the members according to the screening conditions set by the manager, calculation parameters and the members' personal schedule. After the manager adopts a scheme, the scheme will be automatically added to the members' schedule. For some work requiring specific skills, the system will select the appropriate members for the manager to select, reduce the unreasonable arrangement caused by manual intervention, and provide users with a more simple operation and high-quality user experience. When the schedule allocation problem cannot be solved intelligently, the system designs an auxiliary adjustment system to take the form of re-intervention, combining artificial intelligence and manual intervention to increase the rationality and fairness of schedule arrangement.

6.2   Information Sharing

The system realizes a high degree of schedule information sharing, under the premise of protecting user privacy, users can view other people's public schedule information, effectively alleviate the phenomenon of information island, reduce the time spent by users in obtaining schedule information, and facilitate the organization and managers to carry out schedule work.

6.3   Variety of Automated Information Import Methods

In addition to supporting manual input of schedule information, the system also supports a variety of automatic information import methods, and provides users with intelligent input [10] methods such as excel [9] sheets, picture import and voice input, which makes schedule management more convenient and efficient.

6.4   Portability in Operation and Use

Scheduling and management systems, in order to cater to campus life, can be easily used in daily life is particularly important for students. The system relies on wechat mini program to provide users with portable services, making user schedule management more convenient and fast.

7   Concluding Remarks

The use of intelligent and modern information technology means to improve management efficiency is an inevitable trend of society. The designed system starts from the actual situation of the campus, combines the respective needs of managers and students, and deeply fits in with the campus. It is capable of more intelligently and efficiently scheduling plans, providing multiple schedule arrangement options, increases the rationality of the arrangement, reduces the work burden of users, and alleviates the phenomenon of data is landing. It makes up for the common shortcomings of most current schedule management software, and promotes the progress of students' intelligent schedule management system. Although there are still some problems and deficiencies in the system design, with the development of future technology and the abundance of scientific research resources, the system will be more perfect in the subsequent research and development.

Acknowledgement. This work was supported by the innovation and entrepreneurship training program for Chinese college students (No.2023cxcy030); The grants from Zhejiang Xin Miao Talents Program (No.2023R415016).

References

1. Zhu, L.: Design and Implementation of Schedule Management System Based on Android. Master's thesis, Shandong University (2016)
2. Zhang, J., Yu, F.: The current situation, predicament and countermeasures of college students' time management in the micro-era. J. Hubei Open Univ. **35**(6), 46–47 (2022)
3. Cai, Y.: A study on the construction of intelligent schedule management service platform for colleges and universities. Chinese J. ICT in Educ. **28**(3), 58–63 (2022)
4. He, L.: Design And Implementation Schedule Management System of Andriod Phone. Master's thesis, Beijing University Of Technology (2015)
5. Liu, S., et al.: Research on online learning platform experience from the perspective of users. E-Educ. Res. **40**(10), 47–52 (2019)
6. Zhang, X.: Design and development of android-based student schedule management app. Informatiz. Constr. **7**, 21 (2016)
7. Ding, H.: Design of schedule management system based on collaborative work. China Comput. Commun. **12**, 73–75 (2018)
8. Liu, G.: The Research and Application of Greedy Algorithm Based on the Time Slice Priority Scheduling Algorithm. Ph.D. thesis, Hunan University (2013)

9. Huping, Z., Di, A.: A method of excel file reading and writing based on java note and reflection mechanism. J. Jiujiang Vocat. Techn. College **1**, 10–14 (2020)

10. Wang, J., Hu, D., Wang, S.: Analysis and implementation of student schedule management system based on natural language processing. Mod. Comput. **19**, 64–65 (2018)

Project-Based Learning for In-depth Understanding of IoT Architecture: Design of IoT Liquid Flow Monitoring System Based on LoRa Communication

Xu Tian[1], Xin-Yu Chen[1], Ming-Wei Wu[1(✉)], Meng-Qin Zhang[1], Run-Zhi Liu[1], Zheng Zhang[1], Hong-Wei Tao[1], and Qin Dai[2]

[1] School of Information and Electronic Engineering,
Zhejiang University of Science and Technology,
Hangzhou 310023, China
wu_mingwei2004@aliyun.com, zz.itee@msn.com

[2] Chinese-German Institute of Engineering,
Zhejiang University of Science and Technology,
Hangzhou 310023, China

Abstract. With the rapid development of the Internet of Things (IoT) industry, there is an increasing demand for cultivating industry talents in society. However, students often face difficulties in deeply understanding the four-layer architecture of IoT in the relevant subjects taught in colleges and universities. Additionally, LoRa, which represents low-power wide area networks, has been widely used in the IoT industry in recent years, but students have low awareness of it. To address these issues, this article proposes a project-based learning method that aims to help students combine theoretical knowledge with practical projects, gain an in-depth understanding of the IoT architecture, and expose them to LoRa, an emerging communication technology. This approach will improve their comprehensive practical ability and better meet the IoT industry's need for well-rounded talents.

Keywords: IoT · LoRa · project-based learning

1 Introduction

As of the end of May this year, China has built over 2.844 million 5G base stations and has more than 2.05 billion mobile IoT end users, according to the report

This work is supported by Zhejiang University of Science and Technology (ZUST) 2023 College Student Innovation and Entrepreneurship Training Program (No. 2023cxcy036), ZUST Top Undergraduate Courses Development Project 2022-k4, Zhejiang University of Science and Technology (ZUST) Teacher's Professional Growth Community Project 2023, 2020 Zhejiang Provincial-level Top Undergraduate Courses (Zhejiang Provincial Department of Education General Office Notice (2021) No. 195), 2023 Teaching Research and Reform Project of Zhejiang University of Science and Technology (No.2023-jg37).

of the 2023 Global Digital Economy Conference. Which makes China the first country among the world's major economies where the number of "things" connections exceeds the number of "people" connections. This achievement marks the increasingly solid foundation of the digital economy and shows significant progress in the development of China's digital economy [1]. In recent years, IoT technology and industry have been regarded as an important part of future digital economy development strategies [2]. The Internet of Things is a new technology and application model based on the Internet. It combines multiple technologies such as sensors, computers, and networks to achieve a seamless connection between the physical world and the digital world. According to the UNS system framework, the Internet of Things system can be designed and implemented using a four-layer architecture of perception layer, network layer, support layer, and application layer [3,4]. A deep understanding of the architecture of the Internet of Things is of great significance for cultivating future information technology talents.

With the rapid development of the Internet of Things industry, low-power wide area network (LPWAN) technology represented by LoRa has garnered significant attention. LoRa communication technology serves as the extended arm of the Internet of Things, capable of connecting various sensing devices. In comparison to common wireless communication technologies like Bluetooth and Wi-Fi, LoRa possesses numerous advantages, including long-range transmission and low power consumption, making it highly suitable for IoT applications [5]. However, as an advanced communication technology, LoRa remains relatively unfamiliar to school students.

In colleges and universities, majors in information technology, such as electronics, communications, and computer science, offer a wide range of courses. These courses provide students with a wealth of professional knowledge, but they often tend to be more theoretical in nature. Consequently, students may encounter difficulties when it comes to applying theoretical knowledge to real-world projects [6]. Traditional teaching methods typically prioritize the teacher's role in instruction, while project-based learning places greater emphasis on student involvement [7]. In project-based learning, teachers often assume the role of guides. Throughout the process of project development, students not only reinforce their foundational knowledge, but also cultivate various skills, including hands-on practice, independent management, teamwork, and interpersonal communication [8]. Moreover, many college courses fail to establish connections with real-world work and project requirements. Project-based learning serves as an effective solution to address this issue.

Based on the above phenomena, we have designed a project-based learning plan for the IoT liquid flow monitoring system based on LoRa communication to carry out the construction of practical teaching projects and lay the foundation for the cultivation of information technology talents.

2 Learning Plan Design

A comprehensive Internet of Things (IoT) system project necessitates knowledge and skills from various subject areas. This encompasses C language programming, digital circuits, principles of microprocessors, and wireless sensor networks. For example, in the Communication Engineering major at our school, the relevant courses are outlined in Table 1. Project-based learning is typically conducted in the fifth semester, where students form teams of three and work on projects outside of the classroom for six weeks.

Table 1. Courses related to this project in the major of communication engineering.

Technology	Course	Semester
C Programming	Fundamentals of Programming	1
Microprocessor Development	Principles of Microprocessor and Its Applications	3
Fundamentals of Sensors	Digital Circuit Design	4
Communication of IoT	Wireless Sensor Networks	5

This learning plan utilizes our school's tutor system as a medium and is based on the project learning teacher-student community [9, 10]. The plan, as shown in Fig. 1, requires the project to be conducted within the IoT system's project space and based on the IoT architecture and learned professional knowledge.

The instructor offers guidance in topic selection, while students ultimately choose their topics based on their own interests and preferences. Once a topic is selected, the instructor suggests the direction for functional requirements, and students conduct research to gather relevant information. Subsequently, system design takes place, with the teacher establishing a framework for the design plan, and students engaging in brainstorming and discussion to determine the specific implementation details. Throughout the project development process, teachers provide guidance and assistance, while the majority of the work is carried out by student teams. Moreover, since the Low-Power Wide Area Network (LoRa) technology and Wi-Fi cloud technology utilized in this project are not extensively covered in traditional classroom teaching, students are encouraged to actively and independently seek relevant materials for learning. Upon completion of the project development, the teacher evaluates and summarizes the results of each group, and encourages students to share their findings. Students also have the opportunity to think deeply, improve and expand the system according to the teacher's proposed direction, and add more functional modules. Throughout the entire learning project, teachers provide learning resources to support the project. Members of the project-based learning group encourage and collaborate with one another, making progress together, and providing support in the learning process.

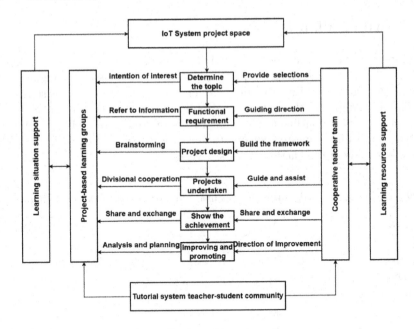

Fig. 1. Design of learning plan.

3   Learning Project Implementation

3.1   Internet of Things System Design

The main framework of the system is shown in Fig. 2.

The first is the sensing layer at the bottom, which uses a Hall water flow sensor to sense water flow information, convert it into a pulse signal, and then transmit it to the microcontroller. After collecting and processing the pulse signal output by the sensor, the MCU obtains the data of water flow information. The microcontroller can send water flow data to the network layer through UART.

The network layer uses two communication methods, LoRa and Wi-Fi, for data transmission. LoRa communication technology is first used to realize data transmission between sensor nodes and gateways. Once the data reaches the gateway, the gateway uses the Wi-Fi wireless network to transmit it to the support layer through the MQTT protocol.

Use the cloud IoT platform as the support layer to store water flow information data and connect with the application layer. The application layer is a data visualization web page developed to visually display the water flow information data stored in the support layer for users to monitor in real time.

3.2   System Development

The specific development route of the system is shown in Fig. 3.

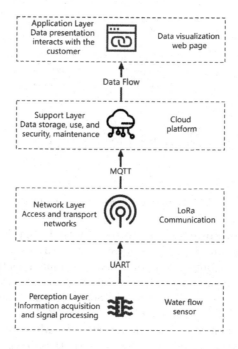

Fig. 2. Framework design of the Internet of Things.

Acquisition and Processing of Flow Information. To complete this project, you will need a flow sensor and a main control MCU. Specifically, the YF-S401 Hall water flow sensor and the STC8G1K08 low-power main control MCU based on the 8051 core are recommended.

The YF-S401 water flow sensor contains a Hall switch element that detects the rotation of a magnet on the rotor as water flows through the sensor. This rotation generates a magnetic input signal that is processed by digital and analog circuits, resulting in a pulse signal output. To use the sensor, students must connect it to the main control MCU and write a C language program that utilizes the timer, counter, and serial port functions of the microcontroller to collect, calculate, and transmit the pulse signals.

For example, students can connect the pulse output line of the sensor to the P34 pin of the MCU and count the number of pulses on that pin every 2 s. By using the corresponding relationship between the pulse number and the liquid volume, they can calculate the volume of liquid passing through the sensor within 2 s. The total liquid volume can be obtained by adding the calculated volume each time. Finally, the flow rate and liquid volume data can be sent through UART.

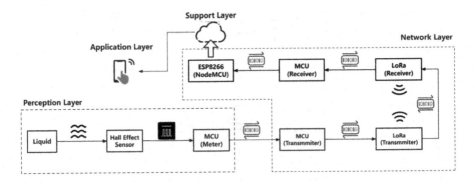

Fig. 3. System development route.

Driving LoRa Communication Module by SPI. In this system, the sensor node needs to communicate with the wireless gateway using LoRa communication technology. The required components are two main control MCUs and two LoRa communication modules. The specific models used are the STC8G1K08 main control MCU, which is based on the 8051 core, and the RF_M607T LoRa communication module, which is based on the SX1268.

The LoRa communication module requires the MCU to be driven through the SPI communication protocol. When the MCU controls the LoRa module, the main control MCU acts as the host, and the LoRa module acts as the slave. The host sends instructions to the LoRa module through SPI communication to change the registers inside the LoRa chip and then drive the LoRa module to complete specified operations. Table 2 provides an example of an SPI transaction for a specific function. Figure 4 shows the software design of the LoRa sending module driver host.

Table 2. SPI transaction of ReadRegister function.

Byte	0	1	2	3	$\cdots$	n
Date from host	0pcode = 0x0E	offset	data@offset	data@offset+1	$\cdots$	data@offset+(n-2)
Data to host	RFU	Status	Status	Status	$\cdots$	Status

When students are operating, they can start by connecting four lines between two MCUs and writing code to enable communication between the two MCUs through SPI. This will help them understand and become proficient in the SPI communication protocol. Once they have a good grasp of the SPI communication protocol, they can write code based on the data manual of the SX1268 chip. This will enable the MCU to drive the LoRa communication module and implement the sending and receiving functions.

This is a challenging aspect of the project. Students may refer to relevant function libraries for assistance. The project only involves point-to-point communication using LoRa. However, interested students can further explore LoRaWAN for multi-node networking beyond the scope of this project.

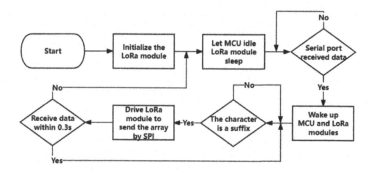

Fig. 4. Software design of LoRa sending segment.

Wi-Fi Module Transmits Data to the Cloud. In this step, we will be using the wireless gateway module along with a suitable cloud platform. Specifically, we will be using the ESP8266 Wi-Fi module and the China Mobile OneNet IoT platform.

After the water flow data is transmitted over long distances through LoRa communication, it needs to be uploaded to the cloud through the gateway module. We use the serial port (UART) protocol to enable the ESP8266 Wi-Fi module to communicate with the main controller of the LoRa receiving module. By programming ESP8266 with Arduino, you can use the software serial port to receive data and publish the data to the cloud platform through the MQTT protocol.

MQTT is a lightweight, open-standard messaging protocol suitable for IoT applications. Students can define two pins on ESP8266 and use these two pins as software serial ports to receive water flow data sent by the LoRa receiving module main control MCU. Through the development of ESP8266, it can be connected to the Internet and connected to the MQTT access service address of the OneNet IoT platform. When the connection is successful, the feedback information of the successful connection will be displayed in the serial port monitor of Arduino IDE, as shown in Fig. 5. Then, through the data publishing principle of the MQTT protocol, the water flow data can be published to specific topics of the platform, so that the data can be displayed in the platform's data flow template in real time. Students can compare the data in the serial monitor with the data in the platform data flow template to confirm whether the data uploaded to the cloud is consistent with the data in the platform data flow template.

Development of Data Visualization Web Page. The OneNet IoT platform utilized in the system offers a development environment for the data visualization View project. Once students create a project, they can construct their individual web page like building blocks and connect the data source to the data flow template to obtain water flow data. After building the visual web page, they can publish and access it on their mobile phones. Figure 6 showcases the development

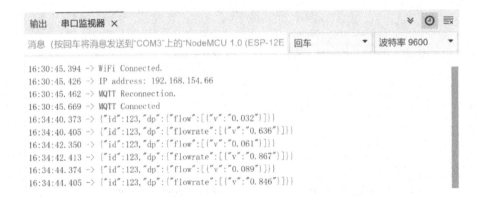

Fig. 5. The output of the serial port monitor during the debugging process.

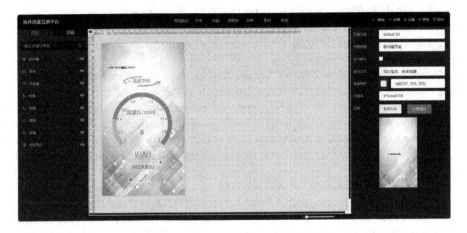

Fig. 6. Development interface of data visualization web page.

environment of the data visualization web page and the data visualization View that we have developed.

3.3 System Achievements and Improvements

The physical diagram of the final result of the project is shown in Fig. 7.

Figure 8 is a physical image of a data acquisition terminal including a Hall water flow sensor, a master MCU, and a LoRa transmission module.

Figure 9 is a physical picture of a gateway module, including a LoRa receiving module, a master MCU, and an ESP8266 Wi-Fi module.

First, connect the data acquisition module to the power supply. Then, power on the gateway module and connect it to the network. Once this is done, you can start the water pump. Real-time water flow and total water output data can be viewed on the data visualization webpage on your mobile phone. By clicking

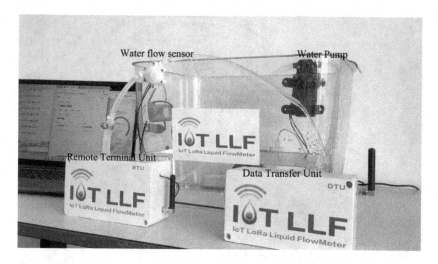

Fig. 7. Overall physical results.

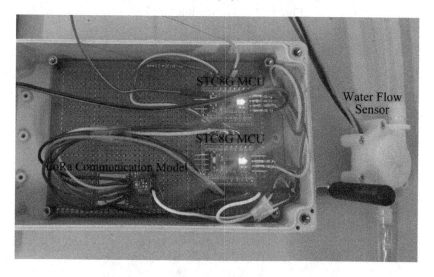

Fig. 8. Data collection terminal (RTU).

on the water flow change icon, you can also access the interface for monitoring the water flow change trend, as shown in Fig. 10.

Although there is still a certain gap between this IoT system and the actual IoT, once students have completed the above-mentioned basic system development, they can think deeply, improve and expand the above content, and add more functional modules, such as local display of data, continuous transmission of disconnected data, and network construction using LoRaWAN.

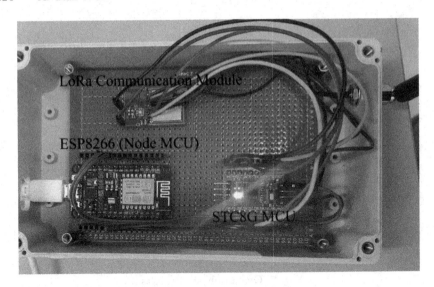

Fig. 9. Gateway module (DTU).

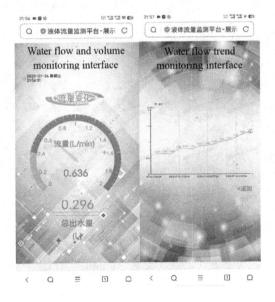

Fig. 10. Data visualization web page.

4 Learning Achievement and Popularization

During the program implementation, we achieved remarkable learning accomplishments that not only gained recognition in competitions but also improved students' comprehensive abilities and knowledge reserves. Firstly, our program won the third prize in the college student physics experiment and technology innovation competition of Zhejiang province, which affirmed our students' skills in hardware design and the Internet of Things. Additionally, our program received approval for the 2023 university-level innovation and entrepreneurship training program, demonstrating the university's recognition and support for our program. This provides more resources and opportunities for our students. These achievements are significant for students' personal development and future science and technology competitions, laying a solid foundation for their future paths.

Subsequently, this project can be transformed from extracurricular project learning into in-class learning projects, such as the integrated design of implementation of IoT course for communication engineering majors, so that more students can be exposed to the practice in the field of IoT, not just Restricted to a small number of students interested in competition. This form of project-based learning serves to bridge the gap between classroom and extracurricular activities, enabling students to integrate theoretical knowledge with practical projects. Additionally, it offers an opportunity for college students to familiarize themselves with emerging communication technology like LoRa, thereby enhancing their overall practical skills and capabilities.

5   Conclusion

The implementation of various communication methods in the system can facilitate students in developing a deep understanding of the different layers within the Internet of Things (IoT) and the underlying principles of communication. The utilization of LoRa communication technology and innovative electronic components exposes students to cutting-edge advancements and stimulates their potential for independent learning. Furthermore, project-based learning nurtures students' practical skills, self-management abilities, teamwork, and interpersonal skills. This project offers students the opportunity to practice their skills, enhance their comprehension of professional knowledge, and achieve the goal of applying their learning effectively.

Through their participation in this project, students can acquire valuable hands-on experience, improve their overall abilities, and make a meaningful contribution to meeting the growing demands of the IoT industry. This project serves as an exemplary model for promoting project-based learning in the field of information technology and aims to guide the development of information technology talents.

References

1. Xu, P.Y.: 5G ushered in a critical period of large-scale development. People's Daily Overseas Ed. **7–10**, 3 (2023). https://doi.org/10.28656/n.cnki.nrmrh.2023.002206
2. Jiang, Z.M.: Development of IT industry in China in the new age. J. Shanghai Jiaotong Univ. (Sci.) **14**(01), 1–24 (2009)

3. Yao, R.H., Li, D., Zhu, J.D.: Analysis of the current status and development trend of the internet of things. Electron. Qual. **07**, 109–114 (2023)
4. Sun, Q.B., Liu, J., Li, S.: Internet of things: summarize on concepts, architecture and key technology problem. J. Beijing Univ. Posts Telecommun. **33**(03), 1–9 (2010)
5. Gan, Q.: LoRa-IoT Network Technology. Tsinghua University Press, Beijing (2021)
6. He, X., Yang, X.P.: Research on the simulation experiment course of "Internet of Things and Sensing Technology" based on project-based learning. Inform.-Res. **01**, 79–81 (2023)
7. Han, T.: The application status and path of project teaching in computer teaching. Adv. Comput. Commun. **4**(3), 119–122 (2023). https://doi.org/10.26855/acc.2023.06.002
8. Zheng, C., Tian, M.: Research on active project-driven learning method based on CDIO. **16**(1), 88–90 (2017). https://doi.org/10.16735/j.cnki.jet.2017.01.037
9. Kang, C.Q., Xiang, D.S., Zhu, L.J.: Practical course of IoT perception based on project learning community. Comput. Educ. **09**, 180–183+188 (2022). https://doi.org/10.16512/j.cnki.jsjjy.2022.09.047
10. Liu, C., Gao, X.Y., He, H.: Theoretical characteristics and practical construction of project learning community. Teach. Adm. **18**, 8–11 (2021)

Enhancing Student Learning in OpenSTEM Labs Through Live Support: The Lab Assist Project

Dhouha Kbaier[✉], Karen Kear, Helen Lockett, Peter Sykes, and Steve Long

The Open University, Milton Keynes, UK
dhouha.kbaier@open.ac.uk

Abstract. This paper presents the Lab Assist project, a two-year initiative at the Open University, focused on enhancing real-time support for students engaged in OpenSTEM Labs (OSL) activities. The project explores the feasibility of real-time support mechanisms. The research includes an in-depth literature review, emphasizing self-regulated learning, live chat technology, cognitive load theory, and real-time collaboration in virtual laboratories. Survey findings from module chairs underscore the diverse experiments benefiting from real-time support, emphasizing the need for flexible solutions aligned with faculty priorities. The paper also outlines pilot live support sessions and future initiatives. Key aspects such as platform selection, staff assignment, scheduling, resource preparation, and feedback collection are discussed in the context of implementing an effective live support system. The paper concludes with a reflection on developing and testing a prototype in 2024, aiming to provide a dynamic, responsive, and accessible support ecosystem within the Open STEM Labs, ultimately enriching the learning journey for all students.

Keywords: Flexible support solutions · Lab Assist project · Live chat technology · Live support · Online STEM education · OpenSTEM Labs (OSL) · Open University (OU) · Pilot live support sessions · Prototype development · Real-time support

1 Introduction

Lab Assist is one of two Enhanced OpenSTEM Labs (OSL) projects aiming to broaden the range of applications and uses of OpenSTEM Labs. The purpose of this two-year funded project is to investigate how enhanced real-time support can be provided to students conducting OpenSTEM Labs activities. Currently, support occurs by a number of mechanisms that are often asynchronous and vary across areas of OSL activities. The concept behind the Lab Assist project is to provide real-time or near-real-time support to students that are having difficulty completing OSL experiments. The project is intended to particularly benefit students with disabilities who may find it more difficult to participate in practical activities without support and also those with additional needs that are a barrier to participation and could contribute to reducing the attainment gap for disadvantaged students. Although the focus is intended to be on students with additional needs, there is potential for broader applicability, depending on what solutions are developed.

The Lab Assist project spans a two-year timeline. The first phase of the project is primarily a research and data gathering exercise and included the trial of a support tool. The objective was to extract information that will guide the development of a real-time support mechanism. We collated and analyzed information about previous real-time support activities in the OSL and the Open University (OU) more widely that might contribute to the project. Then, we investigated possible solutions to provide real-time student support in the OSL and we identified possible solutions to deliver real-time student support through the 'Lab Assist' project. Phase two of the project will focus on the development and deployment of a real-time support system that will be flexible and scalable. The aim is to develop trial solutions for proof of concept by testing real-time support on a variety of modules and evaluating the effectiveness of the trial support solutions. Specifically, the outcomes are envisioned to be one or more systems that will assist students who request and need additional support. Larger scale trials will be carried out with the prototype system(s). There is a desire to incorporate some level of algorithmic approach within associated software, but the project is initially focusing on human support. If software capabilities can be introduced to at least reduce the human workload, then options will be explored.

Throughout the project, we work closely with colleagues with responsibility for student experience and support to ensure that the proposed approach is consistent with wider Faculty's priorities and frameworks. The OSL deliver more than 150 practical learning experiences on more than 40 taught modules in the faculty, providing a key element of our practical teaching and has had more than 55,000 users since 2014.

2 Literature Review

In this section, we summarize the key findings and insights from the literature search conducted as part of the Lab Assist Project. The literature search aimed to explore relevant studies and research related to the project's focus on real-time support for students in practical learning environments, particularly in the context of online STEM labs and software engineering education. The following subsections provide an overview of the literature findings.

2.1 Self-regulated Learning and Help-Seeking

The literature search highlighted the importance of self-regulated learning and help-seeking behaviors in online learning environments. Students in remote or online settings often rely on asynchronous communication methods, such as email and discussion boards, to seek assistance (Kitsantas & Chow, 2007; Koc & Liu, 2016). This asynchronous nature can lead to delays in receiving help, potentially hindering students' progress (Koc & Liu, 2016).

2.2 Live Chat Technology for Academic Help

One significant finding from the literature was the potential of live chat technology to enhance academic help-seeking in higher education, particularly in online and blended learning environments. Students expressed positive responses to live chat technology, highlighting its ability to provide instant, real-time, and convenient assistance (Carter et al., 2017). Compared to traditional face-to-face communication, online learners found live chat to be a valuable alternative (Broadbent, 2020). The use of live chat could bridge the gap in synchronous, private help-seeking between students and teachers in higher education (Cheng and Chou, 2013).

2.3 Cognitive Load Theory

Cognitive Load Theory (CLT) emerged as a crucial concept in the literature search. CLT emphasizes the need to manage cognitive loads effectively to optimize learning outcomes (Kalyuga, 2012). The theory differentiates between intrinsic and extraneous cognitive load, highlighting the importance of minimizing extraneous load through instructional design (Sweller et al., 2011). Strategies to reduce extraneous load include eliminating redundancy, managing split attention, and considering the transiency of information (Kalyuga, 2012).

2.4 Real-Time Collaboration in Virtual Laboratories

The literature revealed studies on real-time collaboration in virtual laboratories, emphasizing the benefits of synchronous interactions for students (Jara et al., 2009). Collaborative e-learning systems that allow students to share experiences while practicing experiments in real-time were discussed (Jara et al., 2009). These findings underscored the potential of real-time support and synchronous interactions in enhancing the learning experience.

The existing literature highlights several potential advantages associated with synchronous interaction in distant educational settings. Synchronous interaction, often facilitated through live chat technology or virtual classrooms, offers real-time communication and collaboration, providing students with immediate access to support and fostering a sense of community (Bülow, 2022; Belt and Lowenthal, 2023). This can be particularly beneficial in situations where timely assistance is crucial, such as during complex experiments or when students face challenges that require immediate clarification.

Furthermore, studies have shown that synchronous interaction can enhance student engagement and satisfaction, creating a more dynamic and interactive learning environment compared to asynchronous communication methods (Broadbent and Lodge, 2021). The immediacy of synchronous interaction can address students' queries promptly, reducing potential delays in their learning progress (Koc & Liu, 2016).

The literature search findings provide valuable insights into the potential impact and benefits of real-time support in online STEM labs, aligning with the Lab Assist Project's goals and objectives. As part of the gathering exercise, we sent a survey to all module chairs who are involved in OSL, so that we could identify the experiments that will benefit from real-time support.

3 Research Methods and Tools

In this section, we provide an overview of the research methods and tools employed in the Lab Assist project, discussing their selection criteria and their contributions to the study's validity and reliability.

3.1 Literature Review

The Lab Assist project initiated with an in-depth literature review focusing on self-regulated learning, live chat technology, cognitive load theory, and real-time collaboration in virtual laboratories. The literature review was chosen as the starting point to establish a theoretical foundation and to understand the existing landscape of real-time support in educational contexts (Booth et al., 2016). By exploring these key areas, we aimed to inform the development of a support system grounded in established educational theories.

The literature review enhances the validity of the study by ensuring that our project aligns with established educational principles (Boote and Beile, 2005). It contributes to reliability by grounding our research in a solid theoretical framework, thus providing a robust foundation for subsequent phases of the project.

3.2 Survey of Module Chairs

A survey was conducted among module chairs to gather insights into experiments within OpenSTEM Labs that could benefit from real-time support. Surveys are a common method for collecting quantitative data and understanding stakeholder perspectives (Ponto, 2015). Surveys were chosen as a quantitative method to collect data from module chairs. They allowed us to understand the diverse nature of OSL activities, identify priorities, and ensure that the project aligns with faculty goals.

The survey contributes to validity by capturing the perspectives of module chairs, who play a pivotal role in curriculum design and implementation. This method enhances reliability by ensuring that the real-time support mechanisms address the actual needs of module chairs and, consequently, the students engaged in OSL activities.

3.3 Pilot Live Support Sessions

The project involved a pilot trial, using Adobe Connect for live support sessions during a specific module (T229 in Mechanical Engineering). Pilot studies are commonly employed to test the feasibility of an intervention before full-scale implementation (Aschbrenner et al., 2022). Adobe Connect was chosen for its real-time communication and screen-sharing features, aligning with the interactive and dynamic nature of educational support (Elekaei, 2022).

The pilot trial enhances the validity of the study by allowing us to assess the effectiveness of live support sessions in a controlled setting. It contributes to reliability by providing insights into potential challenges and facilitating informed adjustments before broader implementation.

3.4 Feedback Collection

Feedback from the pilot T229 live support sessions, including tutor feedback and recommendations, was systematically collected. Systematic feedback collection is a recognized method for gaining insights into the effectiveness of educational interventions and making informed adjustments. It aligns with the need to understand the experiences and challenges faced by both tutors and students during live support sessions.

The systematic collection of feedback enhances the validity of the study by incorporating the perspectives of those directly involved in the pilot sessions. It contributes to reliability by informing iterative improvements based on the experiences and insights gathered from the pilot trial.

4 Key Survey Findings from Module Chairs

The survey conducted among module chairs aimed to identify experiments within OpenSTEM Labs (OSL) that could benefit from real-time support. The survey questions are provided in the appendix. Several key findings emerged. Module chairs identified a variety of experiments conducted within OSL that could potentially benefit from real-time support. These experiments spanned multiple disciplines and highlighted the diverse nature of OSL activities. Module chairs expressed a need for real-time support mechanisms to enhance the learning experience of students engaging in OSL experiments. They emphasized the importance of timely assistance, particularly for complex or challenging experiments. There was a consensus among module chairs that implementing real-time support could positively impact student learning outcomes. They believed that such support could improve understanding, confidence, and overall engagement with OSL activities. Module chairs highlighted the importance of flexibility in designing real-time support solutions. They emphasized the need for solutions that can adapt to the unique requirements of different experiments and accommodate a range of student needs. While there was interest in incorporating algorithmic approaches to support, the initial focus was on providing human support. Module chairs expressed a preference for human assistance but acknowledged the potential benefits of algorithmic assistance in the future. The project's alignment with wider Faculty priorities and frameworks was considered crucial. Module chairs emphasized the need for consistency with the faculty's goals and the importance of collaboration with colleagues responsible for student experience and support. Overall, the survey results provided valuable insights into the potential impact of real-time support within OSL and highlighted the diverse nature of experiments that could benefit from this initiative. The findings will inform the development and implementation of real-time support mechanisms in the Lab Assist project.

5 Pilot Live Support Sessions

Following the survey and analysis, several activities have been selected for focused attention, prioritizing those most likely to benefit from (near) real-time support. These activities were designated as priority 4 or 5 in the real-time support table, considering factors such as inclusion in assessments, pair/group work, multi-stage experiments, and more.

In the provided survey, the priority of activities for real-time support is not explicitly defined in a structured table. However, by examining the responses and comments from module chairs, we can identify some factors and considerations that contribute to the prioritization of activities:

- Assessment weight: Activities with a higher assessment weight may be considered a priority. For example, in the case of S382 (Astrophysics), the group project's write-up contributes to 35% of the Overall Examinable Score (OES), making it a significant component.
- Complexity and difficulty: More complex activities, especially those involving group work or experiments, may be prioritized. Module chairs express a need for real-time support in activities where students work in pairs or groups, as issues in these scenarios could have a more significant impact.
- New or unfamiliar activities: New modules or activities that are being introduced for the first time may be prioritized. Module chairs, such as for the module SM381 (Electromagnetism), express a desire for real-time support in the first run of a new OSL experiment to address unforeseen challenges.
- Accessibility and special requirements: Activities that involve accessibility challenges or special requirements for students, such as those with disabilities or anxiety, are mentioned as priorities for real-time support.
- Real-time experiments with limited slots: Activities where students perform genuine remote experiments in booked slots are considered priorities.
- Time constraints: Activities with short completion time windows or that are expected to be completed quickly may be considered a priority for real-time support. In T193 (Engineering: Frameworks, Analysis, Production), real-time support is valuable for complex activities at the 2nd or 3rd level, where uncertainties may arise in setting up experiments or interpreting output data. This is especially crucial for activities integral to assessments, which are expected to be completed in a short time window.
- Feedback and experience: The feedback received from students and tutors after the initial run of an activity can influence the decision to prioritize real-time support. In S290 (Investigating Human Health and Disease), general feedback indicates that while the tools used in the module are appreciated, some, notably for the ELISA experiment, are perceived as complex by students.

It's important to note that the prioritization of activities for real-time support can vary across modules, and module chairs may consider a combination of these factors to determine the most critical activities for immediate assistance.

5.1 Selection of Activities for Real-Time Support

One such activity chosen for emphasis is T229 (Mechanical engineering: heat and flow), OEL 2.3: Characterizing a wing section (scale 4). Currently, students in this activity can raise queries in the student forum, which are addressed by the forum moderator, the module team, or through direct contact with tutors. Support is provided by both the module team members and Associate Lecturers (ALs), with the forum moderator playing a key role. The introduction of real-time support for this activity would prove especially beneficial for students facing accessibility challenges and those finding it challenging to work effectively in teams. This OEL is conducted in pairs, followed by a group discussion in groups of 3 or 4. Additionally, there is at least one question related to this activity in the assessment TMA02.

To ensure the success of this activity, key factors to focus on include evaluating communication effectiveness within pairs and groups, assessing the allocation of tasks, understanding completion rates and the quality of group discussions, analyzing performance in TMA02, and gauging the engagement and resolution efficiency in the student forum. If real-time support is introduced, careful attention should be paid to the response time for addressing queries, particularly for students with accessibility challenges. This comprehensive evaluation approach aims to enhance the overall learning experience and outcomes for students participating in T229.

5.2 Pilot Trial

The pilot trial introduced an Adobe Connect online room, which was hosted on the Virtual Learning Environment (VLE) of the T229 module, specifically on the Mechanical Engineering: Heat and Flow website, as part of the experiment OEL 2.3: Characterizing a Wing Section. This room, named "OSL Pilot Live Support," was established by Learner and Discovery Services (LDS) Online Services and served as a hub for live support sessions conducted by tutors. Figure 1 and Fig. 2 show the Adobe Connect view during live support sessions for tutors and students, respectively. Throughout the pilot trial, tutors shared the room link with students, a process facilitated by student slot bookings through OSL. The room featured tailored functionalities, such as live chat, with a simplified interface for students, granting them access to interactive discussions. Students had the ability to communicate via chat and voice. In contrast, tutors were equipped with enhanced privileges, including admitting students into the room, arranging students into groups or individual breakout sessions, and facilitating screen-sharing capabilities. The room was designed with specific features, such as live chat, but without the need for recording. It included an end-of-session poll, and tutors had the option to grant screen-sharing permission to students using a secure procedure. Overall, the pilot trial would successfully enhance the learning experience in T229 and other modules by providing a dedicated online space for interactive support and collaboration between tutors and students.

5.3 Cognitive Load Theory Considerations in the Experiment

The design and implementation of the live support sessions in the pilot trial of OEL 2.3: Characterizing a Wing Section in T229 were underpinned by key principles of Cognitive Load Theory. CLT posits that effective learning occurs when the cognitive load imposed on learners aligns with their cognitive capacities. In the context of our experiment, several aspects were considered to optimize the cognitive load for both students and tutors.

- Simplified student interface: To reduce extraneous cognitive load on students, the Adobe Connect interface for students was intentionally streamlined. They were provided with straightforward access to essential features such as live chat and voice communication, focusing on ease of use and minimizing unnecessary complexity.

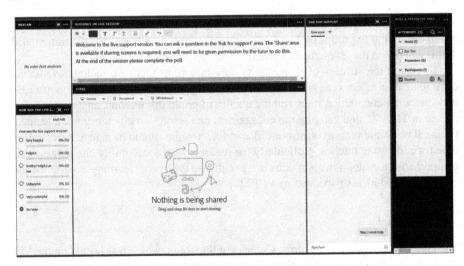

Fig. 1. Tutors' Adobe Connect view during live support sessions.

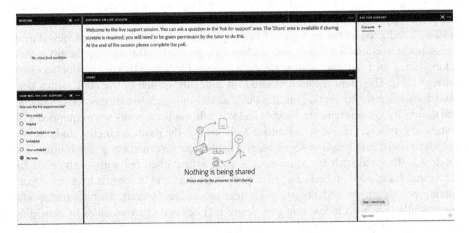

Fig. 2. Students' Adobe Connect view during live support sessions.

- Enhanced tutor privileges: Recognizing the role of tutors as facilitators, the interface for tutors included advanced features and privileges. This aligns with CLT by distributing the cognitive load appropriately—tutors were equipped with the ability to admit students, organize breakout sessions, and manage screen-sharing permissions, facilitating a more interactive and dynamic learning environment.
- Clear communication channels: Effective communication is vital in managing cognitive load. Both tutors and students had designated channels for communication, ensuring a focused and purposeful exchange of information. Live chat and voice communication features contributed to seamless interactions without overwhelming cognitive resources.

- End-of-session poll for feedback: CLT emphasizes the importance of feedback in the learning process. The inclusion of an end-of-session poll in the Adobe Connect room allowed for the collection of valuable feedback. This iterative feedback loop is aligned with CLT principles, promoting continuous improvement in the learning experience.

By consciously incorporating these considerations informed by Cognitive Load Theory, the experiment aimed to create an environment conducive to optimal learning, ensuring that the cognitive load imposed on participants was balanced and supportive of the learning objectives. This explicit reflection on CLT principles underscores the pedagogical foundations guiding the design and execution of the live support sessions.

5.4 Pilot T229 Live Support Sessions Feedback

The pilot T229 live support sessions aimed to assist students in resolving technical issues during experiments. Seven support sessions were offered by two tutors. However, despite students booking slots for experiments, only one student attended a live support session. The reasons behind the low attendance remain unclear as students did not fill out the survey. Tutor feedback indicated that students might not have needed extensive live support because they managed to conduct experiments independently. Positive feedback in the forum chat suggested that students found the recorded video helpful. Tutors recommended providing support, especially during the first experiment when most issues were encountered. Tutors recorded a video of the experiment and suggested using this approach to provide support in the module. However, they noted that being "on-demand" to answer questions was demanding on their time, especially when no students turned up. Tutors suggested gathering students' suggestions on what would help them in the experiment and offering tailored support accordingly. Both tutors recommended scheduling live support during sessions when many students were booked to maximize its effectiveness.

In the next phase of the project, we will explore several key initiatives. Firstly, we will consider the implementation of live support sessions during the initial wind tunnel experiment in T229, capitalizing on the potential benefits of providing immediate assistance to students. Additionally, we aim to further investigate the feasibility of utilizing pop-up messages as a means to offer support during sessions with multiple bookings, ensuring that students receive the help they require when they need it most. Moreover, we will assess the viability of extending the pilot live support sessions to other modules, including S382, SXPS288, and S290, where experiments may also derive significant advantages from real-time assistance.

6 Implementing an Effective Live Support System

Implementing an effective live support system within the Open STEM Labs at the Open University involves several crucial aspects that need careful consideration:

- The choice of the platform for live support sessions is a fundamental step. Adobe Connect has been selected due to its suitability for real-time communication, screen sharing, and text chat features. However, it is essential to remain open to exploring other instant messaging platforms to meet changing needs. Integrating the chosen platform into the Open STEM Labs interface is key for a seamless student experience.
- Assigning qualified staff members to provide live support during scheduled sessions is critical. These staff members may include tutors, project specialists, PhD students, or lab technicians. Proper training and guidance should be provided to ensure they can effectively assist students.
- Creating a clear and accessible schedule for live support sessions is essential. This schedule should be readily available to students to manage their expectations and participation. Additionally, promoting these sessions through module websites, forums, and the OSL booking page is crucial for ensuring students are aware of the support available.
- Preparing necessary resources, such as slides, videos, and demonstrations, in advance of live support sessions enhances the overall learning experience. These resources should be easily shareable with students during sessions.
- Collecting feedback from students after each live support session is vital for continuous improvement. Identifying areas that require enhancement and ensuring students are receiving the assistance they need is an ongoing process.

By addressing these aspects thoughtfully, the Open University can create an effective live support system that enhances the educational experience for students in the Open STEM Labs.

7 Conclusion

In this paper, we discussed the process of implementing a robust and effective live support system within the Open STEM Labs (OSL) at the Open University. Our exploration began with a reflection on the specifications necessary to provide live support sessions, encompassing platform selection, session scheduling, staff assignment, and effective advertising. Recognizing the importance of a user-friendly interface, we also explored functional and technical requirements, including real-time communication, chat functionality, screen sharing, and notifications, while considering compatibility, security, scalability, and accessibility.

The quest to enhance student engagement and satisfaction through live support led us to ponder how to assess its effectiveness. Strategies such as post-session surveys, performance analysis, and monitoring student engagement have emerged as valuable tools in evaluating the impact of live support on learning outcomes and satisfaction.

To implement an effective live support system within the Open STEM Labs at the Open University, we have identified the technical and functional requirements necessary for its success. These requirements form the backbone of a system that promises to enhance the educational experience for our students. Moreover, we investigated the incorporation of a request button for students during OSL activities, emphasizing its functional and technical requisites, integration within the OSL interface, and adherence to accessibility standards. As we look to the future, we are committed to translating these requirements into action. A prototype is currently in development, with plans for rigorous testing in 2024. This iterative approach allows us to refine and tailor the live support system to the specific needs and expectations of our students, ensuring that it not only meets but exceeds their educational support requirements.

To conclude this paper, it is evident that the successful implementation of a live support system requires meticulous planning, adherence to requirements, and a commitment to enhancing the student experience. By weaving these threads together, we lay the foundation for a dynamic, responsive, and effective live support ecosystem within the Open STEM Labs, fostering enhanced learning and facilitating student success. This journey is ongoing, offering opportunities for innovation and continuous improvement. Through this endeavor, we provide a seamless and accessible support system that empowers our students to excel in their STEM studies and reach their academic goals. With continuous improvement at the forefront of our efforts, we are confident that the live support system will play a pivotal role in enriching the learning journey of all those who engage with it.

Appendix

OpenSTEM Labs 'Lab-Assist' Project: Survey to Module presentation chairs.

Feedback from students using the OpenSTEM Labs (OSL) has identified an opportunity to enrich the student experience through tailored real-time support while working in remote teaching labs.

The purpose of the two-year funded project 'Lab-Assist' is to investigate how enhanced real-time support could be provided to students conducting OpenSTEM Labs activities. Currently, support occurs by a number of mechanisms that are often asynchronous and vary across areas of OSL activities.

The concept behind the Lab Assist project is to provide real-time or near-real-time support to students who are having difficulty completing OSL experiments. The project is intended to particularly benefit students with disabilities who may find it more difficult to participate in practical activities without support, and also those with additional needs that are a barrier to participation. The project could contribute to reducing the attainment gap for disadvantaged students. Although the focus is intended to be on students with additional needs, there is potential for broader applicability, depending on what solutions are developed.

If you require any further information, please do not hesitate to contact Dhouha Kbaier who is the lead academic of this project.

Email: dhouha.kbaier@open.ac.uk.

It is greatly appreciated that you take the time to complete this survey. The opinions you provide are valuable and will be considered as one of the first steps in our research and data gathering exercise, in preparation for subsequent trials of one or more support tools.

1. Your name:
2. Which module(s) are you chairing?
3. Please complete the following table. Please copy and paste the table if you are chairing more than one module.

Module Title/code:
How many OSL activities are included in the module?

Activity Name
What type of support is already available for this activity (if any)?
Who is providing the support for this activity (E.g., Associate Lecturers, Module Team members)?
Is the OSL activity included in the module's assessment?
Is the activity likely to benefit from (near) real-time support? Please rate the activity on a scale of 1 to 5 (5 would definitely benefit from real-time support)
Comments/suggestions

4. What are the current metrics you use to measure the success of these OSL activities? If students can complete some specific activities very well without issues, we may prioritise some other activities for the live support.
5. Would you like to share any feedback that you have received from students or tutors regarding the need for additional support in OSL activities?
6. In your opinion, which kinds of activities would benefit most from real-time support, for example in a timetabled session with live support via chat or video conference? Could you please explain why this is important?
7. If real-time support were available, who would benefit and what would be the benefits?
8. How do you think this support could be best implemented? Select one of more of the following options. Do not hesitate to add your suggestions and comments on how a combination of these would be most effective.

☐ Live chat
☐ Adobe Connect Video conference
☐ Email
☐ Telephone
☐ Peer support (students running the experiment at the same time)
☐ Group support (staff member providing support to a group of students conducting the experiment simultaneously)
☐ Pop up message offering live support
☐ Special time slots in the booking system for supported sessions
☐ Separate booking system with special sessions

9. If there were a need to prioritise students who should have access to real-time support, which students should be prioritised, and how could this be done?
10. Would you be interested in participating in a future trial of real-time or near-real time support on your module?
11. Any other information:

Thank you

References

Aschbrenner, K.A., Kruse, G., Gallo, J.J., et al.: Applying mixed methods to pilot feasibility studies to inform intervention trials. Pilot Feasib. Stud **8**, 217 (2022). https://doi.org/10.1186/s40814-022-01178-x

Ayres, P., Sweller, J.: The split-attention principle in multimedia learning. In: Mayer, R.E. (ed.) The Cambridge Handbook of Multimedia Learning, pp. 135–146. Cambridge University Press, Cambridge (2005)

Belt, E.S., Lowenthal, P.R.: Synchronous video-based communication and online learning: an exploration of instructors' perceptions and experiences. Educ. Inf. Technol. **28**(5), 4941–4964 (2023)

Boote, D.N., Beile, P.: Scholars before researchers: on the centrality of the dissertation literature review in research preparation. Educ. Res. **34**(6), 3–15 (2005). https://doi.org/10.3102/0013189x034006003

Booth, A., Sutton, A., Papaioannou, D.: Systemic Approaches to a Successful Literature Review, 2nd edn. Sage, Los Angeles (2016)

Broadbent, J.: The use of instant messaging to support online learning. In: Handbook of Research on Cross-cultural Business Education, pp. 58–75. IGI Global, Hershey (2020)

Broadbent, J., Lodge, J.: Use of live chat in higher education to support self-regulated help seeking behaviours: a comparison of online and blended learner perspectives. Int. J. Educ. Technol. High. Educ. **18**, 17 (2021). https://doi.org/10.1186/s41239-021-00253-2

Bülow, M.W.: Designing synchronous hybrid learning spaces: challenges and opportunities. Hybrid Learn. Spaces, 135–163 (2022)

Carter, M., Lane, A., Golding, V.: Real-time online student support in a blended learning environment. Int. J. Manag. Educ. **15**(3), 236–247 (2017)

Cheng, S.H., Chou, C.Y.: Students' help-seeking behaviors using web-based videoconferencing system within a reciprocal teaching context. Turk. Online J. Educ. Technol. **12**(4), 155–163 (2013)

Elekaei, A.: The use of adobe connect in synchronous online teaching. J. Univ. Teach. Learn. Pract. **19**(2), 60–72 (2022)

Jara, C.A., Candelas, F.A., Torres, F., Dormido, S., Esquembre, F., Reinoso, O.: Real-time collaboration of virtual laboratories through the Internet. Comput. Educ. **52**(1), 126–140 (2009)

Kalyuga, S.: Interactive distance education: a cognitive load perspective. J. Comput. High. Educ. **24**(3), 182–208 (2012)

Kalyuga, S., Ayres, P., Chandler, P., Sweller, J.: The expertise reversal effect. Educ. Psychol. **38**(1), 23–31 (2003)

Koc, S., Liu, X.: Interaction matters: strategies to promote engaged online learning. J. Online Learn. Teach. **12**(1), 52–65 (2016)

Kitsantas, A., Chow, A.: College students' perceived threat and preference for seeking help in traditional, distributed, and distance learning environments. Comput. Educ. **48**(3), 383–395 (2007)

Ponto, J.: Understanding and evaluating survey research. J. Adv. Pract. Oncol. **6**(2), 168–171 (2015). Epub 2015 Mar 1. PMID: 26649250; PMCID: PMC4601897

Sweller, J., Ayres, P., Kalyuga, S.: Cognitive Load Theory. Springer, New York (2011). https://doi.org/10.1007/978-1-4419-8126-4

Frontiers in Educational Digitalization

Human-AI Collaboration: A Study on Anti-ChatGPT Strategies Employed in Innovative Practical Homework Towards "One-Click-Answer" Issue in AIGC

Liu Yiwen[1,2,3], Yang Yahui[1], Fu Jinrong[1], Feng Tao[4], Yin Ting[5], Xiang Yingxi[6], Gao Yanxia[1,2,3], Qu Taiguo[1], and Zhang Xian[1,2,3](✉)

[1] School of Computer and Artificial Intelligence, Huaihua University, Huaihua 418000, China
zx@hhtc.edu.cn
[2] Key Laboratory of Wuling-Mountain Health Big Data Intelligent Processing and Application in Hunan Province Universities, Huaihua 418000, China
[3] Key Laboratory of Intelligent Control Technology for Wuling-Mountain Ecological Agriculture in Hunan Province, Huaihua 418000, China
[4] School of Foreign Languages, Huaihua University, Huaihua 418000, China
[5] Furong School of Xinhong Dong Autonomous County, Huaihua 418000, China
[6] School of Fine Arts and Design, Huaihua University, Huaihua 418000, China

Abstract. ChatGPT as a representative of Artificial Intelligence in Generative Computing (AIGC) has had an impact on higher education. It promotes "human-computer collaboration" in coursework, showing both positive and negative effects. ChatGPT has the potential to provide students with personalized learning support. However, students may become too reliant on these tools and lack independent thinking. Aiming at the above problems, this paper introduces the idea of practical homework resource construction, and provides a series of anti-ChatGPT strategies, which can prevent students ChatGPT's "one-click answer" from the source. By comparing activities such as teaching effectiveness, questionnaires, and talkback interviews conducted in the pilot course, the data illustrate the effectiveness of the methodology.

Keywords: AIGC · Homework Design · Anti-ChatGPT Strategies · Human-AI Collaboration · Teaching Resource Construction

1 Introduction

In November 2022, OpenAI released ChatGPT (Chat Generative Pre-Trained Transformer), a large-scale language generation model based on the Transformer architecture, which drew the attention of global users to the field of AIGC, and was a milestone in the history of AI development [1]. In March 2023, OpenAI provided an upgraded version of the big model-GPT-4 for the ChatGPT Plus service, which has more powerful language capabilities. Major technology companies around the world are actively launching their own AIGC technologies, platforms, and applications, such as Microsoft's NewBee,

W. Hong and G. Kanaparan (Eds.): ICCSE 2023, CCIS 2025, pp. 343–353, 2024.
https://doi.org/10.1007/978-981-97-0737-9_30

Google's Bard, Baidu's Wenxin Yiyin, KDXunfei's Xunfei Xinghuo, and Ali's Tongyi Qianqi [2].

AIGC has become a popular teaching support tool in higher education, and it also promotes the coursework mode from "teacher-student" binary structure to "teacher-machine-student" ternary structure. Compared with offline homework help, AIGC is completely free of time and space constraints, which has significant advantages for students in terms of learning fairness, learning efficiency, personalized learning, etc., and improves the efficiency of teachers' work [3]. AIGC can helps teachers to focus more on providing humanistic care, emotional support and academic guidance for students.

However, it also intensifies the dependence of teachers and students on AIGC, leading to a serious reduction in the function of assignments as a tool for dialog between teachers and students. Some students will use ChatGPT to simply complete their assignments, but the lack of real thinking and understanding of the problem leads to plagiarism and plagiarism. The GPTZero team has launched its latest tools "GPTZero" in 2023 as well as "Origin", which can track a student's writing process to verify that the text was indeed created by that student. But it must be based on the actions and results that the student has taken in order to evaluate the student's behavior. At the same time, borrowing AIGC may lead to copyright infringement issues [4]. Therefore, this study provides a series of anti-ChatGPT strategies based on the known defects of ChatGPT by means of "human-computer co-creation", which can prevent students from obtaining answers by ChatGPT from the source, and thus assist teachers in obtaining the real learning situation and adjusting teaching strategies in time. This will help teachers to obtain the real learning situation and adjust teaching strategies in time to empower students.

2   Related Work

2.1   Human-Machine Collaboration

Human-machine collaboration means that humans and machines work together to create content in a collaborative manner. The differences between humans and machines make each take on the corresponding creative tasks, and the two complement each other's strengths and weaknesses, and mutually beneficial symbiosis [5]. With the development of big data technology, the machine's "natural" weaknesses are exposed. And it is difficult to guarantee the quality of the knowledge and information produced by AI due to the natural deficiencies of algorithms and models, which promotes the basis of human-machine collaboration.

As shown in Fig. 1, the structure of coursework in AIGC has two human-computer synergies, "teacher-computer" and "student-computer", whose goals are not the same. Teachers want ChatGPT to assist with questions that will not be easily solved by Chat-GPT, while students want to ask ChatGPT to get the answers quickly. Therefore, for the teacher, the text $C(x)$ is obtained by searching x on ChatGPT, and then after personal processing, the text $C'(x)$ is finally generated, which is the text published to the students. The "teacher-machine" co-creation can be expressed by the following Eq. (1):

$$C'(x) = C(x) + Input(s) \tag{1}$$

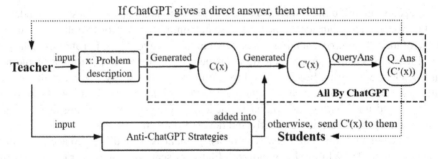

Fig. 1. Human-machine Collaboration for Homework

where s denotes the strategies and Input denotes the part modified by the teacher, which can be understood as removing the "noise" in AIGC. The higher the comprehension difficulty caused by T to ChatGPT, the more the answer given by ChatGPT based on C'(x), i.e., the "answer" obtained by the student, deviates from the correct answer. The more the answer given by ChatGPT based on C'(x), i.e. the "answer" obtained by the student, deviates from the correct answer.

Therefore, in this case, there will be a disconnect between the "student-machine", students will unconsciously doubt whether the answer of AIGC is correct, so that they need to verify whether the generated results are correct, and if the error must be corrected or replaced Output. "Student-machine" co-creation This can be expressed in Eq. (2):

$$Ans(C'(x)) = QueryAns(C'(x)) - Output(s^{-1}) \qquad (2)$$

2.2 ChatGPT Defects

ChatGPT uses the Transformer model, a deep neural network architecture specifically designed to process sequential data such as text, Transformer and introduces a Self-Attention mechanism that allows the model to efficiently capture contextual information in the input text. The hybrid approach of using self-supervised learning in the pre-training phase and supervised learning methods in the fine-tuning phase enables ChatGPT to perform well in a variety of NLP tasks. However, ChatGPT is a generalized natural language processing model, and although it performs well in many tasks, it is not perfectly adapted to all tasks. Examples include domain-specific specialized knowledge understanding, common-sense reasoning, content screening for disinformation and bias, long-form article generation, and accurate answer generation.

3 New Practical Homework Design

3.1 Scientific Research Enlightenment

First of all, the ability to read scientific literature is the key to developing innovative thinking and independent research skills [6]. By reading, analyzing and understanding scientific literature, students can examine problems from multiple perspectives and come up with innovative solutions when solving practical problems.

Second, scientific literature reading initiation helps students build a solid foundation of knowledge. They can access the latest research findings and information on the cutting edge of their disciplines, staying competitive in their academic and professional fields.

Finally, this hands-on type of assignment helps students develop information literacy and academic integrity. Students need to learn how to effectively search, evaluate, and cite scientific literature, which helps them develop information literacy. In addition, colleges and universities can emphasize academic integrity by ensuring that students cite and reference literature correctly and develop academic integrity.

On top of that, this hands-on type of assignment is difficult to replace with tools such as ChatGPT. While AI can aid with literature searching and abstract generation, the ability to deeply understand and analyze scientific literature and apply it to specific problems still requires human critical thinking and judgment.

3.2 Explaining Knowledge Like a Teacher

Video assignments are designed to encourage students to create self-produced learning supplemental resources that explain knowledge from the teacher's perspective. In the current blended learning environment, teacher-made micro-lessons have become an indispensable learning resource. Although these micro-teachings are usually excellent in terms of content creation and sound content, students still tend to be passive recipients of knowledge, and there is a gap between their understanding and true comprehension.

The value of micro-teaching assignments lies in their ability to break through the framework of knowledge established by traditional micro-teaching or textbooks, encouraging students to take the initiative to deepen, understand, organize and reproduce existing knowledge. Students in this process are no longer simple "receivers", but active "explorers", they become "teachers", their understanding of knowledge in the form of microclasses They become "teachers" and pass on their understanding of knowledge to others in the form of microclasses. The process of planning, designing and producing micro-courses provides students with all-round opportunities to show their comprehensive quality and creative ability.

3.3 Designing Questions Like a Teacher

After the course has progressed to a certain stage, the instructor may make a request for students to create their own questions in accordance with the requirements of the specified example questions. Students are strictly prohibited from copying the original questions from the Internet or question banks, and are required to design the questions according to the requirements of the new question types and provide the answers and explanations of the corresponding questions. This process of independent topic design will fundamentally change students' learning attitude from "passive" to "active", so that they can play the role of the teacher, review what they have learned, and focus on the key points of teaching.

When students will need to deeply understand the basic knowledge points of the whole textbook, they may further study or choose to abandon the points that are still unclear. Although plagiarism is strictly prohibited, students usually refer to question ideas on the Internet when searching for relevant questions to enrich their creative ideas and better produce original questions. In the process of question design, students will further consolidate the knowledge they have acquired, and through the process of learning from the past, their mastery of the course knowledge will be enhanced.

3.4 Understanding Concepts Deeply from Practice

By assigning practical-type assignments, universities are able to achieve three key objectives: first, to enhance students' deep understanding of course concepts; second, to develop students' problem-solving and practical skills; and, finally, to improve students' self-confidence and self-directed learning habits. This type of practical assignment bridges the gap between theory and practical application and provides students with valuable career preparation opportunities.

Moreover, this practical type of homework is difficult to be replaced by tools such as ChatGPT. While AI has potential for information retrieval and generation, it still cannot fully simulate the experience of students engaging in real-world tasks and facing challenges and problems firsthand. The key to hands-on assignments is hands-on student engagement and reflection, which cannot be automated. Therefore, this type of assignment remains indispensable for the development of practical skills and synthesis.

4 Anti-ChatGPT Strategies

The implementation of homework should be based on the ChatGPT flaws, with some qualifying strategies to stop students from being able to easily access the answers.

And the importance of academic integrity is emphasized in the course by stressing the importance of academic honesty and making it clear that the use of an external tool to generate an entire video is unethical and may be punished.

4.1 Strategies for Homework Requirements

a. Clarify assignment requirements: Clearly state the constraints of the homework instructions, including word count, content, formatting, and reference resources.
b. Restrictions on Resource Use: Clearly state which resources are allowed and which are prohibited. Either directly give or students indicate the source of the information. For example, use of course materials and specific academic databases may be permitted.
c. Design open-ended questions: Ask open-ended questions, encourage students to think independently and respond creatively, and create PowerPoint presentations to be presented on stage and evaluated by each other, so that the answers are not easily copied or searched for.
d. Anti-cheating technologies: Use anti-cheating and data analytics technologies such as trajectory analysis and anti-cheating browser plug-ins on the eLearning platform or assignment management system to ensure that students are honest and independent in their assignments.
e. Regular interaction: Engage with students on a regular basis to discuss their progress and difficulties, and provide support and guidance to ensure that they are actively engaged in their assignments and understand the tasks.
f. Topic Selection Lock: Allows students to select topics relevant to the course to enhance their engagement and creativity.

4.2 Strategies for Homework Groups

a. Clarify collaboration requirements: In the assignment instructions, explicitly ask students to work in small groups or in a hierarchical way to accomplish the task. Explain how they need to divide up the work and clarify the responsibilities and contributions of each member.
b. Dependency design: Design tasks so that students' work is dependent, meaning that one student's work needs to be based on another student's results. In this way, students need to collaborate and coordinate rather than simply use tools such as ChatGPT to get answers.
c. Regular feedback: Students are encouraged to share their progress and problems by communicating and discussing regularly with their group members or partners.
d. Group assessment: Introduce group assessment or peer assessment to allow students to evaluate each other's contributions and performance in collaboration. This motivates students to participate actively and reduces the likelihood of relying on external tools.
e. Instructional interactions: Teachers can regularly interact with students working in small groups or hierarchies to provide guidance, feedback, and suggestions to ensure that they are making progress in the collaborative process.

5 Homework Application Examples

The course teaching team takes the Principles of Computer Composition as a pilot course. In the context of AIGC, this teaching team mostly set up homework quizzes with practical types and strategies, using the free version of ChatGPT 3.5, which is commonly used by students, as a testing tool, aiming to encourage students to think more, question more, and evaluate more.

5.1 Example 1: Academic Reading Comprehension

Problem Description: Download the PDF attachment and carefully read the full text of the review paper "Review and Reflections on Computing Architecture Research" in Science China: Information Science 2022 (doi: https://doi.org/10.1360/SSI-2021-0163). There are 20 blanks and 6 questions.

Answer Limitations: Each blank can only be answered with vocabulary from the original text (including case-sensitive letters), with a maximum of 4 Chinese characters or a maximum of 6 English characters or numbers, and no mixing of Chinese and English.

Decipherment: Compared with the traditional selection of fragments, the question selected the whole paper comprehension, students can really feel what academic reading is probably like. At the same time to take the anti-ChatGPT strategy students can only AIGC tools as an aid.

- Strategy #1 is to select specific specialized areas of knowledge to understand, the content of the paper is mainly focused on the historical development of the computer general architecture to develop a narrative, and the selection of words that need to fill in the blanks are terminology, to prevent the ChatGPT comprehension.

- Strategy #2 is that the topic is a long article, a total of five chapters, 22 pages, 25,000+ Chinese characters. Students had to locate at least the general scope of the test points in terms of natural paragraphs before they could use them as input for ChatGPT to solve the questions;
- Strategy #3 was that a certain fill-in-the-blank as well as the question answer had to use the vocabulary of the original text, and there was a word limit, which was guaranteed to limit the paraphrasing ability of the AIGC. Through the above types of scientific research questions made a guarantee for student empowerment in terms of quality and strategy.

Evaluation: The fill-in-the-blank questions naturally paraphrased by ChatGPT are easily accessed by the software itself, and the GPT paraphrase retains the word "different", so that it is easier to find out the answer. However, after the teacher's operation of "reducing, changing words and picking special nouns", it interferes with ChatGPT's judgment. As a result, ChatGPT was unable to obtain a standardized answer at this point, and even deviated far from it.

5.2 Example 2: Theoretical Knowledge Encoding

Problem Description: This is Learning to compute serial solving multiplication problems using the idea of *one multiplier in the original code*.

Answer Limitations
The program needs to meet the following requirements:

a) the multiplication operator (*) and the division operator (/) cannot be used, and a zero will be awarded if they are used;
b) library functions other than scanf(), printf(), and abs() may not be used and will receive zero points;
c) addition and subtraction ($\pm$), modulo (%), bitwise operations, logical operators, loops, arrays, basic data types, etc. are allowed (Table 1).

Table 1. Data Comparison of Teaching Activities

Sample	Group1	Group2
Input	+35, 5	−987654,1234567
Ouput	10101111	−1000110111110010101101111000010100101010

Decipherment: This practice problem required a coded implementation of the classical computer algorithm of one-bit multiplication of serial algorithms in the original code, which is the process of empowering students to move from mathematical projections to programming practice. In order to adopt the anti-ChatGPT strategy, the assignment adopted the following specific strategies:

- Strategy #1 is in the form of a picture that requires strict adherence to the process.
- Strategy #2 is to limit the range of programming symbols and functions, e.g., multiplication operation symbols are not allowed.
- Strategy #3 is to add a large number of test cases in the background for serial one-bit multiplication for a large number of large numbers.
- Strategy #4 is to increase the dichotomies of machine understanding by using a number of proprietary conceptual acronyms.

Evaluation: The code generated by ChatGPT runs correctly only within the 32-bit multiplication result, and the large-digit test cases all run incorrectly. Similarly, other the same type of theory to practice programming, such as into the IEEE754 floating-point conversion, floating-point arithmetic, etc.

5.3 Example 3: Application Recording and Presentation

Problem Description: Small Pet Battle Game

a) Use the ChatGPT tool to generate a meaningful C language version of the small pet battle single game, each player is required to have a user ID.
b) Under the condition of not being able to modify the source code, by modifying the values stored in the generated EXE application in a).
c) Mark on the screenshot where all your modified values are stored, and all the methods, and make a report on the stage.

Answer Limitations

a) at least 5 levels of VIP bonus attributes, each small pet has at least 5 different attributes and at least 1 kind of special skills, and the requirements of the battle time to make the fight is not less than 13 ends, and can be a detailed record of the enemy and us. The battle logs of both pets can be recorded in detail.
b) (1) modify the user ID to your full school number; (2) directly obtain the highest level of VIP without recharging; (3) modify various values so that the battle rounds will directly end in 1 round.
c) Other students can raise their hands at any time to raise their doubts, and all students who interact actively will get extra points.

Evaluation
In question a), ChatGPT directly gives the prompt "Please note that this is just a simple example, you can further extend and improve it according to the requirements and game rules.". However, the specific implementation still needs to be done by students themselves.

   In question b), the answer given is rather surprising, prompting the user to say that "it is usually not feasible to modify the data in an executable file (EXE) that has already been generated without being able to modify the source code", with the reason given being that "It is a complex task that may require specialized tools and skills".

In question c), GhatGPT outright refused, giving the reason "I'm sorry, but as a text chat AI model, I can't provide you with actual screenshots, demos, or reports."

6 Teaching Effectiveness

6.1 Data Comparisons

The teaching class of the pilot course of Computer Composition Principles was divided into two groups, and both the control group (79 students) and the experimental group (79 students). In order to reflect the fairness of the teaching data, most of the cases are the same for both groups. Such as major, teacher, syllabus, basic practice homework and exams. The ratio of difficulty of the exams from high, medium to low is 3:5:2.

The experimental group experienced anti-ChatGPT practice assignments to strengthen and empower them during the course, while the control group supplemented their experience at the end of the course. The data collection and effectiveness of the teaching and learning platform were analyzed. As can be seen in Table 2, the experimental group's learning motivation was significantly improved, the number of platform exchanges increased significantly, and the course objectives were achieved to a higher degree.

Table 2. Comparison of Learning Performance

Groups	MOOC studies (times)	Topic Response (times)	Midterm Exam (score)	Classroom Performance (score)	Final exam (score)
CG	197	14	69	22	72
EC	345	31	82	32	83
RCG	60.9%	39.6%	54.8%	68.6%	79.5%

Convention CG = control group, EG = experimental group, RCG = ratio of CG to EG.

6.2 Questionnaires

In order to investigate the teaching effectiveness of the "human-computer collaboration" practical assignments in the teaching class, a questionnaire survey was conducted regularly with all students in both groups, and the results showed that most of the students had a positive view on this kind of anti-ChatGPT open problems (Table 3).

Table 3. Comparison of Questionnaire Results (Partial)

No.	Topics	Options	CG	EG	DCE
1	Do you regularly use ChatGPT responses as a reference when doing other coursework?	Frequency	55.7	57.0	−1.3
		Never	32.9	29.1	+3.8
		Somtimes	11.4	13.9	−2.5
2	Do you trust the answers given by ChatGPT?	Trust, it is correct	79.8	7.6	+72.2
		Distrust, it's for reference only	20.3	92.4	−72.2
3	What are your thoughts on practical homework questions with changes? **(multiple)**	[A] Thinking in many dimensions is difficult	88.6	74.7	+13.9
		[B] Found the ChatGPT helpful	93.7	65.8	+27.9
		[C] (If I find it helpful) I'll still build on AIGC!	21.5	60.8	−39.2
		[D] Proactive in-depth understanding of additional knowledge	26.6	54.4	−27.9
		[E] Actively discusses unintelligible content with teachers	16.5	29.1	−12.7

Convention DCE = Difference between CG and EG

6.3 Discussion

This work is part of the curriculum resource development, which continues to add manual modifications to AIGC to prevent students from being able to easily generate answers through the AIGC tool. In addition to this, the teaching team found the following effects:

a) Using AIGC to monitor previous assignments and re-monitoring the difficulty of assignments through the accuracy of the AIGC rubric.
b) Use AIGC to detect whether there are wrong test cases in previous programming assignments and analyze whether the AIGC tool has easier solutions.
c) When redeveloping new homework resources, use the AIGC tool to measure whether the correct answer or code can be generated, and if it can be generated, review the new interfering statements until AIGC cannot understand the answer.
d) Students will have a greater sense of achievement and confidence when they have accomplished a task that cannot be solved even by the AIGC tool through their own efforts, and they will be more confident that they have the ability to challenge more difficult tasks in the future.

7   Conclusion

Under the impact of AIGC on course education, this paper not only generates homework resources with the help of ChatGPT, but also uses ChatGPT as a testing tool to increase the means of interference, which makes it difficult to obtain the answers to the original questions directly through ChatGPT. In this way, the homework mechanism is more inclined to the form of combining theory and practice, which can not only eliminate the plagiarism phenomenon of the vast majority of students, but also grasp the real learning situation, especially the flipped classroom teaching for student empowerment.

However, the public foundation questions of the coursework are still the bottom core of knowledge, with a single way of asking questions and difficulties in transforming them, so it is not possible to prevent AIGC from passing the answers to all the questions. Therefore, teachers usually also need to educate students more respect for academic integrity, the AIGC tool as a personalized learning tutoring assistant, knowledge and skills still have to be their own have to go deeper understanding and mastery.

Acknowledgment. We are very thankful that this study is supported by Huaihua University Teaching Reform Project (HHXYJG-202305); Teaching Reform Research Project of Hunan Province (HNJG-2019-825 and HNJG-2023-0925); Project of Hunan Provincial Social Science Foundation (21JD046); the Hunan Provincial Social Science Achievement Review Committee Project (XSP2023JYC125); the Hunan Provincial Degree and Postgraduate Teaching Reform Research project (2021JGYB212).

References

1. Zhu, J.J.: The challenges and responses to the regulation of disinformation brought by generative artificial intelligence: upon the application of ChatGPT. J. Comp. Law **2023**(4), 1–24 (2023)
2. Deng, J., Lin, Y.: The benefits and challenges of ChatGPT: an overview. Front. Comput. Intell. Syst. **2023**(2), 81–83 (2023)
3. Yang, Z.K., Wang, J., Wu, D., et al. Exploring the impact of ChatGPT/AIGC on education and strategies for response. J. East China Normal Univ. (Educ. Sci.) **41**(07), 26–35 (2023)
4. Taecharungroj, V.: "What can ChatGPT do?", Analyzing early reactions to the innovative AI chatbot on Twitter. Big Data Cogn. Comput. **7**, 35 (2023)
5. Wang, L.Y., Du, J., Xiong, R.X.: Human-machine co-creation: a new paradigm for the development of digital educational resources based on AIGC. Mod. Distance Educ. Res. **35**(05), 12–21 (2023)
6. Wang, S., Scells, H., Koopman, B., Zuccon, G.: Can "ChatGPT write a good Boolean query for systematic review literature search?", arXiv arXiv:2302.03495 (2023)

A Study on Digital Literacy and Skills Improvement Paths of College Students

Jing Wang[✉] and Tao Liu

Anhui Polytechnic University, Wuhu 241000, China
wjauts@163.com

Abstract. In the context of the digital era, it has become a global consensus to enhance digital literacy for all. As the main force of socialist builders and successors, it is the general trend for college students to improve their digital literacy. This paper analyzes the current problems in college students' digital literacy and skills education, discusses the path to improve college students' digital literacy and skills, builds the basic course objectives and course contents of college students' digital literacy in line with school-running characteristics and positioning, and carries out course teaching with modular and thematic ideas. The digital literacy skills of college students are evaluated through multiple assessment methods, and the evaluation results provide a reference for the evaluation and promotion of digital literacy ability.

Keywords: Digital Literacy · General Technology · Ability Model · Evaluation System

1 Introduction

In 1994, Israeli scholar Eshet-Alkalai proposed the conceptual framework of digital literacy, including image-image literacy, re-creation literacy, branch literacy, information literacy, and social-emotional literacy [1]. Paul Gilster first used the term digital literacy in 1997, defining it as "the ability to understand information and, more importantly, to evaluate and integrate information in the different formats that computers can provide" [2]. In the Program of Action to Improve Digital Literacy and Skills for All, China points out that "Citizens' digital literacy and skills are a collection of a series of qualities and abilities that citizens in digital society should possess in their study, work and life, such as digital acquisition, production, use, evaluation, interaction, sharing, innovation, security and ethics." [3]. College students are the main force of social construction, and comprehensively improving their digital literacy is the most urgent requirement for the survival and development of the digital society. Digital literacy of college students has brought great challenges to the education system [4]. At present, the research on digital literacy of college students mainly focuses on the framework, influencing factors and evaluation indicators of digital literacy [5], but less practice on improving digital literacy ability. How to adopt flexible and comprehensive learning methods is of great strategic significance to enhance the digital literacy ability of college students. Through setting

W. Hong and G. Kanaparan (Eds.): ICCSE 2023, CCIS 2025, pp. 354–363, 2024.
https://doi.org/10.1007/978-981-97-0737-9_31

up digital literacy courses in colleges and universities, implementing digital literacy general education, professional teachers carrying out disciplinary digital literacy education, implementing digital literacy education project practice, and combining theory and practice, the best practice effect can be achieved.

Based on the construction of curriculum resources in the early stage, this paper carries out teaching reform, reconstructs teaching content, innovates digital literacy practice content, and establishes multiple ability evaluation system, which provides thinking for improving digital literacy skills and evaluating digital literacy ability of college students. The main contributions of this paper are as follows:

(1) Compared and analyzed the existing problems of digital literacy education for college students, and proposed a model of digital literacy ability for college students based on three-tier structure, which considered the school-running orientation and school-running characteristics of our university;
(2) Based on the three-tier digital literacy ability model, the curriculum objectives are designed, the teaching resource library of the course "College Students' Digital Literacy Foundation" is reconstructed, and the curriculum teaching and practice are carried out with the general idea of modularization, specialization and case-based, and the curriculum is assessed through multiple assessment mechanisms;
(3) Put forward the mechanism of curriculum continuous improvement to provide ideas and references for future curriculum teaching reform.

The rest of this paper is organized as follows: In Sect. 2, it briefly reviews the problems faced by digital literacy education of college students. Section 3 introduces the teaching system of Digital Literacy Foundation for college students, and Sect. 4 introduces the curriculum evaluation system. Section 5 gives a summary of this paper.

2 Problems Faced by College Students in Digital Literacy

In the context of the digital age, college students are exposed to a lot of digital technology every day, but it does not mean that they are proficient in digital technology. According to the survey data [3], college students' self-assessed digital literacy is generally good, but their content and creative ability are their weaknesses, and they do not have enough digital readiness to adapt to the online learning environment. The daily use time of college students' digital devices only has a significant negative relationship with information and data, content and creation. From the perspective of current educational practice, digital literacy education still focuses on resources, information search and acquisition, and does not highlight the orientation of digital innovation ability, which is mainly reflected in the following aspects.

2.1 Insufficient Access to Digital Content

Students' acquisition of digital content is mostly for entertainment, and less involves original content. In the process of acquiring knowledge in professional fields, there is a simple choice of tools, and students are accustomed to general search engines such as Baidu and Google, and lack of understanding and use of scientific and technological paper retrieval tools in professional fields. Regardless of the use of scientific and technological periodical databases such as "CNKI", students are also limited to graduation projects, and they cannot use digital resources for exploratory learning.

2.2 Inadequate Use of Digital Content Design Tools

In terms of text, forms, presentations, multimedia production and other operational levels, students have different levels of mastery. The main reason is that the application of theoretical knowledge of digital literacy to practice is insufficient, and fewer students can skillfully use tools to reorganize digital resources and choose appropriate media for output and expression. Four years down, the paper will not write, PPT will not do, table data will not calculate and other phenomena are widespread.

2.3 Lack of Comprehensive Understanding of Digital General Technology

Digital literacy is a concept born in the background of "digitalization". In the process of understanding the concept of digital literacy, accompanied by a series of information technology development, it has its era background and knowledge comprehensiveness. Students are only familiar with the background knowledge of the field, and have insufficient knowledge of general technology in the current digital context.

2.4 Weak Critical and Innovative Consciousness

In the digital environment, the understanding of information and public opinion lacks a critical attitude, and it is easy to be influenced by ulterior motives. Some students lack a sense of social responsibility, hold an indifferent attitude in the face of public opinion, and even inadvertently play a role in promoting false information, bringing adverse effects to society. At the same time, the absence of professional education leads to the lack of context, which makes digital skills lack the soil for application, problem solving and reflection, and thus it is difficult to transform digital literacy and skills into lasting creativity in specific disciplines. Digital literacy should be applied to specific life, work, study and innovation scenarios.

To sum up, the concept of digital literacy is technical, contemporary and comprehensive. Combined with the school-running positioning and actual situation of our university, this paper summarizes the connotation involved in the foundation of digital literacy of college students on the basis of existing research, and defines it as: general literacy that can use digital tools to acquire digital content; Creative literacy capable of using critical and creative thinking to design and express digital content; Have the cross-literacy to communicate and collaborate with people in appropriate ways across multiple disciplines. On this basis, the paper puts forward the curriculum ability model of College Students' Digital Literacy Foundation based on three levels of literacy, constructs the evaluation index system combining theory and practice, and the evaluation results will affect the continuous improvement of curriculum teaching.

3 Teaching System of College Students' Digital Literacy Foundation

3.1 Reconstructing the Content of Basic Digital Literacy Courses

Build Personalized Digital Resources

The Program of Action to Improve the Digital Literacy and Skills of the whole People puts "enriching the supply of high-quality digital resources" at the top of the seven tasks, and the construction of digital resources directly determines the improvement effect. On the basis of the existing high-quality digital resources such as Chinese university MOOCs, Fanya general education, and National Smart Education Platform, we can further empower the construction of course resources through the construction of courses on the learning platform to ensure that teachers and students can obtain, sort out, integrate and store beneficial information comprehensively and efficiently.

The resource library is a collection of text, pictures, videos, animations, cases, and exploratory reading materials, which can meet the various learning needs of students at different levels and with different majors. The resource library also retains the relevant resources of the original "College Computer Foundation" course, which provides a learning reference for students with weak foundation.

Build a Competency Literacy Model based on Modularity

The competency model of digital literacy in this paper refers to the certification standards of Digital Capability (DCLC) Level 1 and Level 2 by Computer Education Research Association of Chinese Universities. Based on theory and practice, the course teaching content is divided into three modules, as shown in Fig. 1.

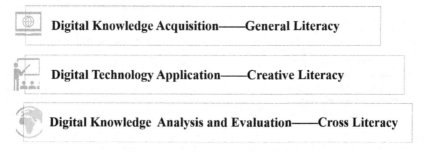

Fig. 1. Three Modules of the Course

Among them, the teaching goal of the general literacy module is to improve the ability of digital retrieval; The teaching goal of creative literacy is to master the ability of digital information analysis, design, evaluation, communication and cooperation. The goal of cross-literacy is to master the digital field of general knowledge, to be able to accurately express the cross-knowledge technology involved in the profession, to be able to identify the digital security ethics and moral norms in the field. The specific curriculum ability model is shown in Fig. 2.

General Literacy	Creative Literacy	Cross Literacy
• General Search Engine • Academic paper retrieval	• Word Processing • Form Processing • PowerPoint • Multimedia Design • Communication and Collaboration	• Digital General Knowledge Technology • Digital Security Ethics • Digital Security Laws and Regulations

Fig. 2. Curriculum Ability Model

Construct Thematic General Knowledge Case Resources

Digital literacy in cross literacy covers the content of six topics. Including: database, big data, cloud computing, Internet of Things, artificial intelligence, blockchain. Thematic case teaching is adopted to organically combine general technology with specific cases, strengthen students' absorption and mastery of new knowledge and skills, and improve students' general literacy. The cases covered by each topic are shown in Fig. 3.

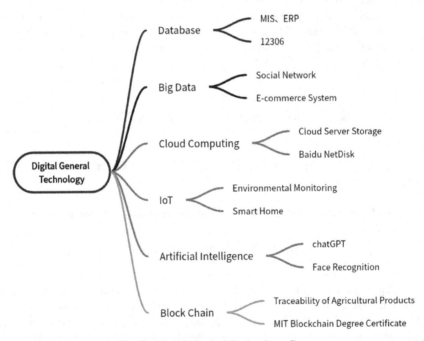

Fig. 3. Digital General Technology Case

Continuous Improvement of Course Resources

The information assisted teaching platform can collect all kinds of digital files created by students, which not only provides an open environment for students' learning, practice and creation, but also ensures adequate resource scheduling and sharing. At the same time, after multiple iterations, the resource library will meet the multiple needs of teaching, scientific research, experimental practice and other requirements, and the analysis results will also play a role in the continuous improvement of subsequent teaching. The continuous improvement mechanism of course resources is shown in Fig. 4.

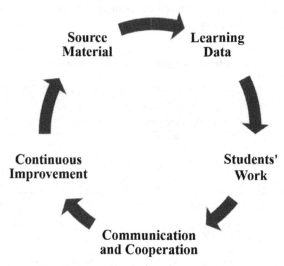

Fig. 4. Continuous improvement mechanism

3.2 Innovative Digital Literacy Practices

Experimental Content Setting

The original course practice mainly focused on the use of operating systems and office automation software. Under the new situation, the experimental content closely follows the digital requirements, and six additional experimental contents are added, including: the search of digital resources, the use of multimedia software, the investigation of digital general knowledge technology, digital communication and collaboration, digital security and laws and regulations and other digital literacy content experiments.

Acceptance Form of Experimental Results

The experimental results are an important part of digital literacy teaching practice and management guidance. The practice of basic digital literacy courses transforms tool orientation into ability orientation, and guides students to effectively achieve learning goals in the digital environment, including reading and understanding media, reproducing or editing data and images with technical means, evaluating and analyzing new knowledge, etc.

According to the different experimental contents, different acceptance forms are set up. The general literacy part mainly involves the use of retrieval tools, and the experimental results are mainly the screenshots of retrieval; The part of creative literacy mainly involves the use of office automation software and multimedia production software tools, and the experimental results are submitted in the form of works; The cross-literacy part mainly expresses the understanding of general technology through communication and collaboration, and the experimental results are mainly based on research reports. Finally, students design and evaluate the content learned in the early stage, and submit a comprehensive practice report on digital literacy in the form of a big assignment. The corresponding relationship between experimental content and submission form of experimental results is shown in Table 1:

Table 1. Experimental content and results

NO.	Experiment Content	Experimental Result
1	Configuration and use of Operating System, Browser and Search Engine	Operation Result Screenshot
2	Document Processing and Academic Paper Typesetting	Design Works & Lab Report
3	Spreadsheet Processing (Chart Visualization) and Presentation Design	Design Works & Lab Report
4	Image and Video Editing	Design Works & Lab Report
5	Digital Technology General Knowledge Application	Investigation Report
6	Digital Communication Collaboration Security and Legal Regulations	Investigation Report
7	Integrated Application of Digital Literacy	Big Project

4   Curriculum Evaluation System

4.1   Curriculum Evaluation System and Evaluation Content

According to the three abilities of digital universal literacy, creative literacy and cross literacy, the curriculum can construct three levels of evaluation system.

The first level of evaluation is students' daily performance, which mainly comes from online and offline teaching, course learning, research learning, professional presentation and students' daily expression. The evaluation is mainly based on the data of the online teaching platform. By setting different proportions, the platform can directly export the peacetime score after the teaching.

The second level of evaluation is the evaluation of students' works. For different projects and topics, students are required to carry out systematic learning of digital post-production, image output and communication of multimedia information, so that students can master the visual communication skills of images and improve the ability of visual expression of information. By teaching the method of document design thinking, it helps students get rid of the low aesthetic level and no new presentation. By learning the design, production and application of presentation, it helps students master the methods and skills of acquiring, processing and integrating multimedia materials.

The third level of evaluation is the comprehensive application ability of cross-fusion. Talents in the digital age are characterized by the same liberal arts and science, strong adaptability, based on the professional course learning at the same time, but also have the ability to cross general knowledge. Through a comprehensive case, the knowledge in this field is combined with digital general technology, and the skills of information retrieval, utilization, evaluation, analysis and integration are skillfully applied in specific digital learning situations, so as to improve the digital innovation ability of students to solve practical problems by using digital technologies or tools in digital learning situations.

4.2 Evaluation Method

Formulate assessment methods according to the curriculum objectives and assessment contents. The scores of general literacy, creative literacy and cross literacy accounted for 30%, 30% and 40% respectively. The content, basis and account of assessment are shown in Table 2. Combined with the data of the three aspects, the total score of this course is obtained, which can be used as a quantitative index to measure the level of students' digital literacy ability. For those who have the ability to learn, DCLC Level 1 and Level 2 certification can be recommended.

Table 2. Assessment Content and Proportion

Capability	Assessment Content	Assessment Proportion
General Literacy	Classroom Performance, Homework, Online Platform Learning	30%
Creative Literacy	Score Works or Reports Submitted According to Practice	30%
Cross Literacy	Final Submission of Comprehensive Assignment Status Score	40%

5 Conclusion

The digital age has raised the demand for digital literacy to an unprecedented level. As the main force of national development, college students' digital literacy level is directly related to national development and social progress. This paper analyzes the problems faced by contemporary college students' digital literacy, and on this basis puts forward the practical path to improve college students' digital literacy. By offering digital literacy courses, students are systematically introduced to the basic knowledge and skills of digital literacy. By reconstructing the content of digital literacy teaching and practice, courses are taught with abundant cases and practices, and a diversified evaluation system is used to evaluate digital literacy ability. The evaluation results provide references for the improvement of digital literacy ability of college students.

However, the cultivation of digital literacy is a complex and continuous process, which is closely related to theory and practice. At the beginning of the course, due to the accumulation of less student learning data, the ability evaluation model proposed in this paper lacks practical verification and discussion. How to evaluate the digital literacy ability of college students effectively is an important direction for further discussion and research in the future.

References

1. Eshet-Alkalai, Y.: A digital literacy: a conceptual framework for survival skills in the digital era. J. Educ. Multimedia Hypermedia **1**, 93–106 (2004)
2. Hwang, H., Zhu, L., Cui, Q.: Development and validation of a digital literacy scale in the artificial intelligence era for college students. KSII Trans. Internet Inf. Syst. **17**(8), 2241–2258 (2023)
3. Cyberspace Affairs Commission of the CPC Central Committee. Platform for Action to enhance Digital literacy and skills for all. http://www.cac.gov.cn/2021-11/0/c_1637708867~331677.htm
4. Tian, X., Park, K.: Learning approaches influence on college students' digital literacy: the role of self-determination theory. Int. J. Emerg. Technol. Learn. **17**(14), 78–93 (2022)
5. Shaowei, S.: A survey of college students' digital literacy: perception level, digital divide and digital experience. library construction. http://kns.cnki.net/kcms/detail/23.1331.g2.2023~0320.1328.004.html. Accessed 31 Aug 2023
6. Yu, D., Xue, T., Chao, L.: Research on the value and path of cultivating college students' digital literacy in the digital age. In: ACM International Conference Proceeding Series, pp. 92–97. Association for Computing Machinery (2022)
7. Nilaphruek, P., Charoenporn, P.: Knowledge discovery and dataset for the improvement of digital literacy skills in undergraduate students. Data **8**(7) (2023)
8. Peng, F., Guo, M., Zheng, C., Wang, S., Wang, X., Xu, M.: An assessment model of digital literacy for the students in vocational education based on principal component analysis in machine learning. In: ITNEC 2023 - IEEE 6th Information Technology, Networking, Electronic and Automation Control Conference, pp. 1382–1386. Institute of Electrical and Electronics Engineers Inc. (2023)
9. Wasis, W., Rahma, Y., Cicik, S., Eko, P., Nanda, P.: Student's digital literacy based on students' interest in digital technology, internet costs, gender, and learning outcomes. Int. J. Emerg. Technol. Learn. **17**(3), 138–151 (2022)
10. Ayesha, A., Agha A., Ihsan A.: Validated digital literacy measures for populations with low levels of internet experiences. Dev. Eng. **8** (2023)
11. Şenol, M., Adem, B.: The predictive effect of digital literacy, self-control and motivation on the academic achievement in the science, technology and society learning area. Technol. Knowl. Learn. **28**(1), 369–385 (2023)
12. Ahmet, K., Ekrem, B., Ahmet, A.: The effect of digital literacy ontechnology acceptance: an evaluation on administrative staff in higher education. J. Inf. Sci. (2023)

13. Oseghale, O.: Digital information literacy skills and use of electronic resources by humanities graduate students at Kenneth Dike Library, University of Ibadan, Nigeria. Digit. Libr. Perspect. **39**(2), 181–204 (2023)
14. Rita, C., Juan, D., Javier, T.: Diagnosing Spanish literature bachelor students' information literacy in digital environments. Digit. Libr. Perspect. **37**(1), 54–69 (2021)
15. Yong, S., Fang, S., Hongkun, Z., Fei, P.: Analysis of learning behavior characteristics and prediction of learning effect for improving college students' information literacy based on machine learning. IEEE Access **11**, 50447–50461 (2023)
16. Janina, K., Hanlie, S.: Knowledge visualization towards digital literacy development: critical success factors. In: Hinkelmann, K., López-Pellicer, F.J., Polini, A. (eds.) BIR 2023. LNBIP, vol. 493, pp. 339–350. Springer, Cham (2023). https://doi.org/10.1007/978-3-031-43126-5_24
17. Khulwa, C., Luthfia, A.: Generation Z students' digital literacy on online learning readiness. In: 2023 11th International Conference on Information and Education Technology, pp. 360–364. Institute of Electrical and Electronics Engineers Inc., Fujisawa (2023)
18. Zhu, S., Li, J., Bai, J., Yang, H., Zhang, D.: Assessing Secondary Students' Digital Literacy Using an Evidence-Centered Game Design Approach. In: Li, C., Cheung, S.K.S., Wang, F.L., Lu, A., Kwok, L.F. (eds.) ICBL 2023. LNCS (LNAI and LNB), vol. 13978, pp. 214–223. Springer, Cham (2023). https://doi.org/10.1007/978-3-031-35731-2_19
19. Kim, D., Ryoo, D.: Learning techniques using study with me: focus on motivational orientations, learning competency, and digital literacy. IEEE Access **11**, 98050–98058 (2023)
20. Li, Y., Li, G.: The impacts of digital literacy on citizen civic engagement evidence from China. Digit. Gov. Res. Pract. **3** (2022)
21. Chen, Y.: Research on comprehensive management of digital literacy education in the era of big data. In: ACM International Conference Proceeding Series, pp. 421–427. Association for Computing Machinery, Online (2022)
22. Wang, W., Yan, L: Construction of the evaluation index system of digital literacy of civil servants - based on fuzzy comprehensive evaluation model. In: CIBDA 2022 - 3rd International Conference on Computer Information and Big Data Applications, pp. 184–187. VDE VERLAG GMBH, China (2022)

Course-Graph Discovery from Academic Performance Using Nonnegative LassoNet

Mengfei Liu[1,2], Shuangshuang Wei[1,2], Shuhui Liu[3], Xuequn Shang[1,2], and Yupei Zhang[1,2(✉)]

[1] School of Computer Science, Northwestern Polytechnical University, Xi'an, China
{mengfei@mail,weishuang@mail,shang,ypzhaang}@nwpu.edu.cn
[2] MIIT Big Data Storage and Management Lab, Xi'an, China
[3] Department of Automation, Tsinghua University, Beijing, China
shliu620@tsinghua.edu.cn

Abstract. This paper focuses on the problem of mining a course graph from students' academic grades in formal education, which is an essential topic for artificial intelligence in education (AIED). However, most current methods often suffer from hardly understanding associations in practice. To this end, we formulate this problem into a feature selection schema that the proposed nonnegative LassoNet can solve. In the study case, we use the course scores of 4,577 records in the computer science department at our university. From the study results, our method achieves about 78% accuracy in score prediction with an acceptable error, which is better than traditional regression models with shrinkage. Based on the sparse self-expressive representation, we create a course map to show the associations behind the student's academic performance, providing pieces of evidence for education studies and triggering exciting discoveries.

Keywords: Course-graph discovery · Nonnegative LassoNet · Academic performance prediction · Self-expressive representation

1 Introduction

Discovering a course map from student academic performance is an important topic in the field of artificial intelligence in education (AIED). The course map is often created to optimize the course assignment [1], analyze course knowledge relationship [2], and implement course recommendations [3]. Hence, many methods using AI models have been developed to mine the relationships between courses from enrollment records, text descriptions, course grades, etc. [4,5].

Due to the fact that educational data suffers from multi-mode, multi-source, and heterogeneity [6,7], studies often employ machine learning-based models to

This work was supported in part by the National Natural Science Foundation of China (62272392, U1811262), the Key Research and Development Program of China (2020AAA0108500), and the Higher Research Funding on International Talent Cultivation at NPU (GJGZZD202202).

extract the concise data representation. Zhang et al. developed a multi-source convolutional neural network (CNN) to learn fused features, followed by using a linear classifier to predict grades and create the course map [1]. Pardos et al. developed a natural language model to achieve course representations and then figure out the relationships between courses to create a visual map of courses. Besides, Leeds et al. computed the Pearson course-pair similarity based on student performance to generate a course network graph [8].

However, the relationships between courses are often nonlinear, as the knowledge concepts commonly contained in courses involve a complex evolution. The simple distance metric is hard to capture the nonlinear relationship, while the high nonlinear model is hard to show a clear explanation. The traditional feature selection model, i.e. Lasso [10], has already been developed to identify key features in student grade prediction [9].

To capture a nonlinear relationship, this study extends the currently proposed LassoNet [11] by enhancing its steadiness and performance. LassoNet is composed of a nonlinear prediction branch and a feature selection branch, accounting for a nonlinear and explainable relationship, and has been extended in many applications, such as Liu et al. [12] proposed a graph-regularized LassoNet model by integrating feature correlations to select a structured feature subset.

In this paper, we formulate the problem of discovering a course graph from academic performance into the LassoNet. We contribute AIED by 1) considering the nonnegativity in course similarity and providing a new method of creating a course graph. This study benefits the route of teaching and learning.

2 Material and Methodology

2.1 Dataset and Pre-processing

We, in this study, use the dataset collected in our university from Fall 2012 to Spring 2018. This study filters the fresh-grade student in the School of Computer Science (CS). We select 23 courses and 4,577 records, as there is a higher overlap between students and fewer missing values in the courses. Besides, we are familiar with CS courses and experts' information. Table 1 shows our data descriptions.

Table 1. Distribution of course categories.

Course Category	Courses	Records
Computer Science	2(9%)	398
Mathematics	7(30%)	1393
Common Courses	14(61%)	2786
total	23	4577

The data used in experiments is extracted based on the above requirements, and the missing scores are filled with the average score of the course. Then, we standardize the data by removing the mean and scaling it by standard deviation.

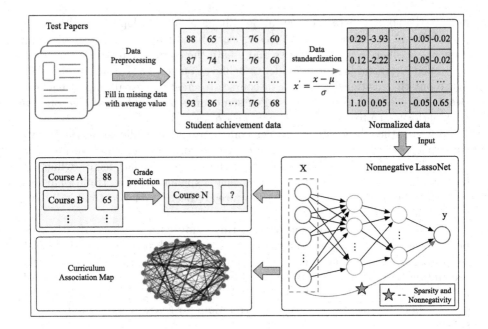

Fig. 1. Workflow of the proposed method.

2.2 The Proposed Method

Our Course-Map Workflow. As shown in Fig. 1, our workflow contains the step of data preprocessing, the step of using Nonnegative LassoNet, and the step of grade prediction and course-graph construction. With the workflow, we aim to predict the score of a target course and meanwhile identify a few courses that contribute the most to the prediction. Thus, the problem can be cast into

$$\min \mathcal{L}(y, X\theta) + \lambda\|\theta\|_1 \tag{1}$$

where $\mathcal{L}$ represents a nonlinear function, $X \in \mathcal{R}^{n \times m}$ is the score-record matrix of n students and m courses, $\theta \in \mathcal{R}^m$ indicates the regression coefficients, λ is a balance hyper-parameter, and the second term is to induce the sparsity.

LassoNet implements feature sparsity by imposing constraints on the skip layer of the residual network, where each neuron of the skip layer corresponds to a feature, shown in Fig. 1 (Nonnative LassoNet). When the weight of a neuron becomes 0, its corresponding feature will be canceled in score prediction.

Nonnegative LassoNet. The problem of our model is written as

$$\min_{\theta,W} L(\theta, W) + \lambda\|\theta\|_1$$
$$s.t. \|W_j^{(1)}\|_\infty \le M|\theta_j|, \theta_j \ge 0; (j = 1, ..., d) \tag{2}$$

where the $L(\cdot)$ is usually defined as $L(\theta, W) = \sum_{i=1}^{n} l(f(x_i), y_i)$, θ and W are the parameters of f, $\| \cdot \|_{\infty}$ gives the max element in a vector, and M is a hyper-parameter. The first constraint and the second constraint term account for sparsity and nonnegativity, respectively. In the first constraint, when θ_j is equal to 0, the whole vector W_j is going to be 0. Then, the corresponding feature j will no longer participate in model training. For the second constraint, θ is enforced to be nonnegative to reduce the solution space. Then, our model is more steady than the original LassoNet.

To implement the Nonnegative LassoNet, we employ a standard feed-forward neural network by adding the skip layer directly from input to output, shown in Fig. 1 (Nonnative LassoNet). The sparsity constraint can be solved by the proximate gradient descent proposed in LassoNet [11]. The nonnegativity constraint is simply implemented by removing negative weights in the training iteration. More details on the implementations can be found at: https://github.com/ypzhaang.

$$d(x, y) = \sum \mathbb{I}(x_i == y_i) \tag{3}$$

2.3   Training and Evaluation

To train the Nonnegative LassoNet, we randomly divide the preprocessed data into a training set and a test set by the ratio of 7:3. When applying the model to forecast student performance, the prediction can be acceptable if the difference between the predicted value and the actual score falls within a predetermined range. In model training, we set $M = 10$ and select λ with a whole solution path through all experiments. The model is iterated by 1000 epochs. To have a steady evaluation, we ran each method five times and averaged the results.

3   Results and Analysis

3.1   Prediction Performance

To evaluate the model, we compare it with the regression models with shrinkage, i.e., the ridge regression, the lasso regression, and the LassoNet. All models are tested on our dataset with the same experimental settings. Table 2 shows the evaluation accuracy for these methods with the accepted range in {3,4,5}. From the results, a greater range leads to higher prediction accuracy. For every range, Lasso is better than Ridge, showing the effectiveness of sparsity; LassoNet is better than Lasso, showing the effectiveness of nonlinearity; Nonnegative Lassonet is the best, benefiting from the nonnegativity. Thus, the proposed model is effective for student academic performance prediction.

To check the steadiness, we list the five-time experimental results in Table 3 and calculate the standard deviations. Note that the results in the Table were rounded off. As shown, Nonnegative Lassonet has a better performance on the result steadiness, coinciding with our motivation.

Table 2. Evaluation accuracy of different methods under different tolerabilities.

Accepted range	Method			
	Ridge	Lasso	LassoNet	Nonnegative LassoNet
3	0.5322	0.5852	0.6591	**0.6612**
4	0.6274	0.6673	0.7095	**0.7140**
5	0.6986	0.7278	0.7728	**0.7818**

Table 3. The variance of the accuracy obtained by LassoNet and our model.

	1	2	3	4	5	Standard deviation
LassoNet	0.6282	0.6530	0.6968	0.6400	0.6773	**0.02496**
Nonnegative LassoNet	0.6652	0.6748	0.6548	0.6635	0.6452	**0.01117**

3.2   Course-Graph Evaluation

To create the course graph from our dataset, we predict the scores of a course j by using all other rest courses, then achieve the relationship vector θ_j. In the 23 courses, we obtain 23 relationship vectors accordingly. The course-graph adjacent matrix M collects these vectors by setting the row vector $M_j = \theta_j$ and the diagonal element $M_{jj} = 0$. Figure 2 illustrates the relationships $(M + M^T)/2$ between the 23 courses, where we remove these edges with small weights.

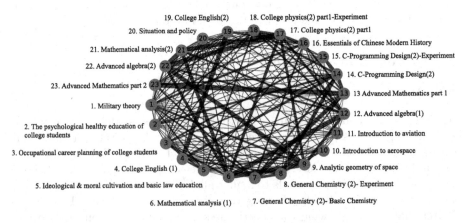

Fig. 2. Course-Graph obtained by using Nonnegative LassoNet.

As is shown in Fig. 2, the courses of liberal education and brief Introduction often have small weights to associate with other courses, such as Occupational carer planning and Introduction to aerospace. While, the courses in Mathematics have more big weights, such as Mathematical analysis and Advanced algebra.

In addition, both College Physics and C-Programming Design are important for supporting other courses. The observations have again arrived in Table 4. Moreover, a subjective evaluation from eight experts shows that these observations are agreed with in real-world cases.

4   Conclusion

In this paper, we propose a nonnegative LassoNet to identify the course graph from student academic performance. On our dataset, the proposed model is evaluated to be effective and more steady. With a self-expression schema, we create the course graph and arrive at understandable relationships. In the future, we will develop more machine learning models to discover more structures hidden in academic data [13–15].

Table 4. The top five courses with high weight rates.

Rank	Course	Sum of weights
1	Advanced Algebra (2)	7.66%
2	College Physics II (Part 1)	7.39%
3	Analytic Geometry of Space	7.00%
4	Mathematical Analysis (1)	6.81%
5	C Programming II	5.69%

References

1. Zhang, Y., An, R., Liu, S., Cui, J., Shang, X.: Predicting and understanding student learning performance using multi-source sparse attention convolutional neural networks. IEEE Trans. Big Data 1–13 (2021)
2. Pardos, Z.A., Nam, A.J.H.: A university map of course knowledge. PLoS ONE **15**(9), e0233207 (2020)
3. Nabizadeh, H., Gonçalves, D., et al.: Adaptive learning path recommender approach using auxiliary learning objects. Comput. Educ. **147**, 103777 (2020)
4. Zhang, Y., Zhou, Y., Liu, S., et al.: WeStcoin: weakly-supervised contextualized text classification with imbalance and noisy labels. In: ICPR, pp. 2451–2457 (2022)
5. Romero, C., Ventura, S.: Educational data mining and learning analytics: an updated survey. Data Min. Knowl. Disc. **10**(3), e1355 (2020)
6. Zhang, Y., Yun, Y., An, R., Cui, J., Dai, H., Shang, X.: Educational data mining techniques for student performance prediction: method review and comparison analysis. Front. Psychol. **12**, 698490 (2021)
7. Perera, L., Richardson, P.: Students' use of online academic resources within a course website and its relationship with their course performance: An exploratory study. Account. Educ. Int. J. **19**(6), 587–600 (2010)

8. Leeds, D.D., Zhang, T., Weiss, G.M.: Mining course groupings using academic performance. In: International Conference on Educational Data Mining (2021)
9. Cui, J., Zhang, Y., An, R., Yun, Y., Dai, H., Shang, X.: Identifying key features in student grade prediction. In: IEEE International Conference on PIC, pp. 519–523 (2021)
10. Ranstam, J., Cook, J.A.: LASSO regression. J. Br. Surg. **105**(10), 1348–1348 (2018)
11. Lemhadri, I., Ruan, F., Tibshirani, R. Lassonet: neural networks with feature sparsity. In: International Conference on Artificial Intelligence and Statistics, pp. 10–18 (2021)
12. Liu, S., Zhang, Y., Shang, X.: GLassonet: identifying discriminative gene sets among molecular subtypes of breast cancer. IEEE/ACM Trans. Comput. Biol. Bioinform. (2022)
13. Zhang, Y., Xiang, M., Yang, B.: Low-rank preserving embedding. Pattern Recogn. **70**, 112–125 (2017)
14. Zhang, Y., Dai, H., Yun, Y., Liu, S., Lan, A., Shang, X.: Meta-knowledge dictionary learning on 1-bit response data for student knowledge diagnosis. Knowl.-Based Syst. **205**, 106290 (2020)
15. Zhang, Y., Xu, Y., Wei, S., Wang, Y., Li, Y., Shang, X.: Doubly contrastive representation learning for federated image recognition. Pattern Recogn. **139**, 109507 (2023)

Author Index

Printed in the United States
by Baker & Taylor Publisher Services